Modern Soviet Society

Modern Soviet Society

BASILE KERBLAY

Translated by Rupert Swyer

PANTHEON BOOKS
NEW YORK

Library of Congress Cataloging in Publication Data

Kerblay, Basile H.
Modern Soviet society.
Translation of: 'La société soviétique contemporaine'
Bibliography: p.
1. Soviet Union—Social conditions—1970–
2. Soviet Union—Economic conditions—1976–
I. Title.
HN523.5.K413   1983   306'.0947   82–24646
ISBN 0–394–51316–9
ISBN 0–394–71111–4 (pbk.)

Contents

Tables and figures

FIGURES

Ruble (R) exchange rates

1897–1914	1 R = 2.75 FF
1937	1 R = 3 FF
1950	1 R = US $0.25
1961	1 R = US $1.11
November 1982	£1 = 1.19 R
	1 FF = 0.10 R
	US $1 = 0.75 R

Preface to the English edition

The reader who expects to find in this book material to fuel an ideological war will be disappointed. Despite undeniable inequalities in living standards and differences in institutions and culture, Soviet society reveals that all people share the same fears, the same basic needs for security, self-development and genuine human relationships. Instead of breeding more division between peoples, whether between individuals or collectives, our intelligence must act to reduce it.

In the present English edition I have updated the statistics and revised the bibliographies. Some paragraphs have been rewritten to incorporate new data which have become available since the first edition. I am indebted to Rupert Swyer who brought both a gift for language and technical accuracy to bear on the translation of the French version.

BASILE KERBLAY
Paris, September 1982

Preface

The subject of this book is Soviet society as we find it today. We shall not be concerned with the different stages in the formation of this society, but we shall be referring to the past whenever necessary, to account for the persistence or revival of a national tradition which, like any other aspect of civilization, is resistant to change. Because this society is being built from day to day, because, like any human society, it is in perpetual movement, we must seek to understand both its structure and its dynamics. This study is therefore concerned not with drawing up an inventory of Soviet society, which must of necessity be immediately obsolete, but with spotlighting the signs of its future development. In a word, our study is intended as a forward-looking one, and in this it represents a break with educational tradition, which stresses knowledge of the past without giving sufficient thought to the future, that is to facts which individuals might hope to foresee and grasp.

Another reason why there has been a need for a synthetic view of contemporary society in the Soviet Union is that less attention has been paid to this aspect of Soviet life than to the Soviet economy. The quality and variety of studies of the economy are evidence of the often enthusiastic interest aroused in the west by the planning and rapid growth achieved by the Soviet Union. However, when we try to spell out long-term development prospects, economic analysis loses its way in the uncharted territory of social process. The future of the Soviet Union cannot be read in this or that growth target alone; it is far more likely to lie in the aspirations and abilities of the individuals and groups that guide its development.

Furthermore, although no attempt has yet been made to produce a general survey for the general reader with no knowledge of Russian, sociology in the Soviet Union has made considerable strides over the past ten years. We shall be referring extensively to these investigations, as well as to official statistics and doctrine, for it is through the Soviets' judgement of their own social system that we can learn how those directly concerned interpret it. Similarly, we shall be making use of Soviet newspaper articles and literary essays which, while making no scientific claims, throw practical light on or bear direct witness to certain specific points. It will be necessary also to refer to foreign sources, because comparative studies may give us a firmer grasp of the specific features of the Soviet social system, and also because, by our criteria of objectivity, we are duty-bound to examine every interpretation, even if it proves necessary to point out their weaknesses.

We shall begin by examining the basic constituents of the fabric of any society, namely those features of social life that strike even the inexperienced observer of the Soviet Union: a territory comprising different populations in their respective geographical settings and with their own national traditions, both town and country, families and enterprises. First, we shall explore the basic groups, or microsociology, of Soviet society, before going on to analyse the structure of social relations and political institutions characteristic of society in general, or macrosociology. With this investigation behind us, we shall then take a look at the nature of Soviet society and at the driving forces specific to it. In other words, we will adopt the opposite approach from the one that seeks explanations of elementary facts in the macrostructure. There are two reasons for this: first, the reader does not necessarily have a grounding in sociology and will therefore find it easier to grasp more familiar facts concerning, for example, his or her family, home town or village − intergroup relations − and gradually, by an accumulation of elementary facts, learn to build up a more complex web of social stratification; also, however, we wish to avoid prejudging the character of the Soviet social system by dressing it up in an ideological straitjacket. Even Marxist critics are by no means unanimous in regarding nationalization of the means of production as sufficient to produce a radical transformation of social relations and in regarding a society of this type as incarnating socialism *ipso facto*. The empiricism of our approach is dictated by a concern to eschew dogmatism.

It is left to the reader to conclude whether or not Soviet society as it appears today matches up to his or her idea of socialism, and to what extent the influence of the past, remnants of the cultural tradition, urbanization and industrialization, the development of the most up-to-date techniques of production and communication, and social and political institutions invite, or discourage, comparison with western society.

Admittedly, any investigation of the real world presupposes a conceptual framework and a set of assumptions, placing the author in the uncomfortable position of having to assert his own preferences. These preferences and intentions are first and foremost pedagogic. We have not set out here to present an exhaustive or definitive picture of Soviet society, still less to judge it with reference to any particular model, value or doctrine; our purpose is to provide readers with a travel guide to enable them to pursue for themselves the never-ending exploration of the contemporary Soviet world, or, more precisely, to equip them with an investigative method and the requisite materials, and to wish them the best of luck − in the field if possible.

Foreword

This book by a noted French scholar is, to my mind, an astonishing achievement. By its structure and avowed aim it does not aspire to be more than a text-book, small, compact and matter-of-fact. In reality, when compared to the existing literature on Soviet Russia, it encompasses so many novel features that the term 'landmark' can be used to characterize its importance and its possible impact.

The book comes at a time when shallow and one-sided statements concerning Soviet Russia seem to be preferred to more pondered reasoning. The media and even part of the academic community, rather than providing analyses, have been projecting a simplified, often misleading picture through the repeated use and abuse of sometimes even the most trivial details of the régime — all to the detriment of a deeper understanding and assessment of a subject of immense importance. The appearance of this book, with its careful statements and balanced views, its refusal to simplify and openness to ambiguity and complexity, its cognizance of failures, achievements, drift and change, is a welcome, refreshing and stimulating antidote to moods of the moment.

But many other traits of this work are of a kind many a teacher or researcher worth his salt dreams of. To begin with, it uses historical data and historical analysis skilfully, allowing the reader to get a sense of change over time, the passing of stages and generations, and to appreciate the unfolding of a broad historical canvas and drama. This key historical dimension is enhanced by what is a genuine multi-disciplinary endeavour where the successful blend of data and concepts offered by sociology, economics, political science, ethnography, cultural studies and literature support each other and contribute to an emerging broader entity. The author achieves this effect not only by a good organization of material and a judicious distribution of chapters, but more importantly by an unobtrusive and flexible conceptual apparatus, implied or suggested rather than dogmatically imposed.

The three hundred or so pages offered to us contain a constant flow of ideas, findings, new formulae and thought-provoking questions; at the same time, an amazing amount of data is crammed into this modest space, on geography, population, social classes and cultural trends, nationalities and economics — not to mention the hobbies, drinking and eating habits, career preferences and fashions of Soviet Russia. Kerblay is equally expert in depicting rural society which he knows better, probably, than anybody else, as well as in the more novel and complex problems of social mobility which he compares constantly with those of the US and France. We learn about universities and the school system, about the industrial world and the realities of industrial enterprise, and are informed in a more detailed way from the best and newest sources about the type of manager workers prefer as compared to the preferences of engineers. We also get enough to whet our appetite, and look for more elsewhere, on values, deviance and criminality. Finally, we turn to chapters dealing with factors or mechanisms that integrate the whole system, the polity and the sphere of culture, subjects that demand great competence to discuss, remain controversial but also exciting and are presented here expertly and concisely.

Obviously, all this and more is needed when the author's aim is to offer an integrated picture of a socio-political and cultural system of a huge and multinational country. And herein lies the most important contribution and the chief novelty of the book. It promises to deal with 'modern Soviet society' — and this is precisely what it does.

The author tells us at the outset why this broader picture is indispensable. Concentration on economic growth or on some other single aspect of Russia is insufficient. Instead, social realities must be studied. But 'social realities' or 'society' is quite a task, intellectually and professionally. No-one can claim that the usual disciplines, like economics or sociology, ethnography or demography, are easy to practise. But at least they are already established and have at their disposal elaborate scholarly tools and professional bodies, university departments and institutes. And this means that important dimensions and aspects of the whole are studied expertly while the whole, the aggregate, is left out. But specialized departments for the study of a country's 'society' are, even in the best universities, almost unknown. Sociology is the one branch that makes the study of society its business, but sociologists tend to leave the study of history, demography and much of what we call culture to others, excluding them from their own constructions altogether. The methodological and conceptual problems of discussing the broader canvas of society still remain unsolved. To make things worse, an established departmental structure creates a tendency to view anyone who tries 'to integrate' the disciplines as being pretentious and, at best, amateurish. Sometimes the established disciplines like economics or political science can give the impression that they can discover almost all there is to be known about the past and present.

Some may think that such tendencies are not representative, but unfortunately they are widespread, regrettable and damaging to scholarship. No-one can do anything without the disciplines, but aggregates must be studied too. An aggregate like 'society' is difficult to handle, but it certainly is a discipline in its own right; yet, as we have noted, no systematic training is available to take on this kind of effort.

In the case of Russia, the absence of global studies is particularly detrimental: one-sided approaches and inadequate theories make us very often miss the deeper springs of the social system and polity, and we end up making proposals and predictions that are constantly belied by events. The study of Russia offers many examples of blunders committed by observers and politicians, friends, foes and neutrals alike. One does not have to go far in search of such examples.

Attentive students of Russia are now aware of a great and growing number of phenomena that should be incorporated into the study and overall picture of the functioning of the Soviet system. Only some of these can be mentioned here and most of them, and more, can be found in this book. Most studies of Russia have tended to concentrate on the state — including its main props such as party and ideology — not unnaturally, of course, for this system and this part of the world. Much has been learned thereby that was and is of great importance. But the almost exclusive insistence on these salient aspects has created a tendency to isolate them or, to put it briefly, to isolate the state from the historical process. The state was pictured hovering above the social structure, shaping it mightily and not shaped by anything itself, certainly not by social relations — they were relegated in many studies to a secondary position, together with 'all the rest' like historical tradition, culture or values. There was some justification for this kind of singling out of the state and of 'statism' during, say, the Stalinist period, but it can be shown that even then such an approach was inadequate. It is even more misleading for the study of the post-Stalinist period and for reflecting on what lies ahead.

In fact the state, however powerful, and even at its most despotic, is always dependent in different ways on the broader social matrix, is part of it and interacts with its components. A study that takes a harder and longer look can show how this interaction accounts for the state's policies, its responses to social pressures and needs, and even for the absence of such responses. The latter happened often enough, sometimes reaching catastrophic proportions, notably at the end of the civil war, during the great purges and in the last period of Stalin's life. Such rifts between state and society lead to mass terror, or mass uprising, or in the decline of the whole system. Sometimes a reaction sets in and some social groups begin to pressure for change and reforms in order to counter the decline or patch up the cracks. Soviet history provides enough examples of ups and downs of this kind, and such trends cannot be excluded when studying the present and trying to look into the future.

But the image of a bureaucratic hierarchy or of overlapping hierarchies running the economy, society and culture with a totalitarian grip, a pyramid of power where orders flow down and information and obedient execution flow up — an image that was widespread during an earlier stage in Soviet studies — is by now probably discarded by most scholars. Sometimes it is even replaced by an opposite view of a Russia where nobody and nothing is obeyed, nothing works and the bureaucracy is just an illegitimate burden on a society that is only yearning to send the whole thing packing. Such a view is even more misleading than the previous one and can become a source of considerable errors of judgement. Much remains to be done to reconstruct a more realistic picture of power, of relations between state and society and within the ruling circles — including the forms and directions of change, and of the character of crises when change occurs, and it does.

A reminder of recent changes in a well-established discipline might clarify the argument. Economists today, for example, understand much better than before the real versus the formal modes of the economy's functioning. They know about the 'second economy', maybe even a third one too, and about a welter of informal but widespread practices without which nothing works — and more relevantly without which the description and analyses of how the economy works (or doesn't) will not stand.

As one moves to the broader social system and its main components — workers, technicians, managers, peasants, intelligentsia, bureaucrats — the picture of the social system becomes a real maze of formal and informal arrangements and mechanisms, open and clandestine, official, unofficial and anti-official; this system is full of pressure groups, ideas and ideologies, complete with different religions, nationalities and nationalisms, which are there for every student to see — and to ask why such things were not always seen before.

Despite their powers, Soviet-style authoritatian régimes often do not really have the power to control or suppress change, generational conflicts, cultural variety, fashions, fads, language and thought patterns. Not in industrial societies in any case. And leaders do recognize and adapt to social realities all the time, however unenthusiastically. This point is worth elaborating upon briefly.

The history and sociology of labour in the Soviet Union show that 'the labour force' — in its narrower meaning of 'workers' and in the broader one of 'the employed' — always exhibited a tendency to act in accord with their own perceptions of their interests; they often ignored orders and plans that ran against their wishes, but also accepted or shared in varying degrees some of the régime's values and aims. On the whole, though, labour showed a high degree of spontaneity in its actions, and labour-force recruitment remained mostly a market phenomenon. To be precise, the labour market was imposed on the planned system after the latter discovered that ordering people around and 'distributing' them administratively to the available jobs were just not feasible. And it always had deleterious effects on productivity which the régime could not afford.

It is also well known that managers, though quite dedicated to their tasks and to the régime, are nevertheless reacting in a variety of ways to the realities of their environment, to its contradictions and inconsistencies, and are thereby considerably influencing the way the system is functioning. They accumulate labour surpluses which the régime doesn't really want, they hide productive capacities from the authorities in order to get smaller plans, or engage in barter of machines and materials with other managers in order to overcome the deficiencies of the official supply system. Much of this is actually now the real *modus operandi* and is either fully accepted or just tolerated. But some such activities are not that benign, even in intention. Cliques and 'family circles', as they are called in Russia, are formed in order to promote their interests, and some engage in illicit activities that clash directly with the law and the authorities, and are prosecuted by the state.

Phenomena of a similar character are known to operate within other administrations — not just among factory managers. The bureaucrats are not only servants of the state; they have always created many headaches for top leadership and frustrate them no less than do other groups of the population. Bureaucrats often fail to perform as expected or to supply truthful data; they have kept developing — not unlike the factory managers — their own informal groups and practices, as well as moods and ideologies that express their aspirations and objectives. They can also impose some of these on the leadership.

We observe similar manifestations of social spontaneity in the sphere of education, and one can quote the well-known example of Khrushchev's educational reforms, which were rejected and finally simply scuttled by a widespread opposition of parents, educators, and many government officials — themselves, of course, also parents. New generations of young people come into the social and political arena and develop their own reactions and preferences, and these are powerful factors of social reality. Career preferences and the scale of values of the young are often far from what the leadership would like to see. We also know that in this supposedly worker-orientated system the real status ladder climbs away from the workers, despite the régime's efforts to turn the system round. The educated layers from different walks of life would consider work at the factory bench a degradation for their children and for themselves — and this would be particularly true for an *apparatchik*, who considers himself the spokesman and carrier of the state's national and revolutionary missions. In fact, those powerful *apparatchiki*, so influential in the political sphere, are not capable of setting the tone and reversing the social status ladder, at least not as it is viewed by most people. They often notice with envy that scholars and writers, or just any Ph.D. (which are not too numerous in Russia), are more respected than even the top officials, and they exhibit a deep need to share in the informal but valued social recognition by trying to acquire academic titles and positions.

In different social groups authorities keep discovering moods and dispositions, sometimes even 'ugly' ones, as well as some that have religious trends, and different types of nationalism have also always been a problem; they were often independent of and stronger than the dictatorship, and imposed their own demands or accommodation.

Thus, the Soviet system is a product of much more than political pressures, controls or an official ideology. The state, which has at times been aggressively active and buoyant, has at other times seemed quite preoccupied with taking numerous opinion polls, as leaders realized that social realities could grow out of control. It is worth repeating that even at the height of the purges, scores of edicts threatening penal consequences in cases of non-compliance often went no further than the state archives.

When the real maze of social, economic and cultural spheres is brought into focus, the story of Soviet Russia, its society and political system, past and present, changes considerably. The study itself becomes much more exacting and interesting, and the theoretical constructs needed for the incorporation of so many aspects and for the interpretation of what is going on and why suddenly need to be rethought. Professor Kerblay is a pioneer in this difficult undertaking. The material to be incorporated in such an endeavour is vast and its organization is far from simple. It is certainly not just a mechanical problem of organizing data. Even the question of what is to go into the picture is not easy to answer. Scholars would certainly agree that data on economics, sociology, politics and demography should be there. But all the rest is controversial. How much of history, if any, and of what kind? And culture, if at all? And exactly how much politics and 'politics' in what sense?

The reader will see for himself how the author has solved these problems and will, perhaps, want to argue about some of his opinions or solutions. But the reader will also find himself immersed in numerous innovative formulae, often elegantly presented.

Kerblay's method of dealing with the state, as we have already noted, consists in treating it historically and incorporating it into the general matrix where it belongs. This is particularly praiseworthy for being methodologically sound — and deserves serious discussion. Concerning the ubiquitous and notorious police surveillance in the Soviet Union, a realistic and flexible formula is offered — without disregarding in the least the system's reliance on police and on other control mechanisms, such as ideology, censorship and monopoly of information. Police and informers (*stukachi*) are facts of life, well known to the population, 'but the vast majority of Soviet citizens escape this surveillance, though knowing full well it could be applied to them' (p. 256). Considering police controls, Kerblay says further that it would have been 'just as dishonest to avoid all reference to them as it would [have been] to imagine a society governed by force alone' (pp. 256–7). To what extent, then, do public opinion, interests and moods influence policy-makers? Kerblay can see the growing weight of these factors, but he points to three main deficiencies in the system that counter their growth. These are, first, the lack of constitutionally recognized procedures for the renewal of leaders; second, the lack of juridically guaranteed procedures for redress and for combatting arbitrary use of power; and, third, the absence of sufficient autonomy within the separate spheres of economic, cultural and political life and of an appropriate separation of powers to guarantee such an autonomy. This particular deficiency puts an enormous 'burden of wisdom' on the national leadership in guiding the system into new stages of development.

This last point could be elaborated upon by adding that other systems which do exhibit a high degree of autonomy in the key spheres of social life can survive even with a very undistinguished leadership, whereas the Soviet system is more vulnerable to crises of confidence and more prone to abuse the levers of coercion. The fact that in recent decades no return to massive violence against the population has occurred inside Russia can be explained by the appearance in the system's *modus operandi* of channels, however rudimentary or informal, for expressing and catering to the specific needs of the main spheres of social life. Kerblay seems to adhere to the idea that economic development leads necessarily to the kind of separation of powers that is needed to assure the autonomies in question – and certainly it is true that growing social and cultural differentiation and variety must find expression, or the system stagnates. For some observers the Soviet system today betrays this kind of stagnation as it responds inadequately – or worse, negatively – to the demands of social development.

It is around these kinds of needs, when inadequately met, that problems and pressures keep accumulating in the Soviet Union and in similar systems. The central issue becomes the system's ability to respond, to evolve and to survive. The historical experience of Soviet Russia is always worth remembering when dealing with such problems. The hurdle of underdevelopment is still in the process of being cleared, and already the problems of a developed society are gathering with great strength. Soviet Russia's position as a superpower adds complexity to these difficulties and dilemmas. But the outcome of pressures and counter-pressures are not known and predictions are difficult. Conservative, authoritarian methods seem to be in force now, probably as a result of not really knowing how to do better; and this is not necessarily just a Soviet predicament at the moment. At the same time, in the course of recent social and economic developments new possibilities are appearing in the social system which could offer solutions and eventually a new, reform-minded leadership. After all, as we have already hinted, this too has precedents in the Soviet Union, and it remains a possibility being no less probable than the violent convulsions some observers keep predicting.

The political system, as Kerblay underlines, 'was not built in a day; no one planned it or created it. . . . It did not spring up on virgin soil but is heir to a secular tradition' (p. 241).

This is an excellent formula and it could be slightly expanded by adding that the sum total of all past social and economic changes are constantly reflected in the state's development, implying a capacity for modernization and change. The system's totalitarian appetites and traits are, according to Kerblay, a result of ideological monopoly — 'a fully fledged religion of the state' (p. 248) — but one could suggest an amendment here too that continues in the direction of Kerblay's own earlier proposition that the system was neither planned nor created. Ideology, too, though certainly a factor of considerable and autonomous impact, can be seen as a product of historical development amenable to change in content and function, and not really the primary cause of a penchant for coercion and conservatism. Leaders of the party know quite well — again from a number of surveys, if any were needed — that the official ideological tenets and the propaganda that go with them have an ever diminishing return, and one can even argue that in real life ideological monopoly doesn't work. It is not true any more that a single official creed is the only operative guide to action. More than one ideology, a mixture of modes of thinking and frames of references, co-exist and not only in society at large but also inside the party and inside the leadership. This phenomenon isn't even new any more and it had to occur because a rigid and codified 'Marxism—Leninism' could not, except in official rhetoric, respond to the régime's real needs in the process of governing.

I do not know whether Professor Kerblay would agree with this treatment of Soviet ideology, but such a view actually reinforces his general findings. If there is more than one ideology in use, or if the official shell keeps accommodating features borrowed from elsewhere, then this could mean that the régime's capacity to learn, to expand its experience and to respond to the problems of the day is enhanced, even if only on a pragmatic basis. Observers of Russia in recent decades would probably have no problems with such an assessment despite the country's lapses into dogmatic and backward practices and its inability to rotate its over-ripe leadership.

The reader will find that Kerblay's remarkable book offers many surprises and provides occasions to argue and to learn on every one of its pages. It remains only to wish this work success in reaching the general and academic reader.

Moshe Lewin
University of Pennsylvania

Introduction

Any study presupposes a certain number of concepts, a method and a frame of reference by which to select from among the facts observed or recorded those that are the most significant. It is also necessary to be able to interpret them correctly.

FRAME OF REFERENCE, CONCEPTS AND METHOD

The facts with which we are specifically concerned are social by nature. What interests us here is not the behaviour of Soviet citizens as isolated individuals, their inner world or psychological aspects of their social relations, but the external aspects of functional relations that grow up between individuals forming groups, the relations of interdependence between these groups and the dynamics of this interaction. Our observational unit will be the *group*. We shall not be looking at Ivan and Natasha's subjective experience of their relations, but at the regular and objective relations of the couple that flow from the functions of the family group they form. Regularity of contact is a necessary condition. Passengers in a bus, who part never to see each other again, do not form a group in the sociological sense of the term. For a group to be formed it must have its own *specific activity*, some *authority* governing its activities, measuring them against the yardstick of values that members of this group hold in common, values that distinguish it from other groups. The behaviour of an individual will be conditioned by his or her place inside the group, and groups.

We shall therefore begin by identifying the different *elementary groups* that make up Soviet society: national communities, residential groups (towns and villages), families, schools, enterprises. Next, we shall try to find out how these groups fit into a network of relations, which, by their regularity, engender the *social structure* of the society in question. We shall be looking at the *degree of mobility* of individuals in the social hierarchy and examining the *institutions* that serve to bind the social system. As in all living organisms, these self-regulatory mechanisms — *power* and *dominant values* — do not rule out the innovations and changes that are essential if a society is to adapt and perpetuate itself. We shall be analysing the dynamics of change in Soviet society in the light of the different *interpretative models* available, in order to shed light on the future development of the Soviet world.

Having thus delineated our field of investigation, we shall conduct our analysis first by defining an operational *concept*, bearing in mind the Soviets' own definitions, for example the criteria by which a built-up area is classified as a town. We shall then go on to try to distinguish, within the compass of this concept, variations on the basis of which we might establish a *typology*; we shall thus be able to distinguish, according to size of population, large towns from medium-sized towns, etc., or, according to their age, new towns, etc. An understanding of the functions specific to each of these types, their structural relations and the factors that produce a shift from one type to another will enable us to form some idea of the *dynamics of change* at work in a milieu or social institution.

We must now determine what means are available to us to carry out this programme.

PROBLEMS OF INFORMATION AND INTERPRETATION

Most of our sources of information are written ones. The general bibliography found at the end of this book and references to more specialist works given at the end of each chapter provide a list of what is currently available. References to works and publications in Russian have been kept to a minimum as this book is not intended solely for Russian-speakers.

Yet, despite this abundance of literature, it must be remarked that certain areas of Soviet life, such as retail prices, morbidity, criminality and the prison system, are not touched on in published sources. The Soviet press only very rarely report political debates, trials, suicides, accidents, natural disasters, etc.

What does get published in the Soviet Union is filtered so as to correspond to the image mass-media officials wish to give of reality, although this does not rule out criticism and self-criticism where these are deemed useful in consolidating the social system. What is more, sociological research, except where it takes the form of overall structural studies, which ought by rights to be regarded as studies in the philosophy of historical materialism rather than concrete analysis, is concerned to facilitate the integration of individuals and groups in the interests of the smooth running of society at large. Thus, it never seeks to question the social system itself, unlike a certain strain of western sociology, which exercises a critical function.

Caution is needed in interpreting figures, for in the Soviet Union as elsewhere statistics may be incomplete, and their degree of representativeness is usually impossible to establish; alternatively, they may be expressed as *global averages*, leaving open the possibility of very broad variations within the mean. For instance, the average earnings of employees tell us little about earnings differentials within this section of society.[1]

Opportunities of on-the-spot investigation are limited, either because of the language barrier or because of the rules and procedures conditioning contacts between the Soviet people and foreigners, especially their freedom to travel about the country.

Fact-gathering, even when rigorously carried out, inevitably brings us face to face with inconsistencies and contradictions. This can come as a surprise only to those who imagine that social systems can be coherent in the way physical systems are. A social system is coherent only in theory; few human groupings act in total conformity with the values they claim to uphold, not necessarily out of hypocrisy or through individual shortcomings, but simply because all societies are rooted in history.

The origin of these contradictions is to be sought in the different paces of change to which the various elements that compose society are subject. Not everything in a given society changes at a single speed. Production techniques or communications evolve more rapidly than institutions. A few five-year plans may alter the economic structure of a country without modifying social behaviour and relations. Group mentalities take root in a cultural tradition, which evolves much more slowly, with the ebb and flow of generations. However good their intentions, individuals change relatively little in the course of their lives. But generations do change.

The key to an understanding of a world which, because it is part of history, is complex and diverse lies in our ability to distinguish the different components of contemporary Soviet life — economic change in the medium term, structural change in the long term — and national culture, which is continuous.

NOTE

1 V. G. Treml and D. P. Hardt, *Soviet Economic Statistics*, Durham, North Carolina, Duke University Press, 1972.

Chapter 1

The expanse of Soviet territory: physical constraints and development planning

TERRITORIAL AREAS AND SOCIETIES

We shall begin our exploration of Soviet society not with its history but with its territory. For time in its continuity lies beyond our grasp and we can only reconstruct the past out of the present: history is merely the endless echoing of our own questions. Geography, on the other hand, is objectively and immediately accessible to the investigator. The first thing we must do before encountering the Soviet people is to cross a border or land on a shore. The first thing we see will be the majestic, silent procession of forests, dotted with myriad lakes, the broad, muddy meandering of rivers flowing across the steppe and the many-hued sands of the arid zones.

For many millions of Soviet people, the constraints and the resources of this territory determine the most elementary details of their everyday life, to the point where, at times of great national peril, national feeling identifies subjectively with the defence of the soil and the fatherland. In the age-old struggle between succeeding generations and their geography, the state has always played a fundamental role in organizing group life and in ensuring the continuity of the nation. So much so that the very title of this book is a reminder of the paramount feature of the society we are about to study, namely its association with a state: the Soviet Union. Soviet society is defined by the collection of populations living within the boundaries of the territory over which the government of the Soviet Union exercises its authority (the limit to territorial waters is fixed at 12 nautical miles and the Soviet borders begin at that distance from the coastline).

We must begin by defining (1) the underlying objective characteristics of Soviet territory and (2) the different ecological zones composing it, not out of a belief in some outmoded geographical determinism, for as is well known, the landscape, or 'nature', in the world's inhabited regions has been modelled by human beings. Rather, the natural environment is both a restraint and a

challenge, which the different groups forming the Soviet Union have interpreted differently, according to (3) the traditions and techniques specific to
the different cultural areas. This deliberate dialogue also contains (4) subjective aspects, which are deeply rooted in the past. To sum up, we might say
that the history of this territory is the conquest, colonization and gradual
winning, by the populations of the Soviet Union, of mastery over a considerable area, which has not yet been fully developed. (5) The fact of analysing the
main patterns of national development amounts to indicating tomorrow's
history.

OBJECTIVE TERRITORIAL FEATURES

Whatever the period being considered, the life of a nation at all times occurs
within a geographical framework, which both imposes certain restraints and
offers resources and potentialities.

A glance at the map reveals one dominant characteristic of Soviet territory,
namely its *continentality*. This term needs to be understood in two senses: first,
in the sense of a territory that embraces an entire continent. The Soviet Union
is the most extensive of all the world's states (22,774,900 square kilometres, not
including the area of the White Sea and the Sea of Azov, which is included in
official data). A distance of 10,400 kilometres separates Kaliningrad and
Vladivostok, embracing eleven time zones; the Afghan border (latitude 36°
North) lies 4800 kilometres from the Arctic Ocean (latitude 82° North), which
underlines the northerly position of the country relative to the equator. Over
two-thirds of the Soviet Union lies north of the 50th parallel, a fact that should
be borne in mind when discussing the handicaps of Soviet agriculture.

Second, this continentality needs also to be understood in a climatic sense.
The average annual temperature in over 60 per cent of the country is less than
0° Celsius. Isolation from oceanic influence contributes to a rising temperature range as we travel eastwards (January: −10°C in Moscow, +3°C in Paris;
July: +18°C in Moscow and Paris); the difference between maximum and
minimum temperatures reaches 35°C at Novosibirsk and 100°C in central
Asia. The short spring and autumn give Soviet life a contrasting, alternating
rhythm between winter and summer. Only the fringes of the Baltic, the
Crimea, Transcaucasia and the maritime province of the far east escape the
rigours of the continental climate.

The physical immensity of Soviet territory and the attendant distances
place a heavy burden on the economy. Goods traffic, which is the only kind
recorded in Soviet national-income figures, represents 6 per cent of Gross
National Product (GNP) in the Soviet Union compared with 2.1 per cent in
France. At the beginning of the 1960s, the Soviet Union devoted a greater
proportion of its primary energy resources to transport than to electricity production. It takes the Rossiya Express seven days to travel from Moscow to

Vladivostok, and it is a twelve-hour flight between the capital and Petro-
pavlovsk (in Kamchatka). Although its communications network is still not
very dense, relatively speaking, the Soviet Union is the world's leading rail and
air transporter. In 1972, for 1000 square kilometres of territory, the Soviet
Union had 6 kilometres of rail track and 23 kilometres of metalled road
(France had 68 and 660 kilometres respectively); even so, in the same year, the
Soviet Union transported 46.5 per cent of world rail-goods traffic, or 2.7 times
as much as the United States. On the other hand, Soviet road traffic represents
only a third of the American figure, which is hardly surprising since the latter
possesses 7.4 times more bitumined roads than the Soviet Union.

Fortunately, the country's relief has facilitated communications. The vast
Eurasian plain, which stretches unbroken as far as the Yenisei, is broken from
north to south by only the relatively easily passed Ural mountains. Beyond, the
plain gives way to the eastern Siberian plateau, whose subsoil has been frozen
since the Ice Age to a depth of between 25 and 300 metres; yet surface
humidity in summer has enabled trees to take root. Close to 50 per cent of the
territory thus lies in the permafrost zone (*merzlota*). This permafrost acts as an
obstacle to the Siberian rivers flowing northwards towards the Arctic seas,
diverting their course in an east–west direction. Consequently, north–south
and east–west communication has always been easy for 150–200 days of the
year, thanks to a network of some 3 million kilometres of waterways (of which
145,000 kilometres are navigable) and 18,000 kilometres of canals. These
rivers permitted the emergence of the first national groups, which grew up in
the region along the Oxus (present-day Amu-Darya), Dnepr and Volga rivers,
in an age when the great empires were of necessity either maritime or river-
centred.

The ease with which it is possible to pass from Asia into Europe has been
illustrated on many occasions over the centuries by a succession of invaders in
the opposite direction; the Russians were the first 'westerners' to reach the
Pacific coast (1649) and to settle in Alaska (1741), whereas the Spanish San
Francisco Mission was not founded until 1776.

Only the mountainous fringes on the southern borders of the Soviet Union,
the Carpathians, the Crimean mountains, the Caucasus, the Pamirs and the
Tien Shan, linking up with the curving chains of southern Siberia, have helped
isolate this territory in the past from the fertile influences of the more
advanced civilizations of India, China or the Middle East. In addition, the
northern seas, which are ice-bound for more than half the year, isolated the
country from the main currents of sea traffic until the foundation of St Petersburg (1703), Odessa (1794), Vladivostok (1860) and Murmansk (1916) and the
annexation of eastern Prussia (Kaliningrad) in 1945.

The position and relief of the country, which affect temperature and
humidity, establish the conditions for a range of vegetation types and
ecological zones. Leaving aside the arid or steeply sloping regions in the south,

the cold or marshy regions of the north, the drought-ridden regions and those where the soil is frozen to great depths, there remains a privileged triangular zone lying between Tallin, Kishinev and Barnaul on the Ob, comprising in particular coniferous and deciduous forests in the west as well as the rich black earth of the steppes (12 per cent of the country's area), where the Slav farmers found the most favourable conditions for settlement prior to the industrial era. Even today, 70 per cent of the population lives in this triangle covering only 20 per cent of Soviet territory, with population density dwindling eastwards towards the steppes as the country becomes increasingly exposed to frost and drought (i.e. into a zone of unreliable farming). In fact, the Soviet population is spread along two main axes: one from north to south, corresponding to the soil and vegetation belts, the other east to west, showing the contrast between the western regions, where settlement is continuous, and the eastern regions, where colonization progresses in scattered islands. This discontinuous pattern of settlement beyond the left bank of the Volga is far more characteristic than the false barrier of the Urals, reflecting the human, rather than geographical, frontier between the European and the eastern regions of the Soviet Union.

Tables 1 and 2 indicate the natural features and resources of the different regions, and the ways in which their populations have made use of them.

From Table 1 we can see that arable land covers only 28 per cent of the total area of the Soviet Union, more or less exactly corresponding to the fertile and temperate regions of the country; 15 per cent of the area lies in the arid zones; and 57 per cent in the northern zone, of which roughly 20 per cent is unsuitable for agriculture owing to the cold. A further 30 per cent has to be eliminated on account of its relief and 8.5 per cent because the ground is too marshy. In the end, 11 per cent of the land is cultivated (compared with 8–9 per cent in Canada and Finland, 10.5 per cent in Sweden). This privileged zone lies on the southern limit of the *merzlota* (i.e. between the 62nd and 63rd parallels in Europe and the 58th and 62nd parallels in Asia), beyond which the number of frost-free days provides an annual total of 1100–1500°C (rye requires 1000–1250°C to ripen, while flax requires 1200–1600°C).

Further to the south, cereal cropping is brought to a halt by the aridity barrier. Cereal farming requires 393 millimetres of rainfall per hectare to produce 2 tonnes of vegetable matter, representing a minimum of 192 millimetres after evaporation. Now, while the water balance stands at 200 millimetres in the central regions, it falls to 15–60 millimetres in the south. The southerly steppes receive in the form of rainfall only two-thirds of the water required to grow wheat. These steppes are ravaged by drought: it occurs one year in ten in the wooded steppes of the Ukraine, one in three or four in the Volga provinces, one in every two in Kazakhstan.

Outside this triangle, Soviet agriculture is highly unreliable and costly. The lack of water has to be compensated for by irrigation schemes or canals. The ability to control the water supply enabled the civilizations of central Asia to

TABLE 1 Soviet territory from north to south

Natural zones	Ecological characteristics							Land occupation		
	% of territory	Mean temperature		Rainfall (mm)		Vegetation (%)		Land under cultivation (%)	Population as % of total	density per km[1]
		Annual	June	Total	Summer	Forest	Prairies			
Tundra	9.3	−10.5	0.14	270	85		} 14.8		} 1	0.4
Forest tundra	15.4	− 7.7		350	160					
Taiga or boreal forest	31	+ 1.6	10−20	300−600 500−600	310			20.4	7	8.0−0.8
Mixed forest	8.2					{ 56.6	10		24	45
Forest steppe	7.7	+ 1.5	17−20	435	270	3.6	} 16.5	69.0	29	64−19
Meadow	4.8	+ 3.3	19−23	380	245				} 17	43−7.5
Arid	2.8	+ 4.4		285	185					
Semidesert	3.9	+ 5.2	24−27	150−250	125		} 42		1	2
Desert	8.4	+10.9	25−32	155	80			5.9	6	5.5
Mountainous regions	8.5					39.9	16.7	4.7	15	4.8
Total or USSR average	100	− 1.4		392	220	100	100	100	100	11.2

Note: 1 Where a range is given, the first figure gives average density in western regions, the second in Siberian regions.

TABLE 2 *Soviet territory from east to west*

Regions	Territory	Natural resources				Land use and development					Economic flows	
		Hydro.	Energy	Gas	Iron ore	Crops[1]	Population		Towns (no.)	Indus-trial output	Tonnage carried[2]	
							1970	density per square km			Import	Export
Europe												
Baltic republics	0.8	0.7	⎱ 0.1			28	3.1	40.2	203	3.5	11.3	6.9
Byelorussia	0.9	<0.1	⎰			30	3.7	44.3	78	2.7	12	7.9
Northwest	7.5	3.9	4.3	3.3	3.0	1.9	5	7.2	114	7.1	14.5	15.9
Centre	2.1	0.6	⎱ 0.2		38.1	31	11.4	57.3	233	14.4	9.3	8.1
Volga–Viatka	1.2	0.6	⎰			30	3.4	31.5	62	3.6	8.1	7.2
Russian black-earth lands	0.9					67	3.3	47.7	48	2.5	12.2	10
Ukraine	2.8	1.5	2.4	6.0	23.4	60	19.5	80	382	17.3	14.7	16.5
Moldavia	0.2	<0.1				56	1.5	110	20		5.9	3.0
Northern Caucasus	1.6	2.3	0.8	5.4		46	6.0	40	88	4.5	9.6	10.0
Transcaucasia	0.8	4.0	0.2	0.4		14	5.1	65	126	3.7	6.7	5.0
Volga	3.1	3.8	0.4	0.6		44	7.6	27	99	9	8.3	10
Urals	3.1	1.1	0.5	5.0	13.4	26	6.3	22	120	9.3	20.6	20.0
Asia												
Central Asia	5.5	13.2	0.9	15.1		5	8.3	16	87	3.2	4.4	3.5
Kazakhstan	12.3	2.5	1.3	1.7	14.8	12	5.3	5	67	3.8	10.9	13.7
Western Siberia	10.6	6.8	13.3	58.1	⎱ 7.3	8	5	5	60	5.6	15.6	19.7
Eastern Siberia and far east	46.6	59	75.6	3.0	⎰	1	5.5	1.2	117	3.9 / 3.1	12.2 / 14.9	17 / 11.6
Total USSR	100	100	100	100	100	10.7	100	11.2	1904	100		

Notes: 1 This column indicates land under cultivation as a percentage of the total area of the region.
2 Tonnage carried by rail per head of population in 1970.

achieve quite startling concentrations of people: in the oases of Tashkent and Bokhara, the population density exceeds 200 inhabitants per square kilometre.

Population density in turn produces sharply varying degrees of farming intensity in the different regions. In Moldavia, the Ukraine, Byelorussia and the Baltic republics, the value of output per unit of arable land is far superior to the Soviet average, whereas in the eastern regions agriculture is characteristically extensive. Land-use patterns are as important as actual areas of cultivated land: this is illustrated by the remarkable productivity of private land plots (3 per cent of cultivated private land produces more than half the potato crop), which receive regular and careful attention.

The development of industrial resources also requires water (100,000 litres of water to produce one tonne of steel). As Table 2 shows, between 77 and 87 per cent of the country's total water reserves (depending upon our source of information) lie in the eastern regions, but three-quarters of this surface water flows out along the great Siberian rivers into the Arctic seas, whereas the inhabited regions, drained by the river basins flowing into the Baltic, Black, Aral and Caspian seas, receive only 16 per cent of available water. It is therefore necessary to supplement this with additional water supplies from canals or reservoirs.

Turning to primary energy sources, the imbalance between east and west is sharper still, with 90 per cent of the total (and 75 per cent of natural-gas reserves) lying east of the Urals, as do more than 70 per cent of all nonferrous ores. This lopsided distribution results in a considerable flow of raw materials and fuel between east and west, as the processing industries tend to be located in the densely populated regions, which generally happen to be those better suited to agriculture than to industry.

DEVELOPMENT POLES AND CULTURAL AREAS

Thus, under pressure from a variety of factors (natural and historical, as well as land-occupation and -use patterns), a number of particularly prominent poles of development have grown up. Two-thirds of Soviet society, indeed three-quarters if we regard the Urals and the Caucasus as belonging to Europe, still lie within the confines of Europe.

At the present time, the Soviet Union's axis of development lies within a zone comprising the Baltic republics, Leningrad, the industrial centre, the Ukraine and the Volga basin; close to two-thirds of the country's industrial and agricultural output is produced on less than 20 per cent of its territory. A second development pole lies to the north and south of the Caucasus and extends into central Asia: 20.3 per cent of the Soviet population inhabit this region, which represents 8.9 per cent of the total area. The regions of Kazakhstan and Siberia, which together represent 68.9 per cent of the total, at present contain only 15.8 per cent of the Soviet Union's inhabitants.

These disparities in land occupation coincide with cultural areas which have been determined by specific ecological conditions: the trappers of the tundra, the nomads of the arid plateaux and the steppes and the farmers of the wooded steppe and forest clearings. Some of these belong to the European sphere of influence, while others are subject to the cultural influence of Asia Minor, Iran or Mongolia. Thus, present-day Soviet territory resembles a juxtaposition of three different regions, distinguished both by their contents and their development dynamics: the *European region*, which is relatively populous and developed; the *Soviet Third World*, made up of Asiatic peoples, which is predominantly agricultural, traditionally backward and only now in the throes of industrialization; and, lastly, the *pioneer lands* of Siberia and the far north, where the development of industrial resources entails a concentration of the population first in camps[1] and subsequently in new towns. Soviet society, whose unity we are concerned to delimit here, occupies a far from homogeneous territory; while, for the sake of concision, we shall subsequently be laying greater stress on the shared characteristics of the Soviet peoples, we shall nevertheless invariably encounter these three distinct environments when we come, for example, to analyse the family or Soviet urban patterns.

Even today, the distribution of eating and housing patterns in the Soviet Union is as much a reflection of ecological as of cultural factors, which may find expression in culinary traditions or local architecture. A Yakut's calorie intake should in principle be 15 per cent higher than a Muscovite's. A Chud in the far north will eat on average 326 grammes of fish, 372 of meat (reindeer and sea mammals), 294 of dairy produce, 35 of potatoes and 8 of vegetables daily, while a Russian peasant on a collective farm has to make do with 5.6 grammes of potatoes, 213 of vegetables, 101 of meat, 768 of dairy produce and only 15 of fish. Where brick 64 centimetres wide provides sufficient protection from the cold in Moscow, a wall twice as thick is needed in Yakutsk. Still, the housing and nutritional maps do not necessarily coincide with ecological zones. In the north, for example, wooden houses (*izba*) are now found well outside the forest zone where they originated, spreading with the Russian and Cossack colonization of the steppe and gradually supplanting the yurt as the Buryat nomads adopt a sedentary way of life. Further to the south, similarly, the dividing line between bacon-eating and sheep-eating Russia is not determined by isotherms but by cultural influences forbidding the Muslim populations, for instance, to eat pig's meat or scaleless fish. For this reason, the Muslim peoples inhabiting the shores of the Caspian Sea do not eat the flesh of the sturgeon they catch to produce caviar from it for export.

SOVIET ATTITUDES TO THE ENVIRONMENT

Lucien Febvre reminds us that 'between man and his natural environment lie ideas', i.e. the individual's conception of the environment and his knowledge and understanding of it are as important as physical constraints (*La Terre et l'évolution humaine*, 1949). This cultural conditioning and these ancestral influences still determine certain aspects of Soviet behaviour and attitudes towards nature, especially among the strata most steeped in peasant traditions.

Respect for or submission to the forces of nature, though not without a desire to conquer or transform the natural environment; a love of the land, which does not diminish the Soviet people's *wanderlust* as they perpetually roam in search of fresh horizons; and a trust in the generosity of the national soil, now mitigated by a growing awareness of its limitations and the need to conserve resources, all reflect some degree of ambivalance as between individual attitudes and the ideas underpinning official policy.

Popular beliefs

Literature, and above all poetry, bear abundant testimony to the nature-worship common to all the peoples of the Soviet Union. In the face of the unknown, small isolated communities become aware of the overwhelming odds stacked against them and seek, by means of propitiatory rites, to conciliate the forces which, according to their beliefs, are present in every living thing, plants, animals and individuals alike. Hunting, and subsequently the domestication of animals and development of pastoral economies, brought these communities into very close contact with both fauna and flora, as we can see from those admirable masterpieces of animal representation left by the peoples of the steppe or in the miniatures painted under Persian influence.

Christianity and Islam merely reinforced the sense of submission to the natural order, to the point where barely a century ago Russian peasants in the Smolensk region refused to replant a crop devastated by greenfly, for 'God created the greenfly, and he must therefore live; it is forbidden to alter the order willed by God'.[2]

However, people do interpret nature differently from one cultural sphere or nationality to the next. Thus, for example, the peoples of the tundra have a very special conception of the principal points of the compass: for them, the Arctic Ocean lies in the south, for the tundra slopes down to its shores, and the fact that they have to climb up towards the taiga gives them the impression that this lies in the north; here, the east is dubbed the 'front' the place where the sun rises, and the west, the 'back'. They hang amulets or *unguns* – animal-shaped figurines intended to capture the prey that are hunted – from the trees around their dwellings in order to drive out evil spirits, for traces of shamanism still exist among these nomads who came from the Siberian taiga several centuries ago. The bear is venerated as much as it is feared. When he kills a bear, the Nenets begs forgiveness: 'It was not I who killed you, but the Russian who made the gun.'

In the Russian villages in the taiga, people no longer believe in the 'forest spirit' (*leshy*); they are no longer afraid of being charmed by the waterspirit (*russalka*), the divinity of the waters who treacherously lured her victims to their fate; she has now ceased to be anything but a decorative motif in folk art. Certain traditional festivals are nevertheless still governed by the solar cycle: New Year and Christmas follow the winter solstice, while Candlemas (*Maslenitsa*) corresponds to the equinox. After a seemingly endless winter, these festivals express the people's longing for light and for the return of summer. Although the summer-solstice bacchanalia have now disappeared, the tradition has been perpetuated in modern forms: Russian students completing secondary school spend the last night before the long summer holiday strolling together until dawn, and the popular song, 'Moscow Nights', reflects this nostalgia for long romantic evenings.

The forest-dweller generally evinces no special love for the tree, with the exception of the birch, symbol of light and young maidens, considering the rest primarily as material to be made use of. The man of the desert, on the other hand, looks upon the tree as a friend, and its welcome shade perpetuates the memory of the man who planted it (filmgoers are referred to Konchalovsky's film *The First Master*, adapted from Aitmatov's novel). Here, the well, water, source of all life, counts for more than land. The Turkmen would be insulted if you were to shake off the water after he had poured it over your hands to refresh you after a strenuous journey across the sands. Wealth here is not counted in acres but in head of cattle, or sheep or goats.

For all these peoples of the forest and the steppe, the horse, which originated hereabouts, guarantees the fertility of the soil and is the very incarnation of power and fertility, which is why the front end of the ridge beam of the *izba* is often decorated with a stylized form of horse. Collectivization robbed the peasant of this faithful companion in whom he confided his secrets. Here, as elsewhere, now that it has been replaced by the tractor, the horse has become an object of display and takes part in races or exhibitions of equestrian skill (*djigitovka*) by Cossack, Kazakh or Caucasian horsemen. Another animal, the cat, is a familiar symbol of wisdom and agility and an indispensable companion for anyone moving to Moscow, Leningrad or Kiev (traditionally, the cat must be the first to cross the threshold of a new apartment). In Russian folklore, the cat is also regarded as something of a usurper (*kot Vas'ka vor*).

The love of hunting, and of fishing especially, dies hard, and Soviet citizens practise them from an early age. Some 3.5 million fishing permits are issued annually, while three times that number actually go fishing.

Herbalism continues to be a highly popular form of folk medicine. The writer Soluhin devotes a high-flown chapter to grass in *Olepinskie Prudy* (1973), as well as a whole book to what he calls 'the third form of hunting'. This is the name he gives to the gathering of berries, nuts and mushrooms, which has grown into a national sport. The newspapers carry stories relating the season's records. The Russians view mushrooms as a kind of manna from heaven, growing mysteriously: no one plants them, and consequently they can be nobody's property. Even the landowners of the past dared not bar the peasants from their forests when they came to gather mushrooms; today, the government tolerates the sale of mushrooms at market by children, even though in principle only adults are allowed to engage in trade.

The rural population is still very much attached to the family farm. As with many farming people, respect for the earth is part and parcel of Russian religious feeling. Which is why, in the past, peasants kept in a safe place the shirt in which they planned to be buried; even today many are reluctant to be cremated and some leave town at the approach of death in order to be buried in their native villages. The theme of the all-providing earth (*zemlya kormilitsa*) lives on in Soviet poetry. Frequently, this attachment does not extend beyond the individual's locality. The notion that the fatherland is conterminous with the national soil only belatedly appeared in the popular consciousness, because for generations the people had grown used to venerating their chief – the Tsar, Lenin or Stalin – as embodying the nation's destiny. The first, and above all the second, world wars were in this respect major milestones in the maturing of national consciousness into less personalized forms.

This growing awareness also finds expression in the relatively recent public interest in the conservation of natural resources: the newspapers are devoting increasing space to campaigns against pollution of rivers and lakes or against the depredations caused by poaching. Does this spell an end to the myth of the fatherland's limitless bounty?

The lure of the wide-open spaces and the habit of wandering is rooted in a long tradition of itinerant workers: the taiga trappers; the nomads of the steppe; the slash-and-burn farmers; escaped peasants seeking to free themselves from serfdom or to evade conscription; members of persecuted sects seeking refuge in remote regions far from the reach of the central authorities; pilgrims aglow with divine love roaming from monastery to monastery; sons of the prophet setting out on the great *hajj* to the holy places of Islam; carters driving loads of food, salt or fodder from fair to fair; artels (peasant co-operatives) or artisans offering their services from village to village; peasants hiring themselves out to the factory or mine in the off-season; and gold-diggers drawn by the eldorado of Siberia. The Soviet people are inveterate wanderers. Some 60 million Soviet citizens aged over 16 spend their holidays away from their place of residence, as many do elsewhere; but they are not alone in helping to preserve this tradition of collective nomadism, for 19.8 per cent of industrial workers in 1972, i.e. 6.5 million people, changed jobs in the course of a year. Further, while 1,450,000 country people left their villages and went to live in the towns, in each of the past 10 years, 1 million seasonal workers signed up for farm work in the collective and state farms. Giving practical effect to an old Russian proverb along the lines of 'the grass is greener on the other side', each Soviet citizen makes an average of 2.8 journeys per year, not including the suburbanites' daily journeys to and from work which involve a daily contingent of 15 million individuals.

Official doctrines regarding development planning

Ever since Peter the Great and Lomonosov, politicians and intellectuals who have given thought to Russia's future have always taken an optimistic view of the territory's wealth while affirming the possibilities of exploiting it and, if necessary, transforming nature. The great chemist Mendeleyev, for instance, reckoned in 1900 that the amount of land suitable for agriculture in Russia was capable of supporting a population of 400 million farmers and an equivalent number of non-agricultural workers by the year 2050. The pioneers who opened up Russia's territory also founded the Russian school of geography, thereby creating a tradition of active geography, which the advent of Marxism as official doctrine has reinforced.

A certain number of correctives were required before the theories of Marx and Engels (which were inspired by their analysis of the industrial countries, especially their proposal to deconcentrate industry in order to weaken opposition between town and country) could be applied in the Russian context. Lenin defined these in his April 1918 *Instructions* to the Russian Academy of Sciences, to which he entrusted the task of drafting the first development plans (*Complete Works*, vol. 36). For him, this entailed: (1) remedying the uneven geographical distribution of industry inherited from the *ancien régime*, (a) by creating on the periphery the industries needed to ensure the economic independence of the nationalities as well as their political independence, and (b) by bringing heavy industry closer to the raw materials supplying it in order to reduce production costs; (2) concentrating production capacities so as to form larger units better able to benefit from the most productive techniques; and (3) electrification, which he regarded as the powerhouse of development.

The idea that sources of energy were the point of departure for the country's development was to remain a constant in Soviet doctrine. In the 1920s, Alfred Weber's principles of localization (*Über den Standort der Industrien* (On the siting of industry), 1909) were fashionable in the Soviet Union, but after the abandonment of the New Economic Policy (NEP) financial criteria borrowed from capitalist economics were replaced by criteria of technical coherence. N.N. Kolosovski developed the theory of the chain of production which, from a given source of energy, determined all the different industries needed upstream and downstream to create a pole of development. According to current doctrine, the pole — known as the TPC (territorial production complex) — is the key to regional planning, although it is necessarily centred upon a source of energy. Nowadays, computers can be used to optimize resource utilization and the location of production units by means of mathematical models designed to maximize output while minimizing harmful secondary effects such as pollution, consumption of non-renewable natural resources and soil use.

Evaluations of industrial resources are constantly altering, partly because new prospecting modifies initial data — as with the recent discovery of Siberian oil — and partly because technological progress affects definitions of natural resources. Thus, the notion is a relative one; relative, that is, to a given state of technology. What is more, prices and costs modify the profitability of production processes. For example, since the 1973—4 oil crisis, the Soviet Union has revised its energy forecasts: the proportion of oil in the 1980 balance has been reduced from 36 to 28 per cent, while nuclear energy will in 1985 represent 14 per cent of electricity generated compared with 2 per cent in 1977. The Peterson report (1972)[3] contains the following comparison of Soviet potential compared with American reserves (=100):

Oil reserves: 135
Natural-gas reserves: 127
Coal reserves: 453
Hydroelectric resources: 350

It seems, nevertheless, that Soviet planners, having, like those in the United States until the second world war, viewed their natural environment as containing unlimited wealth, are now becoming increasingly aware of the need for conservation. Recent years have seen legislation to protect the land (1968), forests and waterways (1970) and natural resources (1972). Soviet economists, who, taking their cue from Marxist theory, formerly thought that human labour alone generates value, now acknowledge that natural resources also have a value, which must be taken into account in order to moderate their utilization: 10,000 hectares of arable land are eaten up each year by urban and industrial growth, while 25 per cent of coal is lost in the process of extraction. Factories now pay a rent on resource utilization, and there is talk of introducing an additional rent for the site they occupy.

THE DYNAMICS OF DEVELOPMENT PLANNING

Populations are constantly shifting around Soviet territory. For thousands of years, they were subject to the constraints of the natural environment; but today they possess techniques capable of transforming it. What are the main directions taken by these human migrations, in what direction does the resulting interregional commerce flow, and what are the main technical and intellectual underpinnings of the relationship between Soviet society and its territory?

Migratory movements

Over the centuries, population movements have conformed to three major patterns.

From west to east. The populations originating in the steppe or the European forests are slowly but surely advancing into the Asian territories. Between 1897 and 1973, the European nucleus to the west of the Volga grew by 44.5 million inhabitants, while the regions to the east of the Volga gained 78 million, practically twice the European figure. This nucleus now represents only 44 per cent of the population, against 65 per cent in 1861. In 1897, only three of the southern European farming regions had a population density in excess of forty inhabitants per square kilometre; by 1940, the industrial centre, Byelorussia, the Donets basin and the Caucasus had all exceeded this mean; in 1973, the Baltic lands and the provinces of the northern Caucasus had caught up with them, while Siberia and Kazakhstan, on the other hand, still had fewer inhabitants per square kilometre than the national average for 1897. Thus, the colonization of the Asian regions is far from complete, although there is unlikely to be any spectacular movement in the coming decades, for long-term forecasts attribute to Siberia only 12 per cent of the total volume of Soviet industrial output in 1990, compared with 9.5 per cent in 1980.

From the agricultural provinces to the industrial regions, and from country to town. This exodus is particularly noticeable close to the development poles. Thus, in western Ukraine, the present-day population of the agricultural centre is lower than it was in 1926, whereas in the Donets region the population has practically doubled. The exodus to the towns is particularly marked in the eastern regions, as a result of industrialization; with the exception of central Asia, these are now all predominantly urban. In 1939, peasants on collective farms represented 42 per cent of the working population in Siberia and the far east, but by 1959, they represented only 24 per cent. Between 1959 and 1970, some 3.3 million rural inhabitants left their Siberian villages to settle in the towns, a matter of some concern to local agriculture officials. At the same time, the population of the Siberian towns has grown 2–2.5 times quicker than in the European towns.

From north to south. A population shift has occurred not only as a result of the attractions of the climate in the Mediterranean or Caucasian regions, but also as a result of the higher birthrates in the Caucasian and central Asian republics: the population of southern Ukraine, Moldavia, northern Caucasus, Transcaucasus, central Asia and Kazakhstan grew by over 28 per cent in 11 years (1959–70), while that of the RSFSR (Russian Soviet Federal Socialist Republic) lost 1 million people, who went to settle in the southern republics, between the last two censuses.

Out of a total increase in the Soviet population of 68 million inhabitants between 1940 and 1979, the eastern regions gained 44.3 million or 65 per cent of the increase. In the 1940s and 1950s, a period coinciding with the second world war when certain industries were shifted eastwards, the urban population doubled in these regions; the 1960s saw a sharp acceleration of the

TABLE 3   *Population dynamics in the eastern regions, 1940–79*
(*in millions at beginning of year*)

	1940			1959			1979		
	Total	*Towns*	*Rural*	*Total*	*Towns*	*Rural*	*Total*	*Towns*	*Rural*
Central Asia	16.6	4.1	12.5	23.0	8.8	14.2	40.9	18.6	22.3
Urals	10.5	3.8	6.7	14.1	8.0	6.1	21.4	15.1	6.3
Western Siberia	9.1	2.8	6.3	11.2	6.0	5.2	11.1	7.7	3.4
Eastern Siberia	4.9	1.7	3.2	6.5	3.4	3.1	9.1	6.2	2.9
Far East	3.1	1.5	1.6	4.8	3.3	1.5	6.0	4.6	1.4
Eastern regions	44.2	13.9	30.3	59.6	29.5	30.1	88.5	52.2	36.3

rural exodus in the Urals and Siberia, where the rural population dropped by
3.6 million between 1940 and 1979; at present, the average annual number of
people leaving the countryside is three times what it was in the previous decade
owing to progress in the exploitation of Siberia's industrial resources.

These population movements are producing a concomitant transformation
of the landscape: dwindling fauna despite protective measures (in the form of
nature reservations); deforestation in certain European provinces where the
forests are subject to intensive exploitation; shrinking arable land as towns and
industries encroach, but also as hydroelectric dams flood vast tracts of land;
river pollution; soil erosion due to wind (now threatening 18 million hectares
of cropland), though this is paralleled by the spread of ground clearance and
irrigated land in the course of agricultural colonization. Since 1917, or in the
space of two generations, 70 million hectares of virgin land have been brought
under the plough, more than half as a result of clearance schemes carried out
in 1954–5, in Kazakhstan especially (2.5 million hectares). Although the
balance to date is substantially positive, towns and industries are likely in the
course of the coming decade to swallow up more arable land than the acreage
capable of being recovered from swamps and desert. Whatever happens, the
sheer size of the territory means that land alone cannot represent a limiting
factor.

Interregional economic flows

The highly unequal distribution of population and resources across the
country produces a series of interregional economic flows between importing
zones and surplus zones. Table 2 illustrates the importance of the peripheral
northwestern regions, the Urals, the Volga, Siberia and Kazakhstan, in the
supply of raw materials and fuel to the central industrial provinces as well as
the relatively modest level of external trade carried on by the least industrial
regions, i.e. Moldavia, Transcaucasus and central Asia.

The opening up of Siberia is generating a greater reciprocity between the
energy surpluses produced in the east and the processing capacities of the

western regions, but it is also generating considerable transport costs: for example, western Siberia exports over 50 per cent of its coal, while the K700 tractors bound for Kazakhstan are made in Leningrad from steel supplied by the Donbass or the Urals.

The long-term (1971–90) territorial development plan jointly prepared by Gosplan (SOPS – the State Planning Commission) and the Academy of Sciences (KEPS) aims at rationalizing the location of activities in keeping with regional characteristics and the state of technology with a view to bringing down unit costs. The main lines of future economic regionalization may be stated as follows:

1 The north and the European centre, with limited energy and labour resources but with a good industrial infrastructure, will be specializing in advanced, high-labour-productive (capital-intensive) industries, and this zone's energy deficit will be made good by the building of nuclear power stations, while farming will focus on establishing a stable food-supply base.

2 The European south and the Caucasus are better endowed than the centre with resources, except water which here places a limit on the expansion both of agriculture and of industry.

3 Siberia and Kazakhstan will attract the major energy-consuming industries (cellulose, aluminium, titanium, nickel, man-made fibres) but those which require little labour.

4 Central Asia, on the other hand, with its rapidly growing population (8.7 per cent of the total population of the Soviet Union today and expected to rise to 12–14 per cent in 1990), might specialize in labour-intensive industry (light industry, radio and electrical assembly, etc.).

5 The Volga-Urals region would seem to be the most favoured region, owing to the presence of energy resources and a few pockets of potential reserve labour from agriculture, as well as more abundant water supplies than in the south, creating conditions for irrigation-based cereal cropping. In addition, this region is ideally situated, between Europe and Asia, to play a decisive role in balancing the anticipated development. Which is why the Soviet Union's centre of gravity will continue to lie in Europe, where between 55 and 65 per cent of its industrial and agricultural output will continue to be concentrated in 1990.

Without in any way minimizing the progress made in the opening up of the Siberian regions, in particular through the creation of a considerable industrial potential over the past thirty years (these regions currently produce as much steel as the whole of the Soviet Union did in 1940) we should guard against succumbing to Siberia's eternal romantic fascination. Generations of Russians and foreigners have, like the Americans setting out to conquer the far west in the last century, flocked to these fabulous virgin lands. Today, however, cold-headed planners armed with computers calculate the cost of settling people in these inhospitable regions, and conclude that it is cheaper to transport

Siberia's resources to Europe than to transfer people to Siberia. New means of communication (roads, oil and gas pipelines, a second Trans-Siberian railway — BAM — 3150 kilometres north of the first one) are currently under construction in order to shift Siberia's forestry, mineral and energy resources to Europe and the Pacific Ocean. Following Canada's example, the Soviets plan to keep to a minimum the labour required to exploit the wealth lying beneath the soil in the northern regions so as to avoid the need to install cumbersome urban infrastructures.

Technical progress in the long-distance transport of electricity by means of higher voltages now makes it possible to eliminate line-loss and to envisage the day when the European grid can be connected to the powerful installations in Siberia (where voltages of up to 1150 kV a.c. and 1500 kV d.c., permitting transport of electricity over 1500 kilometres, are currently being generated). Similarly, pipeline transport is suited to liquid and gas fuels because of the ease with which they can be moved to the refineries and the centres of consumption (oil and gas account for 68 per cent of the 1980 energy budget, compared with 18 per cent in 1950). A programme for constructing pipelines and containers for the transport of minerals and other heavy substances is also at the planning stage. As a result, not only the energy budget itself but also the location of economic activity is being profoundly modified by these new, easily transported forms of energy.

Far more costly and spectacular are the schemes to divert rivers from the northern regions to the water-starved southern ones. The problems involved are considerable, as the possible repercussions of these changes on the ecology of the regions concerned have to be taken into account. Major schemes currently being considered include: in Europe, a navigable waterway between the western Dvina and the Dnepr, a series of civil-engineering projects to increase the water supply to the industrial cities of the Donbass, Moscow, Sverdlovsk and the Baku and Emba oil centres; the linking of the Sea of Azov with the Caspian by means of a series of dams and canals; the diversion of the Vychedga waters towards Kama and the Volga so as to improve the Caspian's resources; similarly, in western Siberia, it is proposed to link the Ob, the Irtysh and the Tobol to the Sea of Aral and the Caspian. The first phase of this project, which represents the marriage of forest-clad, wet, practically uninhabited Siberia with the arid steppes and overcrowded oases of central Asia, takes the form of a 514-kilometre stretch already in service between the Irtysh and Karaganda, soon to be extended to Dzhezkazgan. What once belonged to the realms of science fiction is now a product of the economic and demographic dynamics of the Soviet Union, logically driving it to the conquest of new land in regions suitable for irrigation.

Dynamic conceptions of geography and resources

Not only is the individual's physical relationship to the territory changing, but so also are Soviet conceptions of geography and the natural environment.

As we have already seen, the popular view of the fatherland is no longer confined to the native region or locality: now it encompasses the entire national territory, and a Soviet consciousness is being forged in the mingling of different cultures and population migrations. But, far more than this extension of geographical consciousness to the entire Soviet territory, what seems to be new in the outlook of economic and political leaders is the breaking up of national frontiers due to the special position that the Soviet Union has accorded itself in the community of socialist countries.

In the economic sense of the term, the Soviet sphere now includes the far vaster zone embracing all those countries now engaged alongside the Soviet Union in a common effort of co-operation or integration within the Comecon framework. Materially, this takes the form of supranational firms, an interconnected electricity grid, oil and gas pipelines, a goods-waggon pool, etc., all of which may be regarded as extensions of the Soviet economy.

Modern techniques themselves contribute to this spatial projection by means of extra-territorial communications infrastructures, which are indispensable to meteorology, civil aviation, television, etc. Methods of exploration are no longer necessarily earth-bound, but make use of aerial and satellite exploration. Furthermore, on 27 January 1967, the Soviet Union signed the treaty by which all signatory nations renounced the national appropriation of outer space.

Similarly, politically or strategically speaking, space extends to wherever the Soviet state can assert its control, by coercion if necessary. The occupation of Czechoslovakia on 20 August 1968 by Warsaw Pact troops, illustrates the limits imposed on the sovereignty of member states in the name of the Brezhnev doctrine. Indeed, the Soviet presence extends well beyond its zone of direct political influence: the Soviet Indian Ocean fleet enjoys 'facilities' in Aden; while in Spitzbergen, which is under Norwegian sovereignty, the Soviet Union has the use of an aerodrome under the terms of the treaty of 7 March 1974. The aeroplane has given added importance to the northern regions, since it makes Washington less remote than Vladivostok from Moscow. In other words, the economic and political frontiers of a state shift as much as the isobars delimiting forces of equal pressure.

Not only does technical progress expand the inventory of national resources by means of more systematic exploration; it also helps to reveal latent potential by in a sense creating new resources: Soviet research into the uses of wind, solar and geothermal energy has attracted a great deal of interest on the part of specialists, as has its agronomic research and research into hydroponic techniques (the manufacture of proteins from parasitic aquatic plants in lakes), intensive fresh-water fish-breeding, etc.

Thus, within a few generations Russia has emerged from submission to nature to a position of dominance over nature. At the same time, people are becoming increasingly aware of the need for conservation, though without going to the lengths of those westerners who reject the notion of economic growth in the name of environmental conservation. For Marxists, happiness is synonymous with abundance, which implies growth, but this does not preclude the appeal of a more authentic way of life closer to nature — the Soviets call this 'romanticism' — in whose name thousands of young people go off to work on schemes far off on the country's different pioneer 'fronts'. For, in the final analysis, all these resources take on value only through men and women themselves, the sole true resource. What do all these people, taken together, represent? Are they, or will they be, sufficiently numerous and organized to control the shifting frontiers of their destiny in this territory resembling a garment many sizes too large?

NOTES

1 Throughout history the deportation of labour has been a traditional method of opening up virgin lands in inhospitable regions. One need only think of the history of Australia (see A. J. Youngson, 'The opening up of new territories', *The Cambridge Economic History of Europe*, vol. 6, part 1, Cambridge University Press, 1966, p. 166.) — not that this necessarily morally justifies the existence of what Solzhenitsyn has called the 'Gulag Archipelago'.

2 B. Kerblay, 'La vie rurale dans la province de Smolensk d'après A. N. Engelgardt', *Le Statut des paysans libérés du Servage 1865–1961*, Paris, Mouton, 1963, p. 300.

3 Peter G. Peterson (former United States Secretary of Commerce), 'U.S. commercial relationship in a new area', Department of Commerce mimeograph, August 1972.

SUGGESTED READING

Geographical history

Coquin, F.-X., *La Sibérie: peuplement et immigrations paysannes au XIXe siecle*, Paris, Institut d'études slaves, 1969.
Parker, W. H., *An Historical Geography of Russia*, University of London Press, 1968.
Semenov, V. P., *Rossiya, polnoe geograficheskoe opisanie*, St Petersburg, 1899–1914, 11 vols.
Regional Development in the USSR, Brussels, Nato, Oxford, Pergamon, 1979.

General geography

Cole, J., *L'U.R.S.S.*, Paris, A. Colin, 1969.
George, P., *L'U.R.S.S.*, P.U.F., 1962.
Lydolph, P. E., *Geography in the USSR*, New York, John Wiley, 1980.
Parker, W. H., *The Soviet Union*, London, Longman, 1969.
Sovietskii Soyuz, geograficheskoe opisanie, Moscow, Mysl', 1967–72, 23 vols.

Economic geography

Blanc, A. and Chambre, H., *L'U.R.S.S.*, P.U.F., 1976.
Carrière, P., *L'Économie de l'U.R.S.S.*, Masson, 1974.

Chambre, H., *L'Aménagement du territoire en U.R.S.S.*, Mouton, 1959.

Hooson, D., *The Soviet Union: A Systematic Regional Geography*, University of London Press, 1968.

Whitting, A., *Siberian development and East Asia*, Stanford University Press, 1981.

Ecology

Giroux, A., 'L'environnement en U.R.S.S.', *Le Courrier des pays de l'Est*, no. 442, June 1971.

Goldman, M., *The Spoils of Progress: Environmental Pollution in the Soviet Union*, Cambridge, Mass., 1972.

Komarov, B., *The Destruction of Nature in the Soviet Union*, White Plains, New York, Sharpe, 1980.

McIntyre, R. and Thornton, J., 'On the environmental efficiency of economic systems', *Soviet Studies*, vol. 30, no. 2, 1975. A reply by Ziegler, C.E., in *Soviet Studies*, vol. 32, no. 1, 1980.

'Protection de la nature et ressources', *Problèmes politiques et sociaux*, nos 9 (1970), 149 (1972), 164–5 (1973).

Chapter 2

The populations of the Soviet Union

THE SOVIET PEOPLE AS A WHOLE: NUMBERS

On 1 January 1983, the population of the Soviet Union stood at 271.2 million, and at its current rate of increase, 0.9 per cent, its population in 2054 will be double what it was in 1975. Doubtless this rate of increase depends primarily on individual decisions (marriages, births) and on the physical constitution of the population (morbidity, mortality); but it depends also on the historical context (laws and conquests), economic factors (famine, growth of cities, resources) and cultural patterns (religious views, birth control) characteristic of the society under study. As a result, demographic trends are a reflection of the past hundred years of Soviet history.

Soviet demography and history

There are few reliable data enabling us to retrace the history of Soviet populations because (1) prior to the 1897 census all we have to go on in reconstituting long-term demographic trends are periodical *reviziya* (estimates) of the male population subject to poll tax for military service; (2) frontier changes complicate comparisons over time; and (3) only fragmentary data are available concerning human losses suffered by the Soviet Union.

In the long term, the demographic history of the Soviet Union is similar to that of other major communities that experienced rapid growth from the eighteenth century onwards and especially in the late-nineteenth century. Making allowance for territorial changes, the population of European Russia is thought to have grown from 6.5 million inhabitants around the mid-sixteenth century to 7 million in 1646, 18.2 million in 1744, 57 million in 1850 and 98 million in 1897. Between 1719 and 1857, the annual growth rate was 0.8 per cent, representing a doubling of the population every ninety years; in the period 1897–1913, this rate shot up to 1.7 per cent per year, representing a doubling every forty years. The growth rate has slowed down since the Revolution,

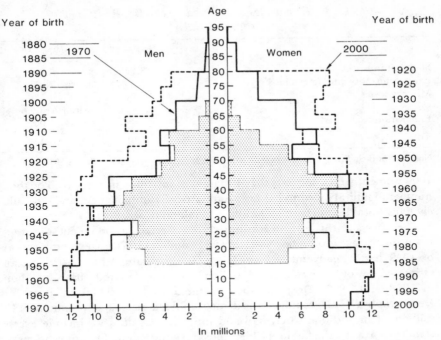

Figure 1   Age structure of the Soviet population on 15 January 1970 and projection to the year 2000

Source: INED, Population, *July–Oct. 1972, p. 810.*

Note: Shaded area represents active population.

since the 1922 population of 136 million inhabitants is only expected to double sometime between 1980 and 1985, i.e. after around sixty years. This more recent pattern is marked by a series of demographic punctures whose outlines can be seen from the age structure shown in Figure 1.

Instead of spreading steadily outwards, the age structure in 1970 contains four indentations from the top downwards.

1 The first one corresponds to the age group born between 1915 and 1920, at the time of the first world war, during which 15 million men, i.e. one-third of the male population, were mobilized, thereby affecting birthrates. In addition, close to 1 million soldiers and 2 million civilians died prematurely. The civil war and its sequels – famine, disease, emigration – make the picture bleaker still (see Table 4). According to the Soviet economist Strumilin, these 6 years of war lost the Soviet Union the equivalent of 70 years of national income, simply as a result of direct or indirect human losses, which he estimates at 405 million working years.

2 The second world war cut deeply into the age groups born between 1916 and 1925, as can be seen from the fact that in 1970 there were 620 men for every

TABLE 4   *Human losses suffered by the USSR, 1914—20*
(in thousands)

	1914—17	1918—20
Shortfall in births	3,855	4,920
Excess mortality among civilians	2,258	7,050
Military losses	975	170
		(Red Army only)
Emigration		2,000
Total	7,088	14,140[1]

Note: 1 Not including 5 million deaths from the 1921 famine (Maksudov, CMRS 1977).

1000 women, which suggests that 1 man in 3 was killed in the war. The total number of military victims has been estimated at 7 million men, and if we add civilians, total losses exceed 20 million inhabitants.

3 The effects of this war on birthrates are reflected in the indentation representing the age groups born between 1940 and 1945. The Russo-Finnish war of 1939 had already made inroads on the birthrate, while births hit an estimated low of between 2 and 3 million in 1942, compared with 4.9 million in 1938 and 1957. Dr J. Biraben of the French National Institute for Demography (INED) estimates the demographic shortfall at approximately 40 million, if in addition to civilian and military casualties we include excess civilian mortality, the fall in the birthrate and emigration. The annexations of Karelia, Poland, Bessarabia, Bukovina and the Baltic republics in 1939 and 1940 add some 20 million; but some of these people, the Poles for example, were substantially repatriated. It took the Soviet Union eleven years to regain its prewar population level, i.e. until 1955.

4 Population losses in the 1930s, represented in Figure 1 by the indentation for the years 1930—35, are due to several factors: the depleted first world war age groups attained reproductive age at this time, famine occurred in the Ukraine and the Volga basin in 1932 and 1933, the abortion laws were liberalized and, lastly, these were the years of forced collectivization. By a sinister paradox, we are better informed as to losses to Soviet livestock in this period than about the number of the regime's opponents who were exterminated, such as the kulaks (1929—34) or those who died in the course of Stalin's purges (1936—9). Roy Medvedev states that 240,757 kulak families, i.e. 1—1.5 million people, were deported early in 1933 (*Stalinism*, p. 147). One can gain some idea of the national drama experienced by the Soviet Union during the years in which Stalinism was establishing itself by comparing the total population recorded by the January 1937 census, 164 million, with demographic forecasts contained in the second five-year plan, which anticipated a Soviet population of 180.7 million for the beginning of 1937, representing a shortfall of 16.7 million individuals. This damning evidence led to cancellation of the census and, from 27 June 1937 onwards, stricter abortion laws.

5 The narrowing of the base of the age structure is a reflection of falling birth-rates, the reasons for which we shall be analysing below; this represents, on the one hand, the cumulative effects of the second world war on the population of child-bearing age (historical causes) and, on the other, a more restrictive attitude towards reproduction on the part of Soviet families (sociological factors). The net annual rate of increase, which stood at 17.8 per 1000 in the period 1946—60, during which the birthrate was high and the mortality rate at its lowest point (owing to the excess mortality of old people during the war), fell to 8.9 per 1000 in 1969, when the mortality rate rose and the shrunken age groups of the second world war reached child-bearing age. The current rate of increase (8.1 per 1000 in 1979) corresponds to 2.3 million individuals, i.e. 1 million fewer than in the period 1950—60.

6 The dissymmetry of this age structure reflects excess male mortality occasioned by war. There were 830 men per 1000 women in 1959, but only 760 men per 1000 women in the 32—34 age group, all of whom had been called up. However, in the 30—31 age group, which had not been called up, the ratio of 921 men per 1000 women was more or less the same as that recorded in the 1897 census and will be restored in the year 2000, when the consequences of the war will have been absorbed.

Soviet doctrine argues, on the basis of this uneven pattern, that there are no such things as general demographic laws applicable in all circumstances, regardless of the economic and social regime. On the other hand, the theory that socialist societies are alone capable of ensuring steady population growth, because planned control of economic development makes it possible to raise the economic potential to the optimum level required by this steady population growth, is not borne out by the behaviour of Soviet couples, who have scant concern for doctrine. We shall be coming back to this question of Soviet attitudes to birth in Chapter 5, which deals with the family.

Demography and the economy

Food resources and population. In a traditional society, the population generally adapts to the capacity of the natural environment to provide subsistence. Wars and epidemics serve as regulators, keeping the population at a level compatible with resources, when production and transport techniques prohibit any increase in the food supply to feed a greater density of population. The abundance of land in Russia has made it possible to extend the area of land under cultivation in line with a rising population, so that in 1913, the new regions — those colonized in the eighteenth and nineteenth centuries — were already supplying 43 per cent of the cereal crop. Between 1897 and 1980, the country's population more than doubled, while the total area sown increased 2.6 times. Meanwhile, a very sharp drop in the proportion of land left fallow, and a slower rise in yields, reflect the adoption of more intensive forms of agriculture.

TABLE 5   *Population growth and agrarian change, 1897–1980*

	1897	1913	1926	1939	1971	1980
Area sown (millions of hectares)	82	105	112	138	207	217
Fallow land (as % of land under cultivation)	37	30		13	8	6
Average wheat yields (quintals per ha)	5	7.3			12.5	14
Total population (millions)	125	139	147	170	244	266
Active farming population (millions)	64	65	68.5	35–40	30–35	27
No. of mouths fed by a single farmer	1.96	2.15	2.15	4.5	7.5	9.8
Area of land under cultivation per inhabitant (ha)	0.65	0.76	0.76	0.81	0.85	0.81

The reduction of the farming population by half in the course of the same period is an indication of improved productivity: a Soviet farmer now feeds 9.8 people on average, compared with 30 people for a French farmer, whereas the *muzhik's* labour managed to feed 2 people only. This trend, which emerges from Table 5, is part and parcel of the industrialization and urbanization of a society which was predominantly agricultural until 1950 (agriculture engaging 48 per cent of the working population) and rural until 1960.

Working and supported populations. We shall defer our examination of the socio-occupational structure of Soviet populations until Chapter 8, confining ourselves here to what is most crucial from the economic standpoint, namely the ratios of working to non-working populations, on the one hand, and of people due for retirement to the age groups about to enter working life in place of them, on the other. Three main categories may be distinguished in this respect: individuals undergoing education or training; the working population; and old and retired people (see Figure 2).

Out of a total population of 241.7 million on 15 January 1970,[1] some 54.1 per cent was of working age, i.e. aged between 16 and 54 years for women and 16 and 59 for men, representing a potential labour force of 130.5 million workers, supporting an average of 0.85 people each.

The burden of the younger generations may be regarded as an investment in training, and costs society slightly more than the assistance given to old people. On average, the state spends 15,000 rubles to train a Soviet worker and 13,000 rubles on his pension over 15 years, representing 60 per cent of his annual salary. In his 40–45-year working life, a worker earns between 60,000 and 65,000 rubles and leaves to the community an accumulation of 65,000–72,000 rubles, from which 28,000 rubles must be deducted for training and pension expenses. Soviet planners calculate that by the age of thirty, a worker has already paid off his training costs through his own work.

The size of the working population varies not only as a result of changes in the age structure: the length of the working week (40.7 hours per week), the

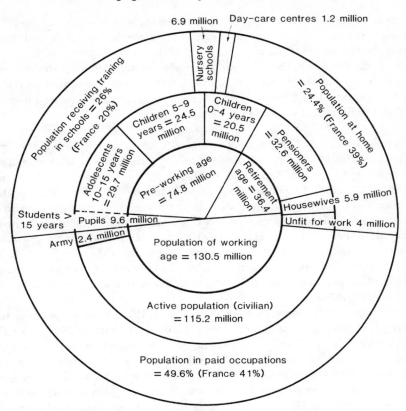

Figure 2   Analysis of the Soviet population, 1970

raising of the school-leaving age, the retirement age and pension schemes, and the proportion of women working outside the home are all factors affecting the overall level of employment. Thus, for example, since the establishment of a compulsory pension scheme for collective-farm-workers in 1964, there has been an appreciable drop in the number of people subsisting solely on the income derived from their family farm, while the number of pensioners has risen accordingly.

In 1970, the real recorded working population represented a total of 115.2 million individuals, of whom 2.6 million were aged 60 or over; this implies that approximately 17.9 million individuals of working age out of a potential total of 130.5 million were not actually engaged in what are regarded as economic activities. Among these we should include: (1) a growing number of students in the final year of secondary school and students staying on in education beyond 16 years, which explains why in 1970 the 16–19 age group contained equal numbers of workers (8,655,200) and non-workers (8,627,000); (2) women obliged to remain at home for domestic reasons, which is why the 20–29 age group, corresponding to the early years of marriage during which fertility is at its highest, is also more strongly represented than the following age groups; (3) able-bodied individuals of working age who prefer to devote themselves to their family farms; (4) invalids; and (5) members of the armed forces and police personnel (3.2 million) and perhaps also – although we possess no official data on this subject – prisoners.

Working women.   There is a high proportion of working women in the Soviet Union. Some 44 per cent of the female population was employed in 1979, accounting for over half the total number of jobs, i.e. 51 per cent, compared with 40 per cent in France and 50 per cent in Japan. But while in the industrial countries long-term trends indicate a rising female labour participation, in the Soviet Union this pattern has to a very large extent been dictated by the demographic upheavals of the 1930s and 1940s, which is why the proportion of women in work is expected to fall as the male labour deficit begins to shrink. Between 1950 and 1976, women contributed 54 per cent of the total increase in the working population of the Soviet Union, compared with 60 per cent of that of the United States.

Of the 64 million women of working age in 1970, some 82 per cent were actually employed in the different branches of the economy, which means that approximately 11.57 million of those aged between 16 and 54 years were not employed. This last figure should be set against the number of married women aged under 54 (there are 40.6 million households), which leads to the conclusion that 1 woman in 5.5 remains at home. An identical proportion of women, over 4 million in all, continues working beyond the legal retirement age.

It is becoming increasingly difficult to free additional labour by means of transfers from the domestic and family economy to other occupations. Indeed, between 1971 and 1975, such transfers contributed a mere 1.5 per cent of the increase in the number of jobs. Furthermore, the working population is ageing. The median age of a worker is expected to rise from 29.7 in 1970 to 32 in 1990. This is due to the raising of the school-leaving age, which means that young people called up to do their national service at 18 do not enter working life until the age of 20. Also, falling fertility rates are reducing annual additions to the workforce: births in 1970 will supply 4.2 million workers, whereas they ought to have produced 5.3 million had fertility remained at its 1960 level. Between 1970 and 1985, there will be a 20 per cent increase in the able-bodied working population representing a growth rate of 1.5 per cent per year (the total in 1980 was 137 million); in contrast, the annual growth rate over the previous 15 years was 3 per cent. The net increase in the working population between 1955 and 1970 was 30 million (a 40 million increase in the state sector, minus a 10 million decrease in the collective farms); 'in the 1980s', however, 'we can expect a sharp slowdown caused by a drop in the size of the potential working population', according to the Gosplan review (*Planovoe Khoz*, no. 3, 1975, p. 146).

This is a matter of concern to economists. For to fly planes and to drive lorries and bulldozers one needs young workers with stamina and fast reflexes. Furthermore, it is frequently possible to promote young people to positions of responsibility only when older workers retire; but the present demographic situation makes it unlikely that the retirement age could be reduced. The issue has been decided until 1996, since the people coming onto the labour market between now and then are already born. What is clear already is that although the rate of renewal remains favourable until 1980 (Table 6 shows a surplus of 14 million young people aged between 15 and 19 over the contingent due for retirement), the situation will begin to deteriorate in 1990, since from then on each person retiring will be replaced by only one new worker instead of two. The arrival on the labour market in the 1990s of the generation born in the 1970s should ease the situation somewhat.

TABLE 6 *Ratio of replacement of persons at retirement age by persons entering the labour force, 1970—85*

Age groups approaching retirement (in thousands at 15 Jan. 1970)	Age groups replacing them
55—59 = 12,026	15—19 = 21,999 (1.83%)
50—54 = 9,088	10—14 = 24,878 (2.75%)
45—49 = 12,270	5—9 = 24,504 (2.00%)
40—44 = 19,024	0—5 = 20,533 (1.08%)

Since growth in employment is being restricted to 1.3 per cent per year over the coming years, the rate of economic growth will depend mainly on productivity gains.

Productivity and population optima. Could it be that the Soviet Union is underpopulated? What would be the optimum population level, one that would give the country a labour force sufficient to exploit its resources to the full so as to cover the general costs of the population while raising per capita consumption?

The answers to these questions depend on the growth rates of both the overall population and the working population and on productivity gains. The optimum population will therefore vary according to the type of economic growth: in some countries, excess *overall* population will increase the burden per working individual and therefore tend to improve productivity, while in other countries — those which rely on immigrant labour — the surplus of *working* people will reduce charges. In the Soviet Union, over-rapid population growth in an insufficiently developed economy has resulted in costly basic investment, which has long acted as a brake on improvements in living standards; but, as we have pointed out earlier, the current drop in fertility is liable in the future to deprive the country of the labour necessary to take over from the older generations.

The Soviet demographer, A. I. Kvasha, calculates that the desirable rate of reproduction for the Soviet Union ought not to fall below the 1.21 per cent needed to guarantee continued growth of the overall population.[3] In other words, the population of child-bearing age will have to grow by 21 per cent compared with the previous generation (corresponding to 300 births per 100 women). This objective still appeared attainable in the 1960s, but now that the net rate of reproduction has fallen to 1.10 in the period 1975–6, this is no longer the case.

No one any longer harbours any illusions as to the possible effectiveness of measures to encourage reproduction, as these would be incapable of reversing an underlying trend observed in all industrial societies. If it is not possible to influence numbers, something must be done about quality, i.e. productivity; this presupposes not only more advanced techniques but also a better-trained labour force. In other words, planners have little room for manoeuvre, which partly accounts for the slowdown in GNP growth (+ 18 to 20 per cent in the 5 years to 1986, compared with + 37 to 40 per cent in 1971–5) and for the fact that stress is now being laid on improving productivity. Does this mean that the Soviets can ignore the problem of numbers, notwithstanding their vast territory with its frontiers subject to pressing political and demographic pressures?

TABLE 7   *Estimated and projected total population by major areas*

Total population (millions)	1880	1939	1970	1979	2000
USSR	88	194	242	262.4	305–306
Other European Comecon members			103	109	122
China		450	800	950	1193
Japan	37	73	103	116	129
USA	50	132	205	220	263–310

The figures in Table 7 show that in the long term the United States could hope to surpass the Soviet Union, whereas at the present time the latter enjoys an 18 per cent lead in overall population and a 45 per cent lead in terms of working population. The American dynamic was undoubtedly influenced by immigration, whereas, on the contrary, the Soviet Union has experienced a greater outflow than inflow of workers (of foreign volunteers who came to work in the Soviet Union in the 1920s and 1930s, of certain Armenian groups from the Diaspora after 1945 and more recently temporary Bulgarian labour).

This leaves us with the problem of the reliability of demographic forecasts.

Frequently in the past these have been upset by unforeseeable changes: the invention of new vaccines or contraceptive pills, political upheavals, shifting moral standards, etc. At all events, we are bound to acknowledge that the population of the Soviet Union is much below its appropriate optimum; with a greater population density, railways would be more profitable and the nation's overheads (which are clearly higher in the Soviet Union than in capitalist countries) could be spread among a greater number of individuals.[2] In 1900, the Russian chemist Mendeleyev calculated that his country could achieve a population of 800 million inhabitants sometime around the year 2050. But at that time the population of the Russian empire was doubling every forty years; at its present rate of growth the Soviet Union would need a century to achieve the same result. This slowdown in population growth is a reflection of the deep-seated changes that have occurred in Russian society in the intervening years.

Demography and society

We cannot hold Marxist doctrine responsible for this trend. On the contrary, it is optimistic by nature and anti-Malthusian on the subject of birthrates. Marx begins his critique of Malthus by emphasizing that poverty in the world is a result not of excessive numbers but of social factors; technical progress can overcome the effects of a rising population, and so it is not this growth which creates the obstacle, but the capitalists.[4] Like the Chinese, the Soviets believe that in a socialist regime population growth is a stimulus to increased output. Presumably, they also admit the existence of a threshold of population growth beyond which the population increases faster than the capital that is required for its subsistence, thereby lowering productivity per worker.

Since 1936, Soviet demographic policy has been inspired by this doctrine favouring an increased birthrate. This policy has scored its main successes in reducing mortality and in improving the health of the population; but it has proved incapable of stemming the drop in fertility, for it conflicts with a sociological factor inherent in the modernization and urbanization of Soviet society, namely birth control.

Morbidity and mortality. The first objective was to raise average life expectancy through improved hygiene, diet and working conditions, which succeeded in bringing the deathrate down from 32.4 per 1000 in 1896–7, to 20.3 per 1000 in 1926, 17.4 per 1000 in 1938–9, 9.7 per 1000 in 1950 and 8.1 per 1000 in 1979.

The fall in infant mortality (death in the first year of life) from 269 per 1000 in 1913 to 182 per 1000 in 1940 and 24.6 per 1000 in 1972 has resulted in a significant rise in the population's life expectancy. In 1887, average life expectancy in European Russia was 32 years, while by 1926–7 this had risen to 44 years and now stands at 65 years for men and 74 years for women (compared with 69 and 76 respectively in France and the United States). This nine-year disparity between male and female life expectancies is interesting, because it is greater in the Soviet Union than in the west (e.g. in France, where it is 7.4). The excess male mortality in the Soviet Union is put down to a higher accident rate among young men, as well as, leaving aside war effects, to more specifically male habits such as alcoholism.

Better health care, particularly in combating epidemics and contagious diseases, has considerably increased the available human potential. Table 8, based on mortality tables and educational statistics, indicates the respective educational chances of a Soviet, an Indian and an American child.

TABLE 8   *Life and educational expectations in the USSR, India and USA*

Probability of a child (%):	*USSR (1970)*	*India (1962)*	*USA (1962)*
reaching the age of 1	94	82	97
entering primary school	93.4	64	96.3
completing secondary school (10 years)	54	2.3	48.7

It is much harder to provide adequate health care in sparsely populated regions. For example, there are 10 doctors for 10,000 Buryats, and though this proportion is higher than in the European regions it represents 1 doctor for every 5000 square kilometres of territory (compared with 25 square kilometres on average elsewhere). This explains why infant mortality is higher among the native Siberian populations and average life expectancy lower than for the Russians.

Despite the rising cost of public health, the results obtained hold out scant hope, given present-day levels, for spectacular gains in life expectancy. Even if infant mortality was totally eliminated, it would be impossible to push average longevity beyond 76–78 years, given the present state of our knowledge. However, it may still be possible, in view of the rising number of old people, to prolong working lives.

Fertility and birthrates. Analysis of birthrate trends is complicated by short-term factors such as the effects of war, which either drag birthrates below the long-term trend line (because of shrunken age groups or sex imbalances) or push them above it (recovery effects). As in all industrial countries, the Soviet trend is currently pointing downwards: 45.5 per 1000 in 1913, 37.38 per 1000 in 1937 and 18.2 per 1000 in 1979. Short-term factors account for only one-quarter of the drop in Soviet birthrates. In the 1970s, one would have expected to see a rise in the birthrate, as the 19–24 age group (in the early years of marriage – the period of greatest fertility) was born in the 1950s and is particularly plentiful as a result of the recovery effect following the second world war. In so far as it is possible to identify causes, the principal cause of the

falling birthrate is the drop in fertility, and this in turn requires some explanation.

R. Pressat of the French National Institute for Demography (INED) calculates that if fertility in 1970 had remained at the level of ten years previously,
today's birthrate would be 20 per 1000 instead of 17.2 per 1000. In 1939, there
were 138.5 births per 1000 Soviet women aged between 19 and 49; thirty years
later, this figure had been halved (65.7 births). In the decade 1890–1900, a
couple produced 5.13 descendants on average; in 1970, the average couple
produces only 2.39 children. A third or further child is exceptional (29 per
cent of births in 1972).

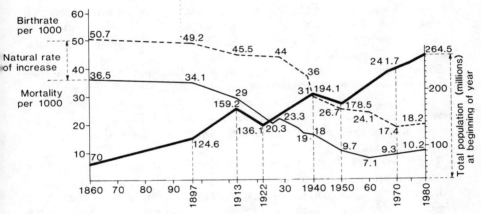

Figure 3   Long-term demographic dynamics

The fertility of Soviet households is high in the first years of marriage,
especially between 20 and 24 years of age, but there is a very marked fall from
the age of 30 onwards: 70 per cent of children born in 1971–2 were born to
mothers aged under 30.

The effect of age of marriage on fertility has led the Soviet authorities to
encourage early marriage, reducing the length of military service from 3 to 2
years and, in 1967, bringing the age of conscription down to 18 so as to free
young Soviet males at the age of 20 instead of 22. Taken by themselves, these
measures are inadequate to exercise a decisive influence on fertility, for this is
bound up with a great many factors causing couples to control and even limit
the number of their offspring. Some of these are: (1) women going out to work,
which places on them, in addition to their professional obligations, a domestic
burden estimated at 6 hours of work daily for 2 or 3 children; (2) the frequency
of divorce (1 marriage in 2–3 breaks down), which is no incentive to raise
children; and, in turn, the absence of children in the home facilitates divorce
(only half of men who divorce remarry); (3) urbanization alters behaviour: in

village society infant mortality is an incentive to breed more children and to marry young so as to provide the community with extra pairs of hands and to ensure the security of parents, who are looked after by their children in their declining years; in contrast the birth of a child in the city, far from improving living standards, reduces per capita family income. In 1970, this difference in attitude was illustrated by an average of 2.24 children per household in the countryside and 1.68 in the towns; and (4) lastly and perhaps above all, rising cultural expectations lead to increased ambitions for the future and for education, both for the parents themselves and for their children; and the more developed education is, the greater these ambitions become. In a survey conducted in Moscow in 1970 of a sample of 5225 married women aged between 18 and 40, those with less than 8 years schooling had 1.33 children on average, while those with higher education had only 0.97 children. Unlike in a traditional society, prestige is no longer associated with the size of one's family, but with one's material and intellectual 'status'.

These observations are not necessarily valid for Soviet society alone, for studies conducted in other countries confirm that, among the different variables affecting family behaviour, those linking fertility to education are the most decisive. From this we must conclude that if measures to encourage people to have children are confined to family allowances alone, they will prove inadequate.

The sociological effects of demographic trends may be summed up in the form of a certain number of questions and observations.

1 If it is true that there is a growing trend in the Soviet Union to single-child families, is this type of family capable of developing a community-minded personality? Some Soviet educators argue that the only child is generally more spoilt, more vulnerable and consequently less well prepared for a demanding social life in keeping with the ideals of the regime.

2 While the dynamics of the generations is tending to increase the number of old people, it would be a mistake to exaggerate the ageing of Soviet society, which is still essentially a young one. In 1970, the median age was 25.2 years old for men and 32.1 for women. Some 10 per cent of the Soviet population was aged over 60 in 1980, compared with 13.9 per cent in France and the United Kingdom. It is true that the Soviet Union has a greater proportion of 100-year-olds, i.e. 16 per 100,000 compared with 0.7 in France, but since this phenomenon is found most frequently among the peoples of the Caucasus, one wonders whether the birth certificates have been correctly recorded. Some people used to hide their true age so as to escape drafting into the Tsar's army; others exaggerated their age in order to win greater respect. At the time of the 1970 census, half the population was aged under 30; today, 45 per cent of the Soviet population was born after the second world war; 81 per cent has not known the old regime. Does this mean that the dead hand of the past is lighter here than elsewhere? To attempt to answer this question at this stage would be

to prejudge a crucial problem that demands more detailed exploration, in particular by analysing social mobility, decision-making mechanisms and values or behaviour patterns specific to a given generation. For the time being, there is every reason to believe that the 3.3 million men and 8 million women born prior to 1900 and still alive in 1970 were far better able to appreciate the changes brought about by the Revolution than those born under the new regime. Among these latter, the 'intermediate' generation, still haunted by memories of the war and the terror, is doubtless more appreciative than the young generations of the changes that have taken place since Stalin's death; it is the youngest generations, with no experience of earlier periods, who feel most strongly the limits to 'liberalization', especially in their thirst for knowledge of the outside world.

3 These differences in behaviour from one generation to the next are noticeable in the labour market. Better-educated youths are more demanding about working conditions, which explains the difficulties encountered in certain units when trying to fill vacancies previously occupied by women aged over forty. We shall be coming back to this problem of relations between demographic structure, working conditions and aspirations in Chapter 6, which deals with the educational system.

4 Alongside the father-son conflict, which is a classic theme in Russian and Soviet literature, demographic analysis reveals two other crucial cleavages in Soviet society: first, the characteristic contrasts between the European regions and the Third World fringes of the Soviet Union; second, the customary, universal differences between town and countryside. For example, differences in the birthrates of urban populations in the different republics are generally less marked than differences between the urban and rural populations of a single republic.

The data in Table 9, which are organized by nationality, reveal a far higher rate of fertility in central Asia and the Caucasus, and in particular in Azerbaijan, with its Muslim traditions. It is also interesting to note the greater fertility of the Catholic Lithuanian families than of Protestant Lett families. Earlier marriage and the rural character of the population account for the greater fertility of certain among these nationalities. Thus Kazakhstan, which ranks thirteenth among the republics in degree of urbanization, takes second place in birthrate, whereas Estonia, which has the highest urban population proportionately, has only the twelfth-highest birthrate.

Are we to conclude from this that, in view of population growth rates among the non-Slavic peoples, the balance of nationalities, which currently favours the Slavs (72.2 per cent of the total population in 1979, of whom 52.4 per cent are Russian), is liable to be upset in the long run? This would presuppose that the Muslim (Turko-Tatar) populations manage to maintain their present growth rates over a long period, which is most unlikely. The falling birth rate in Azerbaijan (42.6 per 1000 in 1960, 27.7 per 1000 in 1970) has caught the

TABLE 9 *Demographic characteristics of major Soviet ethnic groups*

Nationality	Early marriage[1]		Fertility (no. of children)[2]		Children per family		Annual rate of natural increase[4]	% of population living in towns
					Towns	Country-side		
	1926	1959	1926	1959	1970	1970	1959–69	1970
Russians	150	91	1233	863	3.3	3.6	11.3	68
Ukrainians	142	96	1354	714	3.3	3.5	8.2	49
Estonians		42		638	3.0	3.1	1.6	55
Latvians		45		612	3.1	3.1	1.9	53
Lithuanians		47	915	823	3.4	3.5	12.5	47
Georgians	287	107	1483	905	3.9	4.1	17.1	44
Armenians	552	166	1575	1240	4.5	5.1	14.9	65
Azerbaijanis	590	272	1780	1710	5.1	5.8	36.9	40
Uzbeks	564	323	1134[3]	1878	5.8	6.0	39.4	25
Turkmens	636	320	1384[3]	1810	5.9	6.0	38.9	31
Tadzhiks		384	1257[3]	1782	5.9	6.1	39.4	26

Notes: 1 Number of married women per 1000 women aged between 16 and 19.
2 Number of children aged 0–9 per 1000 women aged 20–49.
3 The 1920s were a troubled period in the history of central Asia.
4 Per 1000.

attention of demographers, since it foreshadows what could well happen in central Asia when, as elsewhere, a rural type of demography is replaced by an urban-type one, i.e. when birth control becomes widespread.

We must now look at other aspects of the coexistence of a profusion of nationalities in the Soviet Union.

THE NATIONALITIES

The Russian empire grew up through the annexation of territories belonging to highly disparate national cultures. This 'prison of the peoples' burst asunder in 1917. Differences in the level of material and spiritual development and the very unequal numerical size of the many different nationalities destined to make up the Soviet Union mean that Soviet society is still only very imperfectly homogeneous.

To begin with, we may identify three types of ethnic group: (1) the small ethnic groups of the north and Siberia, which have preserved their tribal mode of organization and have not yet attained national consciousness; (2) ethnic groups that had attained this stage, but which, being subject to the empire, were more or less actively resisting it in the name of nationalist or religious ideologies or of universalist movements (such as socialism, pan-Islamism, and pan-Turanism); and (3) a dominant ethnic group, the Russians, which sought to justify its civilizing mission in the name of pan-Slavism or of Marxism–Leninism.

In dealing with these national liberation movements, some of which were directed against them by foreign influences, the Bolsheviks were quick to grasp the possible benefits they might reap from the situation. Initially (in the 1918 constitution) they thought that the national problem could be settled within the framework of a world confederation of peoples resulting from the spread of revolution to Europe. When these hopes had evaporated, their concern to safeguard the proletarian state pushed plans for autonomy into the background in favour of a federal constitution (1924), which represents a compromise between the 'autonomists' and the 'assimilationists'. It granted the republics a fairly wide measure of autonomy in the social and cultural spheres, but reserved the crucial political power to the Communist Party, which was organized on a unified, not a federal, basis. By means of this structure, the central authorities were able to speed up the mixing of populations through a series of measures designed to integrate the nationalities within Soviet society. But this could not abolish overnight the cultural conditioning that makes a Soviet citizen part of a national group.

The criterion of nationality: language

The Soviet law does not impose nationality by virtue of descent (*jus sanguinis*) or place of birth (*jus soli*) but leaves individuals free to choose their nationalities (by a subjective criterion) at the age of 16, when they receive their internal passports; they may either adopt their parents' nationality (we shall leave aside for the time being the case of parents of different nationality) or make the choice on the basis of mother tongue. In fact, from the moment a child enters school, a nationality is attributed to it on the school register, so that its abilities or difficulties in learning Russian can be assessed.

The Soviets also employ an objective criterion in defining a person's nationality, namely by reference to language (see Table 10), which may or may not be one's mother tongue. Thus, for example, at the time of the last census, 16 million Soviets not declaring themselves as being of Russian nationality nevertheless gave Russian as their mother tongue. This is the case with the Jews, in particular, fewer and fewer of whom speak Yiddish (14.2 per cent in 1979) and 98 per cent of whom are Russian-speaking. The definition of mother tongue varies: it may be the language most frequently spoken at home (the criterion used in the 1926 census) or the language one speaks best (the criterion used in the 1959 census). In addition, the authorities reserve the right to draw up the list of recognized languages and nationalities used in the census: 194 nationalities in the 1926 census, 97 in 1939, 126 in 1959, and 92 in the 1979 census. Numerically, the populations speaking Slavic languages predominate among these different nationalities (189.2 million out of 262.4 million, i.e. 72.1 per cent); they are followed by the Turko-Mongol group of languages (38.5 million, i.e. 14.7 per cent in 1979, compared with 11 per cent in 1959); and these by the Caucasian-speaking peoples (6.8 million) and the Finno-Ugrians (4.2 million).

TABLE 10 Nationalities of the USSR, classified by language

		Population (millions)			Speaking national language 1979 (%)	Speaking Russian as a second language		CCCP[1] 1970 (%)	Students 1979[2]
		1897	1979	+ or − 1970−9		1970 (%)	1979 (%)		
Indo-European									
Slavonic	Russians	55.6	137.4	+ 6.5	99.8	100	100	57.2	219
	Byelorussians	5.8	9.5	+ 4.5	74.2	49	57	5.6	181
	Ukrainians	22.8	42.3	+ 3.9	82.8	36.3	49.8	18.6	175
	Poles	7.8	1.15	− 0.9	29.1	67.5	44.7		
Baltic	Latvians	1.43	1.43	nil	95	45.2	56.7	1.9	188
	Lithuanians	1.66	2.85	+ 7.1	97.9	35.9	52.1	0.9	205
Roman	Moldavians	1.12	2.96	+ 10	93.2	36.1	47.4	0.8	127
Germanic	Germans	1.38	1.93	+ 4.9	57	59.6	51.7		
	Jews (Ashkenazi)	3.77	1.81	− 15.8	14.2	16.3	13.7	0.9	
Armenian	Armenians	1.17	4.15	+ 16.6	90.7	30.1	38.6	2.4	187
Iranian	Ossetians	0.17	0.54	+ 11.1	88.2	58.6	64.9		
	Tadzhiks	0.85	2.89	+ 35.7	97.8	15.4	29.6	0.8	141
	Kurds	0.10	0.11	+ 30.3	83.6	19.9	25.4		
Caucasian	Georgians	1.31	3.57	+ 10	98.3	21.3	26.7	0.8	170
	Abkhazians	0.07	0.09	+ 9.6	94.3	59.2	73.3		
	Circassians	0.04	0.14	+ 10.7	95.7	67.9	76.7		
	Chechens	0.22	0.75	+ 23.3	98.6	68.8	76		
	Dagestan peoples	0.60	1.65	+ 21.4	95.9	41.7	60.3		
Finno-Ugrian	Karelians	0.21	0.13	− 5.5	55.6	59.1	51.3		
	Estonians	1.00	1.02	+ 1.3	95.3	29	24.2	0.9	172
	Komis	0.26	0.47	+ 0.6	76.5	64.8	64.4		
	Udmurtians	0.42	0.71	+ 1.4	76.5	63.3	64.4		
	Maris	0.37	0.62	+ 3.8	86.7	62.4	69.9		
	Mordovians	1.01	1.19	− 5.6	72.6	65.7	65.5		
	Samoyedic Nenets	0.016	0.03	+ 3.4	80.4	55.1	64.2		
	Khants		0.03	nil	67.8	48	52.8		
Altaic	Tatars	2.23	6.32	+ 6.5	85.9	62.5	68.9	0.5	
	Bashkirs	1.32	1.37	+ 10.6	67	53.3	64.9		
	Chuvashes	0.84	1.75	+ 3.4	81.7	58.4	64.8		
	Uzbeks	2.79	12.45	+ 35.5	98.5	14.5	49.3	0.5	173
	Kazakhs	} 4.28	6.55	+ 23.7	97.5	41.8	52.3	2.3	169
	Kirghizians		1.90	+ 31.3	97.9	19.1	29.7	0.5	154
	Azeris	1.47	5.47	+ 25	97.9	16.6	29.5	1.3	172
	Turkmens	0.63	2.02	+ 33	98.7	15.4	25.4	0.6	121
Mongol	Buryats	0.28	0.35	+ 12.1	90.2	66.7	71.9		
	Yakuts	0.23	0.32	+ 10.8	95.3	41.7	55.6		
Tunguz	Evenkis								
	Nanays	} 0.09	0.15	+ 3.2	61.8	52.3	54		
Paleo-Siberian	Chukchis								
	Koryakis								

Notes: 1 Central Committee of the Communist Party.
2 Per thousand.

In addition to the spoken language there is the written language, which is fixed by an alphabet. The alphabet of a language is often connected with a national religion, preserving the cultural identity of an ethnic group, as is the case with the Armenian alphabet, founded in the year AD 405 by Mesrop and adopted by the Crimean Tatar-speaking Armenians, or the Hebrew alphabet, in which Yiddish is written, or the Turkish of the Karait Jews. Often, too, the alphabet is borrowed from a dominant culture. Cyrillic, which is derived from Greek (the language of Byzantium and Eastern Christianity) has now become the alphabet of some forty ethnic groups who had no written language before 1926. The spoken languages of central Asia, as with other languages using Arabic script before the Revolution, have been obliged to adopt Cyrillic; this is also the case with Moldavian, in order to differentiate it from Romanian. The only languages using the Latin alphabet are those spoken in the three Baltic republics.

The criterion of a nation: territorial unity

Language alone is not enough to confer the status of nation upon a national group (*narodnost'*). According to the criteria laid down by Stalin in 1913, in order to be recognized as a nation a nationality (*natsional' nost'*) must possess territorial, cultural and economic unity in addition to its own language. This bars a certain number of numerous though scattered groups unable to achieve territorial unity (Germans, Jews, Poles) from the map of the republics, and also excludes groups too small to form any kind of autonomous economic unity, as with the smaller populations of the Soviet far north and far east, who number no more than 10,000 persons per community on average.

The present-day federation may be taken apart rather like a Russian doll: there are 15 Union, or federated, republics and 20 autonomous republics; these are followed by 18 national districts, which contain the nationalities not eligible for republic status. The equilibrium of these territorial units is frequently brought into question by political and demographic shifts. It is not possible within the present framework to rehearse all the twists and turns by which the Union was formed; we shall confine ourselves merely to analysing the main sociological implications of the present territorial boundaries.

The distinction between Union and autonomous republics is based on a point of law: according to the constitution, the Union republics have the right to secede, which implies that they must have external frontiers. But political considerations must also have played a part in determining the status of a republic. Need one recall that the Tatars were leaders of the Muslim liberation movement within the empire, and that pan-Turanism was at least as influential as communism among the Turko-Tatar populations? Soviet power had considerable difficulty in asserting itself in Soviet Asia: it was confronted by the revolt of the Basmachi in Turkistan in 1918–24, of the Yakuts in 1922 and 1928, of the Buryats in 1929 and of the Kazakhs in 1930–1. Prior to the

Revolution, Turkish was the common language in central Asia (Russian Turkistan) and, for this reason, the populations there were commonly referred to as 'Turks'; at that time, the Kazakhs were called Kirghiz; so one wonders whether these territorial boundaries did not begin as artificial divisions which over two generations have been consolidated.

At any rate, the geographical position of the nationalities relative to the outside world is undoubtedly a key factor shaping the cultural influences and hence the national traditions of the different ethnic groups. The predominance of the Slavs and Baltic peoples lends decisive weight to western and European influences compared with influences emanating from the Middle East or China. Some of the peripheral populations, such as the Moldavians or the Estonians (Finnish broadcasts can be picked up relatively easily in Estonia) are in this respect better off than the enclave nationalities (Tatars).

The density and numerical size of a nationality also influence its ability to perpetuate itself when in contact with other ethnic groups: 10 nationalities each have a population in excess of 1 million, 27 groups a population of between 100,000 and 1 million, and 27 groups a population of less than 10,000. It is these last which are most threatened: one-third of the tiny populations of the far north and Siberia had adopted Russian as their mother tongue at the last census, whereas over 90 per cent of the more numerous Buryats and Yakuts retained their national tongue; the Karelians and the Mordvins, who have been in contact with the Slavic peoples for generations, are being assimilated into the neighbouring populations.

The economic activities of populations and the degree of urbanization of the regions they inhabit also affect the development of their national cultures. An urban civilization, implying a higher population density, is far better suited to this kind of development than are pastoral civilizations. Sedentarization has made great strides in Soviet Asia, but in the tundra steppes or in the mountain regions ecology dictates the terms: even if the Chukchis, Komis, Evenks, Kalmyks, Karakalpaks, Kirghiz and Tadzhiks of the Pamirs and Tien Shan foothills have abandoned their pastoral nomadic way of life, they still migrate seasonally.

Integrating factors: government policy

By their very nature, these different processes of *consolidation* of national cultures, of *integration* within a multinational Soviet society or even *assimilation*, when certain groups ultimately disappear, occur very slowly. Even so, government policy can prove decisive, because it holds the key to certain aspects of cultural development: the degree of autonomy granted to local authorities, the rate and shape of economic growth and migratory movements and, lastly and above all, the precise organization of the educational system.

Degree of autonomy of the republics. This may be measured by certain ostensible criteria, such as the percentage of local people in government and party organs, the size and nature of government credits allocated to the republics, etc. In the Supreme Soviet, the non-Slavic groups are overrepresented: in 1970, 26.1 per cent of the population held 40.3 per cent of the seats. In the Party central committee, on the other hand, in 1972, the Slavic peoples, representing 73.9 per cent of the population had 82 per cent of the delegates, while over 90 per cent of positions in the Soviet Council of Ministers were held by Russians and Ukrainians.

Originally, the shortage of local cadres could be advanced as a justification for Russian control over local administration, but the concern to train local élites − a policy the Soviets evocatively refer to as 'putting down roots' (*korenizatsia*) − has borne fruit, as can be seen from the high percentage of students of all nationalities enrolled in higher education.

The federal budget accounts for 52 per cent of total government spending and the republics' budgets account for 48 per cent (1975), representing a total of 95.8 billion rubles, of which 48.5 per cent came under social and cultural headings; in other words 63.2 per cent of this category of spending in the Soviet Union is handled by the different republics, whereas over 56 per cent of capital spending is controlled by the federal authorities. This economic centralism is not necessarily detrimental to the nationalities, for it permits some measure of revenue-sharing among the different republics making up the Soviet Union, to the benefit of the less developed ones.

Because appointments to positions of responsibility at all levels are made by the Party, the system generally benefits locally born cadres. However, the arrival of new industries, with their need for outside skills may undermine this principle. In 1963, for example, only 10.5 per cent of industrial and transport personnel in Yakutia were Yakuts. In 1973, Tadzhiks accounted for only 44 per cent of blue-collar labour employed in Tadzhikistan, while Buryats accounted for only 13 per cent of the cadres employed in their republic, the remainder being Russians.

Migrations. These can appreciably alter the balance of nationalities in the different regions and republics (see Table 11). In zones open to colonization, such as Kazakhstan and Kirghizia, by 1959 the native population had ceased to be in the majority, and there are now more Russians that Kazakhs in Kazakhstan. Migration in the years 1965−9, preceding the 1970 census, resulted in the RSFSR losing 612,000 inhabitants to the benefit of the Ukraine (+ 325,000), central Asia (+ 198,000) and Armenia (+ 89,000). The Baltic republics gained more immigrants (+ 144,000) than Kazakhstan (+ 68,000). The Russians are gaining ground in Byelorussia, Moldavia, Estonia and central Asia, but are losing ground in the Caucasus. The people with the highest proportion of emigrants are the Tatars, of whom 73 per cent live outside their republic: there are three times as many Tatars as Bashkirs in Ufa, the capital of Bashkiria. On the other hand, the central Asian nationalities generally

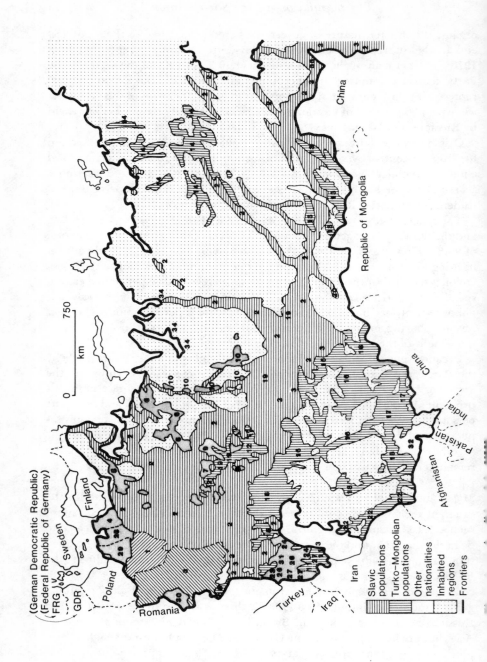

SLAVIC
1 Byelorussians
2 Russians
3 Ukrainians

FINNO-UGRIANS
4 Estonians
5 Karelians
6 Komis
7 Maris
8 Moravians
9 Udmurtians
10 Khanty-Mansians

ALTAIC
11 Azeris
12 Bashkirs
13 Buryats
14 Yakuts
15 Kalmyks
16 Kazakhs
17 Kirghizians

18 Uzbeks
19 Tatars
20 Tuvas
21 Chuvashs
22 Turkmens

CAUCASIAN
23 Abkhazians
24 Dagestan (Avars, Dargins, Lezgins)
25 Chechens-Ingushis
26 Georgians

INDO-EUROPEANS (*excluding Slavs*)
27 Armenians
28 Latvians
29 Lithuanians
30 Moldavians
31 Ossetians
32 Tadzhiks
33 Birobidzhan Jews
34 Paleo-Siberians and Samoyeds

45

TABLE 11 *Distribution of nationalities by republic and selected towns*

	Population			Nationals (%)		Russians			Mixed marriages[6] (%)		
	millions 1979	% 1979	% (2000)	1959	1979	% 1970	% 1979	+ or − 1959–79	1959	Towns	Country-side
RSFSR	137.5	52.4	46.5	83.3	82.6	82.6	82.6	+16	8.3	10.8	5.6
Bratsk	0.214									21[1]	
Ufa (Bashkiria)	0.969					63.2					
Ukraine	49.8	18.9	16.9	76.8	73.6	19.4	21.1	+48	15	26.3	5.8
Kiev	2.144			60		22.9				35.5[2]	
Byelorussia	9.5	3.6	3.6	81.1	79.4	10.4	11.9	+72	11	23.7	5.6
Moldavia	3.9	1.5	1.6	65.4	63.9	11.6	12.8	+73	13.5	26.9	9.4
Kishinev	0.503					30.2					
Estonia	1.5	0.6 ⎫	⎫	74.6	64.7	24.7	27.9	+70	10	14.2	5.1
Tallin	0.430			60.5		35.1					
Latvia	2.5	1 ⎬ 2.9	⎬ 2.5	62.0	53.7	29.8	32.8	+31	15.8	21.3	9.2
Riga	0.835					42.8				35.2[2]	
Lithuania	3.4	1.3 ⎭	⎭	79.3	80	8.6	8.9	+48	5.9	10.4	3
Vilnius	0.481					24.5					
Georgia	5	1.9 ⎫	⎫	64.3	68.8	8.5	7.4	−8.9	9	16.4	3.7
Tbilissi	1.066			48.5		13.9					
Rustavi	0.129	⎬ 5.3		44.3		31.6[3]					
Armenia	3	1.1 ⎬	⎬ 6.5	88	89.7	2.7	2.3	+25	3.2	5.0	1.4
Erevan	1.019					2.8				5.6	
Azerbaijan	6	2.3 ⎭		67.5	78.1	10.0	7.9	−5.2	7.1	11.8	2
Baku	1.550			33		27.7					
Turkmeniya	2.8	1.1 ⎫		60.9	68.4	14.5	12.6	+33	8.5	14.9	2.5
Ashkabad	0.312			29		42.6					
Uzbekistan	15.4	5.9		62.2	68.7	12.5	10.8	+52	8.2	14.7	4.7
Samarkand	0.477			36.1		33.1[3]					
Tashkent	1.780	⎬ 9.8	⎬ 15.4	33.9		40.8				20[2]	
Tadzhikistan	3.8	1.5		53.1	58.8	11.9	10.4	+50	9.4	16.7	5.5
Dushanbe	0.494			18.9		42				44[4]	
Kirghizia	3.5	1.3 ⎭		40.5	47.9	29.2	25.9	+46	12.3	18.1[5]	9.2
Frunze	0.533			9.5		66.1				27.4[5]	
Kazakhstan	14.7	5.6	7.0	29.8	36	42.8	40.8	+51	14.4	17.5	11.9
Alma Ata	0.910			8.1		70.3					
Karaganda	0.572			8.7		74.4[3]					

Notes: 1 1960–2, percentage of births in families of mixed nationality.
2 1963, number of mixed marriages per 100 marriages.
3 1959.
4 1946–66, number of mixed marriages per 100 marriages.
5 1962.
6 Number of families of mixed nationality per 100 families.

live in their respective republics; as a result, the Slavs have been able to colonize Siberia by strengthening their presence on the Chinese and Mongolian borders. The Slavs, who in 1897 represented 68 per cent of the population of eastern Siberia and 57 per cent of that of the far east, represented 85 per cent and 92 per cent respectively in 1959.

The figures in Table 11 also show the often preponderant importance of the Russian communities in the capitals of the Union Republics, as well as in the industrial centres (such as Rustavi, Karaganda and Ufa). In Tashkent, there are more Russians than Uzbeks (44 per cent compared with 33 per cent); in the other cities of Uzbekistan, the ratio is 33 per cent Russian to 37 per cent Uzbek, whereas in the villages the proportion of Russians drops to 3 per cent. This situation, which also exists in many other republics, accounts for the very low percentage of mixed marriages in the countryside.

Urbanization is not the sole integrating factor, for conscription into the Union army also plays, as conscription does everywhere, a vital role in the mingling of the populations (under the new constitution, republics no longer have the right to maintain their own national armies). The launching of new schemes in Siberia and on the Kama, drawing in young people from every region of the country, further enhances the multinational character of the society it is hoped to build.

Schooling. Because of its more or less adequate provision for the teaching of a given language, this remains the key instrument of the government's nationalities policy. In principle, children are taught in their national tongue at primary school; then, in secondary school, Russian becomes compulsory. There are two types of secondary school: those intended for Russians, where the teaching is entirely in Russian (with a few hours set aside for the local language) and national schools, where considerable time is devoted to the teaching of Russian. But this principle is not always adhered to: in percentage terms, there are more Russian schools in the non-Russian republics than there are Russian colonists, so that the local children are often taught entirely in Russian; furthermore, certain nationalities, such as the Karelians, have no schools giving lessons in their language, which explains why only 45.5 per cent of Karelian school-children aged between 16 and 19 speak Karelian. In Uzbekistan, the Russian schools devote 652 hours to Uzbek, while the Uzbek schools devote 2471 hours to Russian literature and language and 1796 to their own language and literature. In Dagestan, Turk Azeri, which was the common language of thirty nationalities inhabiting this territory, has been replaced by Russian.

The spread of Russian throughout the entire population also accounts for the preponderance of books published in this language, which retroactively helps to spread its cultural influence still further. Soviet publishers currently publish books in 57 languages out of the 91 nationalities recorded in 1970;

leaving aside the case of the Estonians, who had on average 10.5 books per inhabitant published in their language in 1971, Russian books come top of the charts with 10.3 publications per Russian reader and 7.10 books per Russian-speaking reader (one with Russian as first or second language), but the average number of titles published then drops to 3.4 books per Yakut, 2.6 books per Uzbek or Turkmen, 2.5 per Moldavian, 2.3 per Ukrainian and 1.8 per Tadzhik. Should we take the fact that 82 per cent of the present-day Soviet population is capable of using Russian to communicate and travel about within the Union as a sign of a far older process of Russification?

There is something ambiguous about Soviet measures in this respect. They represent a quite remarkable effort to bring the benefits of the modern world to ethnic groups who have only been brought into contact with culture in the last generation or two, in particular through almost universal schooling for children. Further, the possibility of being published in Russian gives writers in other languages an audience, while not necessarily forcing them to abandon their traditional culture. However, one cannot avoid observing that Russian is the mother tongue of a growing number of non-Russian Soviet citizens (16.3 million in 1979, i.e. 6.3 million more than in 1959) and that there is a steady penetration of the Slavs into the eastern areas of the country, where their presence is sometimes concealed, as in central Asia, by very high local birth-rates. Even so, the Russians are not the only ones to be engaged in this process of assimilation: the Bashkirs are becoming assimilated into the Tatars, the Tats into the Azeris, the Karakalpaks into the Uzbeks and the Baluchis into the Turkmens. In other words, it is these spontaneous reactions on the part of populations − to adhere, assimilate or resist − which truly test the effectiveness of a policy of integration.

Interethnic relations

Bilingualism, along with everything that is conveyed or communicated by language, is inevitable for any Soviet citizen wishing to pursue his studies beyond secondary level. The resulting acculturation, which can be found in more or less analogous forms in any multinational state, will be examined in Chapter 11, which deals with national cultures and social values. Here, we shall confine ourselves to certain reactions that indicate the true impact of interethnic relations in the cultural, economic and family spheres.

Many Soviet citizens who are accustomed to travelling from one end of the territory to the other make human contacts that ignore considerations of nationality. Solzhenitsyn's *Cancer Ward* remarkably illustrates the fraternal atmosphere of interethnic relations in Tashkent. The frequency of mixed marriages, i.e. between partners belonging to different nationalities (approximately 10 per cent of all marriages), is a reflection of this disappearance of national feeling. Table 11 above shows that these marriages are more frequent in the towns than in the countryside. But for the country as a whole, this frequency is no greater than the theoretical average derived from the mix of nationalities in any given republic; furthermore, while there are frequently mixed marriages among Slavs (Russians and Ukrainians) or between the peoples of central Asia, there are far fewer marriages between Armenians and Azeris than between Russians and Armenians. Religious traditions may account for certain affinities or reservations. The child's choice of nationality, when the parents belong to different nationalities, is revealing in what it tells us about people's preferences for the most advantageous nationality. The Jews, having broken out of the ghetto to which they were confined by the laws of the empire, have the highest level of interethnic relations in their friendships and cultural activities. But cohabitation between different nationalities does not necessarily imply that they communicate with each other, especially in central Asia, where Russian communities sometimes form a separate town from the native one.

The national arts and literary traditions have been opened up to new forms of expression: peoples who formerly possessed only an epic or a lyric poetry have borrowed the Russians' realism; the populations of central Asia have developed a pictorial art freed from the taboos of Islam; national film schools have established themselves in the Ukraine and Georgia. Dramatic art has developed to an unprecedented degree among all the peoples of the Union.

In other fields, such as history and religion, the past has been interpreted in a sectarian Marxist perspective, which certain members of the intelligentsia view with some misgivings.

National feeling is not merely a survival from the past, for it draws sustenance from cultural and economic achievements, which are a matter of pride to the new élites. Much still remains to be done; and, as elsewhere, obtaining more in the Soviet Union involves persistent and persuasive lobbying of the central ministries for additional financial aid. Competition between republics and the tensions between central and local authorities do not necessarily flow from nationalism, although particularisms and even chauvinism (*mestnichestvo*) do often manifest themselves in economic disputes.

As we reach the end of this examination of the diversity of groups and interethnic relations in the Soviet Union, two observations and two questions suggest themselves.

1 Soviet society may be regarded as a two-tier society: each person belongs to a national tradition and inherits its language, but at the same time that individual has the feeling of belonging to a far vaster community whose processes gradually threaten to engulf the frailer national cultures, chiefly because of their rural origins.

2 The formation of the Soviet Union predates the industrialization of the peripheral regions; alongside this, industrial society introduces into interethnic relations a new type of competitive relation, different from the relations of domination previously existing between colonized and colonists. The old

notables (merchants, clergy, landowners) have been supplanted by new local élites of technicians and administrators for whom economic activity offers vast scope to their ambitions.

3 The problem is to know whether the demands of the Union's economic development in any way threaten the present territorial structure and thereby the balance of nationalities.

4 It is unlikely that the populations living on the European frontiers pose any threat to the stability of the Union: elements regarded as hostile — the Finns from the Vyborg region, Germans from former Königsberg and the 'bourgeois nationalists' from the Baltic republics — have been deported. On the other hand, the Asian frontiers are disputed by China, in response to which the Soviet authorities are speeding up their colonization of the eastern regions; but, in the long run, faced with the twofold demographic pressures of the Turko-Mongol peoples within and the Chinese without, political readjustments cannot be ruled out altogether.

NOTES

1 Figures for the age structure as it appears from the 1979 census were not available on 15 June 1981, when this chapter was revised. The working population totalled 134.8 million on 15 Jan. 1979.
2 See the study by A. Sauvy in 'L'U.R.S.S. et sa population', *Population*, June 1958.
3 A. Kvasha, 'Optimalnoe naseleniya SSSR', in *Vaprosy demografio*, Moscow, 1970, pp. 33–47.
4 K. Marx, 'Critique of the Gotha Program', in L. S. Feuer (ed.), *Marx and Engels: Basic Writings on Politics and Philosophy*, New York, Anchor Books, 1959, pp. 112–32.

SUGGESTED READING

Historical demography

Bogarskii, I., *Naselenie Rossii za 400 let (XIV–XXe)*, Moscow, 1973.
Lewis, R. and Leasure, J., 'Regional population changes in Russia and the U.S.S.R. since 1851', *Slavic Review*, vol. 25, no. 4, 1966, pp. 663–8.
Lewis, R., Rowland, R. and Clen, R., *Nationality and Population Change in Russia and the U.S.S.R.* (census data 1897–1970), New York, Praeger, 1976.
Lorimer, F., *The Population of the Soviet Union*, Geneva, S.D.N., 1946
Maksudov, M., 'Les pertes de la population de l'U.R.S.S. 1918–1958', *Cahiers du monde russe et soviétique*, no. 3, 1977.
Rashin, A., *Naselenie Rossii za 100 let (1811–1913)*, Moscow, 1956.

Postwar demographic trends

Balwin, G. and Manning, F., 'Projections of the population of the USSR, 1970–2000', *US Bureau of Census, International Population Reports*, service P-91, June 1975.

Biraben, J., 'La structure par âge de la population soviétique', *Population*, no. 5, 1960.

Brackett, J., 'Projections of the population of the U.S.S.R. 1964–1985', *U.S. Bureau of Census, International Population Reports*, service P–91, 1964.

Destefanis, M., 'La population active soviétique: structure et évolution', *Population*, no. 2, March–April 1971, pp. 241–76.

Feshbach, M., 'Between the lines of the 1979 Soviet census', *Problems of Communism*, vol. 31, Jan.–Feb. 1982. See also *Population Bulletin*, vol. 37, no. 3, 1982.

Pressat, R., 'La situation démographique de l'URSS', *Population*, nos 4–5, 1979.

Itogi vsesoyuznoy perepisi naseleniya 1959, svodni tom, Moscow, 1962.

Itogi vsesoyuznoy perepisi naseleniya 1970, Moscow, Statistika, 1972–4, 7 vols.

'L'U.R.S.S. et sa population', *Population*, June 1958 (special number) (includes a study by A. Sauvy of Soviet thinking on demography).

Naselenie SSSR, po dannym vsesoyuznoy perepisi naselenya, 1979, Moscow, 1980.

The Soviet Union and its peoples

Bromlei, J. and Kozlov, K., 'Izucheniye sovremennykh etnicheskikh protsessov', *Sovetskaya Etnografiya*, no. 1, 1975; *Vestnik Akademii Nauk S.S.S.R.*, no. 11, 1972.

Bruk, S., 'Etnodemograficheskie protsessy v S.S.S.R.', *Sovetskaya Etnografiya*, no. 4, 1971, pp. 8–30.

Dunn, S. and Dunn, E., 'Soviet regime and native culture in Asia and Kazakhstan', *Current Anthropology*, June 1967, p. 147 ff.

Dunn, S. and Dunn, E., *Introduction to Soviet Ethnography*, Berkeley, 1974, 2 vols.

Katz, Z. (ed.), *Handbook of Major Soviet Nationalities*, London, Macmillan, 1975.

Klement'ev, E., 'Yazykovye protsessy Karelii', *Sovetskaya Etnografiya*, no. 6, 1971, pp. 38–44.

Kozlov, V., *Natsional'nosti S.S.S.R.*, Moscow, Statistika, 1975.

Newth, J. 'The 1970 Soviet census', *Soviet Studies*, Oct. 1972, pp. 200–21.

Tokarev, S., *Etnografiya narodov S.S.S.R., Istoricheskie osnovy byta i kultury*, Moscow, M.G.U., 1958.

The national problem

Allworth, E. (ed.), *Soviet Nationality Problems*, New York, Columbia University Press, 1971.

Allworth, E., (ed.), *Ethnic Russia Today*, New York, Columbia University Press, 1979.

Arutyunyan, J., Drobizeva, L. and Shkaratan, O., *Sotsial'noe i natsional'noe*, Moscow, Nauka, 1973.

Azrael, J. R. (ed.), *Soviet Nationality Policies and Practice*, New York, Praeger, 1978.

Bennigsen, A. and Quelquejaj, C., *Le sultangalievisme au Tatarstan*, Mouton, 1960.

Carrère d'Encausse, H., *Bolchevisme et nations, 1917–1929*, Fond. Nat. Sciences Pol., 1977.

Carrère d'Encausse, H., *L'Empire éclaté*, Flammarion, 1978.

Djouba, I., *Internationalism or Russification*, London, Weidenfeld & Nicolson, 1968; New York, Monad Press, 1974.

Holmogorov, A., *Internatsional'nye cherty sovetskoi natsii*, Moscow, 1970.

Korey, W., 'The future of Soviet Jewry', *Foreign Affairs*, Autumn 1979.

Lewis, E., *Multilingualism in the Soviet Union: Aspects of Language Policy*, Mouton, 1972.

Parming, T., 'Population processes and nationality issues in the Soviet Baltic', *Soviet Studies*, vol. 32, July 1980.

Pipes, R., *The Formation of the Soviet Union: Communism and Nationalism, 1917–1923*, Cambridge, Mass., Harvard University Press, 1964.

Ramet, P., 'Linguistic assimilation in Ukraine', *Ukrainian Quarterly*, vol. 35, no. 3, 1979.

Sawyer, T. E., *The Jewish Minority in the Soviet Union*, Boulder, Colorado, West View Press, 1979.

Silver, B., 'The status of national minority languages in Soviet education', *Soviet Studies*, vol. 26, Jan. 1974, pp. 28–40.

Ter-Minassian, 'Le mouvement révolutionnaire arménien, 1890–1903', *Cahiers du monde russe et soviétique*, Oct. 1973, pp. 536–607.

Chapter 3

Where people live: the city

Towns and villages are subgroups of society as a whole. Society affects each of the smaller groups that make it up, but it is these groups that form the everyday environment of each individual Soviet citizen. Whereas his nation and his family are imposed on him by birth, he can nowadays choose his place of residence, depending upon his ability or potential.

We shall begin with the town. While in the west, chronologically, the village gave birth to the town, the history of the peopling of Russia shows the reverse to have been more frequently the case. The *gorod* was a fortified position designed, like the Roman *limes*, to protect Slav colonization from the invader and to ensure the safety of goods convoys. Even today in Siberia, the town still acts as the logistical base for the opening up of the pioneer regions. In the period between these origins and our own times, history has woven a highly disparate urban network, in which a certain number of prestigious names stand out: Kiev, Moscow, Samarkand, St Petersburg and Stalingrad (present-day Volgograd).

Soviet statisticians employ a population threshold to distinguish the town from what we call the countryside. The countryside has no other definition than what is opposed to the town: in the RSFSR, any conurbation of 12,000 inhabitants is classified as a town (*gorod*); one of more than 2000 inhabitants is classed as an 'urban locality' (*poselok gorodskogo tipa*) provided at least 50 per cent of the population is engaged in nonagricultural occupations. The threshold varies from one republic to another, depending upon the degree of urbanization: 10,000 inhabitants in the Ukraine, 6000 in Byelorussia, 5000 in Azerbaijan, Georgia and Turkmenistan, and 8000 in the Baltic lands. On 15 January 1979, some 163.6 million Soviets lived either in towns or in urban localities, representing 62 per cent of the total Soviet population. However, these figures mean different things to the historian, the economist, the sociologist and the town planner, for each has his own distinct conception of what constitutes a town. We shall examine the question from each of these different standpoints, to try and form a fuller notion of the characteristics of Soviet urban civilization.

URBANIZATION AND HISTORY

For the historian, the number of inhabitants is an unsound criterion for defining an urban society, for what sets the population threshold that a town is capable of tolerating at different times in history is its capacity for feeding its population: with 300,000 inhabitants at the end of the eighteenth century, St Petersburg would be comparable to a city of 1 million people today. Moscow was then a very large city with its 100,000 inhabitants; next came Vilno, Kazan, Tula and Astrakhan', all of which are now surpassed by ten cities with populations of over 1 million. In 1863, Odessa took third place, whereas a century later it had slipped to seventeenth place. When, with the abolition of serfdom in 1861, Russia entered the industrial era 640 towns out of today's 2000 were already in existence, and the remainder, i.e. two-thirds of the conurbations, are thus the offspring of industrialization and, with very few exceptions, date from the Soviet period.

It is generally agreed that the building of the railways played a key role in the growth of towns, for without adequate transport the town lacks the means of subsistence; the concentration of population in turn attracts industry, for the division of labour and mass production assume the existence of a relatively large market. In other words, urbanization and industrialization act reciprocally, as illustrated in Table 12. But the remarkable thing about the Soviet case is the way in which this process has gathered momentum in recent decades. Whereas in other industrial countries the expansion of new towns has slowed down, as has the building of new railways (by now an unusual event), in the Soviet Union new towns are being added at a rate of 20 per year, while the rail network is being expanded at a rate of 1000 kilometres per year. This gives the impression that the Soviet Union is in a phase of increasing prosperity, but its expansion is due rather to the lateness with which industrialization took off. In its degree of urbanization and the percentage of its rural population, the Soviet Union is comparable to the United States prior to the first world war and to France in 1940. Japan, which began to modernize in 1868, at about the same time as Russia (1861), had already by 1910 achieved a degree of urbanization not achieved by the Soviet Union until 1940. Since the end of the second world war, however, the Soviet Union has achieved in twenty years an evolution comparable to that of France between 1860 and 1940.

The fact that towns grew up rather later in the Soviet Union than in the west needs to be borne in mind when trying to interpret certain features of Soviet urban society. These should be seen more as the growing pains of industrialization than as symptomatic of the nature of the regime. In particular, the housing crisis, which continues despite efforts over the past twenty years to

TABLE 12　*Rate of urban growth in Russia/USSR in the nineteenth and twentieth centuries*

	Urban population annual growth rate (%)	Average km of railway built per annum
1811–67	1.5	54
1867–1913	2.3	1300
1913–39	2.9	750
1939–59	2.5	985
1959–79	2.8	805

	Russia/USSR		Japan	USA	France
	Urban population (%)	Urban housing (m² per inhabitant)	Urban population (%)	Urban population (%)	Urban population (%)
1860	9		26	20	26
1910	16	7.3	32	52	44
1940	33	6.5	46	57	57
1960	50	8.9	63	69	64
1975	60	12.2	76	74	73

overcome it, is the price exacted for over-rapid urban growth. In 1971, the ratio of dwellings to 1000 inhabitants was 271.4, comparable to the figure for Japan, but contrasting with 320 in France and 338 in the United States. Fifteen years ago, the situation in Japan's cities was just as critical as that in the big Soviet cities which has, however, now improved considerably. In certain major cities, such as Moscow, at the beginning of 1979, some 76 per cent of families lived in separate apartments, whereas in 1960, 60 per cent of all Soviet families living in state-owned buildings had to share a kitchen and bathroom with other tenants.

The extent of the influx into the cities that followed the Revolution to some extent reflects a rejection of the shackles and restrictions of the past. For generations, the Russian nobility had tried to stem the rural exodus and the growth of towns; first for fiscal reasons, for the granting of the status of a town to a conurbation entailed additional taxes that the nobility had no wish to pay, but above all because the proletarianization of the peasantry represented a direct threat to the existing social order. Like its populist adversaries, the Tsarist administration sought to preserve Russia as long as possible from the social upheaval occurring in industrial Europe: towns and railways were hotbeds of revolutionary agitation. Up to the 1905 revolution, the maintenance of peasant communities (*obshchina*) and the host of obstacles to rural exodus, such as the need to obtain the community's permission and a passport in order to leave the village, was thought sufficient to ward off this evil. The 1905 revolution marked the failure of this policy: the general strike, the first workers' soviet in St Petersburg and the Pan-Russian Union of Peasants all signalled the first coalition of town and country.

History also provides an explanation of two further features of Soviet urbanization: the absence of a bourgeois tradition and the clearcut division between town and country. Although twelfth- and thirteenth-century Russia had developed a brilliant urban civilization, as witnessed by its civil and religious architecture, with the exception of Novgorod no autonomous municipal power, no bourgeoisie in the medieval sense of the term, ever managed to withstand the will of a prince. The economic pressures and military mobilization dictated by two and a half centuries of Russian resistance to the Mongols could only be imposed by an autocratic ruler. Thus was forged in Russia a centralizing, bureaucratic tradition to match that of the Mongols, at a time when with the Renaissance and the Reformation the west was embarking upon great individual adventures in thought and action. Nothing comparable was experienced in Russia, where noblemen, officials, tavern-keepers, clergymen and artisans were all in the service of the sovereign; the table of ranks, which existed from 1792 to 1917 specified the position of each individual in the social hierarchy. The first industries were born not in the towns but among the peasants (Ivanovo, the Soviet textile centre, was still only a village in 1853), and from their ranks sprang generations of merchants and businessmen. But the spirit of enterprise never predominated, and the first factories were set up at the behest of the state: Russian capitalism was to be a state capitalism. Briefly, urban life was more closely bound up with the administration than elsewhere; it waned as soon as the seat of authority moved to some other place; sometimes even, the town was indistinguishable from a large village.

For generation upon generation, the rural exodus was the town's chief source of recruitment. Before settling definitively, the worker—peasant long migrated seasonally, periodically returning to his village home; the 1926 census still recorded millions of these *otkhodniki*. The great majority of towns-people, meanwhile, were born in the countryside. At the time of the 1897 census, 43 per cent of townspeople belonged to the peasant class; in 1917, one industrial worker in three in Russia still owned land in the countryside. Between 1926 and 1970, natural increase accounted for only 25 per cent of the 109.7 million Soviets who joined the urban population; the rural exodus accounted for 60 per cent of this increase, while 18 million Soviets, i.e. 15 per cent, became townspeople without even moving, simply because their localities were classified as 'urban' from one census to the next. In other words, more than half of present-day town dwellers have scarcely one or two gener-ations of townspeople behind them.

This conquest of the town by the surrounding countryside sometimes makes the clearcut division between the two somewhat arbitrary. In 1910, in a now

classic book (*Gorod i derevnya*, 'Town and Country'), the Russian geographer
P.V. Semenov-Tyanshanskii confessed his perplexity when attempting to
define what constituted a town. Even today, many old towns or suburbs, with
their low houses, their village pumps and gardens, have retained a village
appearance. Among the crowd thronging the town centre, one can distinguish
the rural origins of the recently arrived townspeople by their rugged build,
their clothes and their slow gait. People have kept up the peasant custom of
making preserves; the allotment garden (*uchastok*) which many suburbanites
cultivate, provides a chance to engage in a favourite hobby as well as supplying
vegetables, and in the summer evenings many old people love to sit on a bench
near their apartment block to gossip, as they used to beneath the windows of
their *izba*.

The rural exodus is likely to play a smaller role in urban growth in the fore-
seeable future. Between 1959 and 1970, nearly as many children were born in
the towns (14.6 million) as arrived there from the countryside (16.4 million).
Since 1970, natural increase has accounted for 43.5 per cent of urban population growth, compared with 20.2 per cent in the period 1939—59.[1] The
peasantry has ceased to be the principal source of recruitment to industry (the
RSFSR's unskilled and semiskilled labour force increased by 6.9 million
between 1965 and 1972, while the number of people working on collective
farms dropped by only 1.6 million, i.e. only 20 per cent of new unskilled and
semiskilled jobs). However, new town—country relations are emerging, in the
form of daily commuting by workers who live in rural areas and come to
work in the big cities — their way of perpetuating the tradition of the
otkhodnichestvo. The city has not yet lost its vitality (indeed, it is planned to
create a further 400—500 new towns in the country by the year 2000) nor its
irresistible power of attraction.

THE SOVIET TOWN: POLARIZER AND CATALYST OF DEVELOPMENT (URBAN ECONOMY)

The polarization of increasingly vast tracts of land modifies not only the limits
but also conceptions of the town. It is no longer the historical character of the
city which holds the economist's attention but its power of attraction. The
town is likened to a living organism, which absorbs the resources and information (inputs) necessary to its multifarious activities, and finally restores to
the outside world its products and its services (outputs). While industry has
been and still is for many cities the dominant function (*gradoobrazuyushchii*),
the number of jobs in the services sector is now rising more quickly than in
industry, especially in the very large cities such as Moscow and in the new cities
devoted to scientific research. A city's dimension is the expression of its polariz-
ing power and serves as a classificatory criterion.

Different categories of town have grown up at varying speeds at different

periods in Soviet history. Between 1897 and 1926, it was the large cities (of over
100,000 inhabitants) which grew fastest (2.6 times); between 1926 and 1939, the
medium-sized towns (50,000–100,000 inhabitants), which had generally grown
up under the pressure of industrialization, took the lead, tripling their populations. The growth of this category of towns then slowed down, and they
increased their populations by only 34 per cent between 1959 and 1970, whereas
the large cities grew from 48 million to 82 million inhabitants, in other words
twice as fast as the medium-sized towns. Small towns (less than 50,000
inhabitants) are growing steadily, doubling their population from census to
census. The average population density in the large cities (over 100,000
inhabitants) remains relatively stable: 314,000 inhabitants on average in 1897,
329,000 inhabitants in 1939 and 1959 and 342,000 inhabitants in 1970. Meanwhile, the appeal of the very large cities (over 500,000 inhabitants) is undeniable,
and these have doubled their populations every sixteen years; of the cities in this
category, those with populations of over 1 million inhabitants – there were 18 at
the beginning of 1979, including 8 republic capitals – have a lower growth rate
because of measures taken to inhibit the concentration of industry in some of
them. Old cities such as Moscow or Kharkov enjoyed a boom in the 1930s, when
their industries produced the capital goods required for the new industrial
regions: the annual influx of population to Moscow (currently around 16,000
immigrants, as in the last century) had swollen to 200,000 individuals in 1931–2.

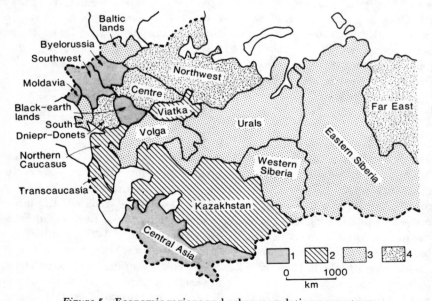

Figure 5 Economic regions and urban population percentages

Note: Urban population %: 1 less than 40%; 2 41–50%; 3 51–60%; 4 over 60%.
Source: J. P. Cole, Geography of the USSR, *London, Penguin, 1967, p. 69.*

Comparing the distribution of the Soviet Union's urban population in 1970 (see Figure 5) with that of, say, West Germany, we find a higher concentration in large cities (over 100,000 inhabitants) in the Soviet Union (55.5 per cent of the total) than in West Germany (40 per cent). Furthermore, the rather denser German network contains about the same number of localities of under 10,000 inhabitants (3095, representing 80 per cent of German conurbations) as the Soviet Union (3576). Because of its belated urbanization, the Soviet Union had no network of small towns when rapid industrialization got under way; this contributed to the rush to the big cities, where the concentration of population is akin to that of the United States. The 18 cities with a population of over 1 million now account for 13 per cent of the total Soviet population and contain 51 per cent of the students in higher education, one-third of them in Moscow alone.

A city's power of attraction can be measured not merely in terms of the size of its resident population, but also by the yardstick of how much daily or seasonal migration it gives rise to. Suburbanites account for 91 per cent of Soviet rail-passenger traffic (compared with 61 per cent in France and 75 per cent in Japan), and each year the Soviet railways transport the equivalent of twelve times the Soviet population. An estimated 4 million people live in the countryside and work in town. In the central provinces, this category represents 20 per cent of the rural population, while in the Moscow region the proportion climbs to 26 per cent and in the Leningrad region to 28 per cent (including students and school-children).

A city's sphere of influence varies according to the speed of the available means of transport. Daily commuting to work ceases when the journey takes over two and a half hours; the peak frequency lies around the 15-kilometre mark and drops beyond 30—40 kilometres from the city centre (in London 70 kilometres and in Tokyo 120 kilometres). For shopping trips, visits to the doctor or administrative formalities, the radius of polarization may stretch as far as a 3—4-hour journey, for such journeys are not a daily necessity although the total number of journeys of this type (12—15 million) surpasses those of regular commuters. In Moscow, for example, with 7.4 million inhabitants (1973), the population expands to 9 million in the daytime if we include those who come in for work but not the 6 million inhabitants of the province of Moscow who occasionally come into the city: it is estimated that half the purchases made in the city's shops in summer are made by non-residents. In the case of certain firms or government agencies, a city's influence may extend well beyond its regional perimeter. Moscow and Leningrad exert their influence over practically the entire country.

Towns also interact with one another, leading to new forms of urban growth: mergers of conurbations and clustering through the creation of twin cities (e.g. Volgograd—Volzhskii). In 1960, the population of Moscow increased from 1 to 6 million by absorbing 5 towns and 12 localities; in 1966, Tashkent expanded by annexing 35 localities.

Analysis of transport patterns has enabled us to identify some 500 clusters of towns accounting for close on 80 per cent of the country's urban population: among these conglomerations (*goroda blizhnego sosedstva*), the Donets (17 towns), the Moscow region (44 towns) and the Kuznets Basin (8 towns) are the most important, although they do not form real conurbations as in the Ruhr or the east coast of the United States. Even so, the drawing power of the Moscow region is not as great as that of (for example) the Paris region, as it contains only 9 per cent of the total urban population of the Union (compared with 27 per cent around the French capital). Moscow has a higher population density per square kilometre (7403 inhabitants) than Paris (4470); on the other hand, the Moscow region (260 inhabitants per square kilometre) is far less populous than the Paris region, which contains 770 inhabitants. Also, the city of Moscow contains 63 per cent of the urban population living in the province of Moscow, which means that it exerts a slighter power of attraction than the Siberian cities: Omsk absorbs 82 per cent and Novosibirsk 71 per cent of the urban population of their respective provinces (1973).

These movements are not always only one way. Summer migrations carry hordes of holiday-makers to the beaches of the Black Sea or the Baltic: Sochi, which had a population of 241,000 in January 1970, receives over 3 million tourists each year. In the suburbs of the big cities, and in the environs of Moscow, the shutters of dachas, or summer homes, are thrown open; suburban traffic rises by 18 per cent during this season. Leningrad, with a population of 4 million, has some 850,000–900,000 country homes. This trend is bound to develop as the number of private cars increases.

The drift outwards from the centre towards the periphery, characteristic of American cities and even the Paris region, has not yet occurred in the Soviet Union. Indeed, even on public holidays, the centre remains lively and bustling — none of the Sunday lethargy so common in western cities — because of the often excessive concentration of shops, which stay open on public holidays, and places of amusement. Old people remain very attached to the amenities that the big city affords, which is why one finds a relatively higher proportion of retired people living there. So, despite all the government's efforts to halt urban growth and encourage the population to take advantage of the healthier life to be had in smaller towns, the big city continues to exert its magic fascination. 'To Moscow! To Moscow!' Chekhov's three sisters cried in *The Cherry Orchard*; and to this day this has remained the rallying cry of many Soviet people, who regard the road to the city as an essential stepping stone to success, and Moscow as its crowning glory.

THE SOVIET CITY: WAY OF LIFE AND MEETING PLACE (URBAN SOCIOLOGY)

General features

For many Soviet citizens, city life begins with signing a contract to work in a factory. As we have already pointed out, in 60 per cent of cases it was the factory or the mine which gave birth to the town: Magnetogosk yesterday, the Kama factory (Naberezhnye Chelny) or Togliatti today; the residential quarter where the newcomer will be making his home stands close by the buildings of the firm he will be working for. Old cities and a few suburban dormitory-towns (Saltykovka near Moscow, with 80 per cent of the capital's workers, Vsevoloysk near Leningrad, etc.) are the exception to the rule. A job in the city gives single people the right to accommodation in a workers' hostel, while families will have a right to accommodation in an apartment block; in either case, the accommodation will generally be owned not by the local council but by an enterprise. From this, there flow a certain number of sociological consequences specific to the urban way of life.

First, the move to the town represents a break with the family for young single people or couples. Parents are no longer there to interfere in their daily life, nor are the grandparents on hand to take care of their little grandchildren. The social control exerted by the family and the pressure of village traditions are replaced by a more anonymous, more impersonal way of life.

The new city dweller, having just left family and village, looks to a new employer for security: in addition to accommodation, the enterprise provides the worker with an apprenticeship school, club and dispensary. The enterprise's collective will take the place of the village community, with all the advantages and the drawbacks that this kind of patronage entails. Drawbacks include the heavy dependency of the worker with regard to living conditions and the way in which work and the zeal with which it is done are noted. Membership of an enterprise or of a government or local authority agency is one's visiting card, establishing a person's position in the social hierarchy of the town.

The diversity of contacts characteristic of the urban way of life, in contradistinction to that of the country, is only really found in the long-established big cities, where a great variety of age and occupational groups mingle. Elsewhere, officially provided housing somewhat restricts the individual's choice of friends. These will be chosen out of personal affinities rather than from among colleagues at work, although this by no means rules out mutual assistance between immediate neighbours, especially among the less well-off sections of society. Lacking more deeply rooted social integration, the city dwellers seek to conform to their neighbours' way of life by possessing certain articles or adopting certain patterns of behaviour as outward signs of their membership of urban society.

The great obstacle to integration is excessive mobility on the part of certain sections of the urban population. These people change residence frequently, either to take up new appointments or, putting into practice the old proverb 'the grass is greener on the other side', to give expression to their wanderlust. Of all the features of urban life, this mobility of Soviet families is the key factor differentiating them from their counterparts in western urban society. When we come to discuss the enterprise (Chapter 7), we shall take another look at this mobility; it is felt to be excessive because of the social costs it entails; but it is also a necessary condition for the opening up of the nation's territory, for without it there could be no new towns. However, this want of stability makes it difficult to stimulate urban life and to settle the population.

Typology: categories of city dweller

What emerges from the foregoing is that the *age* of the town and the *length of residence* of the individual in the town are decisive criteria in the typology of urban areas. Accordingly, depending on the moment of their arrival in a town, we may distinguish between 'the patricians' (*starozhily*), who have been living there for at least a generation, townspeople of rural origin but who are already settled and, lastly, the newcomers. Housing surveys allow us to quantify these different categories by types of dwelling, as in Table 13.

TABLE 13 *Analysis of urban population by type of accommodation, 1965 (%)*

Type	RSFSR (mean)	Leningrad[1]	Gorky	Novosibirsk		Barnaul, number of years' residence[3]			Novopolotsk[4]
				long-estab-lished residents	new-comers	less than 2 years	2–5 years	10 years	
Private individual homes	31.6	6.4	10	17	3–6[2]	18	15	34	20
With parents						14	4	6	
Apartments: shared	} 55.6	55.6	30	} 58	} 24–17	} 24	} 51	} 56	6
separate		31.6	50						66
Private sublettings	6.4			22	60–66	41	27	4	
Hostels	6.4	6.4	10	3	13–11	3	33	8	8
Income bracket						76–85 R	90 R	95 R	

Notes: 1 In 1964, when the survey was carried out, 57.3 per cent of working-class families lived in a single room, 20.6 per cent in two rooms and 9.2 per cent in more than two rooms.
2 The first figure refers to people born in the city, the second to those coming from the countryside.
3 Barnaul was then a city requiring no residence permit (*propiska*).
4 A new town founded in 1963.

Housing conditions to a large extent shape the townsperson's way of life. Depending on whether one lives in the town centre or on the outskirts (i.e. with or without the convenience of proper drainage and running water) depending on whether one lives in a modern building or in an old house, depending on whether one lives in a separate apartment or shares one's bathroom and kitchen with other families, so the degree of intimacy of family life, relations with neighbours, availability of schooling for children, the degree of comfort and furnishing will differ.

The Soviet town has abolished the ghettos and the neighbourhoods of ill-repute, where the jobless, the rootless and the criminal classes congregated. But it has not yet completely resolved the problems connected with the integration of young people newly arrived in town, who form a kind of subproletariat with few ties; they are less well paid because they are unskilled, and are employed in jobs (building, roadworking, waitressing, etc.) that the older-established city dwellers shun. Also, they are less well housed, as can be seen from the high percentage of those forced to subrent a room or even a simple 'corner' of a room (41 per cent of those living in Barnaul for less than two years, 60–66 per cent of newcomers to Novosibirsk) from another individual. The fact of having a relative in town makes the move easier, which is why a greater number of those arriving from the surrounding countryside manage to find a detached home of their own. Their favourite occupation in their free time is to gather with people from their own villages, for theatres and concerts are frequented by citizens of longer standing.

Some 3.5 million Soviet citizens live in furnished accommodation in hostels (*obshchezhitie*) for young workers. Some 70 per cent of enterprises run such hostels, under the management of a 'commandant'. Young workers spend no more than three years in these hostels on average, as they are too noisy to allow residents to concentrate on their studies and because couples are not allowed to live in these nurseries for young fiancés. In spite of the supervision of the 'educators' (*vospitateli*), of whom there are too few, moral standards in these hostels are not always the best. Consequently, the hostel system, which was supposed to perform an educational function and facilitate the integration of young workers, is coming under increasing criticism; although more expensive, preference now goes to 2–3 person rooms incorporated into the more recent working-class housing estates, such as at Togliatti or at Naberezhnye Chelny.

In the older towns, people who own a house of their own, even if it is not as comfortable as the apartment blocks, are generally attached to their memories and their independence. Young people are willing to live in a tiny apartment for the sake of the comfort that this affords them. The situation of couples living with their parents in the town is different from that of people with an apartment of their own or of those putting up relatives from the country. In the first case, both the style of the apartment and the way of life will be dictated by the tastes of the previous generation (iron beds, cushions and embroidery, potted plants, etc.), while in the second case, the younger generation imposes its own lifestyle.

The number of people forced to live in communal apartments with shared washing and cooking facilities is dropping (compare in Table 13 the percentage of communal and separate apartments in Gorky, an old town, and in Novopolotsk, a new town). For these people, relations with their neighbours have to be regulated. They take turns to clean the shared portions of the apartment, they have a timetable for doing the laundry, etc., although even this does not entirely preclude conflict. Each family's living space is marked off by sideboards and cupboards, and family gatherings have to be held in a restaurant as there is no dining room. In separate apartments — the ideal, which the great majority of city dwellers have now attained — the first room is used as a living room, where the family places its status symbols (television set, rugs, vases, statuettes, and so forth), while the second room, with its bookcase, is used for study and for the parents to relax in.

The distance between place of residence and the town centre (shops and amusements) and place of work also varies according to one's social category. In Pskov (population 141,000), 75 per cent of workers live less than 2 kilometres from their place of work and travel there on foot, which takes an average of 4.9 hours per week for men and 4.2 hours per week for women; 2.3 per cent travel by bicycle or motorbicycle. In the Moscow region, 25 per cent of workers (in the median population) live less than 10 kilometres from their place of work, while managers, engineers and technicians, who enjoy better transport facilities, tend more frequently to live in the suburbs and 20 per cent of them (median population) live 50 kilometres from their work. In Kharkov, on the other hand, where metalworkers represent 24.7 per cent of the population and engineers and technicians 11.5 per cent, 34.8 per cent of metalworkers and 4 per cent of managers live in the suburbs; the contrast is sharper still among people working in the cultural and scientific spheres: 5.1 per cent in town and 0.9 per cent in the suburbs (1959 census).

Our information on the big Soviet cities is not sufficiently detailed to allow us to identify neighbourhoods or streets that might be reserved for privileged categories (or conversely to marginal ones) of the population. Co-operative building programmes financed by a number of subscribers could ultimately lead to the formation of areas inhabited by families belonging to a single socio-occupational group. Andrei Sakharov has mentioned property developments that result in the expulsion of ordinary citizens from the centre of Moscow in order to build luxury housing for a carefully selected élite on the site of older houses (*My Country and My World*, Harvill, 1976, p. xxi). Such cases have been relatively rare until now; examples include the locality of Peredel'kino, south of Moscow, reserved for writers and artists; the co-operative dachas reserved for members of the Georgian Academy of Sciences near Tbilissi (Tiflis); and the academic and university town of Akademgorodok.

In towns where growth has altered the balance of nationalities, certain ethnic groups tend to gather in distinct areas. This has happened in certain old cities of central Asia, where Russian and native districts have grown up. The same phenomenon can also be seen in more recent cases of urban growth, such as at Ufa (821,000 inhabitants in 1972), capital of the Bashkir Republic, where 63.2 per cent of the population is Russian, 20.5 per cent Tatar and only 5.4 per cent Bashkir. The town centre is occupied by the Russians, who hold down most of the non-manual jobs; recently built apartment houses in the suburbs are inhabited by skilled workers, while the

Bashkirs working in the least-skilled trades are concentrated in detached homes on the city outskirts.

Typology: small towns, pioneer bases and dormitory towns

Age or the inhabitants' length of stay are not the only criteria by which we can differentiate urban areas in the Soviet Union: size, location and the function of the town have as much influence as housing conditions on population structure, occupations, forms of social life and the degree of mobility among the inhabitants. Three types of town emerge from monographs on urban problems: small towns that have preserved their character as a rural centre, the new town in the pioneer zones and the dormitory town in the suburbs of the big cities.

The small town. From the distant past, the small town has inherited its function as the administrative centre of a rural district (*raion*) which is why it is sometimes known as a *raigorod*. The small town often lies some way distant from the railway and has not been much affected by industrial growth: 22 per cent of localities with between 10,000 and 20,000 inhabitants and 39 per cent of those with less than 10,000 inhabitants belonged to this category in 1970; they included the historic city of Suzdal (population 9000 in 1959), the market town of Makarevo (2000 inhabitants in 1861 and 4400 in 1959), seat of the ancient national fair, and Vetluga (9000 inhabitants in 1959), refuge of the Old Believers in the nineteenth century.

Apart from a few architectural gems — a citadel, church or monastery — the small town differs little from a large village in appearance, with its small houses nestling in lush green gardens and its vegetable gardens supplying the locality with food, which elicits the accusation that it is populated by a higher than usual proportion of people catalogued as 'idle' who devote all their energies to their own patches of land. The small town really only comes to life on Sunday, market day, except during the season of the thaw and of the autumn rains, which turn the roads into a quagmire (350 towns do not have roads with stable surfaces). There are no queues and no harassing crowds here. People do not come simply for the Sunday market; gossip and the exchange of news are part of the ritual of these small communities, where everybody knows everybody else. The population consists mainly of officials and retired people, the young having gone off to find work elsewhere.

Efforts are now being made to revive these small and medium-sized towns by creating industrial jobs. During the eighth and ninth five-year plans (1966–75), over 200 towns in this category were earmarked for the creation of some 2600 new enterprises. Difficulties have emerged, because planners have apparently overestimated the ability of these towns to absorb larger populations, as they generally lack both adequate social amenities and a sufficient supply of labour. It is now intended to direct them more towards tourism, schooling — to supplement the educational system in the big cities — and above all food industries (stockbreeding centres, dairy industries and other rural industries).

The pioneer city. This is the exact opposite of the previous example. The striking thing about the pioneer city is its youthfulness in terms both of its still inadequate amenities, because these mushroom cities have grown up too quickly (the population of Bratsk, for example, has expanded from 43,000 in 1959 to 219,000 in 1980) and of its population which is recruited from the Komsomol, by volunteer contracts or when young men complete military service. These people need no residence permit. Wages are 30—100 per cent higher because of distance and the harshness of the climate. The majority of the population is made up of young unmarrieds: in Magadan, 70 per cent of the workers are aged between 20 and 39, compared with 36 per cent in the rest of the country; men outnumber women, as in most of the world's pioneer fronts, and the amount of alcohol consumed is reminiscent of clichés about the far west.

But these workers have trouble settling down, which has earned them the nickname of 'fliers' (*letuny*). People stay long enough to save a little money, a year or two, then go off elsewhere (certain independent teams, paid by the amount of gold they manage to extract in the eastern Siberian placers, manage to earn the equivalent of five years' average wages in four weeks in the summer). The reasons given for leaving include the desire to pursue one's studies in one of the big university cities, and, because these workers marry quickly and the birthrate here is higher than anywhere else, that living conditions (housing, nursery schools, etc.) are insufficient to encourage a family to put down roots in these towns. In the town of Kachkanar (population 35,000), in the Urals, where the average living space per inhabitant is 7.3 square metres, 72 per cent of the workers are aged under 26: in a period of 10 years, 58,000 people left this town, while 40,000 arrived.

New residential districts in the big cities. These are known as Novye Cheryomushki, on the model of the one in Moscow. They have burgeoned with exemplary speed in the past twenty years and have helped mitigate, if not totally abolish, the housing crisis. Widespread use has been made of industrial prefabrication methods, the quantity of flats being more important than their quality. The problems that these dormitory towns breed are familiar to many westerners living far from the city centre, with its shops and amusements, and far from their place of work. These problems include not only the material difficulties resulting from lack of amenities in certain developments, shortage of transport or living together in poorly soundproofed jerry-built apartment blocks but also the psychological problems of monotony and isolation for old people accustomed to a different environment and for the young mother in need of help in the home. In other words, despite its bright lights, the city has yet to satisfy the profound need to communicate felt by every person in this lonely crowd. Have town planners been short on imagination, or have they failed to appreciate the aspirations of city dwellers as they really are?

URBAN IDEOLOGIES AND THERAPIES (TOWN PLANNING)

In principle, the Soviets are well equipped to combat the growing pains and problems connected with urban underdevelopment. Legal and financial obstacles to ground occupation, and land speculation, have been eliminated by nationalization and the fact that land is virtually free; it is the job of centralized economic planning to co-ordinate regional development and urban growth. Furthermore, Soviet cities do not yet suffer to the same degree as elsewhere from traffic congestion, since space is more abundant; still, the great diversity of ecological conditions and cultural traditions is ill-suited to stereotyped prescriptions.

The planners and architects who took over from the patrons of building under the *ancien régime* (noblemen, clergymen and merchants) are no longer exclusively concerned to perpetuate their memory by some monumental building, palace or sanctuary; their mission is to create vast complexes of factories and offices, housing and schools for the multitude as quickly and as cheaply as possible. They work to technical directives devised by the Gosstroi, the state committee responsible for standardization of construction, and their plans are the outcome of discussions with the elected representatives of town councils, the city soviet (for a discussion of its workings, see Chapter 10). In the very large cities, the chief architect heads all planning and development operations, and in some of them, a construction trust, modelled on Moscow's Glavmosstroi, is the sole main contractor for all construction work. Town planning is conducted on a 20-year timescale or a longer one still; one result of this is that it is inspired by a certain conception of the city of the future.

Town-planning doctrines

For the founding fathers of Marxism, the ideal to be attained was the suppression of any distinction between town and country, less (as is currently happening) through the gradual building up of rural areas than by the dispersal of industrial activities. For Engels,

> the elimination of the division between town and country is not a utopia in as much as it is conditional upon the spreading of large-scale industry as evenly as possible throughout the territory. In the big city, civilization has assuredly bequeathed us a heritage that is going to take us a great deal of time and trouble to rid ourselves of. (*Anti-Dühring*, vol. 3, pp. 72–4)

For Marx who saw at first hand the poverty engendered by the industrial revolution, the city was 'the crudest expression of the individual's subordination to the division of labour and to a determinate activity imposed upon him, a subordination of the blinkered animal of the city' (*German Ideology*, vol. 6, pp. 201–2). Was the city, then, doomed to disappear along with capitalism? Many contemporaries in Russia, as elsewhere, hoped for just that, despite their very disparate political backgrounds: Dostoevsky (in *Crime and Punishment*), Leo Tolstoy, and Peter Kropotkin, who proposed to alternate farm work with factory work (in *Fields, Factories and Workshops*).

These anti-city prejudices died hard. In 1920, A. Chayanov published under the pseudonym Ivan Kremnyov a populist-inspired 'peasant' utopia in which he prophesied the disappearance of the big cities and that Moscow would have a population of 100,000 in 1984.[2] Then, the inauguration of the first five-year plan, which involved the foundation of new towns, stimulated Marxist theoreticians to reflect on the forms of the socialist city. They hesitated between a naturalist model of the garden city (*The Green City* by M. Ginzburg) and the culturalist model of the commune city (*Sotsgorod* by N. Miliutin and G. Strumilin). The latter's theories re-emerged in 1960 on the occasion of the discussion of the Communist Party programme, approved in October 1961 by the twenty-second Congress of the Party, which is responsible for laying down long-term policy. Strumilin then published a study on 'The everyday life of the worker and communism' (see Suggested Reading), in which he develops the idea of a relatively small city (with a population of 30,000), equipped to 'socialize' to the utmost certain functions traditionally performed by the family: the children would be brought up in boarding schools, meals would be taken in communal canteens in each building and residents would form fully fledged communes near their places of work but in distinct residential areas. This vision of the future was to be condemned as utopian; evolution, it was claimed, showed it to be false, for people prefer big cities to small towns, and families have rejected it, having experienced the unpleasantness of shared apartments, and now thirst for a life of independence.

Discussion of the ideal or optimal dimensions of the city is by no means dead. It has given rise to controversy between economists, who reject policies aimed at limiting industrial activities in the very big cities, and town planners favouring medium-sized towns. The former are chiefly concerned with questions of labour productivity. The criterion of optimization governing planners' choices, they argue, ought to be the value of output per inhabitant, which is greater in the metropolis where enterprises enjoy better conditions for research, employment of skilled labour and industrial co-operation; in addition, enterprises enjoy external economies in infrastructure costs already borne by the city. To which the town planners reply that this is precisely the problem, and that the economists' criteria ignore the costs of urban development borne by the city council. Big cities have a voracious appetite for space, entailing spiralling transport and general utility costs. On the contrary, this expansion needs to be slowed down by ridding the city of all non-essential activities.

Urban development costs are far lower in medium-sized towns, and the real question, in the final analysis, is to know which formula corresponds not to higher profitability for the enterprise, but to the aspirations of the city's inhabitants.

Gradually, these two extreme positions have drawn closer together, for by taking as their point of departure a functional conception of the city, everybody now agrees that the optimum population will necessarily differ according to whether one is talking about a metalworking centre or a spa town. Further, the traditional town/country distinction is now being absorbed within a more unified global system of territorial development known as ESR (*edinaya sistema rasseleniya*). Town planners are now concerned with the entire network of urban and rural interdependencies, because the spread of towns into the countryside is altering the basic terms of the problem. What planners now try to do is devise a community that respects a certain balance of green belts and inhabited zones, built up according to a hierarchy of specialized elements on a cellular model. The basic module is a series of dwelling units designed for 1500–2000 inhabitants which, consisting of several buildings with educational and commercial amenities, form neighbourhood units (*mikro-rayon*) of 8000–12,000 inhabitants; these cores are linked together to form districts with their attendant services (cinemas, hospital, etc.), or *rayon*; a certain number of districts in turn go to make up the town (between 50,000 and 100,000 inhabitants). Wherever possible, residential areas are situated about walking distance from the areas where other activities are carried on and from the traffic routes, as has already been tried experimentally in other countries, in Sweden in particular.

The originality in Soviet doctrine is not to be found in town planning, for it rejects the idea that town planning can be separated from control of the forces of production. Its specific feature is the belief that what determines the fate of the town is its location and the expansion of the forces of production. The distribution of industry and research institutes and labour-market forecasts all combine to dictate the terms on which the architect works; town planning is merely a by-product of economic planning.

Achievements and realities

The priority accorded to economic planning in Soviet town planning means that the enterprise is responsible for providing social amenities for its staff. This is not always particularly economical – each enterprise tries to found its own cultural club – nor particularly advantageous from the point of view of housing construction as managers are generally in more of a hurry to get their factory working than to complete residential buildings and their attendant services; nor is it particularly aesthetic, as the town grows up according to no particular plan but around the factories as these spring up. Even today, many of the financial and technical resources are in the hands of the enterprises, on whom local councils depend for much of the town's infrastructures and social amenities; unless, as in the very big cities, all development work is concentrated in the hands of a single authority.

Government agencies are not the only main contractors, for in order to rebuild, after the devastation of the second world war, in some 1700 localities private individuals were invited to take part in the work of reconstruction. In the early days, private involvement took the form of the building of individual houses, and a great many homes were put up by traditional methods with help from the state, on land provided free of charge, which resulted in an extension of land occupation and increased costs for the provision of utilities. Since 1962, housing co-operatives have once more been permitted, in which subscribers (who pay 40 per cent of the value of the apartment, which comprises 15 square metres per person with an upper limit of 60 square metres) are partnered by the state, which lends the balance outstanding (60 per cent) at very low interest rates repayable over 10–15 years. The private sector accounts for 28 per cent of the urban housing stock; in other words, one urban family in four lives in its own home. In the course of the ninth five-year plan (1971–5), out of a total of 580 million square metres of housing space built, the state accounted for 63 per cent of the programme, individual houses 13 per cent and housing co-operatives 6 per cent (the balance is rural building by collective farms and their members). These co-operatives attract people with savings who are looking for an investment, and above all single people and childless couples who are not eligible for priority housing allocation in the public sector (even though 1 square metre costs 160 rubles for owner-occupiers in comparison with rents which are charged at an annual rate of 1.6 rubles per square metre).

The urgency of the problem facing the authorities during the period of massive population influx to the big cities meant that, for many years, priority had to be given to water supplies, public transport (*metro*) and housing. In the 1930s, there could be no question of building ideal cities out of nothing, as recommended in certain schemes for a new Moscow to be built beside the old. Town planning had to be confined to bringing order out of chaos, carving through the ancient fabric of the cities in the manner of Haussmann.[3] In Moscow, 426 churches, monasteries, monumental gateways and so on were demolished between 1935 and 1941. This process is still under way, the solutions being adapted to each historic city; but everywhere one turns new, tall buildings now stand where once stood old houses. Much still remains to be done, judging from the fact that in 1960 derelict single-storey houses accounted for 55 per cent of total available living accommodation in the towns of the RSFSR, a phenomenon found also in Japan, as in every part of the world in the throes of rapid expansion, where traditional homes rub shoulders with modern buildings.

Where the past imposes no restrictions, town planners are freer to realize their dreams, as can be seen in the new academic city of Akademgorodok, the seat of twenty-odd institutes of the Siberian branch of the Academy of Sciences, a garden city where residential zones alternate with working and leisure zones, a 'satellite' (or sputnik) town situated 25 kilometres from Novosibirsk. 'Sputnik' is the name given in the Soviet Union to built-up areas designed to disperse industrial activities (Kryukovo, near Moscow, or Sestroretsk, near Leningrad) or research centres (Dubno, the atomic research centre, Serpoukhov, Obninsk, Pushkino and Chernogolov in the Moscow region). These are sited some way from the metropolis so as to avoid a fresh flow of commuters, and out of a concern to preserve a non-built-up area around the capital on the model of the Greater London green belt.

Strumilin's avant-garde visions have inspired the 'house of the new life' (*dom novogo byta*) built in Moscow in the 1960s by Nathan Osterman and his colleagues. This housing unit consisting of two 15-storey buildings was designed to house 2000 people. Each apartment was only equipped with a corner kitchen, since meals were supposed to be served at snack bars on each floor or in a big restaurant in the central wing, which also contained all the community's social, educational and recreational amenities. But although the experiment involved volunteers, it failed (communal houses failed to provide their tenants with the hoped-for satisfaction) and the building has now become a hostel for students attending Moscow University.

Does this mean that Soviet society has been evolving too fast to allow it to develop an urban style of its own? Leaving aside the avant-garde ventures of the period 1928–35, it would be true to say that Soviet architecture, like all other contemporary architecture, is the daughter of concrete and the metal frame, with its resulting uniform landscape of rectangular boxes. Even so, certain features do lend to the socialist town a symbolism all its own, with its immense esplanades for military parades and mass meetings, its imposing (or pathetic) monuments perpetuating the cult of heroes of national or revolutionary struggles. Here, educational concerns prevail over mercantile considerations, the blare of commercial advertising gives way to hoardings boasting of achievements or announcing the Party's directives, or more prosaically inviting the citizen to give up smoking or to keep a lookout when crossing the road. Even the town's gardens are pressed into the service of the cultural revolution and bear the significant name of 'parks of culture and rest'. More attention is paid in the Soviet Union to the setting of collective life than to individual living conditions; certain Moscow underground stations are subterranean replicas of great palatial salons, with their marble and their chandeliers. But there is less contrast there between everyday life and the holiday atmosphere (except for the greater number of people drinking to celebrate payday); shops and recreational amenities take days off by turns and one-third of the working population works on Sundays. The fashion for cafés reflects a certain desire for a rather less austere way of life and more spontaneous social relations.

As to the future, Soviet urban growth is unlikely to slow down, as planners expect 240 million city dwellers in the year 2000 out of a total population of 305 million. On the other hand, it is less easy to imagine the impact of changes brought about by new forms of transport, as well as by new information and communication techniques. With a turbotrain travelling at 300–400 kilometres per hour, it would take only 12 minutes to cover 100 kilometres whereas the real rate of travel in the Moscow area is at present only 12.3 kilometres per hour. Will the car, which has wrought far-reaching changes in town and country relations in the west, produce the same upheavals in the Soviet Union when traffic grows denser? The private car fleet (4 million in 1976) reached 6.3 million at the end of 1980, giving 24 cars per 1000 inhabitants (compared with 289 per 1000 in France, 256 in the United Kingdom and 526 in the United States). The number of Moscow's private cars in 1973 (250,000) is estimated to have risen to 500,000 in 1980. At the same time, it is planned to extend the metro network from 146 to 320 kilometres as the government continues to give priority to public transport.

In the final analysis, is what once appeared to be the characteristic feature of urban society — namely greater diversity and mobility in human relations coupled with individual autonomy and isolation within a less restricted environment than that of the village, giving an impression of a huge spectrum of opportunities for everyone — is this merely a by-product of a certain industrial technology, not of a residential environment? With the spatial extension of this technology, the traditional town/countryside contradiction tends to disappear. Will tomorrow's village be nothing but a myth, perpetuating the memory of a human-sized community, of a more harmonious lifestyle in which nature still had its part to play, a lifestyle of which the city dweller, yesterday's villager, dreams in his moments of relaxation or leisure? But what does today's village look like?

NOTES

1 *Istoriya SSSR*, no. 6, 1980, p. 135.
2 I. Kremnyov, *L'Âge d'homme*, 1976, p. 2: 'Voyage de mon frère Alexis au pays de l'utopie paysanne' (My brother Alexis' journey to the land of the peasant utopia).
3 Baron Haussmann, prefect of Paris under Napoleon III, who pulled down much of ancient Paris in the mid-nineteenth century to build the broad boulevards we know today (Transl.).

SUGGESTED READING

Urban development

Barter, J., *St. Petersburg, Industrialization and Change*, London, Edward Arnold, 1976; *The Soviet City, Ideal and Reality*, London, Edward Arnold, 1980.

Blackwell, W., *The Beginnings of Russian Industrialization, 1800–1860*, Princeton University Press, 1968.
Brower, B., 'L'urbanisation russe à la fin du XIXe siècle', *Annales*, A. Colin, Jan.–Feb. 1977.
Harris, C., *Cities of the Soviet Union*, Chicago, 1970.
Kerblay, B., 'La ville soviétique entre le possible et l'imaginaire', *Annales*, A. Colin, July 1970.
Razhin, A. G., *Formirovanie rabochego klassa Rossii*, Moscow, 1958.

Town Planning

French, R. and Ian Hamilton, F. (eds) *The Socialist City*, New York, John Wiley, 1979.
Kopp, A., *Ville et révolution*, Anthropos, 1967.
Osterman, N., 'L'habitat de l'avenir', *Architecture d'aujourd'hui*, no. 147, 1969, pp. 94–9.
Starr, S., 'L'urbanisme utopique en U.R.S.S., 1928–1931', *Annales*, A. Colin, Jan.–Feb. 1977.
Strumilin, G., 'La vie quotidienne de l'ouvrier et le communisme', *Archives internationales de sociologie de la coopération*, Jan.–July 1966 (from *Nory i Mir*, no. 7, 1960, pp. 203–20).

The big cities

Berton-Hogge, R., 'Recherches pour un urbanisme au XXIe siècle', *Problèmes politiques et sociaux*, nos 59–60, Feb. 1971.
Berton-Hogge, R., 'Plan directeur de Moscou', *Problèmes politiques et sociaux*, nos 35, 36, 37, 1973–74.
Kerblay, B., *Moscou, Notes et études documentaires*, no. 3493, 24 May 1968.
Kurman, M. and Lebedinskii, I. *Naselenie bol'shogo goroda*, Moscow, 1963.
Morton, H. W., 'Housing in the Soviet Union', *Soviet Studies*, vol. 32, April 1980.
Rozhdestvenskaya, S. B., *Zhilishche rabochikh gor'kovskoi oblasti*, Moscow, Nauka, 1972.

Urban development in the eastern regions

Carrière, P. and Maurel, M.-C., 'Urbanisation et croissance de la population urbaine en Asie soviétique', *Inter-Nord*, no. 12, 1972, pp. 101–17.
Perevedentsev, V., 'Migrations et conditions de vie en Sibérie', *Démocratie nouvelle*, Nov. 1966.

Chapter 4

The village and rural society

The population of settlements that cannot be classified as urban is regarded as rural; the countryside is therefore regarded as a *residual*. The village is whatever the town is not.

Indeed, the very size of the average Soviet village (225 inhabitants) makes it the reverse of the town. Far from being a pole of attraction, it rejects its children; for want of roads open to normal traffic it is cut off from the world. Access to a great many villages is difficult in spring and autumn; the winter snows fill in ditches and peat bogs, making this the ideal season for travel by sledge; in summer, the state of the roads and bridges keeps traffic down to an average speed of 25 kilometres per hour (*Izvestiya*, 16 July 1971; 23 August 1982).

Although turned in on itself, the village is nevertheless obliged to obtain the wherewithal for its survival. Essential food requirements are provided by the family economy jointly with the big collective farms. Farming and craft activities remain a common feature of the entire rural population. Consequently, the pace of rural life is dependent far more on the vegetable-growing cycle, with its alternating periods of unhurried activity in the winter months and weeks of feverish activity (the Russians speak of the 'period of labour', *stradnoe vremya*) during the haymaking and harvest seasons. Out of the 21 million collective-farm workers in 1968, only 13 million were productively engaged in the month of January. In brief, notions of work and leisure, of full employment and underemployment do not have the same meaning here as in the towns.

What confers upon this population group its community of characteristics is similarity of occupations and preoccupations No one can remain anonymous here; everybody knows everybody else. The commune assembly (*skhod*) and the brigade or collective-farm assembly provide a framework for direct participation in municipal affairs or in the running of the enterprise. Age-old traditions − folklore, village festivals, propitiatory rites − bear witness to the vitality of peasant culture, while the emergence of a different social hierarchy, in contrast with the traditional one, and new behaviour patterns, reflect the changes currently in progress in the Soviet countryside.

These residential, demographic, economic, social and cultural features of the rural world are even more diverse than in urban areas, owing to the particularism of traditional peasant cultures (formerly an obstacle to the growth of a shared peasant ideology), but also as a result of the differing impact of modernization on different regions.

RURAL HABITAT AND POPULATIONS

General features and tendencies

According to Soviet statistics, the rural population is defined as residing in localities of less than 2000 inhabitants; its activities, which may be either agricultural or non-agricultural, are not specified. This population is not only declining in percentage terms as a result of urban growth, but also, since the end of the second world war, in absolute figures as well. Until 1940, the towns steadily absorbed the natural rate of population increase in the countryside, thereby keeping the rural population stable; now, however, the exodus is outrunning the natural rate of increase and the countryside is fast becoming depopulated: between 1959 and 1970, the rural population fell by 3.1 million, and between 1970 and 1979, by 6.9 million. The population has fallen fastest in the RSFSR (6.7 million) and the Ukraine (2.2 million), while in central Asia the rural population continues to grow. In all, 58.5 million peasants left the countryside for the towns between 1926 and 1970, and 18 million country dwellers became townspeople without even moving, their locality having become a town.

As the rural exodus absorbs the population of working age, the age structure

TABLE 14 *Structure of the rural population and educational level of population aged between 20 and 30 (at the 1970 general census)*

Age groups	Towns	Countryside	Countryside towns = 100	Educational level	Towns	Countryside
		%			per 1000 inhabitants	
Under 15	24.8	34.4	139	Higher	126	44
15–19	25.4	17.4	68	Specialized	140	98
30–44	25.5	20.9	82	Secondary	339	225
45–59	14.0	13.6	97	Uncompleted secondary	322	431
60 and over	10.3	13.7	133	Primary	73	202
Total	100	100			1000	1000

Source: *Nash Sovremennik*, no. 1, 1974, p. 147.

of this residual population contains a higher proportion than in the towns of old people and children (Table 14). It will be noted, moreover, that it is the 15–19 age group which is least represented, because the better-educated boys and girls are the first to leave their villages, so that the educational level of young people aged between 20 and 30 who remain behind in the country seems lower than in the towns. Taking the rural population as a whole, differences are even more marked: in 1970 some 26 per cent had attended secondary or higher education as against 50 per cent in the towns; but, compared with the figures for 1939 (when only 4 per cent of villagers had pursued their education beyond the primary level as against 18 per cent in the towns), remarkable progress has been made.

The numerical predominance of women in the countryside was already noticeable prior to the Revolution, owing to the large number of men engaged in seasonal work (*othhodnichestvo*) away from the community. Since the war, the chief factor responsible for this situation is loss of lives among the male population. Most of the unskilled farm labour force is female: in 1970, the collective farms employed 1 million more women than men, whereas men outnumbered women on the state farms. Still, the Soviet agricultural labour force was more markedly female before the war: in 1939, women accounted for 58 per cent of agricultural labour (and agriculture occupied 59 per cent of women regarded as 'active') compared with 56 per cent in 1970; but agriculture now occupies only 26 per cent of female labour.

As in all industrial countries, there has been a steady drop in the percentage of agricultural jobs in the Soviet Union: 50 per cent of the total in 1939, 39 per cent in 1959 and 21 per cent in 1979. These percentages are calculated on the basis of the number of days actually worked: the total number of days worked in 1959 gives an annual average of 24.5 million agricultural workers (conventional units) whereas the January 1959 census indicated that 32.3 million individuals were actually engaged in agriculture. The numbers of people working in agriculture, which remained remarkably stable between 1939 and 1959, fell by 25 per cent between 1959 and 1970. Even so agriculture is still the principal activity, with 64 per cent of the working population living in the country in 1970, compared with a rural employment rate of 69 per cent in 1959. During the same period, the number of people employed in the services sector increased by 30 per cent.

The growth of rural industry has resulted in the creation of 1 million additional jobs. On 1 January 1980, 17,000 industrial enterprises run by the collective farms provided employment for an annual average of 713,000 collective-farm workers. These changes are first of all affecting the central provinces – Moscow, Gorky, Kalinin, Vladimir – where branch factories in an extremely broad variety of sectors, from the manufacture of laboratory equipment to perfumes, are now moving out into the country. In certain collective farms, these industrial activities not only ensure full employment but also make a bigger contribution to total turnover than agriculture, and are more profitable as well. The creation of agro-industrial combines is expected to wipe out certain peasant features of rural society in the Soviet Union within a relatively short space of time.

Another, and by no means negligible, change is that today 56 per cent of the rural population depends for its income directly on the state as employer, whereas ten years ago, most of this population depended on collective farms. Thus, it is becoming less and less appropriate to equate the rural world with the peasants on the collective farms, even though these still outnumber the state-farm labour force by 2 to 1.

The process of concentration, both administrative (at local-council, or *sel'soviet*, level) and economic (involving the amalgamation of farms), has been particularly marked over the past twenty years (see Table 15). In 1979, there were 41,258 rural soviets and 47,000 large-scale farms, regrouping some 319,000 localities, compared with the 70,034 soviets, 241,000 farm enterprises and 572,500 villages that existed on the eve of the second world war. Although these farms, all of which incorporate several villages, have expanded, it does seem as if the people involved tend to look to their enterprise rather than to the rural soviet as the focal point of collective and cultural life. The smaller villages are being deserted in favour of rural centres of more than 1000 inhabitants, which in 1970 accounted for 44 per cent of the rural population. However, the bulk of the villages, close to 63 per cent of all rural localities in 1979, had populations of less than 100, but these now account for only 12 per cent of the population, having lost over 6 million rural inhabitants in 10 years. Medium-sized localities, with populations between 200 and 1000, have lost only 1.9 million, while the rural centres, where the seats of the collective and state-farm administrations are located, gained 6.9 million between 1961 and 1970.

The contrast between the village, which in most cases is still a leftover from the past, with its average population of 225 inhabitants (scarcely more than in 1897), and the large-scale farm, with 3000–6000 hectares of crop land, shows just how far peasant agriculture has come since 1929 (the year of the 'great turn', of forced collectivization) to the mechanized agriculture of today.

Typology of rural regions and of the Soviet peasantry

The degree of agricultural modernization, the level of industrial development in a region, the dominant type of agricultural enterprise, population density and cultural traditions, all serve to differentiate the pace of change in the rural world according to a great variety of criteria. We have selected three types of criteria: (1) ecological factors (i.e. the natural conditions of a given region), which are the most stable criteria; (2) historical factors and traditions or beliefs, which give rise to very distinctive peasant cultures; and (3) economic criteria, which, as in the past, to a large extent govern the pace of social change in the countryside.

TABLE 15 *General features of long-term rural change*

	1897	1913	1926	1940	1959	1970	1970, of which women	1970, 1959 = 100
Total rural population								
1945 frontiers (millions)	106.2	131.1		130.3	108.8	105.7	57.3	97
1939 frontiers (millions)		114.6	120.7	114.5				
Rural working population								
Total (millions)					52.3	44.3	21.9	85
(a) manual occupations					46.4	37.3	18.1	80
intellectual occupations					5.9	7.0	3.8	119
(b) Branches:								
administration					1.0	1.3	0.5	130
education, health					3.4	4.8	3.4	141
commerce					15.4	19.7	13.1	128
industry, transport					7.8	8.9	2.9	114
fishing and hunting					0.16	0.09		56
forestry					0.72	0.52		72
agriculture					36.2	27	13.7	75
Non-working population			71.3	54				
Family economy					8.7	1.6–5.6[1]	1.5	18
Living on grants					0.16	0.36	0.16	225
Retired and pensioners					4.2	16.7	11.6	398
Dependants					43.3	42.9	22.3	99
Habitat and communities								
No. of localities (thousands)	524.7		613.6	572.5	704.8	469.3		67
Population per village	201		197	200	154	225		146
Localities of less than 500 inhabitants	91.3		91.3	91.1	92.6	88		95
Localities of over 1000 inhabitants	3.7		3.8	3.5	2.9	4.9		169
Municipalities (soviets) (thousands)	10.6		55.8	41.1	27.4	22.6		82
Farms								
Sovkhoz (state farms) (thousands)			1.4	4.2	7.4	15.0		203
Kolkhoz (collective farms)			14.8	236.9	44.9	33.6		75
Sovkhoz workers (millions)			0.34	2.3[2]	7.1	9.8		138
Active kolkhoz workers				29.0	22.3	17.0		76
Areas under the plough								
(10⁶ ha)		113		150	203	207		102
per sovkhoz/ha		80		2800	9000	6200		69
per kolkhoz/ha		40		500	2700	3000		111
no. of households per kolkhoz		18		81	383	431		113
total no. of peasant households (millions)		25		18.7	17.1	14.4		84
no. of tractors per 1000 inhabitants		0.23		3.5	5.5	9.5		173
Agricultural labour (millions)								
Kolkhoz and sovkhoz management					0.29	0.21	0.02	72
Agronomists and veterinarians					0.47	0.62	0.23	132
Brigade and shift leaders					0.78	0.47	0.07	60
Tractor-operators					2.4	3.3		137
Unskilled manual labourers					24.2	12.8		52

Notes: 1 The second figure gives the total, expressed in number of hours worked in the family farm by the total active population.
2 Including MTS personal (which merged with the kolkhoz in 1957).

Ecology and patterns of farming. In Chapter 1, we showed the gradations of heat, cold and humidity as one traverses the country from north to south, and from west to east. In the *forest zone*, the abundance of water encourages scattered rural habitats. Lakes and rivers mirror the villages, which generally have a population of no more than 250 inhabitants. Here, wood offers the best protection against cold; the *izba*, generally in modernized form, is the most common type of dwelling. The primitive slash-and-burn technique of farming in this area has left a heritage of small patchwork fields constantly at odds with stones and brushwood.

The hills of the Desna and the Oka form a barrier beyond which spread the *black-earth lands*. The population density rises sharply to 25 inhabitants per square kilometre; forest-clearing farming gives way to large-scale *steppe* farming: tractors inch their way towards a seemingly endless horizon. Here, villages are more concerned to protect themselves against heat than against cold. The houses are built from clay, bricks or stones; the thickness of the walls helps to maintain a steady temperature (in central Asia, the mud houses are built to withstand temperature variations of 60° between winter and summer, and of 20° between day and night at certain times of the year). The trees and vines growing around the houses add welcome shade, whereas the villages of the north have no trees at all. In the Ukraine, the farm is kept separate from the dwelling place, for the closeness and warmth of animals that is preferred in the compact farms of the north would here be highly inconvenient in the summer heat. In the Caucasus and in Asia, the houses are often huddled together, like a swarm, so as to prevent the heat from penetrating into the maze of alleys.

As the degree of aridity rises, so does the density of settlements: the villages of the Ukraine and the provinces in the northern and southern Caucasus average 700 inhabitants. These large villages sprawl in an often unbroken string down the valleys (as on the left bank in the Ukraine, in Moldavia and in Kuban) or along the Georgia coastline. The area between valleys was formerly the domain of the Kalmyk, Kazakh, Kirghiz and Buryat nomads. Today they have practically all been sedentarized, although the yurt has been preserved as a temporary dwelling place in the summer pastures for shepherds and their families (*chabany*). New forms of temporary occupation are arising in the eastern steppes, where seasonal workers are employed during the harvest, as in the western plains of the United States (absentee farming).

Further to the south, in the *semidesert regions*, population settlement depends on control of the water supply. A variety of techniques are employed: in the Caucasus, and especially in Dagestan, terraced cultivation; in Turkmeniya, traditional Iranian techniques of irrigation by means of underground conduits and wells (*qanat*); and, in the valleys, open-air irrigation, prior to the gigantic river diversion and broad canal schemes of the Soviet era. The density of the villages is dependent upon the capacity of the irrigation system, the more populous ones standing at the head of the system.

What the *Siberian village* fears most, on the other hand, is too much water. It cannot live without the river, which is its principal means of communication in summer and from which it obtains fish; but it stands by preference on the steeper bank of the river so as to avoid flooding when the ice breaks up. These villages are denser than in the European forest zone, for it is necessary to live in a community in order to cope with the isolation and the climate of Siberia. As in the northern part of the RSFSR, farms are much more spacious, as wood and space are unlimited. Today, railway stations and geologists' and lumber-jacks' camps, as well as mining communities, are moving into the rural land-scape and altering its character: the rural population now accounts for only 40 per cent of the population of Siberia and the population engaged in farming does not exceed 25 per cent. There is a shortage of labour on Siberia's farms.

History and cultural traditions. Natural conditions are interpreted in the light of a given cultural tradition, making any clearcut distinction between ecology and history rather tenuous. Thus the very high density of Kazakh localities (*stanitsy*) is as much the result of hydrology as of the need for safety. On these unsheltered 'frontier' steppes, it was necessary to band together in order to resist the nomad invaders. Even in 1897, the *stanitsy* in Kuban had populations averaging 1000; today these have increased to 5000–10,000 inhabitants. In these regions, a locality of 400–2000 inhabitants is regarded as a hamlet (*khutor*).

In the Caucasus, invasions have driven the settled populations to the natural defences of the mountains. Villages are scarcely distinguishable from the rocks in which they nestle (*aoul*); except possibly in Georgia and Armenia, where the Romanesque church rises like a citadel upon a peak, because for generations this has been the repository of Georgian and Armenian national traditions. The houses climb terrace-like up the hillside, the roof of the lower house serving as a courtyard for the house on the terrace above; in times of danger, people could go from one to another by means of secret doors. In the valleys, the houses have slightly pitched, tiled roofs divided into four sections; the roof covers a floor with an open or glazed gallery, around which the living rooms are arranged, while the kitchen is on the ground floor. In summer, cooking is done on an outside range in the courtyard, as throughout the Mediterranean south.

In the Ukraine (literally, this word means 'on the frontier' and serves as a reminder that for centuries this region constituted the marches of the Russian empire), the large villages stretching along the road (*ryadovaya derevnya*, the *strassen-dorf*) gradually give way, as one travels southwards, to 'nest-like' villages (*gnezdovaya derevnya*), so called because it was necessary to guard the communal livestock in the centre of the village and the pebble-lime *khatas* are built in a circle so as to afford better protection against the Tatars.

In the western provinces, on the other hand, there are a great many separate

farms (*khutora*) left over from the capitalist period. The Stolypin reform
(1906) sought to increase the number of 'independent' farms on American
lines and to break up the communal pattern of farming (*obshchina*). Many of
those who had asked to leave an *obshchina* were subsequently forced to rejoin
it after the revolution. The combining of lands which followed collectivization
put an end to the patchwork of holdings. Even so, the hill and dale landscape
of isolated farms is still a typical feature of the Baltic lands and western regions
recently attached to the Soviet Union: out of the 469,300 rural localities
counted at the 1970 census, 185,100 were hamlets in these regions of
Byelorussia and the Baltic republics.

On the frontier between the Baltic peoples and the Slav world, it is not only
the size of the village or the ancient church which distinguishes the Lutheran,
Catholic (Lithuanian) and Orthodox communities, it is also the steep-roofed,
flower-bedecked houses with their windows opening on to the farmyard, and
the roads snaking from hamlet to hamlet (certain collective farms embrace
100–150 hamlets, but these are currently being regrouped).

In contrast, the Russian village is identifiable by its rigid planning, dating
from eighteenth- and nineteenth-century regulations dictated by the frequent
outbreaks of fire. Houses, their windows overlooking the street, line the broad,
straight roads; they may lack the gaiety of flowers in their gardens, but these
villages do reveal a developed artistic sense in the way the church blends in
with the landscape, or in the outline of a farm gateway or the carved window-
frame of an *izba*.

Villages built in the Muslim tradition, whether in Tatar localities, with their
izbas hidden behind high palisades of woven wood, or the *kishliaks* of central
Asia with their mud houses, are relatively unplanned, except those built
recently. One wanders through a maze of alleys, between high, windowless
walls (*duvaly*), family life being concealed from outsiders. Men who are not
members of the family are allowed only into an outside courtyard (*tashkari*),
and family intimates alone are admitted into an inner courtyard (*ichkari*),
which leads to the different rooms and to the female occupations. Here, unlike
the church in Christian villages, the mosque is not the centre of community
life; for in Islam each head of household is expected to conduct prayers, and
the family is the centre of religious life. The social promotion of women, which
is bringing them out of their seclusion, is breaking down this tradition and
naturally resulting in the modernization of the environment. Walls of beaten
earth are disappearing and windows are increasingly being opened onto the
outside world. People gather either on a terrace in the house (*aivan*), or on an
adjoining veranda or in the garden (*suri*) beneath the shade of a vine, to drink
tea and enjoy the cool air. Men prefer to meet in the village *chaikana*, the local
café, even if as the root *chai* suggests all they drink is green tea; the *khauz*, a
rectangular pond, quietly mirrors the skies above.

Certain regions stand at the crossroads of several different cultural traditions.

Kazakhstan is an example of this diversity: broad streets of Russian or Ukrainian villages along a *trakt* (the Siberian road), the winter quarters of Kazakh shepherds, characterized by the higgledy-piggledy arrangement of the houses, as the livestock is accustomed to wander or stand beside them, and the *agrogorod*, an urban-type state farm built on newly cleared land and heralding the shape of the rural locality of tomorrow.

The economics and dynamics of social change. The speed of change of material civilization and of mentalities in rural society depends on the greater or lesser impact of industrialization and urban growth in the different regions, and on the degree of modernization or intensification of agriculture. In the light of these economic criteria, we can identify three types of rural regions.
1 Industrial regions in which agriculture plays a secondary role only for the supply of perishable foodstuffs (milk, vegetables) to the big centres. Heavy demand for non-agricultural labour has gradually emptied the countryside of its inhabitants, and the rural population now accounts for only 27 per cent of the total in the northwestern and far eastern provinces of the RSFSR, 29 per cent in the centre of the RSFSR, 31 per cent in the Urals, 37 per cent in the Donets basin, and 38 per cent in Siberia. In order to supply essential needs, it has become necessary to develop the state farms, which in all these regions (with the exception of the Donets), employ over half the agricultural labour and are therefore rapidly losing their peasant character.
2 The traditional agricultural regions engaged in intensive production, such as the Ukraine or the Baltic republics. Here, the rural population accounts for approximately 42 per cent of the total population or more, as in Moldavia, Transcaucasus and central Asia, all of which specialize in fine produce; most of the labour in these regions is supplied by the collective farms (66–70 per cent). Intensive methods are used, to judge from the cereal yields per hectare and from the average area cultivated per agricultural worker, which totals around 5–7 hectares and even falls to 2–3 hectares in the heavily over-populated farming regions such as the southwest Ukraine, Moldavia, the Transcaucasus and central Asia.
3 The new agricultural regions engaged in extensively mechanized large-scale production, such as the Volga plains and Kazakhstan, where the average area cultivated per worker on the state farms comes to 17–23 hectares, although yields per hectare (9–13 quintals per hectare) are lower than those produced in the black-earth regions of the RSFSR and the Ukraine (20–26 quintals per hectare). It is the fluctuating yields in these regions of uncertain agriculture which determine the success of the overall harvest from one year to the next.

Turning now from production conditions to incomes, certain regions such as Estonia, Latvia and Kazakhstan appear to be 'richer' than others, e.g. Azerbaijan Uzbekistan and Tadzhikistan. In 1970, Estonia, Turkmenistan and Kazakhstan had the highest collective-farm incomes and paid their collective-farm workers the highest wages (between 25 and 65 per cent above the national average), whereas those paid to collective-farm workers in Georgia, Moldavia, the Ukraine, Azerbaijan and Byelorussia were roughly 10 per cent below the national average. On the other hand, among this last group, with the exception of Azerbaijan, incomes from individual plots of land and family farms were higher than the national average, as was also the case in the Baltic lands. The number of days worked per worker on the collective farm was also the lowest: 196 and 122 days per year respectively in Lithuania and Georgia, the two republics having the highest incomes in the family sectors, compared with an average of 239 days in Siberia and 254 days in the centre.

The conditions of peasant families depend not only on total incomes, collective and private, but also vary according to the number of people in the household. Karl Wadekin has shown that while Turkmenistan had the highest income per family in 1970, the average income per person in the household dropped to 78 on the index (national average = 100), whereas Estonia came top of the index with 182; per capita incomes differ by a ratio of 1 to 3 as between Tadzhikistan (58 on the index) and Estonia.

Consumer spending in the countryside confirms these income disparities on the whole, except in Georgia; but it is difficult to reach conclusions on the basis of purchases made in the countryside alone, for we do not know the proportion of purchases made by peasants in towns. We also find a good correlation between family incomes and the average level of savings for the rural population in each republic, but for a given income level per family the Armenians save twice as much as the Uzbecks, while the Moldavians save less than the Ukrainians or the Russians.

The amount spent on food and drink per inhabitant in the countryside, compared with townspeople, reflects the relative degree of monetarization of consumption. This is lower where the family economy is most developed, notably in the Transcaucasus, the Ukraine, Byelorussia, Lithuania and Latvia, where spending on food and drink is less than 35 per cent of the amount in the towns. Purchases account for more than 50 per cent in only Kazakhstan and the RSFSR, owing to the importance of the public sector − state farms − in these two republics. But even here, home produce still accounts for a considerable proportion of consumption and underscores the vital role played by family agriculture in all rural regions.

THE FAMILY ECONOMY

The nature of the family economy and Soviet policy

Subsistence family agriculture is a universal phenomenon. It represents the dominant sector in the less-developed countries; in others, such as the Soviet Union, it is a leftover from the traditional peasant economy. The entire family helps to build the farm, and its chief function is to satisfy virtually all its members' needs: food, care of livestock, the cost of festivities and celebrations, and the payment of taxes. Authority was wielded by the head of the household, and under him labour was traditionally divided between the men, who tilled the fields, reaped and engaged in 'outside' crafts, while the women looked after the house, brought up the children, made clothes and ruled over the farm itself, taking care of the animals and the vegetable patch.

The first aim of marriage was to produce the number of children needed to run the farm and provide for old age. The horse provided the manure needed to fertilize the land. Propitiative rites implored the heavens for good weather or to protect the animals. In other words, the entire organization and ritual of the peasant economy was directed towards one major concern, namely to preserve the family group.

The greater the number of hands in the family and horses in the stables, the greater the economic viability of this social group, enabling it to cultivate more land and allocate its labour more efficiently. This system presupposes abundant land and periodic share-outs within the rural community (*mir*). As over-population on the land and the development of the market economy bred growing social differentiation, the workings of the *mir* seized up, and new forms of agriculture (capitalist) emerged. It was this evolution which gave rise to discussions in the Soviet Union on the nature of the peasant economy. Marxists emphasized the spread and the dangers of capitalism in agriculture; the populists, on the other hand, argued in favour of the specificity of a peasant economy based not on profit but on the family's needs.

This controversy raged until the end of the New Economic Policy (NEP), having been revived by Bukharin's theses on the agrarian crisis. According to him, the agrarian reform carried out after the Revolution, together with the tax system, eliminated the extremes, and this levelling process reinforced the 'middle' peasantry (*serednyaki*) and not, as the Trotskyists claimed, the rich peasants (the kulaks). These diverging analyses had enormous practical consequences, since Stalin had speeded up collectivization in the face of peasant opposition on the ground that there was a danger of capitalism arising in the countryside.

The Soviets have long hesitated over the correct policy to adopt towards small-scale family agriculture, which has survived collectivization, albeit on a reduced scale. While everyone agrees in rejecting the term 'private sector' (*edinichnoe khozyaistvo*), which westerners often used to refer to this form of agriculture, preferring the term 'auxiliary economy' (*podsobnoe khozyaistvo*), they often disagree as to what ought to be done about it. Should they, as Stalin held before his death, rapidly abolish this family sector, which he regarded as an obstacle that must be eliminated before collective farming could really progress, or would it be preferrable, on the contrary, to wait for growth in the output of the large-scale farms and rising farm wages to eliminate the need for family farms in the countryside without any outside intervention? It looks as if present policy has adopted the latter alternative, with the raising of certain restrictions imposed on the private sector between 1937 and 1953 and from 1956 to 1964. But although it is tolerated, the family-farm economy is strictly regulated.

The limits and evolution of the family economy

In 1970, some 34 million Soviet families possessed some kind of auxiliary economy (individual home, plot of land and possibly even some livestock). This feature was not necessarily confined to collective-farm families (15.5 million households) but extended also to the Soviet rural population as a whole: 14 million non-collective-farm households, of which 7.5 million state-farm families were in the same situation. To this should be added a further 4 million blue- and white-collar workers living in towns but with access to a plot of land. So the total is substantially higher than the number of families and individual people living in the countryside. Article 12 of the new constitution recognizes the right of each Soviet citizen to private ownership of a house and a farm.

However, the importance of this auxiliary sector varies from one socio-occupational group to another, not only on account of income differentials but also because the size of the farm permitted by law varies according to the category of family and rural region in question. We also have to distinguish the family's private property, the *dvor* (i.e. the house and the farm, livestock and poultry, machinery and small tools, with the exception of a horse, a tractor and a lorry, which are prohibited) and what is not owned but merely available to the family to use: the land attached to the house (*usad'ba*) or a plot of land outside the village (*uchastok*).

In the collective farms, a single working member in a family is sufficient to earn the right to the use of a plot of land up to a maximum of half a hectare, under the terms of the existing legal statute (December 1969). In regions under irrigation, the maximum is set at 2000 square metres but this ceiling is rarely observed, for the actual average is around 2500–3000 square metres, not including some tolerance of grazing and mowing on common land. Since the decree dated 6 March 1956, collective-farm assemblies have exclusive authority to fix the area of individual plots of land with reference to the collective work of the collective farm, thereby establishing a threat to those who might be tempted to neglect their obligations (a legal minimum of work on the collective farm was introduced in 1940, varying according to age and sex). The same decree also instituted the payment of monthly advances on wages so as to encourage people to take part in the collective work.

With regard to livestock, the 1969 statute makes republics responsible for establishing norms in keeping with local traditions. As a general rule, the farm of a family on a collective farm may contain a cow and her calf, a sow and piglets, three sheep and their lambs (but no draft animal), 30-odd poultry and a few beehives. Exceptions to this rule are permitted in republics with a tradition of stock-breeding: in particular the Buryats are allowed to own a horse and a greater number of cattle, and the peoples of the far north are allowed to own a small herd of reindeer. The donkey's meagre appetite qualifies him for a fair measure of tolerance, as he can live off a diet of a bunch of thistles and salt in the Caucasus and Asian regions, where he is a vital auxiliary on the mountain tracks. In actual fact, livestock statistics show that fewer than 60 per cent of rural families own a cow or a pig; however, 80 per cent of goat herds are privately owned, presumably because this 'poor man's cow' is much easier to feed. Family-tilled land accounts for 3 per cent of total land under cultivation in the Soviet Union, but for 7 per cent in the Ukraine, 9.2 per cent in the Baltic republics and 21 per cent in Georgia.

Where family farms do exist on state farms, these are merely tolerated and have no legal existence. Private plots are kept to a maximum of 1000 square metres, except in the state farms recently created out of former collective farms, where the old norms have been maintained. *A fortiori*, other categories of population living in the countryside can only hope to obtain a plot of land if the available reserves of land permit, and they must apply to the executive committee of the rural soviet, which is responsible for their administration. In any case, the person concerned, collective-farm worker or otherwise, can be deprived of his individual plot of land if it is used for commercial purposes or is left untilled for more than two years. The agricultural tax on private income is doubled when legal norms concerning the possession of livestock are exceeded. The agricultural tax is based on a sliding scale to take especially favoured situations into account; for instance, it is twice as high in Uzbekistan as in the RSFSR. Another effect of regulations concerning the sale of farm surpluses at market is to preserve the auxiliary nature of the family farm and to prevent it degenerating into a profit-orientated economy.

The various limitations imposed on individual farming activities, the difficulty of obtaining fodder and rising money incomes have not resulted in any appreciable decline in the private sector in absolute terms over the past twenty years. On the other hand, there has been a considerable decline in the area under cultivation since 1940, especially in land assigned to cereals, but this is a rather unrepresentative comparison inasmuch as it was in 1940 that the Soviet Union incorporated regions where non-collectivized agriculture was being practised. Between 1953 and 1972, the decline in private livestock and areas cultivated went hand in hand with the decline in the rural population. In relative terms, however, owing to the expansion of collective farming, family output of vegetables and animal foodstuffs declined appreciably: one-third of total output in 1972, compared with over 70 per cent of meat and milk produced in 1940. Some 60 per cent of potato and fruit production is still in private hands, although now representing only a third of the produce available on the market. What has happened to private egg production is even more remarkable — it declined from 69 per cent of the market in 1953 to 14 per cent in 1972, the result of recent progress in industrial poultry farming.

In all, the family economy accounted for 28 per cent of gross agricultural output in 1970 (but the percentage falls to less than 20 per cent if we deduct the value of fodder supplied to the private economy by the collective economy) and approximately 12 per cent of total output marketed. This latter figure confirms the traditional purpose of the family sector, namely to satisfy the family's own needs. Soviet estimates put the proportion of private output intended for sale at only 20 per cent, leaving aside certain products (such as meat and eggs) for which this proportion is more than 20 per cent.

Private consumption and incomes

When asked the reason for their attachment to the family farm, 55 per cent of respondents stated, in the first place, that it supplied them with virtually all their food requirements; 30 per cent mentioned its role as a source of additional income; while 12 per cent said that it helped to fill their spare time. To this should be added the satisfaction of owning one's own house and of being master in one's own home.[1]

The very low proportion of food purchases per inhabitant in the country — 41 per cent of the average figure per inhabitant in towns — confirms that for a given level of consumption and income, the rural family supplies more than 70 per cent of its needs (except for spending on drink, and on vodka in particular). The family farm was estimated to contribute 623 rubles per collective-farm family on average in 1961 (in the RSFSR). More recent figures — 200 rubles per member of each family in 1971 — show that this income has not dropped in absolute terms. In relative terms, on the other hand, owing to rising farm wages and state benefits, the proportion of private income had fallen from 43 per cent in 1960 to 27–23 per cent in 1972, while incomes paid by the collective farm had risen from 25 per cent of total family income to 43 per cent in 1972.

Among families on state farms, the number of family farms is far less, for in 1971 they represented only approximately 20 per cent of total income (compared with 23 per cent 10 years previously, giving an average of 465 rubles per month per family). This percentage drops to 4 per cent among the families of industrial workers. Taking the average industrial and white-collar wage of 163.3 rubles per month as 100 (1979), average monthly incomes varied as follows: the industrial worker earned 180.3 rubles for 280 days' work, and the state-farm worker 144.9 rubles and the collective-farm worker 112.9 rubles (index 69) for 215 days' work. The lot of this last category has improved considerably since 1967, when it was decided to pay collective-farm workers a minimum monthly wage in place of the former system of sharing out the profits at the end of the year on the basis of the number of days' work recorded.

Income in kind from the family sector generally helps to supplement the incomes of the least-well-paid categories, and particularly those of pensioners (who long formed an underprivileged category on the collective farms, as pensions depended upon the wealth of the collective farm; since 1964, the state has assumed part of the cost of collective-farm pensioners, the minimum pension being 20 rubles per month at present).[2] A survey conducted in 1969 in Lithuania indicates the correlations between the scale of collective incomes and the corresponding size of the family economy. Figures on farm incomes in 1969 are given in Table 16.

TABLE 16   *Labour input and structure of farm incomes, 1969*
(district of Vilnius, Lithuania)

Collective incomes (per family)	% within group	Hours worked per member				Income per capita		
		on the kolkhoz	in the home	on private plot	Total	Collective	Private	Total
up to 600 R	33	350	170	330	850	105	480	585
from 601 to 1200	40	571	179	289	1039	304	435	739
from 1201 to 1800	16	469	151	210	830	464	425	889
1801 and over	11	555	141	234	930	722	391	1113
Mean	100	462	180	288	930	296	443	739

It is not always so obvious that the family economy serves to equalize incomes. In a certain number of regions, and especially in the Baltic republics, the advantages accruing from the farm's resources are additional to the high wages paid by the agricultural enterprises. Furthermore, the peasant farm is not just a source of income. The upkeep of buildings, transport and tilling all involve additional costs that do not fall upon other categories of society, even when neighbours or relatives lend a hand (6 per cent of the rural family's budget is spent on housing, compared with 2.5 per cent in the towns). These material costs are compounded by the number of hours spent working on the farm: an average of 160–170 adult days' labour per family, and approximately 200 days per year if one takes into account the work put in by all the members of the family.

Intensification of labour and the productivity of the auxiliary sector

Soviet economists estimate that 31.2 per cent of the collective-farm worker's time is devoted to the auxiliary sector. The actual degree of involvement in these activities varies according to age and sex. Men devote on an average

36 days per year to their farm, out of the total 268 days worked, while the women spend 108 days out of a total 292 days, representing 4 hours daily, in addition to the 7.5 hours taken up by work on the collective farm. A survey conducted in the RSFSR in 1967 showed that among people of working age, men contributed 13 per cent of all time spent on the family sector, women 52 per cent and people not of working age 35 per cent (nearly all of the last being women). When able-bodied men do work on their plot of land, they do so only temporarily; these may be youths after school or after military service, while waiting for a job, or a relative on a visit to the country. The family economy is therefore dependent essentially on women.[3]

The Soviet Union has not yet reached the stage found in certain parts of the French countryside, where peasant women are achieving liberation through the abandonment of animal husbandry and through the proliferation of home appliances, which take some of the backbreaking work out of domestic chores. The Soviet peasant woman works particularly hard in summer because, in addition to her work on the collective farm, the family economy takes up an average of 46 hours per week. True, certain domestic tasks, such as bread baking or butter churning, are gradually disappearing. Everything depends on the supply situation in the countryside, for the family cow is very often the only way of making sure the children get milk. The shortage of day-care centres in rural areas is another cause of absenteeism (32 per cent of women of working age remaining at home give this as their reason for doing so), since, in 1968, there was room for only 29 per cent of children aged under 7 in day-care centres and kindergartens.

Now that men have lost their prerogatives as head of the farm, becoming, like their wives, workers or employees on a collective or a state farm, they have lost the prestige that formerly attached to the master (*khozyain*). Even so, they are vital to the smooth running of the family farm: without them, how would one manage to bring home the cartloads of hay and the fuel necessary for everyday life?

The family farm is a joint undertaking, and it is not always possible to distinguish each person's contribution with precision. The family's property (home, cow, etc.) is even more difficult to apportion, which is why even today, as under ancient law, the *dvor* is the common property of the family, not owned exclusively by the family head.

The secret of the remarkable success of these auxiliary activities lies in the extraordinary intensity of family work that goes into them, more akin to horticulture than to agriculture, the plot of land being regularly watered and abundantly fertilized. Some 3 per cent of the total area of land under cultivation supplies 20 per cent of gross output, after allowing for fodder obtained from the collective-farm system (on which the family economy is thus dependent).

Complementarities and contradictions between the family economy and collective farming

The large-scale mechanized enterprises, collective and state farms, enjoy a virtual monopoly of cereal growing and industrial crops (beet and cotton). In the past ten years, they have been introducing industrial animal-rearing methods (for poultry and baby beef). However, the private sector continues to play an appreciable role in making good the shortfalls in the collective system in the supply of vegetables, fruit and farm produce which require regular and careful attention. Some degree of division of labour has thus taken place between family and collective farming.

For many years, this complementarity was imposed by the compulsory deliveries exacted from rural families by the state, but since January 1958 these levies in kind have been abolished. Deliveries are now voluntary, and are governed by contractual relations: tobacco is grown for the state monopoly and piglets are fattened on the family farm on behalf of the collective farm. Close to 12 million calves are handed over to the collective farms each year, for subsequent supplying to the state as part of the collective and state farms' compulsory deliveries. In the final analysis, there has been no drop in the proportion of the commercial output of the family economy sold to the state: 24 per cent in 1970 compared with 20 per cent in 1950.

Conversely, the peasant family remains dependent on the collective farm for cereals, which it does not produce (or at any rate not in sufficient quantity), and for fodder. Privately owned livestock could not survive without these outside supplies. As in the past, sheep and cattle graze on the common land, watched over by a herdsman from the collective farm. The herdsman used to stand right at the bottom of the social ladder, but today he warrants special consideration, now that he is entrusted with the care of the cow, the family's principal source of wealth.

Despite this complementarity, the existence within the large-scale farm of a family sector governed by criteria different from its own creates a certain amount of friction. The peasant woman cannot work simultaneously on her own plot of land and elsewhere. This contradiction is resolved in practice by a crushing burden of work for people in certain occupations, such as dairy-maids; the other consequence is a sharp rise in absenteeism at harvest time, when perishables cannot wait upon the whims of the administration.

A second cause of friction lies in farm prices. Unregulated prices on the collective-farm markets can, depending upon the time of year, be as much as 20, 100 or even 200 per cent higher than official retail prices, which are themselves higher than the prices paid to farmers. These differences are an incentive to engage in family farming. In 1970, the rate of pay for a day's work on a collective farm was 3.90 rubles (the average for the Soviet Union, including payment in kind) and the rate for work in the fields was only 3.42 rubles, whereas 8 hours' work on one's own private plot of land could bring in 4.80 rubles.

In the vicinity of the big cities, the profits waiting to be made in the market are a further incentive to absenteeism. For, at certain times of the year, prices in the city markets are three or four times higher than those paid by the state to producers. For this reason, it has proved necessary to prohibit individual sales of milk by making it mandatory to hand over surplus milk to bulk-buying centres and to expand the system of sales on commission by means of contracts between peasants and consumer co-operatives, so as to cut down on the number of journeys into town. Thus, since few families are able to go regularly to market to sell their produce, most choose to pool their surpluses in order to travel to town no more than once or twice a year, taking care to choose the town that offers the highest returns and affords an opportunity of acquiring articles not available in the provinces.

In the medium term, the existence of the family sector is in no danger, so long as it makes an indispensable contribution to the food requirements in small towns and in the countryside. Even the country school teacher would have difficulty surviving without a plot of land. In other words, as long as collective production is incapable of taking over from family production, there will be objective reasons for its continued survival. At present, there is even a tendency to encourage the development of private stock-breeding, by permitting grants of additional grazing rights over and above individual allotments in exchange for contractual obligations to deliver a portion of the animal produce to the state. Restrictions imposed in the past on private-farm activities have generally worked to the disadvantage of city dwellers. This, independently of factors specific to the rural world, accounts for the apparent vitality of the family economy which until now has managed to survive all the upheavals of history.

But it is a precarious existence, constantly dependent on decisions that may be taken by the authorities through the agency of the collective assemblies. The price at which fodder is sold to collective-farm workers has a decisive influence on patterns of private livestock-owning. The state is the sole employer in the final analysis, with the power to apportion land and fodder and to fix wage and pension levels. Another long-term threat to the family economy comes from the growing disaffection for farm work among young people, who dislike the demands it makes on their time. Furthermore, current rural planning schemes propose to reorganize land-holding patterns, providing for more compact housing arrangements, which would leave only 100—400 square metres of garden around each house, thereby directly undermining the family economy in its traditional form. In other words, as in the past, the future of the family is going to depend upon its relations with the community — village or farm — to which it belongs.

THE RURAL COMMUNITY

Institutions

Today, as in the past, the existence of the peasant family is only conceivable with reference to that of other families. Relatives provide the help needed to build the *izba*; the village assembly lays down communal duties and decides whether or not to provide assistance to needy families. Membership of a collective farm is more than just a right for anyone reaching the age of sixteen: it carries with it the right to vocational training, to assistance, to work suited to one's age, sex and family situation; in other words, the community takes the individual in hand, and this is what differentiates this particular type of farm from other public enterprises (where, among other things, recruitment is subject to regulation). Even so, there are fundamental differences between the old community institutions and the new.

The village tradition and collectivization. The *obshchina*, which until the Revolution served as the administrative unit of the rural community (*mir*) in Russia, performed more than economic functions: it laid down cropping rotations, the date for seeding and grazing rights and above all it periodically redistributed the common land being worked individually (roughly every twenty-five years); most of all, its role was a fiscal one. Prior to the abolition of serfdom, the community assumed collective responsibility for the gathering of taxes and duties *vis-à-vis* the landlord and latter *vis-à-vis* the state. The egalitarian distribution of land on the basis of the number of 'mouths to be fed' or 'hands' derived from this fiscal solidarity. If the accident of inheritance assigned two lines of descent to the peasants in a single village, they would form two distinct communities within the village. Mostly, though, the *obshchina* and the village were one and the same thing. The assembly of heads of household (*skhod*) of the *mir* elected a *starosta* (literally, the 'eldest') to represent it at the district assembly (*volost'*).

The populists long entertained the hope that this original form of agrarian socialism might one day serve as the basis for a new society, dispensing with the capitalist stage. With the development of the market economy and the formation of differentiated strata of peasants, the preservation of the original equality proved illusory. Merchants, money-lenders and tavern-keepers swelled the ranks of the notables (the squire and priest) who possessed either good manners or learning. Stolypin, the minister of the interior, saw that the 'strong', prosperous peasants were likely to be the most reliable defenders of the Tsarist regime.

The Bolsheviks, on the contrary, looked for support to the poorest categories (*bednyaki*), to fan the flames of the class struggle in the countryside against the kulaks, thus transposing to Russian rural society, still barely emerging from its feudal servitude, an analysis borrowed from western Marxism. In actual fact, the power of the kulaks flowed less from the possession of substantial means of production or from the hiring of labour (the criteria of capitalism) than from their network of relations. The kulak was more feudal than capitalist, and his real enemy was less the 'little' peasant, who was his client, in his debt, than the middle peasant (*serednyak*) who felt insufficiently powerful to be able to stand up to him in the *mir* assemblies (renamed *sel'skoe obshchestvo*). When the breakdown of the New Economic Policy (NEP) turned the peasantry against the new regime, thereby triggering the acceleration of collectivization and the extermination of the kulaks, a new form of agrarian socialism took shape before even capitalism had had time to develop a production and marketing organization appropriate to the needs of the countryside. In the Soviet Union, the large collective farms exceeded industrial capacity, and the redistribution of peasant lands preceded the advent of the tractor, which could not fail to affect the efficiency of collective farming, independently of political factors.

The traditional and new forms of community are similar in appearance only. Under the term 'collective farm', which is the translation of the Russian word *kolkhoz*, there began to function, from 1918 onwards, a variety of systems which differed from the traditional community system in that the work was to be done jointly: whether by simple temporary collaboration for ploughing and harvesting in the TOZ (association for the joint cultivation of the land), by the pooling of machinery and sharing of income based on each individual's contribution in the artels, or through out-and-out common ownership of goods and equal shares for all in the communes. In 1935, the artel became the only form of collective farm, but henceforward income was shared on the basis of work done (recorded in units of work days, or *trudoden'*). It was no mere accident that the Russians preferred a familiar term, an ancient word, to refer to something new (the word *artel'*, unlike the word *commune* which was associated with communism, was more readily acceptable to the peasants, because under the old regime it had been used to designate voluntary associations of peasant artisans). While it was true that on the eve of the Revolution only 20 per cent of the empire's peasantry was emancipated from community bondage, this bondage had never entailed any collective labour obligations, apart from certain corvée obligations; only the collective ownership of the land formed part of peasant tradition. Every peasant dreamed of becoming a master (*khozyain*), a prosperous farmer; social status within the community flowed from economic success. It took the climate of terror against the kulaks in the countryside to cure them of such ambitions.

Even before the decision to collectivize the peasant economy by brutal methods (December 1929), a parallel network of 'rural soviets' had begun to be established from 1918 in order to supervise the distribution of land, thereby depriving communities of one of their traditional prerogatives. In 1924, the rural soviets also took over administrative functions; then, in 1926, through a process of gradually nibbling away at the functions of rural society, they took over the communal budget as well, in other words the financial resources which had been the mainstay of these communities. This explains why the village community, which had originally been an administrative and economic unit, is now split into two distinct institutions, neither of which coincides with the village: the big collective operations (whether collective farm — kolkhoz — or state farm — sovkhoz), and the *sel'sovet*, the purpose of one being economic, the other administrative, although there is considerable overlapping of responsibility (which does not always facilitate dealings between them). These new rural institutions do, however, retain their links with the past in one important way: they have retained their tax-gathering powers, which used to be the principal *raison d'être* of the *obshchina*, while adapting this to the demands of gathering and physically controlling agricultural produce in a period of rapid industrialization. As in the old days, they maintained for more than two generations strict control over rural migrations, by granting or withholding the internal passports without which no one aged sixteen or over was allowed to leave the countryside.

However, certain privileged categories of rural inhabitant already held this passport. Marriage with a person in possession of a city residence permit also qualified one for a permit. Many young people left the village before reaching the age of sixteen, the age at which a passport was required, thereby accelerating the exodus of teenagers anxious to acquire as much freedom of movement as possible. The 25 December 1974 issue of *Pravda* announced that, starting in 1976, a new internal passport would be delivered to all Soviet citizens regardless of their place of residence. The age-old inequality of treatment in this respect was abolished in 1981.

The sel'sovet, or rural council. The rural soviet is the basic administrative unit for all rural populations, whether engaged in agriculture or not (differing in this from the ancient *obshchina*, to which only heads of farms belonged). Between 1928 and the present day, the number of rural soviets has fallen from 73,000 to 41,000, in line with the changing shape of agriculture. Nowadays, the rural soviet administers 10 or so localities, covering an average of 2700 inhabitants. But it still sometimes happens that a kolkhoz or a sovkhoz lies inside the boundaries of several rural soviets, as the amalgamation of farms gets ahead of the process of administrative concentration in certain densely populated regions. The rural soviet itself is dominated by a higher administrative echelon, the district (*raion*), heir to the *volost'*, which embraces a dozen rural soviets.

In addition to the traditional functions performed by a town hall (registering births, deaths and marriages, conserving land-ownership records, managing local finances, educational and social services), the rural soviet has also preserved the functions of the *ancien régime*: delivering passports or identity cards to people wishing to leave their village, distributing available land to office and factory workers, organizing the corvée for the upkeep of the roads (6 days yearly for men aged 18–45 and 4 days for women aged 18–40) and tax-collecting (farm taxes, income taxes, etc.). It also performs new functions connected with: (1) the planned economy, such as the distribution of chits for the allocation of building materials or fuel; and (2) the communist regime, such as organizing the rural masses in liaison with the Party and the Komsomol and ensuring that official directives are implemented, including on the collective and state farms within their boundaries.

These fairly general functions of the rural soviet duplicate those of the big farms, which also perform social and cultural functions but whose material and financial resources are in fact much superior to those of the rural soviets. Without the collective farm's trucks and tractors, without its financial assistance in building the school or the club, the rural soviet is just about able, with nothing but the communal revenues, to pay for the upkeep of the school teacher and the health officer (*fel'dsher*) and is totally dependent on the prosperity and goodwill of the collective or state farm. It is true, however, that the rural soviet in turn comes to the aid of the farms, mobilizing all available hands to help bring in the harvest.

Some people have suggested putting an end to this system of dual power, as the social responsibilities of the collective farm (which include schooling, health and retirement pensions for farmworkers) are incompatible with the growing economic specialization of production units whose finances have to carry the burden of these social costs, thereby placing the farms at a competitive disadvantage in comparison with public enterprises. A decree dated 8 April 1968 strengthens the powers of the rural soviets, transferring to them certain of the functions performed by the *raion* committees.

The executive committee (*ispolkom*) of the rural soviet, which meets once every two months, is elected by all the constituency's voters on the same conditions as for the urban soviet (see Chapter 10). The chairman of the executive committee, who performs the functions of mayor, is assisted by specialist commissions employing paid officials and made up of elected representatives and members of the administration (*upravlenie*). One feature specific to the rural administration is the existence of a citizens' assembly which perpetuates the tradition of the *mir* by involving the population in the management of public affairs.

The citizens' assembly (*sel'skii-skhod*) is convened by the executive committee of the soviet, or at the request of 20 per cent of the voters. The assembly does not necessarily include the entire population of a constituency: it may be confined to a village or a neighbourhood, and it meets to discuss local-planning issues or matters connected with public order, market bylaws or the gathering of farm surpluses. These assemblies can also raise taxes (self-taxation) to supplement communal revenues, although they are not entitled to exceed a certain ceiling per head of population. The *sel'skii-skhod* appoints for two years the handful of officials (5–11 people) needed to organize road sweeping and maintenance, help for old people and child care.

In certain regions of central Asia and the Caucasus, the assembly takes a form derived from the ancient tradition of respect for old people and is called the Council of Elders. In this way, awkward decisions have the backing of those who to this day incarnate the wisdom of the people.

Petty offences are brought before the people's courts (*tovarishcheskii sud*). These are made up of local citizens whose judgments are grounded not in written law but in commonly accepted standards of morality. The victims most frequently hauled up for public rebuke are drunkards, hooligans, 'lead-swingers' or just plain malingerers. The trials are held in public and, before deliberating, the jury asks the assembly's opinion. This is generally more tolerant towards women than towards men for petty theft of articles for personal use and not for sale, while the women find the courts sometimes a little too indulgent towards drunkards or moonshine distillers.

The kolkhoz and the sovkhoz. Looking at today's kolkhoz (collective farms) and sovkhoz (state farms), one wonders whether farms of their size can still be called communities: 6100 hectares of agricultural land and 3200 hectares of sown land for the average kolkhoz; 20,000 hectares of agricultural land and 6200 hectares of sown land for the sovkhoz. Although the latter, taken as a whole, cultivate roughly the same area of land as the kolkhoz, they employ half as much labour. How are we to account for these differences, and for the gigantic size of Soviet farms?

The distinction between kolkhoz and sovkhoz stems in the first place from their origins. The kolkhoz are heirs to the overpopulated precollectivization villages; the first sovkhoz were the successors to some of the big estates, which the Soviet authorities felt it expedient to preserve at the time of the nationaliz- ation of the land, in order to serve as model farms. Like all state enterprises, the sovkhoz are not free to increase their work force beyond stipulated norms. So, in the beginning the kolkhoz coincided with the village, whereas the sovkhoz remained outside the community.

This difference widened at the time of collectivization, when the government set up almost 3000 giant sovkhoz in the newly cleared steppes (fully fledged cereal factories, as they were then called) in order to remedy the difficulties caused by the famine of the years 1931–2. Then, in 1954–6, a second campaign to clear the eastern steppes raised the area under cultivation by sovkhoz from 7.7 million hectares in 1940–53 to 22.4 million hectares in 1956. Thereafter, the public sector expanded still further by transforming more than 23,000 kolkhoz into sovkhoz. This recent trend has led to a narrowing of the differences between these two categories of enterprise, because in the meantime, the smaller kolkhoz of the past have merged to form very large farms which no longer bear any relation whatever to the ancient village communities.

Another and indeed a key consideration explaining the Soviet authorities' preference for big farms, is political. Marxist doctrine, which calls for the abolition of all distinction between town and country, considers that, as in industry, technical progress in agriculture demands concentration of the smaller units and mechanized production methods. But in 1929, when the Soviet Union still had only 18,000 tractors and 7000 trucks in the countryside, the first priority was to gather in the farm produce. The physical appropriation of farm surpluses which followed on the freezing of the agricultural market seemed to be the only solution, and this control of production at its source was easier to achieve in large units supervised by reliable political cadres than among 25 million peasant smallholdings.

Nevertheless, an attempt was made to preserve the community façade of the kolkhoz by giving them the status of workers' co-operatives. Unfortunately, the dramatic circumstances of their birth distorted relations between peasants and the administration, because unlike in a co-operative, where it is the members themselves who decide, decisions relating to production or the distribution of income were for years imposed by the supervising authorities, with the rank and file only recovering its rights at the end of the year when it came to sharing out the residue according to each person's recorded number of work points. Since the adoption of a new legal framework for the kolkhoz, in December 1969, they have ceased to be defined as co-operatives even though the administrative mechanism has been left unchanged; on the other hand, over the past ten years the kolkhoz have won greater freedom in planning their output and profits.

The chairman of the kolkhoz continues to be elected for a three-year term by the assembly of kolkhoz members, after being nominated by the Party secretary for the *raion*. The assembly also votes to admit or expel members, to modify the statutes or to merge. But the kolkhoz has now grown so large that it is practically impossible to convene a meeting of all the workers spread among several different localities. The rural community, therefore, is now re-forming around the brigade or the sovkhoz subdivision, which is generally equivalent to a village. The brigade assembly elects a council of 5–9 members and delegates its representatives to the kolkhoz assembly.

In the sovkhoz there is, as in all state enterprises, a production council whose purely consultative role will be examined later, in the chapter on the enterprise (Chapter 7). But it is in the financial sphere, even more than in the administrative, that the sovkhoz have until now differed most from the kolkhoz. The kolkhoz still, doubtless temporarily, owns its plant, equipment and income, which can bring about substantial variations in the wealth of individual collective farms. Everything concerning the income of the kolkhoz automatically affects each of its members. Sovkhoz workers take a more detached view, as they can easily obtain state loans and subsidies, and, as in all public enterprises, wages paid are independent of operating results. An investment

decision affecting the future and the portion of income available for distribution will not necessarily elicit the same reactions in a collective farm as in a
state one.

These differences between the collective and the state farms are bound to
narrow as time passes. For one thing, as an incentive to the sovkhoz to tighten
up their management, it has been decided to grant them a degree of financial
autonomy comparable to that enjoyed by industrial firms; they are no longer
to be subsidized. Second, since 1967, kolkhoz workers have been paid regular
monthly wages based on sovkhoz pay scales. Therefore, the kolkhoz worker is
now paid as an employee and no longer out of the co-operative's profits.
Lastly, the kolkhoz are tending to form federations or regional 'unions' in
order to set up joint-venture industrial firms and to finance their pension
funds, with the result that kolkhoz incomes are tending to level out in any given
region: in brief, a major step has been taken towards the marriage of kolkhoz
property with public property – the goal of this development.

But how are these huge agricultural enterprises, now grown well beyond the
dimensions of the rural community, going to re-create it? For it is in the nature
of farmwork that those engaged in it need a sense, if not of ownership, of at
least some direct interest, i.e. not only adequate pay but also a chance to
exercise initiative and responsibility. Large, unwieldy brigades, and pay rates
based on the amount of time worked and not on output, have turned out in
practice to be relatively inefficient in stimulating productivity: It has proved
necessary to re-establish a direct link between the farmer and the land he
works, by permanently detailing a small team of about ten people (*zveno*) to
cultivate a given field; in this way, the yields obtained can be personalized.
This form of labour organization is particularly well-suited to intensive farming, as incomes here are proportional to yields; another advantage is that it
allows the team (*beznaryadnoe zveno*) a broad measure of autonomy, as it is
free to choose its members, who are usually relatives or friends, and thus by
way of some small-scale self-management revives the traditions of the artel'.
However, the *zveno* is still regarded as an 'experiment'. The authorities are
reluctant to broaden its application, as it results in some dispersal of farm
machinery and leads to fluctuating income in years when the harvest is bad. It
could manage to stimulate or re-create a new collective consciousness; but
then again it could merely strengthen or revive the age-old yearning for private
property, which still lives on in the peasant mentality.

Social stratification and hierarchy

In traditional society, prestige was dependent upon age and the economic
success of the head of the household. Old people were the incarnation of
knowledge and wisdom. But in the rural hierarchy, the peasant yielded before
those who because of birth, wealth or learning – the nobility, merchants,
clergy – were the principal intermediaries between the village and the town.

These former notables were eliminated, either in 1917 or at the end of the NEP, and with them disappeared not only the opponents of the new regime, but also the most dynamic elements of peasant agriculture. It took a generation of collectivized farming for new peasant élites to emerge.

As with the former hierarchy, the new one is based on the position of the individual *vis-à-vis* the established authorities. The 'heads' (*golovki*), as they are colloquially called, are all either Party members or appointed by its various organs. At the apex stands the Party secretary for the *raion* (*pervak*), followed by the chairman of the collective farms, the state-farm managers, the chairmen of the *sel'soviet*, the secretaries of the Party cells in the kolkhoz or sovkhoz. The average Party membership in a collective farm is forty-eight, so that the Party is now able to control the kolkhoz from within. The chairman of the kolkhoz is nominated from the *nomenklatura* of the *obkom* (see Chapter 9). Prior to 1957, the MTS (Machine and Tractor Station) managers also had a place on this list, as they wielded authority over the farms through the *politotdel* (political section).

In the early days, these cadres were recruited on the basis of their capacities for leadership and loyalty to the Party. A military record with the Red Army, or working-class origins, i.e. absence of rural connections, served as criteria for selection. Now that the collective farms have become gigantic enterprises equipped with up-to-date machinery, technical and economic expertise are as important as character. Out of the 35,000 kolkhoz chairmen in 1970, 7000 were self-made men (*praktiki*, i.e. had learned the business on the job and had no paper qualifications), but the great majority were experts, compared with only 2.6 per cent in 1950.

Next, the qualified personnel: agronomists, veterinary surgeons, engineers and school teachers, who form a rural intelligentsia that differs somewhat from the rural intelligentsia of the past. The doctor or the agronomist in the *zemstva* was more of a humanist than a technician. The kind of life that these managers lead helps to propagate urban models of consumption in the countryside rather than to breed a new rural culture.

School teachers have preserved their traditional prestige: their functions now extend to every aspect of extra-scholastic activity, and they now have more adequate resources at their disposal (libraries, clubs, etc.); but they also play a vital part in the selection process which, together with the Komsomol competition, picks out those who will be entitled to continue their studies. Even so, theirs is a precarious position, and they often feel isolated. What is more, food shortages in the countryside oblige them to cultivate their private plots of land, or even farms, in order to obtain enough food for their needs; this robs the teacher of time that could otherwise be spent on studying, and educational standards suffer accordingly. Furthermore, the young women who make up the bulk of primary-school teachers are not regarded as particularly desirable wives, as farmers want a woman capable of running the farm without obligations outside the home. Even so, for a young country girl, the regional teacher-training college, which trains secondary-school teachers, is a classic path of upward social mobility.

A new category is now emerging, consisting of agricultural-machinery specialists: tractor, truck and other heavy-machinery drivers and mechanics, whose living standards and status are reminiscent of the rural bourgeoisie.

But the broad masses of the peasantry are still more or less unspecialized, unless one happens to regard those working on the poultry- or livestock-breeding farms as being more specialized than those engaged in crop-growing, because the former use milking machines. Furthermore, the mechanization of agriculture has benefited men more than women. Generally, it is the men who drive the tractors and the women who do the manual work in the fields. With very few exceptions, moreover, the men occupy all the top jobs. In other words, the rural world is still misogynous.

TABLE 17   *Occupational structure of the rural population (%)*

	1959	1970	1970 Kolkhoz	% Party members
1 Intelligentsia (management personnel and graduate specialists, school teachers, doctors, accountants, agronomists)	9.6	14.1	3.5	95% of chairmen 41% of specialists
2 Subordinate administrative personnel. Service personnel	5.5	8.5	3.5	
3 Skilled manual labourers in agriculture (mechanics, etc.)	4.8	7.6	12	17
in other branches	13.6	18.8	8.8	
4 Unskilled manual labourers in agriculture and stock-breeding	54.5	39.6	69.9	2.5
in other branches	12	11.4	2.3	

Table 17 shows the relative percentages of these different rural strata. To this list, at the bottom of the scale, we should add the marginal categories represented by pensioners and widows with dependent children, for the composition of the family is as important, in the countryside, as its members' occupations.

J. Arutjunjan, in a series of epoch-making studies on Soviet sociology, has shown that Soviet rural society can be divided into four social strata according to the nature of the work done: manual or intellectual (and the degree of qualification), skilled or unskilled labour. Each of these broad groups possesses a certain number of shared objective characteristics: income level, level of education, make-up of personal wealth (function of the family farm, degree of home comfort, objects owned), and cultural habits.

One thing that emerges from his study is that the type of ownership – public ownership in the state farms, co-operative in the collective farms – is less important as a differentiator among peasant strata than the nature of the work done. And indeed, we do find that for each category of worker educational levels, wages, tastes and occupations are relatively similar, irrespective of the type of farm on which they are employed.

Only half the managers are of rural origin themselves, and 75 per cent of their spouses are not employed in manual occupations. More than half their children live in the towns. Their family plot of land is smaller than those of other categories, and less than half own a cow; but on the other hand they own more domestic appliances.

Among manual workers, the tractor drivers and mechanics are worth a closer look on account of their age (60 per cent of them are aged between 16 and 34), their secondary education and their income, which is higher than that of white-collar workers. It is presumably because people working with tractors have less difficulty obtaining fodder than other categories that 92 per cent of the collective-farm workers belonging to this group own a cow. The age structure of other semiskilled manual workers, on the other hand, reflects the ageing of the peasantry; this has now become a residual population with little education, a fact that is having repercussions on their children (one-third of the children of people in these categories go to the towns to pursue their education).

Subjectively, the hierarchy in the rural world is probably perceived differently, inasmuch as social distances are far less clearcut in the countryside than in the towns; family relations also help to bridge distances. Furthermore, within the network of village obligations, certain occupations are held to be 'strategic'. Thus, for example, the chairman of the collective farm is obliged to stay on good terms with the manager of the official agency responsible for keeping the countryside supplied with manufactured goods (*sel'khoztekhnika*) as well as with the inspector of forests. For a peasant woman, the people who count are the carpenter, without whom she cannot keep her *izba* in good repair; the truck driver, who delivers her fuel in return for payment; the herdsman who looks after the cattle on the commonland, including her own cow; the midwife or the health officer; and the teacher, upon whom her children depend for their upward social mobility. In other words, we have here a whole hierarchy founded upon the peasant psychology, which is not necessarily attuned to the sociologist's classifications.

Soviet literature dealing with rural themes is an inexhaustible source for the study of social relations. These writings abound in those imponderable distinctive signs designating the new notables – possession of a passport permitting travel without special permission, the way of dress (a tie for the men, high-heeled shoes for women), and the fact of being addressed by one's patronymic; to this we should add the precariousness of a situation in which Party secretaries or kolkhoz chairmen are obliged to pick their way with the utmost care through the maze of parallel hierarchies while keeping a weather eye open for shifts in political line. They demonstrate the customary resistance of peasants to innovation imposed on them by 'campaigns' or directives that are often poorly suited to local conditions.

Thus, new divisions have taken the place of the ancient opposition between rich and poor; today they are based on decision-making powers, or access to goods and qualifications. But whereas formerly the peasants all shared in a single culture, today the gulf created by education and the influence of the town are tending to sap the foundations of the rural community and to erode the content of traditional culture.

RURAL CULTURE

The coexistence within village society of the older generations, who have still not broken completely free of the influence of the past, and of younger generations or people from outside the rural community with urban roots makes it impossible to describe rural culture as a coherent and stable whole. We shall try to describe (1) what has survived of traditional culture and (2) the factors that are helping to modify that culture, or their impact on the future of rural society.

Modernization and traditional culture

The term *culture* will be used in its broadest anthropological sense, designating material goods, behaviour and moral thought.

Material civilization. Whatever the regional peculiarities of the rural habitat (these have already (pp. 79–89) served as a basis for outlining the principal cultural areas), there are nevertheless a certain number of characteristics that are common to every part of the country. Houses are detached and generally one-storeyed and 70 per cent of them are owner-occupied. While not necessarily roomier than in the towns (31.2 square metres for 3.8 people on average in the province of Novosibirsk), at least they offer greater scope for arrangement according to individual taste (cellar, verandah, mezzanine, etc.). In 77 per cent of cases, there is a farm adjoining the house.

Conditions are now becoming more comfortable, with almost universal electricity, butane gas replacing the old-fashioned stove, and running water, although this is still generally limited to a communal pump in the street. Even this represents a considerable step forward for a peasant woman until now obliged to go and fetch her water from the well or the river each day (48 per cent of peasant households in the province of Novosibirsk were still having to do this in 1972). The tasks of fetching water (12—14 hours weekly) and wood (20 cubic metres per year) are still a heavy burden on the peasant woman. On the other hand, the baker's shop is now tending to replace home-baked bread, especially in the southern steppe provinces, where wood is scarce. Meat-salting is still widespread, as there are few freezers. Diet has grown more varied (including noodles, confectionery and preserves), although people still prepare the traditional dishes, formerly associated with religious feasts: pancakes on Shrove Tuesday or Candelmas (*maslenitsa*) and cakes at Easter (*paskha*, *kulichi*); as elsewhere, however, fasting and abstinence have fallen from favour.

Domestic weaving is unusual, but 74 per cent of rural families own a sewing machine. Young girls still prepare a trousseau, but they generally prefer the gay dresses sold in town and workman's trousers for work. In winter, felt boots (*valenki*) are invaluable. As everywhere, young men are attracted by urban models of consumption: cars, motorbicycles, motorboats, television and so forth attract their curiosity, in the way in which horses or cattle used to do in traditional society. A survey of the wealth of rural families in the province of Novosibirsk, conducted in 1972, shows that 1.6 per cent owned a car (9.2 per cent expressed a wish to buy one) and 55.4 per cent a television set.

Compared with the urban worker's budget, rural families' spending patterns appear to reveal certain similarities: less is spent on consumer durables and services, while more goes on food (including home produce), housing and savings. These differences are due to the very rudimentary state of food supplies in the countryside and to the shortage of services, as well as to the demands of the farm (the cost of buying a cow, fodder, repairing the roof, etc.), which curtail a family's consumption. Major family events, such as marriage or death, are also an occasion for heavy spending, as well as for community celebrations.

Folk art and traditions. The secularization of country life, which began in the 1920s, represents a far-reaching change in traditional peasant culture, which used to be rooted in religious cosmogony. This secularization, which was imposed by the shutting down of places of worship, has still not done away with certain rites of passage, such as the baptism of children or the commemoration of the dead (*pominki*); nor has it removed the icons from the home. Propitiative rites, on the other hand, such as processions and sprinkling of holy water on livestock and fields, have disappeared. In certain regions, attempts are being made to introduce new rituals associated with the cycle of agricultural life (harvest festival) or civil life (marriage or presentations of a passport on attaining majority), although these have not completely supplanted certain traditional feasts such as the parish feast, which is still a public holiday.

Every feast day, whether civil or religious, provides an outlet for the vitality of the community at rest, both in rivalry among the men (who enjoy excelling in games or friendly wrestling matches) and in displays of drunkenness (the alcohol flows particularly freely on such occasions). Marriage is an important event. The Russians have an expression for 'getting married' which plays on the double meaning of the word, suggestive of both marriage and riotous living, which graphically conveys the spectacular character of this occasion for collective rejoicing. Nowadays, the festivities are not as lengthy as they used to be, but the Russians still have their *druzhka* or best man to act as master of ceremonies, while in the Caucasus, it is the *tamada* who presides over the banquet. In the old days, a wedding was not a wedding without a piano accordion, but the spread of recorded music is now putting the accordionist out of business.

Mechanical music would also pose a threat to folk songs — as would the rural newspaper, which reports on local events, to the satirical song (*chastushka*) — were it not for choirs organized by the village clubs precisely for the purpose of preserving them. Not all villages, unfortunately, are able to afford these choral or dramatic activities. Generally, the club has film projections each week, followed by a dance; the young people attend, but the older people take little part in cultural activities. For some years now, however, the authorities have been encouraging a revival of folk art in certain villages or regions renowned for their traditional handicrafts: the santons, or statuettes, of Dymkovo (in the province of Kirov), lacquerware in Palekh (in the province of Ivanovo) in the tradition of the ancient icon-painters, the gossamer-fine shawls of the province of Orenburg, lacework from the province of Vologda, and so forth. But popular imagery has given way to printed posters, with themes inspired by official directives.

Peasant attitudes and the peasant ethic. People are still deeply attached to their individual farms and land for objective reasons analysed above (p. 87). More recent surveys[4] show that 80—85 per cent of collective-farm peasants want to preserve their smallholding. Only a tiny minority say they would like to see these plots of land either reduced in size or abolished altogether. This minority is made up of state-farm workers, whose incomes are more stable, and younger people who baulk at the drudgery that the family farm entails. Most peasants, however, given the choice between a more comfortable home without an adjoining garden, and keeping a relatively uncomfortable home with its adjoining land, prefer land to comfort. As a result the peasant, who is not yet a worker, still has the mentality of a smallholder: his dream is to have a house of his own and to be master in his own house (*khozyain*). The poor productivity of collective labour, the rather nonchalant attitude towards farm machinery not owned by the peasant himself, and the high rate of theft of public property suggest that, with some exceptions, collectivization has not yet bred a new social ethic.

Educational progress has presumably broadened the peasant's outlook and political education; but the ethic underpinning everyday behaviour is still steeped in acceptance of a natural and immutable order, which helps the individual to face trials bravely, in compassion for the destitute and in suspicion towards everything foreign to the village (such as marriage outside the circle of friends and acquaintances), which may lead the peasant to dissemble.

Everybody in the community knows and greets everybody else. Nothing can be kept secret, and the fear of gossip is a powerful factor of conservatism. The village store is the focal point of gossip, as all human dealings pass through it; the composition of one's shopping basket is an infallible telltale of every household event, great or small. While the importance of collective opinion is one fundamental trait of the peasant's mental make-up, his feeling of inferiority *vis-à-vis* the town dweller is another, sometimes expressed in malevolent gibes at those 'townsfolk, who just twiddle their thumbs'. On the other hand, the peasant is generally more tolerant of his own kind's foibles: of petty theft, for example, provided private property is not involved and no profit is gained thereby, and above all of drunkenness, the scourge of the countryside.

The factors and patterns of change

Underlying the transformation of rural culture described above we find a series of economic, technical and cultural factors whose intensity can be measured by the greater or lesser impact of urban civilization, depending upon the degree of isolation of the region concerned.

Education. Now that schooling is universal, it is tending to lengthen. In 1938, some 51.1 per cent of rural inhabitants aged between 15 and 25 had had less than 5 years' schooling; 20 years later, only 6.6 per cent of adolescents had had so little schooling, while 55.4 per cent had had 8 years' schooling (uncompleted secondary education) compared with 9.4 per cent in 1938. This pattern cuts both ways, inasmuch as the raising of the cultural level makes it possible to apply agricultural techniques requiring more skilled personnel, but on the other hand it implies the introduction of a cultural model that is ill-suited, or even foreign, to the rural world.

The rural exodus tends to rob the countryside of its best-educated elements, since the very fact of pursuing one's studies entails leaving home to become a boarder where local conditions rule out the organization of school buses. In 1970, the average number of people per rural school was 158. A secondary school with between 300 and 600 people corresponds to a population of 1000–2000; but this density only occurred in 23,500 out of the 469,000 Soviet villages in 1970. The flight from the countryside, to which we shall be returning in the chapter on social mobility (Chapter 9), is today, and will long remain, the overriding social problem. In the industrial provinces, the annual percentage of departures from the countryside was 18 per 1000 in 1973, while the average for the Soviet Union as a whole in the period 1959—65 was 15 per 1000. At this rate, the rural population can be expected to drop from 98 million in 1980 to 83 million in the year 2000. In actual fact, national averages conceal the gravity of the situation, for high population growth rates in the Caucasian regions, Moldavia and central Asia are continuing to add to the rural population in these parts, whereas in the RSFSR the number of young country people aged between 20 and 29 dropped from 9.47 to 4.58 million between the 1959 and the 1970 censuses.

The mass media do not appear to be capable of slowing down the rural exodus. Indeed, television tends to paint an alluring picture of life in the towns while at the same time emptying the streets, which used to be the vital focus of traditional village culture. Guest lecturers at the clubs no longer speak to packed audiences; as elsewhere, young people are tiring of propaganda (34 per cent of them stated that they had attended more than three lectures a year in 1969, compared with 47.5 per cent in 1938), and, like advertising in other countries, political activism tends to standardize opinion rather than stimulate creative activity in the sense of the development of a new rural culture.

Military service merely helps to strengthen the appeal of the city, as it offers recruits internal passports which allow them to satisfy their deepest craving, namely to become somebody, which means leaving the village.

The urbanization of the countryside. This is a universal and ineluctable fact of life. It takes several different forms in the Soviet Union. First, town-country relations are engendered by the rural exodus itself, since the friends and relatives of yesterday's rural inhabitants still live in the village. They return home more or less regularly, depending upon how far away they have moved, surrounded by general curiosity and laden with gifts symbolizing the fact that they now live in the town, to lend a hand at mowing time, harvest the potatoes, repair the *izba* or hunt and fish. Other urban influences are now reaching the village with the arrival of summer holiday-makers who rent rooms with the inhabitants, as well as of seasonal workers mobilized for the harvest and, more especially, student brigades, coming to help in construction work in the countryside in summer, and enjoying great prestige in peasant eyes.

Second, villages are merged to form urban-type rural centres (*agrogoroda*) as a result of the emptying of the countryside and with the intention of creating living conditions for the people remaining behind comparable to those in the towns. This is a long-term operation, and its aim is to reduce the number of localities from 469,000 to 120,000 in the course of the next few decades. At the time of the 1970 census, 90.2 million rural inhabitants, i.e. 85 per cent of the total, lived in the 121,300 villages of over 200 inhabitants; but, in terms of town-planners' norms for the kind of social amenities envisaged, this average is still too low. Some people are concerned about the cost of the operation; and nor are all the communities affected enthusiastic about it. It would be cheaper to modernize the road system and motorize the population, which would avoid the need to abandon the land. At all events, here as elsewhere, the small town or rural centre is bound to replace the village as the focus of country life. This tendency is bound up, moreover, with another factor of social change, namely the industrialization of agriculture.

The industrialization and professionalization of farming. The development of processing industries in the countryside, the gradual industrialization of certain agricultural activities, such as stock-breeding, the emergence of agro-industrial combines incorporating both agricultural and industrial enterprises, all inevitably entail a steady rise in the non-agricultural population as well as a change in the nature of the farm activities themselves. In 1970, the statisticians identified 197 different specialities in agriculture. To be a farmer is becoming an occupation and is no longer a status inherited by birth. In 1975, the collective-farm peasants accounted for no more than 44.5 per cent of the rural population. The pace of this change will depend on the scale of investment in rural development; in other words, on the ability ultimately of industry to satisfy the needs of the countryside, which, despite the progress made by modernization, remain considerable.

Does the dwindling number of peasants and the rise in the worker and intellectual strata in the countryside necessarily point to the disappearance of rural culture?

It follows from the fact that modernization has not made an equal impact on all cultural areas, that the tendencies which we have just examined are not present in equal degrees in all regions. Estonia, or the rich localities of Kuban, for example, are at the head of this movement, while the Caucasian and central Asian republics lag behind. We may take it, therefore, that for some time to come rural communities will live side by side within a single region yet conform to different cultural models, just as within a single family each generation has its own pattern of cultural behaviour. Furthermore, the car has not yet made the deep impact on country life in the Soviet Union that it has in the west; the lack of suitable roads is currently impeding this means of communication, and only 8 per cent of rural families owned a car in 1975. Doubtless the widening use of the car will in the future facilitate the penetration of urban influence. Even so, traditional cultures will never completely disappear, because it is they which underpin the different national traditions and because the consolidation of national cultures presupposes this diversification.

In addition, despite the erosion of traditional culture, country life will still stand apart from town life because of its different way of life: the detached house, the contact with nature, the use of a garden or plot of land on which children very early learn to observe and acquire the habit of manual labour, all help to socialize and shape the personality of the child. Which is why, despite the unified streams in the educational system, it will probably be a long time before the distinction between the country child and its urban peer vanishes completely. The unanswered question is whether that imperishable cell, the family, has not also been undermined by the change in the residential environment.

NOTES

1 Survey conducted in 1971 in a district of the province of Novisibirsk (in *Izvestiya Sibirskogo otdeleniya Akad. Nauk*, no. 11, 1974, p. 39).
2 40 rubles planned for 1985.
3 V. Churakov, *Aktual'nye problemy ispol'zovaniya Trudouykh cesurov sela*, Moscow, 1972, p. 210.
4 *Sovetskaya etnografiya*, no. 5, 1970, p. 105; *Sotsio. issled.* no. 4, 1975, p. 95.

SUGGESTED READING

Rural regions and the peasants

Beaucourt, C., 'Le potentiel agricole soviétique, une approche régionale', *Courrier des pays de l'Est*, no. 170, Jan. 1974.
De La Breteque-Maurel, M. C., 'L'évolution recente de la population rurale de l'Union soviétique', *Bulletin de l'Assoc. des géographes fr.*, nos 404–5, Jan.–Feb. 1973.

Rural change

Aymard, M., 'Une charte nouvelle pour les kolkhoz', *Cahiers du monde russe et soviétique*, Dec. 1970, pp. 497–575.
Chombart de Lauwe, J., *Les Paysans soviétiques*, du Seuil, 1961.
Dumont, R., *Sovkhoz, kolkhoz ou le problématique communisme*, du Seuil, 1964.
Kerblay, B., 'U.R.S.S.: du mir aux agrovilles', in Mendras, H. and Tavernier, Y. (eds), *Terres, paysans et politique*, Futuribles, S.E.D.E.I.S., 1969, pp. 276–312.
Lewin, M., 'Who was the Soviet kulak?' *Soviet Studies*, vol. XVIII, no. 2, Oct. 1966, no. 3, Jan. 1967.
Maurel, M.-C., *La Campagne collectivisée: société et espace rurale en Russie*, Paris, Anthropos, 1980.
Shanin, T., *The Awkward Class, Political Sociology of Peasantry, Russia 1910–1925*, Oxford, 1972.

Rural population and society

Arutjunjan, J., 'Essai de sociologie du village', *Archives internationales de sociologie de la Coopération*, no. 32, July–Dec. 1972.
Arutjunjan, J., 'La structure sociale de la population rurale de l'URSS', Cahiers ISMEA, série AG15, *Economies et sociétés*, vol. XIII, 1979.
Chayanov, A. V., *The Theory of Peasant Economy*, Chicago, Richard Irwin, 1966.
Cox, T. M., *Rural Sociology in the Soviet Union*, London, Hurst, 1979.

Ladenkov, V. and Gorina, N., 'Opyt izucheniya urovnya zhizni sel'skogo naseleniya', *Izvestiya Sibirskogo otdeleniya Akad. Nauk SSSR*, no. 11, 1974, pp. 33–40.

Millar, J., *The Soviet Rural Community*, Urbana, Illinois, 1971.

Sakoff, 'Société rurale et société urbaine en U.R.S.S.', *Bull. mensuel économie et statistiques agricoles*, FAO, Oct. 1972.

Staroverov, V., *Sotsial'no-demograficheskie problemy derevni*, Moscow, Nauka, 1975.

Staroverov, V., *Sotsial'naya struktura sel'skogo naseleniya SSSR*, Moscow, Nauka, 1979.

Wadekin, K. E., *Fuhrungskräfte im Sowjetischen Dorf*, Berlin, Duncker Humblot, 1969.

Wadekin, K. E., 'La rémunération du travail dans l'agriculture soviétique', *Revue de l'Est*, Oct. 1972, pp. 5–27.

Wadekin, K. E., *The Private Sector in Soviet Agriculture*, Berkeley, 1973.

Wadekin, K. E., 'Income distribution in Soviet agriculture', *Soviet Studies*, no. 1, Jan. 1975.

Peasant civilization

Belov, V., Ocherki o narodnoy estetikie, *Nash Sovremennik*, Moscow, nos 10–12, 1979, no. 3, 1980, no. 1, 1981.

Dienes, L., 'Pastoralism in Turkestan', *Soviet Studies*, vol. XXVII, no. 3, July 1975.

Dunn, S. and Dunn E., *The Peasant of Central Russia*, New York, Holt, Rinehart, Winston, 1967.

Kerblay, B., 'L'évolution de l'alimentation rurale en Russie, 1896–1960', *Annales*, Sept.–Oct. 1962.

Kerblay, B., *Les Marchés paysans en U.R.S.S.*, Mouton, 1968.

Kerblay, B., *L'Izba d'hier et d'aujourd'hui*, Lausanne, L'Age d'Homme, 1973.

Pascal, P., *La Civilisation paysanne en Russie*, Lausanne, L'Age d'Homme, 1969.

The Village of Viriatino (an ethnographic study of a Russian village from before the Revolution to the present), New York, Doubleday, 1970.

Tul'tseva, L., 'La fête agraire', in Rambaud, P., *Sociologie rurale*, an anthology, Mouton, 1976, pp. 266–71.

The village in Soviet literature

Abramov, F., *Chronique de Pekachino*, A. Michel, 1975.

Belov, V., *Affaire d'habitude*, Julliard, 1969.

Doroch, E., *Pluie et soleil*, Gallimard, 1972.

Mojaiev, B., *Dans la vie de Fedor Kouzkine*, Gallimard, 1972.

Ovietchkine, V., *Les Visiteurs au hameau de Stoukachi*, Les Editeurs réunis, 1956.

Rasputin, V., *L'adieu a l'île*, R. Laffont, 1979.

Shukshin, V., *I Want to Live: short stories*, Moscow, Progress, 1973.

Solooukhine, V., *Une Goutte de rosée*, Stock, 1963.

Solzhenitsyn, A., *Matryona's House and Other Stories*, Penguin, 1976.

Bibliography

Armand, M. and Aymard, M., 'Le village soviétique, bibliographie sélectionnée des travaux en langues occidentales', *Archives internationales de Sociologie de la Coopération*, July–Dec. 1974, pp. 149–94.

Chapter 5

The family

The previous chapters have discussed some of the more important factors governing the Soviet family's living conditions. Thus, the demographic situation is as much the outcome of individual attitudes as a factor influencing the marriage rate, when, as was the case in 1959, there is an imbalance of over 20 million people between the sexes. Also, the age at which people marry, the size of the family and its cultural habits vary, as we have seen, from one ethnic group to another. Place of residence, too, in town or countryside, conditions type of housing, social amenities and the pace of family life. Thus, the family may be viewed as a microcosm reflecting the degree of modernization of Soviet society and the profound changes that have occurred, and are occurring, in the behaviour of its members. The reason why all regimes pay special attention to the family unit, whether to venerate it, or to execrate it as the root of all oppression, is that, whatever the external circumstances, it manages to preserve its autonomy: its formation, its growth, its dissolution, all depend in the last analysis on personal decisions. Today's woman has the right to refuse a husband or a child. What is more, the stamp that the family leaves upon the child in its earliest infancy is generally the longest-lasting. This is why an individual tends to identify primarily with the group whose name he or she bears and why a person maintains the closest bonds with this group throughout his or her life.

As we explore the traditional functions of the family — to ensure the biological survival of society, the upkeep of its members and the transmission of its cultural heritage — we shall see this dialectic of relations between the family and the Soviet state emerging; as everywhere, it evolves under pressure of dominant ideologies, of growing permissiveness, rising living standards and, above all, the education and status of women. Because the evolution of the family is shaped by changing behaviour patterns, this process of change is necessarily slow and hence intimately bound up with history.

THE FAMILY AND SOVIET HISTORY

From the extended family to the nuclear family

When we take a long-term view of the family as an institution in the Soviet Union, we note first a characteristic common to all countries in the throes of modernization, namely the break-up of the patriarchal, extended family, which began in Russia with the emancipation of the serfs in the second half of the nineteenth century. The distribution of land in 1917 merely served to accelerate this fragmentation during the 1920s. Not only has the size of the nuclear family changed — now cut down to the basic couple with their under-age children — but so also has its purpose. It has ceased to be a quasi-dynastic alliance of two families designed to perpetuate the family heritage which itself dictates the choice of spouse; it is a union founded on the mutual attraction of two people and geared for planned parenthood, for the family group no longer performs the same productive functions in industrial society as it did in traditional rural society. Still more importantly, the need for the wife to work outside the home accentuates the dispersal of the family, especially in the Soviet Union. On the other hand, the fact that the welfare system now takes care of pensioners and old people frees children from the duty to aid and live with their parents.

Inevitably, uneven economic and cultural development in the different regions of the Union explain why the family has not reached the same stage of evolution in every part of the country. If we take women's education as our criterion, the 1970 census showed that out of every 1000 people, 41 men and 63 women had graduated from higher education in the RSFSR, and 62 and 85 respectively in Georgia, but only 59 and 38 in Tadzhikistan and 58–43 in Turkmenistan. Furthermore, one no longer finds anywhere in the country those extensive families belonging to the nobility or to the merchant class, who before the Revolution maintained a considerable domestic retinue — nannies, servants, relatives (*prizhival'shchiki*), all more or less part of the family — who had no private life in the service of their master.

Cultural traditions and ideologies

Religion, superstition even, always played an important part in family life in the past, so much so that under the old regime marriage, divorce and the recording of births were matters concerning the religious rather than the civil authorities. There were, moreover, Russian, Polish, Baltic, Jewish and Koranic laws to say what property belonged to which spouse in marriage. Nowadays, different ideologies underpin the individual's behaviour, and the attitude of the state towards the family. These new influences, which have not necessarily supplanted traditional beliefs, are not all inspired by Marxist doctrine; the latter may be seen rather as a superimposition upon more specifically Russian currents.

Russian literature contains an extremely rich range of observations on family life, from descriptions of peaceful domestic felicity – such as S. Aksakov's *Family Chronicle* (1852) or Tolstoy's Natasha in *War and Peace* – to all-out hostility towards the family and marriage. Examples of the latter may be found in Rakhmetov, in Chernishevsky's *What Is To Be Done?*, who renounced carnal knowledge in order to devote himself body and soul to the cause (the rejection of love was to be a constant feature of the revolutionary hero) or Tolstoy, in his *Kreutzer Sonata*, denouncing the enemy, woman, and the works of the flesh. These two examples contrast with V. Rozanov, who venerates procreation in *The Dark Face* (1906). Whatever the trends emerging from these works of the imagination, alongside the fallen woman, and confronting the idle nobility (*Oblomov*) or infatuated intellectuals, we very often find a model heroine, such as Katerina in Ostrovsky's *Groza*, Vera in Goncharov's *Obryv* or Gorky's *Mother*, prefiguring the strong woman of Soviet literature. Thus, the notions of women's emancipation, propagated in particular by the Marxists, fell upon particularly well-prepared soil in Russia.

Basically, the position of Marx and Engels with regard to the family was as follows:

> The economic emancipation of the workers will deprive the family cell of its economic function, as household and educational tasks would be performed by society. Far from destroying the family, this will reinforce it, since the union of the couple will henceforward be based exclusively on natural inclination. (F. Engels, *The Origin of the Family, Private Property and the State*, New York, 1972, pp. 83–9)

Marx added that the family would only become human 'when it is as human beings that other people become necessary to us'. From this it follows that: (1) the life of the couple must be founded upon true love, and that it must be possible to terminate a marriage if the bonds that presided over its birth should ever loosen; and (2) the family does not have a monopoly over the education – socialization, in the sociological sense of the term – of children.

Attitudes of revolutionaries towards feminist movements (*Soyuz ravnopravykh zhenshchin*), on the other hand, have always been more reticent. Thus, at the first All-Russian Congress of Women, held in St Petersburg in 1908, A. Kollontai, who spoke in defence of the Marxist view (*Social Foundations of the Woman Question*),[1] stressed that the emancipation of women depended upon the social revolution, and that it would be an illusion to create a unified women's movement so long as class interests divided them. Her ardent, free-thinking temperament took her well beyond the socialization of housework and the assumption of child-rearing by society to the point of envisaging free love, like certain utopian socialists; the family would cease to be a necessity (*The Family and the Communist State*): a mother would be a mother not only to her own children but to all the children of the workers. Lenin disagreed with her on this last point, rejecting temporary union as 'a mere glass of water' (in his letter to Clara Tsetkin[2]). On the other hand, Marxist principles regarding divorce and the role of the state in the socialization of the child have inspired Soviet policy towards the family from 1917 to the present day.

Government policy: evolution of family law

From 1917 to 1926. In the first phase, family policy was designed to encourage the break-up of structures inherited from the old order, whose values the family perpetuated: attachment to private property, religious sentiment and the subservience of women. A. Kollontai, appointed people's commissar for social security in October 1917, was given responsibility for putting into effect the early legislation abolishing religious marriage and instituting civil marriage, the protection of unmarried mothers and freedom to divorce. This legislation, enacted in 1917 and introduced into the 1923 Code of Civil Law, had the following principal aims.

1 To undo marriage ties in households that had been torn apart by the ideological and economic upheavals of the postwar era; this meant that it was now possible to divorce either by mutual consent or at the request of one or other of the spouses (Article 87) by a simple entry in the civil registry (*ZAG-otdel aktov grazhdanskogo sostoyaniya*).

2 To establish the equality of all children, regardless of their descent (legitimate or illegitimate), which led to the legal recognition of all unions hitherto unrecognized under religious laws.

3 To establish equal rights for men and women under matrimonial law, by abolishing the predominance of the husband and giving the wife identical rights over children and property, as well as with regard to work, the home and choice of name (this entitled her to keep her maiden name).

Economic difficulties and the growingly permissive moral climate led to the legalization on 18 November 1920 of abortion during the first three months of pregnancy; the aim of this was to reduce the number of backstreet abortions. Lenin took a personal interest in the development of day-care centres or crèches, which he regarded as nurseries for communist society and as a means of improving women's conditions.

Some people wished to go further still: abolishing inheritance, prohibiting the adoption of children in order to defuse the proprietorial instincts of adoptive parents over their adopted children. In the climate of anarchy that reigned in the early years of the regime, people opened free-love agencies. A decree was issued in Vladimir, in 1918, proclaiming all women state property on reaching the age of eighteen. People were not ready for such radical measures, and adoption was once more permitted in the aftermath of the 1921 famines in order to keep down the numbers of abandoned children (*bezprizornye*). For the same reason, that society was as yet unprepared, family communes, as extolled by the poets and town planners of the 1920s, never went beyond the experimental stage, once the famine period was over. But it was in central Asia that the new status of women encountered fiercest resistance and where activist women were murdered even.

From 1926 onwards. In the second phase, with the onset of Stalinism, the social-ist reorganization of society presupposed a stable family basis. Stricter legis-lation (the 1926 Code of Common Law) laid a multitude of obligations upon husband and wife, when the child truly created the family. Henceforward, the family was legally responsible for the care of children, and common-law marriage was the same as civil marriage in so far as its consequences were con-cerned. As a result, the courts were deluged with alimony suits.

The new 1936 constitution confirmed the equality of men and women (Article 122) and recognized private ownership of domestic chattels and their transmission by inheritance. Further decrees improved terms of assistance to women in childbirth and instituted the payment of allowances to large families (over a period of five years for seventh and subsequent children). To halt the sliding population, after the heavy toll exacted by collectivization, restrictions were placed on abortion (decree dated 27 June 1936), prohibiting it unless the woman's life or health was in danger. Divorce too was made more difficult by obliging couples to publish the divorce decree.

Similar concerns lay behind the legislation enacted on 8 July 1944 to regulate marriage and divorce. Henceforward, civil marriage alone was con-sidered legal, and people living maritally were obliged to legalize their union. Divorce was no longer free but subject to the discretion of the courts, while stamp duties and legal publication fees were increased. Actions for affiliation were no longer permitted outside legal marriage, but a system of aid to un-married mothers was introduced and family allowances now became payable from the fourth child onwards. Distinctions such as the Order of the Mother Heroine were awarded to mothers of ten children, while special medals were struck for mothers of 5-6 and 7-9 children respectively.

After Stalin's death. The domestic thaw that followed Stalin's death produced a relaxation of legislation, the third phase, in recognition of changing family-behaviour patterns and material problems.

In 1955, abortion on economic grounds was once more authorized in state hospitals. It was made available free of charge for working women, while for others the fee was 5 rubles (2 rubles in the countryside). In 1965, divorce by mutual consent was authorized once more, subject to a reconciliation pro-cedure (a mere formality), but the obligation to publish the decree was lifted. Lastly, since November 1974, family allowances have been paid for each child up to the age of three years, when per capita income in the family does not exceed 50 rubles. Some Soviet demographers believe that the family-allowance system ought to take into account variations in the fertility rates of different ethnic groups.

One thing that stands out clearly from this historical process is that family life is no longer, as it used to be, a private matter, and that, like it or not, the state is today the chief arbiter of the source of support of the family — so much so that family values and behaviour patterns have been modified by government policy and economic change: the traditional image of the mother at home has been replaced by a new model, that of the woman committed to the building of socialism and going out to work. This could not fail to influence family size.

THE FAMILY AS AN INSTITUTION TODAY

Definition of the family and number of families

Up till now, we have considered the family from a legal standpoint, in the sense of people united by blood ties or marriage. To the anthropologist, the family embraces the whole of the kinship network, and the family system is merely a method of exchanging women in a society in which incest is prohibited; a mechanism for the consolidation of wealth and transmission of goods. Here, though, we shall be adopting the economist's narrower outlook, in which the family is limited to the household, that is to the stable group of people living under the same roof or, at least, those maintaining a permanent financial link with this group, such as students, conscripts and seasonal workers.

At the 1970 census, 90 per cent of Soviet people lived in a family; of those living alone, 4 per cent were temporarily separated from their families, because they were studying away from home, were on military service or were away for professional reasons, and 6 per cent had no family. We do not know how many of these people living alone were single, widowed or divorced. Out of the total population aged between 20 and 40 in 1970, some 7.9 million men and 9.4 million women were unmarried. Table 18 shows that women living alone outnumbered men doing so, and the latter accounted for 70 per cent of those living separated from their family while preserving financial links with it, presumably doing their military service.

Family size

As in other countries, the Soviet family has drawn physically closer together; out of a total of 59 million families, 34 million live in town, which means mostly in apartments. It is still not uncommon to find several generations living under the same roof: we find three generations cohabiting in 25 per cent of families in towns which gives an idea of the importance of the *babushka* (grandmother) in the life of the family, in the countryside especially. In the towns, the percentage of three-generation families varies between 15 per cent in Moscow and 25 per cent in Leningrad. In the countryside, we find that 26 per cent of rural Ukrainian families are three-generation ones while the

The family

TABLE 18 *Analysis of households in the USSR and France*

Individuals		1970 census (millions)			USSR 1970 (%)	France 1962 (%)
		alone	linked to family			
Living alone	men	3.8	6.9	10.7	4.4	6.4
	women	10.4	2.9	13.3	5.5	13.6
Living in a family				217.5	91.1	80
Families	A childless couple			11	18.7	20
	With children			35.7	60.8	58.7
	Plus parent			9.4	16	4.5
	Two couples			2.2	3.7	
	Without spouse but with children and parent			8.7	14.8	16.3
	Total families			58.7	100	100

percentage rises to 29 per cent in rural Armenia, 31 per cent among Uzbeks and 48 per cent among the Bulgars.

The trend to nuclear families (the couple and its children) has been hastened by urban housing conditions and by improved old-age pensions since 1956. Three generations living together implies a common budget, often leading to grandparental interference in the younger couple's spending; but the younger generation is less and less ready to put up with this, owing to inevitable differences in lifestyle from one generation to another. However, the grandmother is often irreplaceable for looking after the children and the housework, to the extent that certain demographers point wryly to the likely consequences on the birthrate of the separation of generations (a survey conducted in Leningrad in 1967 revealed that 10.5 per cent of female factory workers depended on their own mothers for the housework, and 4.7 per cent on their mothers-in-law).

Further, the number of births per Soviet family is not as high as it used to be. This drop in the fertility rate is the chief factor in the decline of the number of people per household (Table 19), which is currently 3.7 on average, compared with 7 a century ago (1861).

Average family size varies more between ethnic groups (the Turkmen family is twice as large as the Estonian family) than between socio-occupational categories: the Soviet average is 3.9 people per household among collective-farm workers, 3.4 in urban working-class families and 3.1 among office workers.

The number of children per family can be seen to be declining from one generation to the next. At Nizhniy-Tagil, for instance, 55 per cent of couples married in 1920 had three children or more; the figure falls to 45 per cent for marriages celebrated in 1940 and to 6 per cent for couples married in 1957.

TABLE 19 *Average number of persons in a household*

		Towns	Countryside
1897	Russia	4.7	5.9
1923		3.9	
1939	USSR	3.6	4.3
1970		3.5	4.0
1979		3.3	3.8
1970	Russian families	3.4	3.6
1970	Uzbek families	5.8	6.0
1979	Estonian families	3.1	3.1

Even so, the transition from the large to the nuclear family does not abolish relations of kinship. These have adjusted to a more mobile society. Although country people now live separately, albeit often in the same house, garden or cow still remain common property. Parents with a cellar look after their married children's potatoes, and the latter come to help them in the harvest season or at mowing time. On important occasions (birthdays, Easter, New Year), people invite their in-laws; the extended family is reunited at weddings and funerals. An uncle or aunt will assume responsibility for an orphaned nephew or niece. In town too, parents and married children remain in close contact if they live nearby.

The size of the house naturally varies in the course of the family's life.

The family cycle

Like any social group, the family goes through phases of expansion and contraction. The problems of family life differ greatly according to whether a couple is in the first year of its marriage and awaiting the birth of its first child, in the twenty years of growth between this birth and the marriage of its first child, or in the period of dispersal of its children which comes to an end with the last child's marriage.

Many young couples in the Soviet Union continue to live with their parents after marriage, either because they do not have priority on the housing list before their children are born, or because their income makes it expedient to turn to their parents for help. Parental aid is the rule when one or other of the spouses is still studying, for grants are insufficient and daytime students are forbidden to hold a paid job (which results in 'disguised' jobs, in which one of the grandparents officially has the job while the grandson does the actual work).

Couples newly arrived in a locality live separately from their parents, but 70 per cent of childless young couples live with their parents during the early years of marriage, and close to 52 per cent of them are in addition prepared to depend on them financially. Consequently, in this initial phase of the couple's development, the process of psychological adjustment is bedevilled by the parents' interference; this accounts for the number of early divorces attributed to housing problems (19.5 per cent of reasons given) or to conflicts with parents (18.3 per cent of reasons).

Relations between generations undergo a change with the birth of the first child. If the couple manages to obtain separate housing, the grandmother's presence ceases to be anything but occasional. In the last century, mothers used to devote 12 to 15 years of their lives to their children, either in pregnancy or feeding the newborn baby; nowadays this period is much shorter, lasting 3 to 4 years on average, until the child is ready for the day nursery or kindergarten. On the other hand, the period of a family's dispersal has lengthened considerably owing to the couple's greater longevity.

The Russian economist Chayanov has demonstrated the influence of the family cycle on per capita needs and income: to begin with, the ratio of workers to mouths to be fed in the family is unfavourable; it subsequently improves as the children reach working age and make their own contribution to the family income.[3]

But family income and outgoings are not the only factors to vary from one phase to another in the family cycle: the group's relations with the outside world are affected too. Prior to the birth of a child, the couple is freer to participate in joint activities outside the home; subsequently, the division of labour between husband and wife hinders such shared outside activities. It is worthwhile recalling these different phases, for though not all the families necessarily pass through them, and though they are obviously not specific to Soviet society, these distinctions underpin any family typology.

THE FORMATION OF THE LEGAL FAMILY

Now that considerations of property no longer lie at the root of a couple's formation, emotional relations may lead to a stable union officially recognized by marriage. In the Soviet Union, as elsewhere, behaviour patterns reflect a certain dissociation of sex and marriage.

Sex before and outside marriage

A survey of Leningrad adolescents shows that 52.5 per cent of boys and 14.5 per cent of girls had their first sexual experience between the ages of 16 and 19, while 2.1 per cent of men and 10.5 per cent of women married between these ages.[4] Public opinion very largely does not disapprove of these non-marital relations. Some 53 per cent of male and 38 per cent of female students interviewed approved of them, 31–35 per cent expressed indifference, while 16 per cent of boys and 27 per cent of girls disapproved. Among female research workers, the percentage disapproving fell to 7 per cent, while 55 per cent took a favourable view. Sex education appears to be neglected, since 72 per cent of young people stated that they had learnt about sex from their peers, 3 per cent from their parents and 3 per cent from a teacher. Another indication of the morally tolerant attitude of Soviet society is that 50 per cent of happily married women see nothing wrong with extramarital sex. However, the penal code (Article 226) punishes severely (five years' imprisonment and then exile upon completion of the sentence) anyone found guilty of 'running a bawdy house or living off immoral earnings'; soliciting is prosecuted as vagrancy (Article 209). There is no prostitution on the streets, with very rare and very discreet exceptions.

Housing conditions of young people on arrival in a new town (see Chapter 3), especially of those living in hostels, do not make it any easier to set up a home, while in the countryside the disparity between the sexes and looser morals breed short-lived affairs. This explains the growing number of births out of wedlock, even though the percentage of unmarried women has fallen since 1959. For the Soviet Union as a whole, 400,000 illegitimate births were recorded in 1970, i.e. 9.5 per cent, Novosibirsk coming top of the league with 23 per cent. (For purposes of comparison, the proportion is 21 per cent in Sweden, 8.1 per cent in the United States, 8.2 per cent in France and 2.7 per cent in Belgium.)

The courts can order a father who refuses to recognize his child to assume material and moral responsibility for it when he cohabits with the mother, but the law takes a different view when, in cases of irregular relations, there is insufficient proof.

Cases of couples living together maritally without legalizing their union are fairly frequent. In the 1970 census, the number of women stating that they lived with their husband exceeded the number of men stating that they lived with their wife by 1.3 million. It could be that this difference is an indication that, where morals are fairly free and easy, women attach greater importance than men to appearances.

Legal marriage

Age at marriage. The legal age for marriage is 18, but this may be lowered by two years if necessary. One-third of marriages celebrated before the age of 20, and approximately 20 per cent of those before 25, legalize an existing situation; in other words, births occur within the first eight months.

The effective average age of marriage in 1973 was 24 years and 5 months for men and 22 years and 7 months for women; in France, the average age of marriage is respectively 24 years and 4 months for men and 22 years and 4 months for women (1970). Marriage takes place later in the Soviet Union than it did 50 years ago, for in 1926 12.2 per cent of men married before the age of 20, compared with 4.9 per cent in 1973. However, there has been a slight drop in the average age compared with 1965, since the passage of a law in 1967 freeing young men from military service at 20 years of age instead of 22.

The age differential between partners is less than two years at present, compared with four years in Russia at the end of the nineteenth century. The age at which girls marry varies greatly from one republic to another. In Tadzhikistan, 43.4 per cent of girls marrying in 1973 were aged under 20, whereas the percentage of brides in the same age group elsewhere was 17 per cent in Estonia, 23.8 per cent in Byelorussia, 25.7 per cent in Armenia, 28 per cent in the Ukraine and 37.4 per cent in Uzbekistan. Nevertheless, there has been a very marked decline in early marriages over the past generation or two. The percentage of women marrying when aged under 20 has fallen from 29 per cent in 1926 to 19 per cent in 1970 in the RSFSR, from 71 per cent in 1939 to 27 per cent in 1970 in Armenia and from 65 per cent in 1897 to 25 per cent in 1970 in Uzbekistan. Regional differences narrow when we turn to the age at which men marry, for whatever their nationality, they all do their military service between the ages of 18 and 20. Moreover, in central Asia, possibly due to the hidden survival of the *kalym* (the fiancé purchases the girl from her parents), it is customary for the husband to have a decent material situation at the time of marriage: in Tadzhikistan, twice as many men as women marry after the age of 24.

Longer schooling seems to have no effect on marriage rates, since the percentage of married women in the 16–19 age group was 19 per cent in 1970, compared with 17 per cent in 1957. Among unmarried women, we find a higher percentage (33 per cent) of girls with a secondary education, while 68 per cent of girls in the same age group with only a primary education are married. A survey conducted in Kiev in 1971 showed that 17.9 per cent of boys and 23 per cent of girls who marry continue to study.

Choice of spouse and the wedding ceremony. Young people attain economic independence much earlier than in the past, which means that they are far freer to choose their marriage partner. Marriages are no longer arranged; they are desired, even if for the sake of form parents are still consulted, or at least informed.

Some 70 per cent of marriages (more in the countryside) are between partners from the same socio-occupational background. Seventy per cent of blue-collar men marry blue-collar women, while 10 per cent of the men in this category marry students. Male students, on the other hand, show a greater tendency (25 per cent) to marry blue-collar women. It frequently happens that the husband is better educated than his bride owing to age differentials. Some 20 per cent of female office workers continue their studies after marriage. At Nizhniy-Tagil, out of a sample of 822 families, 66 per cent of people born in that city and 72 per cent of newcomers to the city belonged to the same social group as their partners. Among families of mixed origin, in 52–81 per cent of cases the husband was a blue-collar and the wife a white-collar worker; male-female blue-collar families, and families in which one spouse is a member of the intelligentsia accounted for only 13–20 per cent of cases.[5] The rising number of women employed in the services sector ought, in principle, to produce a growing number of mixed marriages with either intellectuals or blue-collar workers.

Race prejudice has not yet been banished entirely. Andrei Amalrik mentions the hostility of his fanatical, narrow-minded future parents-in-law when they learned that their daughter, a Tatar, wanted to marry a Russian.[6] A survey in Armenia revealed that although 20 per cent of the population was non-Armenian, only 5 per cent of marriages were mixed. Among the latter, it was found that marriages between Armenians and Azerbaijanis were far less common than between Armenians and Slavs, which could possibly be due to a greater sense of affinity between populations belonging to the Christian tradition. In a big city like Leningrad, 16.4 per cent of marriages were mixed in 1960, half of them between people of Slav nationality (Byelorussians, Russians and Ukrainians).

Cultural level, which determines a family's lifestyle is a far more important discriminating factor than race, religion, occupation or income. In 1965, it was found that 90 per cent of engineers had married women from the same social group; in 47 per cent of these marriages, both partners had had the same level of education.

The circumstances in which future couples meet are, in descending order of frequency: place of work (22.1 per cent), leisure activities (21.6 per cent), while studying (15.7 per cent), holidays (8 per cent), the fact of living in the same house (6.8 per cent) or the same street (6.5 per cent); lastly, 4.5 per cent stated that they had met in the street. Soviet sociologists account for the precariousness of certain marriages by the fact that the couples do not know each other well enough and that engagements are too short. The safest solution would be to marry a childhood friend, but this is uncommon (1.2 per cent of marriages celebrated in Kiev).

Couples have known each other, on average, for 1–2 years (29.6 per cent), 2–3 years (18.8 per cent), 3–5 years (17.1 per cent), and sometimes as much as 5–10 years (10.3 per cent). There is a legal wait of one month between the declaration of intent at the Registrar's office and the actual wedding ceremony; this is enough for 10–15 per cent of intended couples to change their minds.

The civil marriage ceremony itself is a public, even a solemn affair. In the big cities, where people marry in the palace of marriages, the bride often wears a white dress and white stockings, while the groom dresses in black suit and white shirt, sometimes with a jabot. They step forward in procession, to the strains of Mendelssohn's *Wedding March*, in company with their witnesses; they then lay a wreath at the foot of the war memorial (the way French brides used to lay a bouquet before the altar of the Virgin). After the ceremony, relatives, and above all friends, gather in a restaurant for the wedding feast and dancing. The couple leaves the restaurant in a taxi bedecked with ribbons for the occasion and a plastic doll attached to the bonnet. Employers grant three days' leave and the government provides priority vouchers for the purchase of clothing and household articles.

Fertility patterns

At the 1970 census, 21.2 per cent of Soviet families had no children, 35.4 per cent had one child, 26.4 per cent two children and 17 per cent three or more. The Soviet average was 2.4 children per household in 1970, compared with 2.8 in 1959; but the figure varies considerably from one republic to the next: the RSFSR 1.97, Ukraine 2.04, Georgia 2.62, Armenia 3.2, Azerbaijan 4.63, Uzbekistan 5.64, Tadzhikistan 5.9 and Turkmenistan 5.95. The average is higher in Catholic Lithuania (2.35) than in Protestant Latvia (1.94).

Fertility varies not only according to ethnic group (in 1959, there were 863 children per 1000 Russian women aged 20–49 and 1870 children per 1000 Uzbek women in the same age group) or place of residence (there is an average of 1.4 children per family in Moscow, while 61.2 per cent of Muscovite families have only a single child), but also according to social status: there are 177 children per 100 blue-collar mothers, 253 per 100 rural women and 152 children per 100 mothers belonging to the intelligentsia. This is because rising educational levels bring increased cultural demands on the part of parents and ambitions for their children, as well as more effective birth control.

Almost 80 per cent of couples interviewed (in a survey conducted in Kiev in 1971) about their intentions at the time of marriage stated that they would like to have children, 3 per cent replied in the negative and 13 per cent did not know. Ideally, people in Uzbekistan and Azerbaijan would like to have 4.5 children and in the RSFSR 2.6 (3.3 in the countryside and 2.3 in Moscow), giving an average of 2.9 children for the Soviet Union as a whole, which is greater than the actual average. This suggests that living conditions too play a considerable part in deciding how many children a couple will have.

Indeed, among reasons given by blue- and white-collar women not wanting any more children, housing conditions came first with over 50 per cent of interviewees. On the other hand, there is no evidence that a rise in family income would increase fertility. The reverse is generally the case, but E. V. Urlanis, a Soviet demographer, disputes the conclusion drawn from this, arguing that people confuse cause with effect and that incomes are low because there are more children in the home.

The mass media have been enlisted in the service of a campaign to encourage earlier marriage and larger families. Public opinion, however, is not convinced that mothers ought to have lots of children. Women with big families complain of the hostility they encounter in shops when buying large quantities and of the mother's lack of prestige, her role being honoured but once a year, on 8 March, whereas women's involvement in civic, occupational and military life is constantly extolled.

While the appearance of the first child is welcomed joyfully, this hardly solves the problems that ensue: housing conditions, lower per capita income (especially if the mother stops working until her child is old enough to go to the day nursery), reduced participation in working life and less leisure time. Legal abortion appears to be regarded as a substitute for contraception, recent surveys conducted in Leningrad and Moscow indicating that over 70 per cent of women interviewed have had at least one or two abortions in the course of their married life. If it is true that there are 6 million abortions per year, this greatly exceeds the number of live births.

These different behaviour patterns point to the existence of several types of family in Soviet society: some still cleave to tradition, while others are heavily influenced by ideas of female emancipation, as witnessed by falling birthrates and the high divorce rate. In Latvia, there are 491 divorces per 1000 marriages and 14 births per 1000 inhabitants; in Tadzhikistan, there are 123 divorces per 1000 marriages and 36 births per 1000 inhabitants.

BROKEN HOMES: DIVORCE

Couples do not always find the satisfaction that they expect from marriage, for they frequently lack full psychological maturity and encounter difficulties of communication in their everyday life; also, the fact that women enjoy material independence allows them to assert their rights. But this independence may in itself be a source of conflict. In other words, the family unit is more fragile than it used to be.

The divorce rate

This reached 2.8 per 1000 inhabitants in 1966, the year following the easing of legislation in 1965 (when the rate was 1.6 per 1000). Subsequently, the rate has gone up to around 3.5 per 1000, which is very high compared with the 1940 rate of 1.1 per 1000 or with that of other countries.

TABLE 20   *Divorce rate per 1000 marriages*

	1910	1940	1960	1967	1979
Russia/USSR[1]		167	104	303	340
France	46		82		266
USA	87		259		320[2]
UK	20		100		

Notes: 1 The Soviet divorce rate peaked in 1935, when it reached 44 per cent of marriages (*Izvestiya*, 4 July 1935).
2 1970.

Divorce is more frequent in the towns (4.2 per 1000) than in the country (2.7 per 1000), while in big cities such as Novosibirsk or Moscow (6 per 1000), 1 marriage in every 2 ends in divorce. The divorce rate is highest in Magadan (8.9—9.4 per 1000), a 'frontier' province in the far east which attracts individuals because of the high wages offered on short-term contracts; where many separated couples regularize their situation in order to remarry. Latvia (with 4.2 per 1000) and the RSFSR (3.7 per 1000) come top among the republics, while Catholic Lithuania (with 1.8 per 1000), Armenia and Georgia (1.0 per 1000), Kirghizia and Tadzhikistan (1.1 per 1000) bring up the rear.

Since we know that the average age of divorce is 21—23 for women and 24—27 for men, we may conclude that 62 per cent of divorces occur in the very first years of marriage. Some 48 per cent occur in the first four years and 18 per cent after ten years of marriage. A great many divorces merely serve to legalize an existing separation at the time of the divorce decree, since 20 per cent of people divorcing have already set up a new family and produced children.

Circumstantial, or objective, reasons for divorce

In the Soviet Union, as elsewhere, family upheavals led to a large number of divorces subsequent to the first and second world wars. Many adolescents grew up without any experience of paternal authority, as many women lost their husbands or were unable to marry. This reservoir of 20 million surplus women was doubtless a factor in the postwar loosening of moral standards. On the other hand, fewer women instituted divorce proceedings during the years 1960—5, since they were unsure of finding another husband. Today the sexes are once again evenly balanced and a woman who divorces need no longer fear that she will not remarry.

In normal times the geographical mobility of the Soviet population entails a weakening of social constraints for the approximately 12 million Soviet citizens who change their place of residence each year. They no longer have relatives and friends to guide and help them. In addition, accommodation for new city dwellers is not always conducive to a happy family life. In 1973, some 31.7 per cent of couples divorcing in Leningrad lived with their family or in a hostel, 63.2 per cent in a shared apartment and 5.1 per cent in a separate apartment. At Naberezhnye Chelny, 70 per cent of young people were living in hostels (*obshchezhitie*). Married men could visit their wives there, but this was hardly a good beginning to conjugal life.

Being financially independent, working women can more easily cope with the practical consequences of a break-up. On the other hand, it is likely that a woman who lives a full professional life and in addition shoulders most of the domestic responsibilities must often feel exhausted. This will lead to irritability and sometimes tension within the family.

The drop in the birthrate may also encourage divorce: it has everywhere been observed that divorce is far more common among childless couples (50 per cent of divorces in the Soviet Union) than in families with several children. This development is only one aspect of more far-reaching changes in behaviour brought about by the urbanization and secularization of Soviet society. The religious taboos that used to stand in the way of divorce have been replaced by a much more tolerant attitude.

Subjective reasons for divorce

Subjective reasons are those most commonly cited by couples in court. Under the old regime the Orthodox Church granted divorce in the case of prolonged absence (5–10 years), loss of civil rights (condemnation to hard labour or deportation), adultery, impotence or bigamy. The Code of Civil Law of 1918 and 1926 required only the mutual consent of the couple, or even an application by only one of them. Today the courts accept as legal grounds: absence of children through inability to procreate, marriages entered into under duress, misrepresentation, actual long-term separation, infringement of Soviet laws and cruelty towards wife and children. However, this list is not exhaustive, as modern life is considered too complex for anyone to be able to foresee every situation likely to lead to a breakdown in marriage. Thus, in Turkmenistan, in the summer of 1974, 65 cases of *kaitarma* (imprisonment of the fiancée in her parents' home for non-payment of the *kalym* by the fiancé) were brought before the courts.

Alimony is usually fixed at a quarter of the husband's salary for one child, a third for two children and a half for three, all up to the age of eighteen.

TABLE 21   *Reasons for divorce in the 1960s*
(as a percentage of all cases)

	Lithuania	Leningrad	Moscow	USSR
Previous marriage not dissolved	21	5		
Adultery	17.5	28	16	15
Alcoholism	14.2		20	19.5
Incompatibility	13	17		
Transfer of affections	7.5		12	5.6
Enforced separation (prison, etc.)	7.7	3	4	4.2
Religious, social, professional incompatibility	6.5			
Quarrels, insults leading to assault	3.8	9	16	6.2
Sickness of spouse	2.8		5	1.2
Failure to produce children	2.5			} 10
Sexual dissatisfaction		17		
Parental interference	3		3	3.2
Husband not returned from war		17		

Children also have the right to a third of the goods acquired during the marriage. Ex-husbands' failure to pay alimony is often reported in the Russian press.

Among the legal reasons advanced, it is not always easy to identify the real motive. For example, is drunkenness on the part of the husband − cited in almost half of cases − the cause of the conflict or its result? Widely differing situations are concealed beneath the heading 'incompatibility of character'. What are we to understand by 'transfer of affections'? Does it imply an outside affair (although adultery, the most common ground for divorce in France, for example, is only mentioned in a quarter of divorce cases in the Soviet Union)?

The percentage of remarriages after divorce may help to provide an answer. In the Soviet Union only half of divorced couples remarry, as against 70−80 per cent in the United Kingdom and in the United States. This percentage is higher than the intentions expressed at the time of divorce: 55 per cent of men and 70 per cent of women then state that they do not intend to commit themselves again. The number of single people between the ages of 25 and 55 increased between 1959 and 1970. However, some of these live maritally, either permanently or at weekends.

Some sociologists ascribe the high divorce rate to early marriage, pointing out that sexual maturity is attained before psychological maturity. Others believe that prevention of family troubles depends on improved housing conditions and leisure facilities, which would help reduce alcoholism. One is also inclined to wonder whether the fact that Soviet women usually go out to work (encouraged by the political environment and by practical necessity) may not contribute to family instability. Where there are two salaries there are also two professional careers, whose demands do not necessarily coincide. A more detailed examination of family life shows how difficult it is for women to reconcile their role as wife and mother with professional commitments.

HOW THE FAMILY LIVES

In traditional peasant society, most food and clothing requirements were met by the family's own efforts. This productive function continues to some extent in the countryside (see Chapter 4). Elsewhere the family is primarily a consumer unit, by virtue of the community in which it resides, though this does not exempt it from the fundamental need to provide the wherewithal of subsistence and, consequently, to decide who has to work and where.

Working women

At the 1970 census, 68 per cent of households (71 per cent in the cities) contained at least two active members. Only 22 per cent of households had a single partner at work, and 11.3 per cent of families in the country and 6.8 per cent in town did no work outside the home. (In France, in 1968 a single partner worked in 42 per cent of households, and in 35 per cent of cases both partners were salaried workers.) In all, 86 per cent of women of working age in the Soviet Union have an occupation outside the home, 7.5 per cent of them being students. Therefore, 44 per cent of the total female population currently work, with a particularly high percentage (80 per cent) between the ages of 20 and 39, i.e. during the years when women are most fertile (we have already noted the effect of this on the birthrate). In 1959, some 11.4 million women between the ages of 16 and 54 were not considered 'active'; of these 6.8 million had dependent children aged under 14. Among women between the ages of 55 and 59, some 55 per cent continued to work outside the home, though they had reached retirement age. We can estimate that since this date the 'reserve' of unemployed female labour has diminished considerably — from 18 million to 6 million — and that the proportion of women in the active population as a whole must have risen, despite a one-third reduction in the agricultural labour force.

Women prefer jobs in the services sector, particularly where hours of work are more flexible (e.g. teaching and health care) (see Table 22). However, there are also a large number of women in unqualified and little-mechanized jobs, for example agriculture, light industry and the building industry, despite the fact that since the war their level of training has very rapidly been brought up to that of the active male population (see Table 23).

TABLE 22 *Percentage of women in the active population and in selected occupations, USSR and France*

USSR			USSR 1970	France 1975
1928	24 (excluding agriculture)	Agriculture	44	30
1939	43.4 (including agriculture)	Industry	48	22
1959	48 (including agriculture)	Building	29	
		Commerce	75	59
1968	50 (France 35%)	Administration	61–78	65
1980	51 (France 40%)	Education	72	64
2000	44 (forecast)	Public health	85	79
		Total	51	38

More young married women go out to work than older married women. In families with two dependent persons, there were, in 1970, two salaries in 70 per cent of cases and a single salary in 17 per cent of cases. Among city families with three dependants, 52 per cent had two salaries and a third one salary.

The size of the husband's salary also affects the wife's decision to work. Thus, when the husband works in the steel industry or coalmining, which pay considerably higher wages than light industry (where women predominate), the wife tends to remain at home. The young women employed in the Ivanovo textile industry — only 44 per cent of them are married — do not settle there since they are unlikely to set up a family in an area where there are 154 women for every 100 men.

TABLE 23   *Comparative educational levels of male and female labour*

	Women	Men
Per 1000 of active population		
Graduates from:		
secondary education in 1959	95	120
in 1981	725	729
higher education in 1959	9	16
in 1981	104	108
Percentage of total employment in 1970		
factory directors	16[1]	84
doctors	74	26
engineers	40[2]	60
Qualifications at Taganrog in 1974[3]		
Highly skilled jobs	4	31
Medium-skilled jobs	30	50
Jobs requiring little skill	66	19
	100	100

Notes: 1 In France, 9.6 per cent of company heads are women.
2 16 per cent of chief engineers are women.
3 *Kommunist*, no. 17, 1974, p. 54 (Taganrog has a population of 282,000).

Among the factors encouraging them to work, the women questioned in Leningrad in 1971 and in Moscow in 1974 put financial considerations first (53.5 per cent and 91 per cent respectively); 34.9 per cent and 86 per cent respectively stated that they wished to have some form of group activity and to do socially useful work; 11.4 per cent wished to be independent of their hubands. The same survey showed that 73 per cent of women questioned accepted work as a necessity; in only 27 per cent of cases did husbands fully approve of their wives working. However, when the interview took place at work and not at home, diametrically opposite replies were obtained: 70 per cent of women stated that they would continue to work even if their husband's wage was sufficient to enable them to stop. These divergent findings are a matter of controversy between demographers, concerned to increase the birthrate through a policy of aid to the housewife, and economists whose job it is to plan future developments in the labour market. The latter prefer to encourage part-time work for women, setting sex-differentiated industrial norms for work, a situation that has long been current in agriculture.

A decree dated 10 July 1967 provides for the organization of part-time work in factories. However, application of this measure is meeting with resistance on the part of factory managers, who are reluctant to complicate their task. The measure is welcomed, on the other hand, by young women under twenty who have left secondary schools and are keen to go on with their studies (23 per cent of persons interviewed) and by women with young children (46 per cent of replies) when per capita income is insufficient.

Prevailing attitudes in the Soviet Union see no conflict between the image of the housewife and the ideal of the working woman. The latter is apparently less likely than in the west to feel guilty for not discharging her role as housewife to the full. Indeed, the reverse is often the case, with women considering that their obligations as wife and mother impede their careers, which are interrupted for one year in four, their promotion, chances of retraining, etc. For this reason women with comparable qualifications are promoted less rapidly than men. However, for many women bringing up children on their own, particularly in the country, there is no choice. For the others, relinquishing a second salary means a drop in income which cannot be offset by promotions for their husbands.

Family resources: living standards

The family is no longer a self-sufficient productive unit, although domestic tasks are almost as time-consuming as salaried work. In an industrial economy based on the division of labour, the major part of income now derives from outside activities. In addition, given the collectivist approach to life in a socialist regime, the state assumes responsibility for an ever increasing proportion of needs.

Income is thus diversified by origin and type (see Table 24). We may distinguish: (1) resources in kind and money income originating from family farming; (2) remuneration of work (salary, bonuses); (3) payments by the state or social transfer payments (pensions, scholarships, family allowances); and (4) lastly, what is often called 'indirect salary' or 'fringe benefits', namely social benefits available to workers in the form of free medical care and education. Note that in the Soviet Union, in theory, income from capital or from property does not exist (with the exception of rent paid to private individuals who sublet rooms).

In the Soviet Union, the individual pays for basic needs (for food, clothing and personal care) from his own income. Training and health care are, on the other hand, increasingly paid for by the state in the form of transfer payments or free benefits (28 per cent of direct and indirect family resources in 1975 as against 2 per cent fifty years ago). The Soviet state also covers a large proportion of housing outlays in the form of grants (the rents paid by city dwellers bear no relation to real costs) and similarly helps with the upkeep of holiday homes or grants holiday vouchers (*putyovki*). Official sources have estimated these indirect benefits at 64 rubles per worker per month in addition to the average monthly salary of 168.9 rubles in 1980. In France, the state covers 68 per cent of expenditure on training and health, as against 71 per cent in the Soviet Union.

Another factor that needs to be taken into consideration is taxation and other deductions from gross income: direct taxes, different types of insurance, penalties and loan repayments. Taken overall, these charges represent around 5.6 per cent of total family income since direct taxation is only very slightly graduated in the Soviet Union (with a ceiling of 13 per cent for the top brackets).

The family

TABLE 24 *Soviet family income and expenditure*

| | Average income per family (%) | | | | |
| | Working-class families | | | Kolkhoz families | |
	1972	1940	1979	1940	1979
Resources derived from family activities					
market sales	10.3	8	0.8	48.3	26.9
miscellaneous income			1.8	1.3	1.6
Income from work					
Blue/white-collar wages	87.7	77	74.3		8.8
Kolkhozian earnings				39.7	43.4
Monetary payments by the state					
transfers (pensions, grants, allowances)	2.0	15	23.1	4.9	19.3
Total private consumption	100	100	100	100	100

| | Monetary expenditure (%) | | | |
| | Working-class families | | Agricultural families | |
	1940	1979	1940	1979
Expenditure on food and drink	59.1	37.1	69.6	39.8
Clothing	12.2	18.2	11.3	17.4
Consumer durables	1.9	8.1	1.2	6.9
Fuel	1.3	0.2	3.9	1.8
Paid services	9.3	10.9	1.3	7.0
of which housing	3.0	3.1		2.4[1]
Miscellaneous	6.4	7.9	4.2	15.6
Taxation	4.5	9.9	1.4	1.6
Savings	5.3	7.7	7.1	9.9
	100	100	100	100

Note: 1 Building materials.

Family allowances are only paid from the fourth child onwards, for four years unless monthly per capita income is less than 50 rubles, in which case 12 rubles per child is paid up to the age of eight. It is only fairly recently, as a result of demographic studies (by Belova and Darsky) on the relationship between birthrate and income, that this minimum-income threshold has been taken into consideration.

What in fact determines family living standards is mainly per capita income and only to a lesser extent the salary scale and increases in the minimum wage (see Table 25). An average money salary of 135 rubles per month in 1973[7] represented a family budget of around 230 rubles per month for 1.7 active

TABLE 25   *Comparative average net monthly wages in the USSR, France and the USA*

1973	USSR (R)	France (F)	USA ($)
Gross wage	134.60	1422.90[1]	717.77$
Tax witheld	12.70	nil	69.28
Social Security	nil	114.70	41.78
Supplementary family allowance	nil	188.41	nil
Total net wage	121.90	1496.61	606.71
in US dollars	168.14	361.64	606.71
per hour worked	0.90	1.90	3.41

Note: 1 Gross income per working-class household in 1970 was estimated at 29,736 FF (J. Delors).

persons, that is 65 rubles per capita. We can reckon that in 1974 around one-third of families had a disposable per capita income of no more than 50 rubles per month. Certain economists consider this a threshold below which basic needs can no longer be met. According to these same estimates a monthly per capita income of 100−150 rubles was necessary for purchasing power to meet the rational norms set by Soviet consumer institutes: in 1967, some 10 per cent of families were in this category.

To money income we must add resources from subsistence farming when the family has access to a plot of ground near to its dwelling (*usad'ba*) in the country, a private garden in the suburbs (*uchastok*) or a plot in a firm's collective kitchen garden (*pashnya*). In an average town, 60−70 per cent of working-class families have access to a plot of land, which provides almost all their potato requirements; this of course implies the existence of cellars to store the crop (3−5 per cent of food requirements in Moscow and Gorky according to Trivous). Private livestock has become increasingly rare, however, now that milk is regularly available in the shops. For some categories of worker (e.g. miners and white-collar workers) the family garden provides an opportunity to relax outdoors. Its contribution to the family budget is estimated at 50−60 rubles per month in the country and 5 rubles in town.

It is much more difficult to estimate the irregular earnings that sometimes supplement the family income, in particular income from sideline activities (jobs done for private individuals, private coaching, private consultations and occasional dealing). For these activities, which are more often than not illegal, are not counted in official statistics. The importance of these additional earnings is attested by surveys of how people spend their time: 23 per cent of time among the intelligentsia and 3 per cent among unskilled workers is spent on these jobs. Similarly, statistics do not take into account the financial help that parents usually give young couples during the first years of marriage, though this help is vital when either husband or wife is pursuing advanced studies.

Bearing in mind these various extras, we may reckon the median income of a 3.5-person family at around 230 rubles per month, that is between 60 and 70 rubles per capita. Western estimates put the net monthly salary at around 122 rubles in 1973.

Expenditure and family property

It is difficult enough to determine a family's overall income and to estimate how representative this income is. Analysis becomes even more complex when we turn to expenditure. Although income enables us to pinpoint the standard of living, the latter differs from one family to another (even though their incomes are equal) due to cultural needs and objective conditions which determine lifestyles and even differences in social status. A skilled worker may earn as much as a young couple of intellectuals, but the latter's lifestyle (food and leisure activities) will be qualitatively different. In addition, consumer habits are influenced by national tradition, place of residence, type of accommodation, how well shops are stocked, the services network and the quality of social amenities.

In Table 24, which compares changing consumption patterns over a period of time, official figures at national level are not corroborated by local surveys of actual money expenditure. Making due allowance for these ambiguities, a number of comments suggest themselves:

1 Over the long term, in the Soviet Union as elsewhere, the proportion of expenditure devoted to food (40 per cent in the Soviet Union and 35 per cent in France) is tending to diminish. It remains higher in the country than in the towns. However, whereas before the war collective-farm families devoted two-thirds of their income to food, today they spend only half (including the proportion accounted for by subsistence farming). Expenditure on clothing remains relatively stable (18 per cent in the Soviet Union and 10 per cent in France), while purchases of consumer durables (furniture, household equipment, cultural articles, radio, television, bicycles, etc.) are on the increase.

2 A special feature of Soviet budgets is the heavy expenditure on alcohol (although concealed under the heading 'miscellaneous'). Both in working-class and in agricultural families expenditure on drink outstrips the proportion spent on paid services.

3 The small proportion of budgets devoted to paid services (less than 10 per cent in the Soviet Union and 35 per cent in France) is primarily due to the fact that many services are provided free of charge (e.g. education and health care), and because state subsidies keep rents low. Another factor, however, is the slow development of the services sector. At present the most popular services are those provided by seamstresses, tailors and shoe repairers (an indication that everyday articles are either in short supply or of shoddy quality), plus expenditure on home repairs, particularly in the country. However, dry-cleaners, laundries and hairdressers will come to occupy a larger place in the

future as these services become more widespread. Paid services, which in 1960 accounted for 9 per cent of total private-consumer expenditure, should rise to 21 per cent over the next decade when expenditure on private transport and leisure activities reaches levels comparable with other industrial countries.

4 Differences between town and country are particularly marked when it comes to housing costs. The city dweller has the advantage of a subsidized rent. The country dweller, on the other hand, is generally responsible for his own building and maintenance costs. There are fewer opportunities to spend money in the countryside because goods are in short supply. This partly explains why rural people save a higher proportion of income (17 per cent of gross family income in France). Average savings in the country went from 157 rubles per savings book in 1960 to 1189 rubles in 1980, while the number of rural depositors rose from 13.9 million to 35.5 million.

Analysis of food-consumption patterns brings out other contrasts between rural and urban families, while also revealing long-term improvements in living standards (see Table 26). Despite considerable improvements, vegetable calories predominate over those of animal origin. The scientific criteria which serve as guidelines for the planning of agricultural production targets are intended to redress this dietary balance, allocating to fruit, vegetables and meat a proportion equal or superior to western standards, although no prescriptive value is ascribed to them.

Quantity and type of diet vary according to income and cultural tradition. Paradoxically, average per capita consumption of animal produce, vegetables and fruit seems to be slightly lower in the country than in towns. This is because farm produce is a source of income for agricultural families. A characteristic of rural nutrition is its irregularity: the frugal everyday diet is interspersed with feasts: weddings, funerals and departures for the army are an excuse for revelry and outside purchases (preserved foods, biscuits, confectionery and vodka).

City working-class families eat meat every day when per capita income reaches 75 rubles. Otherwise people usually fatten up a pig, which means that they eat meat less often; but then they consume more sugar and milk (up to 3 litres per day in families with four children). A typical menu would be composed of meat broth (*borshch*) or milk or fish soup; a meat dish, either minced or as a goulash with mashed potatoes or cabbage, or sausage with fried potatoes; stewed fruit or jellied fruit with potato flour (*kisel'*) added, and tea with sweetmeats, biscuits or jam. In summer, less meat and more eggs and salads are eaten. On important occasions, puddings are made, also meat pies (*pirozhki*) with cabbage and mushrooms if an oven (*pech*) is available.

The midday meal is usually eaten in a canteen when both father and mother work. In Ivanovo, 70 per cent of female textile-workers and in Leningrad 60 per cent of families resort to what the Soviets call 'collective catering'. However, this type of consumption as yet only occupies a very minor place in total

TABLE 26 *Consumption of principal foods and household goods in the USSR and France*

	Annual per capita consumption (kg)				No. of minutes' work required to buy 1 kg			Ownership of household goods — per 100 families 1979		no. of hours work required	
	USSR 1922	USSR 1979	France 1975		USSR	France		USSR	France	USSR	France
Cereals (flour equivalent)	241.8	139	72	flour	34	13	Sewing-machine	64	48		
Potatoes	140	119	94	rye bread	15	3	Washing-machine	70	79	178	194
Vegetables	58.4	95	113	potatoes	8	3	Vacuum-cleaner	12[1]	91	289	77
Fruit	5.9	38	38	cabbage	8	8	Refrigerator	82	91	39	13
Sugar	4.1	43	38	oranges	115	20	Radio (transistor)	84	84		
Meat	11	58	99	sugar	85	26	TV (black-and-white)	83	89	585	151
Fish (and preserves)	10	16	15	pork chop	216	144	Bicycle	50	49	73	34
Dairy products (in milk equivalent)	62.1	319	230	milk	25	11	Motor bicycle (scooter)	10	49	482	119
Eggs	0.6	11	13	eggs (dozen)	89	47	Private car	24%	269%	43.3[2]	11.7[2]

Notes: 1 1970.
2 Number of months worked for Zhuguli car in USSR, Fiat 124 in France.

food expenditure. Although canteen prices are very reasonable, many families consider it cheaper to eat at home. The evening meal is taken at home fairly early (6 pm) when hours of work permit. Breakfast is usually a hearty meal (of two courses).

There have been changes in styles of dress: women no longer wear the traditional very long skirt and blouse. Now they wear dresses made of sateen, and a suit when they go out. Today, neither men nor women own clothes kept for very special occasions only. During the week they dress up to go out to the theatre, etc. During the 1920s, women cut their hair short; since Stalin's death, however, hairstyles have become better groomed. Women will go without a meal in order to buy a pretty blouse; they like to dress smartly and wear stockings, bracelets, earrings and a wedding-ring, even if they are not married. Men's trouser-widths sometimes give a clue as to age; young men often wear matching tie and handkerchief.

Expenditure on durable goods is also perceptibly affected by changing habits. Washing- and sewing-machines are more often to be found in the homes of couples aged over thirty. Young couples prefer to buy televisions, motor-cycles and sports equipment. The adjective 'cultural' is applied to the latter because for many Soviet citizens they are the hallmark of culture. Demand for all these articles still far outstrips supply. In low-income working-class families, where expenditure on food and housing accounts for 70 per cent of the budget, durable goods are often bought on hire purchase. This is why such families always appreciate receiving this kind of article as a reward for work, or as a lottery prize.

If one adds to the above list about ten other articles (e.g. tape recorder, piano and books) we have the major items of the Soviet family's inheritance. A survey of 1740 families in Chelyabinsk in 1969 showed that 12 per cent of them owned all these goods, and that most of the families interviewed considered them essential to contemporary life.

Owning durable goods is less a matter of ostentation than in western societies. In the west, social inequalities are more evident in the extent of the family's wealth, which includes not only furniture but also buildings and stocks and bonds; in the Soviet Union, there is much less opportunity of amassing these, and so greater importance is attached to personality than to external signs of wealth.

Despite very rapid progress in the production of consumer durables, inequalities still exist in this sphere, as the extent of household equipment testifies (with a few exceptions such as cars and telephones,[8] primarily between town and country). Inequalities can also be ascribed to cultural levels. The intelligentsia attach greater importance to musical instruments and books to develop their knowledge, and prefer to spend more money on mind-broadening travel and less on acquiring goods. The working classes prefer amusements and goods to lighten the housewife's work, particularly among non-manual workers, who are quicker to grasp the usefulness of these goods and who earn more. Opportunities of acquiring these goods are in reality limited not only by income but also by housing conditions (see Chapter 3). Consumer durables only make their way into the house when the family has an apartment of its own.

By combining the main material and social characteristics of Soviet families, we may attempt to develop a typology (Table 27) based on a distinction between: (1) standard of living, derived mainly from per capita income and housing conditions, and (2) lifestyle, as expressed in husband–wife relations, in the extent to which they participate in social activities and in their leisure patterns, and which, in the final analysis, is governed by people's cultural levels.

Organization of family life

We must now look at how the family organizes its social relations.

Division of responsibilities. As in traditional society, the husband still remains the head of the family in working-class and agricultural society, though the wife holds the purse strings, since she shoulders most of the day-to-day responsibilities. Within the intelligentsia, however, married couples share the burdens, with the wife handling everyday expenditure and the husband deciding on large outlays and where to spend holidays. It is obviously impossible to generalize in an area where sex is less important than strength of personality. Moreover, many young Soviet couples reject the very idea of a head of the family, claiming that their decisions are taken jointly.

Surveys indicate that the wife does 60–70 per cent of the work: the husband – apart from minor everyday repairs – plays a fairly small part in domestic tasks. In Leningrad, a similar survey in 1973 indicated that around 10.5 per cent of working-class women received help from their mothers and 5 per cent from their mothers-in-law. In 28 per cent of Moscow families the husbands take the children to nursery school or school and bring them home, which indicates, according to Soviet sociologists, a low level of responsibility with regard to education.

Some observers have noted that intellectuals play a much smaller part than workers in domestic tasks: though working-class women are overwhelmed with work they do also receive more help. Shiftwork in industry is convenient for families with young children, since the parents can take turns at home and prepare meals alternately according to their hours of work. When a child is old enough to work, its salary replaces that of the mother, who then stays at home.

Free time after work. From the above division of labour it is clear that the housewife's timetable is markedly different from that of her husband. Before marriage she had forty-two hours of free time per week, but with children and domestic responsibilities her free time is reduced by half. Consequently, greater equality in the professional sphere has yet to trickle down into domestic life.

TABLE 27 Typology of the Soviet family[1]

CRITERION	High standard of living	Modest standard of living	High standard of living	Modest standard of living
Per capita income	120 R	Less than 80 R	Between 90 and 120 R	Between 40 and 60 R
Occupation	Manager, technician, officer	Researchers, students	Blue- and white-collar workers with intermediate qualifications	Unskilled workers
No. of years married	5 years	Newly married	10 years	11 years
No. of children	12.5% have two	45% have two	60% have a single child	38% two, 62% one
Type of accommodation	94% live in separate apartments	Cramped	Separate	60% in separate accommodation / 40% in shared accommodation
Household goods	Wide range of appliances	Few appliances	Overequipped	Refrigerator 60% / Vacuum cleaner 8% / Washing machine 10%
	Families with a developed lifestyle		*Families with a restricted lifestyle*	
Marital relations	Cooperation and equality between spouses		Husband takes decisions, but gives little help in the home; wife does all housework	
Use of leisure time	78% go to the theatre, concerts, own a library[2]		Little reading, rare visits to theatre; visits to relatives	
Degree of social involvement	92% participate in social activities		Few social interests outside a narrow circle of relatives	
Education	Higher or secondary		Secondary or primary	

Notes: 1 Survey sample: 470 Muscovite families.
2 In the Soviet definition of this term, 100 volumes constitutes a library.

The working week was reduced to an average of 58.5 hours in 1913, 47.8 hours in 1955 and 40.7 hours in 1970 (it has been reduced to 37.6 hours in the coal industry and 30 hours for some unhealthy jobs). In addition, a decree dated 14 March 1967 instituted the five-day working week as far as possible in every occupation (with the exception of railway-workers, sailors, etc.), though weekly hours of work remained the same. This means an average of 8 hours 12 minutes work per day. Actual time worked exceeds legal hours at the end of the month, when overtime is necessary to fulfil the plan, or in sectors such as agriculture, where there are wide seasonal variations in hours of work. The total number of days worked corresponds to 266 days in industry and less than 200 days in agriculture, though the collective-farm worker works more than the industrial worker when we take the burden of the family farm into account.

Nowadays, free Saturdays are usually devoted to domestic work — washing and housework. Sunday is usually taken up by visits to the dacha, gardening, forest walks to gather berries and mushrooms, or fishing.

To time actually spent at work must be added unpaid time spent on transport, in the cloakroom, in showers, etc. (1.4 hours for an industrial worker, 0.6–0.9 hours for an agricultural worker, rather less than 1.2 hours and 0.8 hours respectively for women). The amount of time spent in work-related activities varies according to the size of the city (Moscow 1.45 hours, Novosibirsk 0.53 hours). Overall, if we compare the Soviet worker's timetable in 1924 with that in 1959 (worktime + transport) we find that the reduction in legal working hours has been cancelled out by longer travelling times (7.38 + 1.17 in 1924 and 7.13 + 2.30 in 1959).

In the 1920s, Strumilin, in particular, examined the way people used their free time after work.[9] Conditions for men and women only become equal when society is able to release the housewife from some of her obligations through the development of community services; another condition is the husband's readiness to co-operate more in household tasks. This presupposes a fairly long period of time, as in the case of all changes in habits of thought. In short, for both objective and subjective reasons, equality in leisure time — that is time available after domestic work — is still far from being a reality in the Soviet Union, as recent surveys have shown (see Table 28).

In summer, the countrywoman has around 7.87 hours free time per week and her husband 20.37. In the winter, the collective-farm worker's wife enjoys 21.55 hours free time and her husband 39.19. The situation is just as unequal in industrial working-class families, where the husband has 32.4–34.8 hours free time per week and his wife only 17.8–21.5 hours.

Among the housewife's different domestic tasks, preparation of meals and shopping take up 10–12 hours and 6 hours per week respectively. It has been estimated that the nation as a whole wasted 30 milliard hours per year in shops in 1970, either because shops are too far from the home, or because it is

TABLE 28   *How working-class and collective-farm families spend their time (average, expressed in hours per day in any given week)*

	Workers 1963		Collective-farm workers 1963		Moscow 1964		France¹ 1963–64			Workers 1967		Collective-farm workers 1967	
	Men²	Women²	Men²	Women²	Men²	Women²	Men	Female working	Female non-working	Weekdays	Days off and public holidays	Weekdays	Days off and public holidays
Work													
Paid	5.8	5.8	7.6	5.5			7.5	6.2	0.2	5.14	0.02	6.28	3.29
In connection with paid work	1.4	1.2	0.9	0.8	1.45	1.86				1.04	0.03	0.58	0.31
Domestic work	2.1	4.5	3.0	6.6	2.03	4.46	1.2	3.2	5.6	5.27	6.13	6.19	7.30
Free time													
Care and education of children	0.3	0.5	0.1	0.5			0.8	1.3	2.9				
Physiological needs (sleep, meals)	9.6	9.0	9.0	8.4	7.20	7.10	10.8	10.7	11.3	9.05	10.43	8.17	8.46
Leisure	4.5	2.7	3.0	2.0	4.18	2.38	7.4	6.6	9.2	2.54	6.29	1.25	2.53
Miscellaneous	0.3	0.3	0.4	0.2						0.16	0.30	0.33	0.51

Notes: 1 Data for France taken from surveys conducted in Arras, Besançon, Chalon-sur-Saône, Dunkirk, Epinal and Metz.
2 Mean established for all days in the week (including days off and public holidays).

necessary to queue, since shops are too few in number or badly supplied. Some 95 per cent of families eat their meals at home. The canteen is only used occasionally: 36 per cent of households interviewed in Leningrad in 1964 ate only occasionally in the canteen, and only 1.8 per cent ate there on a permanent basis. Hence the meal retains its traditional place in family relationships.

Laundering too remains a household task. It takes up an average of six hours per week (in Leningrad 24 per cent of families make use of laundry services). All these household occupations — which take up an extra hour during holidays — mean that women have much less time to devote to themselves than have their husbands. Women sleep less: when on night shift they sometimes get only four hours sleep, as housing conditions rule out a separate bedroom in which they might sleep alone. In 1964, 55.5 per cent of working-class women in Leningrad lived in communal accommodation, and 47.2 per cent had access to only one bedroom.

Housework differs greatly in town and country. In a big city like Moscow there are more services available, and so household tasks take up 20–30 per cent less time than in Novosibirsk. In contrast, a collective-farm worker's wife finds that her family and farm demand an average of forty-six hours per week in June, over and above her work on the kolkhoz. Cow-owners (13.2 million in 1980) are tied to the home at all times, or else must find someone to replace them. Elsewhere, growing vegetables and fruit takes up any spare time available. Here the main obstacle is not really shortage of income: the real reason is each family's urgent need to provide for its own requirements so long as food is in such short supply in the country areas.

Obviously the timetable varies according to the day of the week, per capita income, wife's age and number of children. However, the most important differences in lifestyle are apparent in the organization of leisure time.

Leisure time. Leisure is no longer a class privilege in the Soviet Union, as in every industrial society. Although inequalities may still exist, they are probably less important in the Soviet Union, where the entire working population is salaried. In the Soviet Union, as elsewhere, the weekend has become a time for spending with the family. In addition to the weekly rest days, there are eight legal holidays plus annual holidays. People do not spend their free time in the same way during the week, as at the weekend or during the holidays.

Generalizations about *weekly leisure* are harder than about other activities. The way people use their free time varies greatly and is also influenced by the whims of fashion and changing technology. As late as the 1960s, surveys only very imperfectly reflected the growing influence of television and neglected the impact of the private car. In 1973, some 70 per cent of the population regularly watched television for an average of one and a half hours per day (7–10 hours per week). In the country, television occupied half people's free time, as against 20 per cent in the towns. This passive form of relaxation is tending to supplant reading (only half the working-class families were readers at the time of Gordon and Klopov's survey, while in the larger towns 64–75 per cent of families watched television). A few general trends may be noted however:

1 Over the long term we find that in working-class circles free time devoted to social activity diminished perceptibly (by 92 hours per year) between 1924 and 1959, while amusements took up 330 extra hours. Time devoted to study increased by only 7 hours, and time devoted to sport by 56 hours per year. These developments reflect the transition from a society where attendance at public meetings and, above all, religious services was commonplace to a family life in which leisure activities have tended, with the advent of radio and television, to withdraw into the home and where religion and political activism play a diminishing role.

2 A feature of this growing amount of domestic leisure time is the time given over to reading books (4.35 hours per week on average for both men and women before marriage, 1 hour to 1 hour 50 minutes when the couple has young children). Men spend up to 2 hours 40 minutes reading newspapers per week, while married men watch television for 9–10 hours and women for 4–5 hours per week. The Soviet family acts as a miniature cultural club, where information is passed on, ideas exchanged and amusements enjoyed. We shall see later (Chapter 6) the role of the father and mother in their children's education, a role whose importance increases with the parents' level of education.

3 Some forms of recreation, such as the theatre, reading, television, walking and sport, are today enjoyed by all occupational categories in the large towns. Members of some sedentary occupations prefer sport. Manual workers seek relaxation in their leisure time, for example in fishing or entertainment. Television is the favourite pastime of country people: this tends to encourage passiveness and means that they lag behind city dwellers in cultural matters. The most educated classes devote more time to pastimes that develop the personality: study, creative activity and social relationships.

4 The widespread notion that Soviet citizens devote a lot of time to study is borne out by surveys of family life. Some 38 per cent of unmarried girls and 43 per cent of boys pursue their studies while working. Once they marry the percentages drop to 13 per cent and 35 per cent respectively, then when a child is born, to 4 per cent of women and 12 per cent of men. Within the family overall, 20 per cent of men and 15–17 per cent of women devote some time each week to study.

5 The frequency of study, book-reading and visits to museums in the Soviet Union contrasts with the minor importance of these leisure activities in the lives of French people: only half the French read books, 2–5 per cent visit museums (22 per cent in the Soviet Union) and 13 per cent of French working men go to the café every day. Soviet citizens spend less time in cafés, not because they are less fond of drinking (see in Chapter 11 the section on social

anomie) but because the social climate is unfavourable. In comparison with French citizens, who today more often than not own a private car, the Soviet citizen has less opportunity to escape at weekends and for his annual holidays, for the present at least. Cars are particularly prized in the Soviet Union because they are scarce (see p. 72): a 'Zhuguli' (Lada) cost 8800 rubles in 1980, i.e. the equivalent of over 4 years' salary.

Holidays in Yalta and Sochi used to be reserved for the aristocracy under the old regime. Today 60 per cent of Soviet citizens go on holiday. Holidays are nowadays an established habit and an occasion for spending (around 8 per cent of a family's annual income). The average length of holiday, for all occupations combined, is 20.9 working days (12 days in the collective farms, 33.7 days in teaching). However, 44 per cent of Soviet citizens are only allowed 15 working days and around 35 per cent one month or more (among the latter are managers in industry, with an average of 24.3 working days against 19.7 days for a worker).

Two-thirds of Soviet citizens, like the French, prefer the summer months for their holidays. Factories do not, however, as in France in August, shut down for the summer except for a few that take the opportunity of doing their stocktaking or repairs (*remont*). There is a second season, in winter, in particular for those whose occupations prevent them from taking their holidays in summer (farmers, sailors, fishermen and geologists). Among the intelligentsia it is the growing custom to take two holidays so as to be able to go away in winter as well.

Where people spend their holidays depends on the availability of accommodation, income and personal preferences. At the top of the hierarchy of facilities extended to the family come holiday vouchers, which cover the cost of transport and reduced-rate accommodation in a union-run rest house (*putyovka*). However, fewer than one holiday-maker out of five has the opportunity of an organized stay, whether in a rest house (where standards of comfort are higher, but discipline more strict) or in a holiday camp or boarding house (the rules are more relaxed but meals are not provided). In 1973, almost a third of Moscow families benefited from a *putyovka* or, in the case of their children, a stay in a pioneer camp. Some 10 per cent of rest-house guests are admitted free of charge (20 per cent in the sanatoriums). Those admitted as paying guests pay 30 per cent of expenses, that is around 36 rubles for 24 days (care and full board).

Soviet citizens who pay for their own holidays can either go in a party with an organized itinerary (*marshruty*), or they can rent accommodation (a dacha or in a private home); rates depend on how fashionable the area is. This solution is often chosen by those who wish to spend their holidays as a family, since not all rest houses are currently equipped to receive both parents and children. However, it is not unusual in the Soviet Union for couples to take their holidays separately.

In the Soviet Union, as in many other countries, where one spends one's holiday is an indication of social standing, although to go on holiday today is no longer a social privilege but a mass phenomenon. The intelligentsia has a predilection for the Black Sea and Baltic coasts and the shores of Lake Baikal, although there is also a fashion for exploring historic sites and visiting old churches and monasteries. A suntan is in any case aesthetically acceptable. Young people between 18 and 39 spend their holidays at the seaside or climbing in the Caucasus mountains. Older people like to return to the forests (47 per cent) or lakes and rivers (30 per cent) where they spent their childhoods. This mass exodus in summer is a way of compensating for urban life, to which many still have difficulty adjusting. It is an opportunity to return to the country, visit relatives and friends and go hunting with them.

The doubling of the summer migration during the 1980s, as forecast by sociologists, may well pose problems due to lack of hotel accommodation and to the latter's slow rate of expansion. In the Soviet Union, potential demand has no influence on where investment is directed, and no real leisure industry has emerged yet, as it has in the countries of the west.

One development is already clear, however: free time, as a factor in self-development and personal satisfaction, is much more important to the younger generation than it used to be. This attitude is largely responsible for the drop in the birthrate in all sections of society. The departure of young people from the countryside is encouraged by propagation of the urban lifestyle in the villages. These new city dwellers hope to find more acceptable working hours and services that do not yet exist in their isolated villages.

In the long term, town planners expect to see a gradual reduction in hours of work from 8 hours to 4 hours per day, and a considerable increase in free time – from 3 to 8 hours per day. These forecasts have led sociologists to recommend that leisure time be planned, doubtless forgetting that for Marx the value of free time was precisely the absence of coercion. This development towards increased leisure time is inherent in our lifestyles, partly because for the great majority of people work is a necessity imposed upon them, and not a creative activity, but also because the speed at which techniques evolve requires the individual to adapt continually, which means more time spent on keeping abreast of affairs and on personal development in particular.

Before examining the part currently played by the family in the educational function of socialization, which in all societies remains one of its traditional roles, we might wind up this first look at the family with three remarks:

1 The much vaunted equality between men and women cannot be measured only by the latter's legal and professional status or by the number of women engineers and doctors. Also important are the number of water taps in the countryside, the number of washing-machines and separate flats with bathrooms and the number of retail outlets near the place of residence. Socialization of the means of production does not in itself create equality for women.

2 Nor can equality be created by extension of services and town planning. Though women have won the right to have children when they wish — despite official encouragement to do so more often — and to work in the professions of their choice, they have not given up what in their eyes constitutes an honour, namely being mistress in their own home. Similarly, men cling to an image of women that absolves themselves of domestic responsibilities. Although there is no necessary conflict between the ideal of the woman at home, giving her full attention to her children's education, and the idea of the woman committed to her job, nevertheless 20 per cent of women admit that they have difficulty reconciling their own roles. Some 52 per cent stated that their situation was 'tolerable': this word seems to be a euphemism concealing the total exhaustion that is the daily lot of the majority of the world's women. Despite this, and because of their natural need to assert themselves, few of the women working in a profession of their choice would ever dream of sacrificing their careers to confine themselves to their maternal functions.

The authorities themselves seem to be torn between a policy in favour of a higher birthrate, according to which the woman at home is paid to perform a recognized social function, and the need for labour. They count on reconciling these conflicting demands by longer maternity leave and more flexible arrangements for working mothers.

3 In the Soviet Union, as elsewhere, the demands of industrial society have wrought great changes in the family unit; the many divorces testify to the precariousness of the family. The family has relinquished its economic role as a productive unit and is left with only its role as consumer. Though it still, as in the past, serves to reproduce workers, it has transferred to the state educational and welfare system much of its responsibility to hand down values and to provide assistance. In an anonymous world, splintered by the division of labour, the family today remains the only unit capable of providing an outlet for the need for interpersonal communication and emotional expression. Without its support, the individual finds it more difficult to learn to exercise responsibility and solidarity in a wider context. In order to fulfil this psychological and cultural role, which is so vital today, the family unit can no longer withdraw into itself: it is still wide open to society, stimulating it and breathing life into it. In its turn society impresses its own image upon the family.

NOTES

1 A. Kollontai, *Sotsial'nye osnovy zhenskogo voprosa* [*Social Foundations of the Woman Question*], St Petersburg, 1909.

2 'Slaking one's thirst is an individual act; in love, on the other hand, there are two individuals about to give birth to a third, a new being. This concerns society and entails duties towards the community' (Lenin to Tsetkin, in Clara Tsetkin, *Reminiscences of Lenin*, New York, 1934, p. 48).

3 B. Kerblay, 'Chayanov and the theory of peasantry as a specific type of economy', in

T. Shanin (ed.), *Peasants and Peasant Society*, Harmondsworth, Penguin, 1971, pp. 150–60.
4 *Chelovek i obshchestvo*, vol. VI, 1969, p. 137.
5 *Kul'tura i byt gornyakov i metallurgov Nizhego Tagila 1917–1970*, Moscow, 1974, p. 161.
6 A. Amalrik, *Voyage involontaire en Sibérie*, Paris, Gallimard, 1970, p. 215.
7 177.3 rubles per month in 1982.
8 In 1973, there were 53 telephone subscribers per 1000 people in the Soviet Union compared with 199 per 1000 in France.
9 S. Strumilin, *Problemy ekonomiki Truda*, Moscow, 1957, p. 288.

SUGGESTED READING

History

Cuisenier, J. and Raguin, C., 'De quelques transformations dans le système familial russe', *Revue française de sociologie*, no. 8, 1964.
Geiger, K., *The Family in Soviet Russia*, Cambridge, Mass., Harvard University Press, 1968.
Atkinson, D., Dallin, A. and Lapidus, G. W. (eds), *Women in Russia*, Hassocks, Harvester, 1978.

Women

Berton-Hogge, R., 'La condition féminine en U.R.S.S.', *Problèmes politiques et sociaux*, nos 31–2, 1970.
Brown, D., *The Role and Status of Women in the Soviet Union*, New York, 1968.
Dodge, N., *Women in the Soviet Economy*, Baltimore, Johns Hopkins Press, 1968.
Fisher, W. A., *The Soviet Marriage Market*, New York, Praeger, 1979.
Gasiorowska, X., *Women in Soviet Fiction, 1917–1964*, Madison, 1960.
Lapidus, G. W., *Women in Soviet Society*, Berkeley, University of California Press, 1978.
Lublin, N., 'Women in Soviet central Asia', *Soviet Studies*, vol. 33, April 1981.
Porohnyuk, E. and Sepeleva, M., 'O sovmeshchenii proizvodstvennykh i semeynykh funktsiy zhenshchin rabotnits', *Sotsiologicheskie issledovaniya*, no. 4, 1975, pp. 102–8.
Sacks, M., *Women's Work in Soviet Russia*, New York, Praeger, 1976.
Slesarev, G. and Jankova, Z., 'Zhenshchina na promyshlennom predpriyatii i v sem'e', in *Sotsial'nye problemy truda i proizvodstva* Moscow, 1969, pp. 416–38.

Formation and break-up of the family

Belova, V. and Darsky, L., 'L'opinion des femmes sur la formation de la famille', *Annuaire de l'U.R.S.S., 1969*, Paris, 1970.
Berton-Hogge, R., 'La crise de la famille soviétique', *Problèmes politiques et sociaux*, no. 392, July 1980.
Cuyko, L., 'Molodozheny, sotsial'nyi portret', *Lit. Gaz.*, no. 9, March 1972 (*L'Expansion*, April 1973).

'Fondements de la législation soviétique sur le mariage et la famille', *Problèmes politiques et sociaux*, no. 4, July 1968 (série U.R.S.S.), pp. 27–36.

Kharchev, A., *Brak i sem'ya v S.S.R.*, Moscow, 1964.

Jankova, Z., *Gorodskaya sem'ya*, Moscow, Nauka, 1979.

Perevedentsev, V., 'Sem'ya vchera, sevodnya, zavtra', *Nash sovremennik*, no. 6, 1975, pp. 118–31.

Vasil'eva, E., *Sem'ya i eyo funktsii*, Statistika, 1975.

Yvert-Jalu, M. H., 'Le divorce en U.R.S.S.', in Michel, A. (ed.), *Femmes, Sexisme et Sociétés*, P.U.F., 1976, pp. 179–98.

Way of life

'Aspects de la consommation en Union Soviétique', *Problèmes politiques et sociaux* (documentation française), no. 404, Dec. 1980.

Aspects économiques de la vie en U.R.S.S., Colloque de l'OTAN, Brussels, 1975.

Baranskaya, N., 'Cette semaine comme une autre', *Novy Mir*, no. 11, 1969, transl. by H. Sinany, Lausanne, L'Age d'Homme, 1973.

Grossman, G., 'The illegal private economy', in *Soviet Economy in a Time of Change*, Joint Economic Committee, Congress of the U.S., October 1979.

Krupyanskaya, V., Budina, O., Polishchuk, N. and Yukhneva, N., *Kultura i byt gornyakov i metallurgov Nizhnego Tagila 1917–1970*, Nauka, 1974.

McAuley, A., *Economic Welfare in the Soviet Union*, Madison, University of Wisconsin Press, 1979.

Problemy byta, braka i sem'i, Vil'nius, 1970.

Smith, H., *The Russians*, London, Sphere Books, 1976.

Trivous, J., 'Enquête sur l'évolution du budget des familles ouvrières en U.R.S.S. (1951–59)', *Cahiers du monde russe et soviétique*, Oct. 1961, pp. 487–503.

Leisure time

Dumazedier, J. and Lagneau, J., 'Société soviétique, temps libre et loisirs', *Revue française de sociologie*, no. 11, 1970.

Gordon, L. and Klopov, E., *Chelovek posle raboty*, Moscow, Nauka, 2 vols, 1972, transl. into French as 'L'Homme après le travail' ('Man after working hours'), Moscow, Progrès, 1977.

Kolpakov, V. and Patrushev, V., *Byudzhet vremeni gorodskogo naseleniya*, Statistika, 1971.

Panetrat, P., 'Les budgets temps des ouvriers soviétiques, *Cahiers ISMEA*, série G 37, *Economies et sociétés*, vol. XIII, July–Oct. 1979.

Chapter 6

The educational system

The socialization of the child is one of the fundamental functions of a social system. It refers to the entire educational process by which the child evolves from simple biological to adult consciousness, through the acquisition of language, knowledge, behavioural standards and the values by which it will fulfil its role in society. Education is crucially important, moreover, in a country whose leadership proposes to transform society, promising equality of opportunity for the greatest number. Family, school, mass media, town planning even, all are pressed into the service of the 'cultural revolution'.

HISTORICAL BACKGROUND

From the start of the new regime, Russian educationalists concentrated their efforts on three areas in which the educational system was backward: (1) adult literacy; (2) compulsory, universal primary education; and (3) the democratization of secondary and higher education.

The ground had been prepared by a long tradition of reflecting on educational methods. N. Novikov, K. Ushinsky, Pirogov and Leo Tolstoy under the old regime and Lunacharsky, Lenin, Krupskaya, A. Makarenko and V. Sukhomlinsky in the postrevolutionary era are evidence of the interest that the Russians have always shown in education, an interest which still finds expression today in regular features in the press. Few other societies, China and Japan excepted, have attached as much importance to culture.

Adult literacy

At the time of the 1897 census, 21 per cent of the population of the Russian empire was able to read and write; the level had risen to 28 per cent by the outbreak of the first world war, but the illiteracy figure was still over 70 per cent. If we analyse these figures in terms of age groups, excluding very young children below school age and the elderly, we find that young people were already well on the way to achieving literacy before the Revolution: in 1915, 51 per cent of children aged from 8 to 11 years had attended primary school and in 1912 68 per cent of conscripts knew how to read and write. On the other hand, literacy among women aged between 10 and 49 did not exceed one-third of the age group, decreasing to less than 10 per cent for the higher age ranges; this state of affairs had repercussions on the entire cultural environment of the family. The situation was better in the towns than in the country if the workers in the cotton industry are anything to go by, as over 50 per cent of the under-25s in this group were literate in 1918. Among the ethnic groups of Siberia or central Asia, the literacy rate was less than 5 per cent at the beginning of this century.

One of the priority tasks was adult literacy. A mass campaign was launched in 1931–2, affecting some 6–10 million people and addressed chiefly to people aged between 18 and 35 years. The general literacy rate rose from 51 per cent in 1926 to 81 per cent in 1939, when 6.9 million people were still recorded as attending adult-literacy classes. The most remarkable results were obtained amongst the non-Russians, some of whom still had no alphabet: in Uzbekistan and Turkmenistan, the illiteracy rate had fallen from 88–99 per cent to 32–33 per cent by 1939.

TABLE 29   *Soviet literacy*

	population aged 9–49			*Population aged 50 and over*	
	Men	*Women*	*of whom peasant women*	*Men*	*Women*
1897	40.3	16.6	12.7	20.5	6.5
1926	71.5	42.7	35.4	40.6	11.4
1939	93.5	81.6	76.8	48.7	23.1
1959	99.3	97.8	97.5	—[1]	—[1]

Note: 1 Figures not given by the 1959 census.

It was far easier to put young people into school than to instruct the older age groups. The figures in Table 29 show that the literacy rate in 1939 among the over-49s was not very different from the percentages recorded in 1897, 42 years earlier, for people aged 9–49. The 1959 census contains no details about those aged over 49; but, judging by the literacy rate of the least privileged category, rural women, the gap has undoubtedly been filled today.

Compulsory schooling and the democratization of education

The first schools to be opened in Russia in the eighteenth century were reserved for the privileged classes of the nobility. In the nineteenth century, these schools began to admit increasing numbers of commoners. An enquiry into the social origins of students at the St Petersburg Polytechnic, conducted in 1909, showed that the majority were the sons of businessmen (25.5 per cent), the clergy or civilian or military officials (29.6 per cent); if we combine the professions with the nobility, their sons together with students from the land-owning nobility represented 26.4 per cent of the total, as against 11.7 per cent from the petty bourgeoisie (artisans and employees) and 6.5 per cent from the working classes and peasantry.[1]

The democratization of education implies, first of all, compulsory schooling for the children of the people. In theory, this was enacted for the first time by the Duma on 3 May 1908, and confirmed by a decree dated 30 September 1918, instituting a uniform system of free schooling for all children aged eight and over. In fact, this did not become a practical reality (providing four years of compulsory schooling) until 1930-1, when sufficient numbers of schools and above all teachers became available (see Table 30).

TABLE 30 *Increase in schooling in the USSR*

	1914	1928	1940	1959	1975
Primary and secondary schools (millions of pupils)	9.9	12	37.2	36.3	49
of whom students in classes 8–10	0.152	0.170	2.5	2.8	16.3
% of children in these age groups enrolled in school	24.7	31.9	80		
High-school students (millions)	0.127	0.169	0.811	2.15	4.7
No. of students per 1000 inhabitants	8	12	40	102	187

The democratization of education was accompanied by measures to make higher education more accessible to workers and peasants. To this end, the Proletarian University of Moscow was founded in 1918, together with workers' faculties (*rabfaki*, in which enrolments expanded from 38,000 in 1922 to 339,000 in 1932) for the purpose of training workers and peasants from the ranks of the Party to the point where, after three to four years' studies, they would be qualified for admission to university without examination. Until 1927-8, the majority of students were still recruited from amongst the liberal intelligentsia; it was then that restrictions were introduced to limit the number of students from 'socially alien milieux'. Political organizations and the unions played a role in the allocation of university places, as a result of which the number of workers and peasants attending increased to 58 per cent in 1935. But, from 1936 onwards, when the *numerus clausus* restricting the numbers of children of the bourgeoisie admitted to institutes of higher education was lifted, the percentage of workers and peasants fell once again to 36 per cent in 1938. The predominance of students of bourgeois origins was strengthened with the reintroduction in 1940 of fees in the final classes of secondary school and in higher education.

Thus, the hopes that the partisans of Proletkult (among them Lunacharsky, appointed commissar of education in 1917) had entertained regarding the possibility of creating a proletarian culture freed from the shackles of the past, a past that they identified with bourgeois ideology, proved illusory. The spirit and the content of soviet pedagogy (non-denominationalism, emphasis on collective values, Marxism–Leninism) were profoundly modified; nevertheless, certain aspects of the educational system have maintained their links with the past: brown dresses and black aprons for young girls, uniforms for the boys, the role of the schoolmistress (yesterday the *klassnaya dama*, today the *klassnaya rukovoditel'nitsa*), the names of diplomas (*attestat zrelosti*) and, finally, and above all, the central role of the family in the child's socialization.

THE EDUCATIONAL ROLE OF THE FAMILY

Relations between the family and the state

Compulsory schooling was not introduced without resistance. In the traditional family, the father, who knew how to do everything, taught his own children. The learning process began very early on: by the age of 6 or so, boys were already minding the cows or sheep; between 9 and 13, they would be given horses to look after; at 15–16 years of age the adolescent was admitted to the *skhod*, the assembly of heads of family, like an adult. Daughters busied themselves at their mother's side from the age of 7–8 onwards. When the first primary public schools (*nachalnye narodnye shkoly*) were founded in around 1864, under the control of the Zemstva, to supplement the parish schools (*prikhodskie shkoly*), the peasants reacted with suspicion: 'What could one teach in school that the children do not already know, if not principles foreign to the rural community?' The same resistance was encountered in the 1920s and 1930s when compulsory schooling was introduced in the republics of central Asia, where Muslim tradition perpetuated the segregation of the sexes and early marriage for girls. Everywhere, families had to be taught the rudiments of hygiene – it was necessary to insist that each child be provided with a bed of his own – to combat the influence of faith-healers.

To keep the child away from the one-sided, conservative influence of the family, the new regime immediately began experimenting with children's communes along lines reminiscent to us of the Israeli *kibbutzim*. Makarenko's educational work with delinquents was based on this experience. Despite the keen interest shown in this new departure by the Soviet intelligentsia, it proved short-lived.

Nevertheless, the prewar generation continued to favour the idea of placing very young children in boarding schools in order to relieve women of some of the burden of domestic work and to enhance the educational role of the community, developing in the child a greater measure of emotional independence by placing him amongst educators who were assumed to be more neutral than parents. In his proposed city of the future (1960), Strumilin suggested the setting up of communes consisting of all the families living in a given building. The building would contain all the necessary communal eating facilities, while schools would be very close at hand. These proposals, which stepped well beyond the bounds of educational theory, were not well received. Similarly, Khrushchev's plans to increase the number of children educated in boarding schools to 2.5 million by 1965 were unfulfilled, for Russians associate this type of education with the orphanage, and therefore dislike it. Roughly 1.6 million children were enrolled in boarding schools at the end of the 1960s. Half of the Leningrad mothers interviewed about the kind of community services they thought might ease their daily burden replied that their presence was an irreplaceable part of child care.

Observation of children brought up in groups, outside the family, has shown that excessive community life often breeds frustration and that excessive emphasis on 'us' may lead to antisocial attitudes. These considerations, coupled with the probable cost of total collectivization of education, has led the authorities to acknowledge the family's paramount rights in this respect, especially regarding the very young child. Later, as the child grows older, parents are prepared to recognize that specialized institutions offer their offspring a better preparation for life than they themselves could give them. But if the two models, parental and community, are too different, then the contending influences can make it very difficult for adolescents to fit in.

Parent-child relationships

The influence of the family upon the child during the process of socialization spans three phases, corresponding to the different stages of its psychological and physical development.

Early childhood. In the first stage in the child's life, from birth to six years old, or until the child enters primary school at the age of seven, the family's influence is, if not exclusive, at least preponderant. Mothers are given maternity leave of 112 working days, two months prior to birth and two months after. For a difficult delivery or the birth of twins, maternity leave is prolonged by one month; an allowance of 20 rubles is paid at the birth of the third child, and up to 250 rubles for the eleventh. In addition to this maternity leave, women may also take part-paid leave until the child reaches one year of age (35–50 rubles per month depending upon the mother's residence) and a further year's unpaid leave. At that age, the mother must decide whether to go on looking after her child herself or, if there is no grandmother (*babushka*) to help her, to place her child in a day-care nursery. Children are admitted to these from the age of three months onwards, but only 5 per cent of children aged under one are looked after in this way; in other words, most arrive at the crèche having already acquired a great many habits and stereotypes.

Not all parents send their children to the crèches, either because there are not enough places in them, or because, in the absence of a *babushka*, they prefer to have some individual look after their infant, as not all crèches enjoy a good reputation. When the crèche is situated near the mother's place of work, she is legally entitled to 30 minutes' absence for every three and a half hours worked in order to visit her child. Some people would prefer to see the crèches installed on a floor specially reserved for children in each large building, so as to avoid wasting time in journeys back and forth.

Since 1959, there has been a tendency to combine crèches and kindergartens in a single establishment, under the supervision of the national ministry of education (whereas isolated crèches are run by the health ministry). According to statistics, these two categories embrace a total of 10 million children, or roughly a third of the age group concerned, which represents a very high attendance rate compared with other countries. In France, in 1972, there were 40,500 places in crèches for 350,000 working mothers with children aged under 3, compared with 60,000 places in Sweden, for 325,000 children in the same age group. In the Soviet Union, the crèches can offer places for 1.2 million small children out of a total of 4 million children aged under 1 in 1970, i.e. 29 per cent. There were kindergarten places for 27 per cent of children aged between 1 and 6 in 1970; more recent unofficial estimates put the figure at 50 per cent in towns and 30 per cent in the countryside.

Family income is not a determining factor in the placing of children. The cost of having a child looked after at home comes to around 50 rubles per month. In the crèches, parents are charged between 4 and 10 rubles per month for 12 hours per day (3—9 rubles in the countryside), depending on the parents' income. Families earning less than 60 rubles per head per month have been exempted from crèche and nursery-school fees since 1981. It has been observed that families with high per capita incomes (over 50 rubles) are more willing to send their children to preschool establishments; here, the income level is not the cause but rather the consequence of two salaries entering the home, making it necessary to have the child cared for outside, whereas in the lower-income groups, where the proportion of children placed in crèches is lower, there is only one income-earner, as the mother stays at home. It is generally thought that, as living standards rise, many families prefer to keep their child at home, as conditions are better than at the crèches. The Soviet press has reported understaffing and consequent overcrowding: one employee to feed and change 20 babies, and 1 paediatrician for 250 beds.

Some demographers doubt the wisdom of investing in an extended network of existing establishments; they recommend transferring this money to the mothers themselves, to enable them to look after their children up to the age of three at home. Not all working women view this proposal with favour, however: some fear disqualification as a result of prolonged absence from work, but the great majority claim that they send their child to the crèche because there is no one to look after it at home (*Lit. Gaz*, 10 Sept. 1975, p. 12).

Paediatricians and psychologists agree that this is a decisive period for the development of the child's sensibility, its acquisition of language and the awakening of musical aptitudes. At this age, words are less important than the subtle intonations of the mother and close relatives. The Russians are accustomed to close physical contact with children. Breast-feeding is recommended, and parents carry their children around in their arms as much as possible, even when cooking. They show exaggerated concern to protect the child from all bodily harm. Yet at the same time children quickly learn to consider outside adults as uncles and aunts (*dyadya, tyotya*), which helps to soothe the child when left with other people.

On entering nursery school, children come into contact with another kind of language: that of their mistress and peers. They learn to live among equals with schoolmates, whereas with parents the only kind of relationship is hierarchical. Imitation plays an important part in this introduction to community life, and the mistress encourages children to take an interest in what their comrades are doing, throwing a ball into the same basket or practising somersaults. This early familiarization with the outside world is conducive to greater equality of opportunity among children, by rectifying inadequate supervision in some cases, or excessive attention in others. The kindergarten is optional, and compulsory education only begins at the age of 7.

Childhood. From the age of 7 to 14, parents hand over many of their prerogatives to the school. According to surveys carried out by Gordon and Klopov ('Man after working hours', p. 131), a father or a mother can only devote four hours *per week* on average to their child's education, whereas the same child spends between four and six hours *per day* in the classroom, and more still if he belongs to a group undergoing supervised education. Where there is a grandparent in the home (15–20 per cent of households in towns and cities), he or she assumes these responsibilities. As in most families both parents are at work, it would be a mistake to underestimate the role of the street and the peer group.

In the countryside, it is with its parents that the child learns very early on to tend the garden or wield an axe, but most abstract knowledge is learned in school which, as in the towns, shares the burden of the child's moral education with the youth organizations that boys and girls join as soon as they start school: the octobrists (*oktyabryata*) from 7 to 9 years of age and later the pioneers from 10 to 14. This Soviet-style scouting teaches the child to fit in with his or her age group and to engage in social activities − recreation, ecology and patriotic work. If need be, the child will assume the duties of *starosta* or *kommandir*. These two bodies, which are legally under the ideological control of the Komsomol, are in fact run by the school authorities.

The moral code places the highest value on the positive virtues such as fatherland, Lenin, socialism, work, study, solidarity: all virtues encouraging the sacrifice of personal desires to the interests of the group, respect for the Party, devotion to the welfare of the people and defence of the oppressed peoples of the world. Negative values are personified by imperialism, capitalists and the exploiters and speculators of the old regime. Children learn to obey their elders, and punishments are modelled on those meted out in the enterprise: reprimands, warnings and deprivation of an advantage. At home, mothers express their disapproval by cold-shouldering their children, giving them a sense of withdrawal of affection, which is far more effective than direct pressure.

Adolescence. Between the ages of 15 and 20, family influence dwindles, as the adolescent tends to take a more detached view of received values, not necessarily rejecting them, but in order to internalize them, make his or her own selection of values and test them in the light of the individual's own experience. He often becomes quite critical of his family.

This is a crucial age, coinciding with the young person's first experience of love and work, an age when communication with parents becomes more difficult and strained. This stems from the inevitable frustration at the gap between desire and reality, at differences in the lifestyles and ideals of one generation and another, which tend to be exacerbated by the lengthening of schooling. The generation gap is particularly noticeable in rural areas, especially after military service. Girls no longer spend their evenings at home preparing their trousseau while they wait for a fiancé; they prefer city manners and dream of leaving their village at the first opportunity. Their mothers take a very dim view of such yearnings.

Relations used to be very different when the son inherited his father's occupation and a long string of brothers and sisters in the family helped to attenuate the age gap. In a family of no more than one or two children, the adolescent has no other recourse but to turn to his own age group. In the city, for instance, a survey of children in classes 7−10 showed that young Soviet people prefer to confide in their friends or classmates of their own age, and spend their free time with them rather than with their parents. They tend to confide more in their mothers, but get more understanding from their fathers when contact can be established. Soviet sociologists would like to see rather more paternal influence in order to produce emotional stability in children who are overprotected by their mothers. This predominance of the mother in education, which is reinforced by the fact that the great majority of the teaching profession is female, is a feature of the Soviet system.

In unstable families, or where children are 'over-mothered', which happens frequently in Russia, the school and youth organizations prove powerless to counteract family crises and disorders.

Such opposition as formerly existed between the values of the family and those of the state school have now disappeared. Co-operation between parents and school has been institutionalized by parent-teacher meetings (*roditel'skie sobraniya*), although the climate of these meetings is sometimes more like that of a magistrate's court, with the parents appearing to answer for their children's behaviour and studies, or even being obliged to discuss family problems in public. For the Soviet school assumes goals that go well beyond mere education of the individual. While the family plays a decisive role in the awakening of aptitudes, the school has the last word in the direction the child's career takes and is the key to social mobility: hence its immense prestige.

THE ROLE OF THE SCHOOL

The aims of education and the evolution of Soviet policy

Like all educational systems, the Soviet school exists to transmit knowledge and select the ablest students. However, owing to the cultural backwardness of certain particularly deprived sections of the population under the old regime, the school was also seen as an instrument contributing to greater social equality and integration. We have already noted, in this respect, the influence of the Russian language on the emergence of a common culture among the different nationalities.

Unlike state-run schools in the west, which claim neutrality as regards ideologies, the Soviet school system is an instrument for indoctrination, for the purpose of shaping the collective consciousness to fit official ideology. Article 2 of the secondary-school statutes states that the school should ally the Marxist-Leninist conception of the world with an elevated sense of patriotism and respect for the best traditions of the past. In addition, it is entrusted with the task of supplying the economy with the requisite skilled labour, thereby making the educational system an integral part of economic planning. The close links between school and production lie at the heart of Marxist doctrine. The growing need for specialists has conditioned the constant modification of school curricula and streams in the Soviet Union.

The length of compulsory schooling has grown steadily from 4 years in the 1930s to 7 from 1949 onwards, and subsequently to 8 in 1959. The aim is to provide full secondary education (10 years) for all children, thereby instituting compulsory general education (decisions of the central committee of the Party and the council of ministers of the Soviet Union, *Pravda*, 25 June 1972). In fact, the average length of schooling among the active population increased from 6.8 years in 1959 to 8.1 years in 1970.

To facilitate the generalization of secondary education, evening classes have been opened for working-class and rural youth deprived of a normal schooling. In the 1930s, the aims were rather more modest: there was an urgent need to train rapidly an army of skilled industrial workers in the technical colleges (1930–1) and short-course training centres (factory apprenticeship workshops – FZO – and 'Labour Reserve' schools in 1940, when youth was brought in to replace workers mobilized for war). These priorities account for the re-introduction of school fees in classes 8, 9 and 10 of secondary schools and in the universities in June 1940. The average annual salary in 1940 was 4054 rubles, and the fees introduced in that year were 150–200 rubles per annum in the secondary schools and 300–400 rubles in higher education. The number of full-time admissions to higher educational institutes in 1940–1 fell by a third. In 1944, gold and silver medals were re-introduced for students coming top of the class.

Until 1954, and for demographic rather than purely academic reasons, the number of students graduating at the end of ten years' compulsory schooling never exceeded the quota admitted to higher education. As in many countries, secondary education was designed to prepare future managers and technicians. Between 1946 and 1953, however, the number of secondary-school graduates quadrupled, whereas the universities were gradually restricting their intake. Increasingly stringent selection favoured the children of the intelligentsia, who were better prepared for university entrance. In 1958, Khrushchev waxed indignant on learning that between 30 and 40 per cent of Moscow University students were of working-class or peasant origin. From this we may deduce that 60 per cent came from the intelligentsia, a social stratum representing only 20 per cent of the population at that time.

The aims of the school and university reforms decreed after Stalin's death were: (1) to revamp the secondary school in recognition of the fact that it was now a mass institution and no longer the stepping stone to university, and (2) to prevent the selection process from restoring the privileges of any given social category. In 1958, Khrushchev tried to introduce compulsory vocational training in the secondary schools in classes 8–10, either in the form of school workshops or by means of part-time courses in the factory. But this initiative raised more problems than it answered, since the range of specialities offered did not always match the pupils' own preferences, and factory managers were unenthusiastic about this influx of schoolchildren to complicate their jobs. In 1966, these obligations were reduced to two hours' practical work, and only a third of all secondary schools still continue to provide training in the form of factory courses.

To facilitate admission to university for students with two years' prior factory or farm experience, Khrushchev introduced a special entrance scheme in 1958, giving priority to candidates recommended by their employer. By 1964, these students with production experience (*proizvodstvenniki*) represented 62 per cent of students in higher education, and as much as 80 per cent in certain institutes. In this way, Khrushchev sought to re-introduce a greater degree of social mobility. He may well have been influenced by the Hungarian revolt in 1956, for a period of factory training makes it easier to select more mature, or more reliable, students, with the aid of the trade unions. The thirteenth congress of Komsomols, held in Moscow on 18 April 1968, formally recommended that political criteria be taken into consideration in the selection of applicants to higher education.

Leaving aside the abolition of school fees in 1956, these innovations, like their predecessors, were to prove ephemeral. After Khrushchev's departure, the contingent of students sent by their employers dwindled to only 30 per cent (1967), as it was found that the results of these grant-aided part-time or correspondence students were inferior to those of full-time students.

In other words, while not altogether doing away with the opportunities offered to young workers, 1965 saw a return to a competition-based selective system which, instead of giving them priority, reserved for them a certain quota in proportion to the number of candidates in each section (if, for example, there are 500 places to be competed for and 3000 secondary-school graduates and 2000 workers apply for them, then the places will be split 300 : 200). While in 1964—5, the majority of students were enrolled in evening classes or correspondence courses, by 1980 full-time (daytime-course) students had come to represent 57 per cent of the total student population.

With the number of applicants to university and the institutes rising yearly, the competitive entrance examinations are becoming stiffer and stiffer, thereby tending to favour the children of the intelligentsia, who are better prepared for these entrance competitions than are the *proizvodstvenniki*. A special stream has been set up for peasants' and workers' children in the form of a year's intermediate study to coach them for the examinations. Does this mean that, as in any other society, Soviet society tends to reproduce the culture of the dominant strata?

But all this leaves unresolved the definition of the type of vocational training best suited to the needs of an economy in the throes of rapid technical change. Lenin, in common with the rest of the Marxists of his generation, considered that overspecialization bound the worker to manual tasks and that the worker could only achieve promotion if given a polytechnic training. But interpretations of this term have varied, and vocational training has in fact remained specialized, for a factory is only capable of training specialists to fit its own profile; consequently, they are not all-rounders. Which is why there is a current preference for the development of professional schools, which are better fitted to provide the kind of polytechnic training able to ensure the requisite degree of professional mobility in a period of rapid technical progress.

Meanwhile, the fact that four-fifths of secondary-school pupils do not go on to higher education has made it necessary to set up specialized secondary schools to provide technical professional training. Taken as a whole, these different training courses form a coherent network enabling people of all ages to improve their skills, so that culture need not be regarded as the privilege of certain classes.

Streams and the organization in public education

The unity of general public educational policy is supervised by the science and education department of the central committee. Three central government agencies are responsible for application of the General Education Act (21 July 1973), namely the ministry of national education, the ministry of higher education and specialized secondary education and the state committee of the council of ministers for vocational training. Each republic also has its own public educational authority.

General education. This is divided into three cycles: primary (three years), first-cycle secondary (five years, from classes 4 to 8) and second-cycle secondary (classes 9–10) (certain non-Russian-speaking republics have an eleventh class to enable pupils to perfect their Russian, which is essential in higher education). In the countryside, the first three years of schooling are available locally, but beyond that, children are often obliged to leave their village, so that longer schooling exacerbates the rural exodus. In each class (*druzhina*), patrols (*zvenya*) are formed to encourage competition between the classes and groups.

The first selection takes place at the end of class 8 (see Table 31). According to educational statistics, approximately 46 per cent of secondary-school pupils had gone through the complete course in 1974, in other words pursued their studies through class 9 and 10 (58 per cent in Moscow, compared with 92 per cent in Japan). Some of those who leave school to go out to work on completion

TABLE 31   *Extent of selection on completion of secondary school*

	Completing secondary school (thousands of pupils)		Entering higher education (thousands of students)			
	7–8 years (col. 1)	10–11 years (school certificate) (col. 2)	Full-time		Evening classes, correspondence courses (col. 4)	Cols 3 + 4 as % of total of cols 1 + 2
			(col. 3)	(as % of col. 2)		
1928–29		50	42.8	85.5		85.5
1940	1850	303	160	52	103	12.2
1950	1491	284	237.5	83.6	111.5	19.4
1960	2383	1055	257.9	24.5	333.4	17.3
1970	4661	2591	500	19.2	411.0	12.5
1980	4270	3996	640	16.1	412	12.8

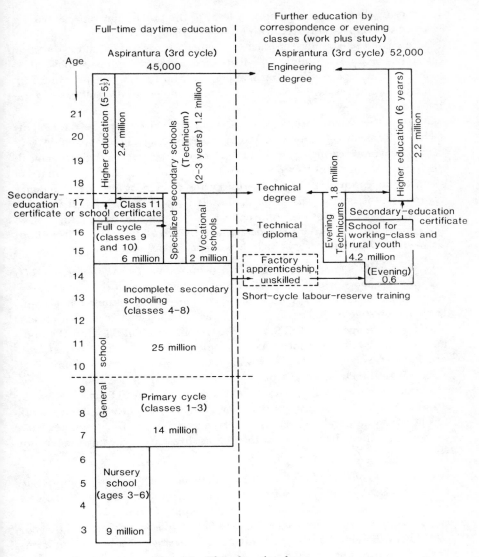

Figure 6 The educational system

of class 8 will go on to complete their secondary education by enrolling in evening classes run by the worker and peasant youth school (20 hours of classes per week, plus 8 hours' work at home for 36 weeks in the year in town and 26 weeks in the countryside). Most people make do with a short training course in an apprenticeship centre, either in a factory (FZO), or in an appropriate centre run by the state committee for vocational training. At the last census, the average educational level of the population represented 8.4 years of schooling, compared with 6 years in 1959.

The second selection takes place at the end of upper-secondary education (after ten years' schooling). One-fifth of a year's secondary-school-leavers will have the opportunity, after competitive examination, of pursuing full-time higher studies, while most of their erstwhile comrades will enter working life.

Many of these young people, who go to work in a factory in one of the highly technical branches of industry at seventeen years of age, hold a school-leaver's certificate (representing up to 40—50 per cent of recruits in the mechanical-engineering industry in Moscow, Novosibirsk, Barnaul, etc.). A great many of them try to continue their studies by means of evening or correspondence courses, in the *technicums* in particular. It may be reckoned that approximately 11.4 per cent of the children in a given age group gain admission to full-time higher education; this percentage rises to 28 per cent of those born between 1957 and 1959 if we include students attending the *technicums*.

The vocational schools. These fall into two groups. The *short-cycle (PTU) vocational schools*, which train skilled workers, generally at the end of lower-secondary education. There is no entrance competition to these schools, and they lack prestige (only 15 per cent of young people leaving class 8 at around 16—18 years of age in the RSFSR and the Ukraine enrol in this kind of school, and twice as few do so in central Asia). People generally prefer the *technicums*, or specialist secondary schools, to which admission is by examination. They offer two- or three-and-a-half-year courses to turn out middle-rank supervisory-grade personnel, such as nurses, teachers or technicians. On graduation, at around nineteen or twenty years of age, students obtain a diploma of full secondary studies and a specialism, carrying with it, as for graduates from higher education, the obligation to work as directed by the government for three years.

Admission to colleges of higher education or universities. With a few exceptions,[2] this is subject to competition, which is becoming stiffer every year owing to the rising number of secondary-school pupils. Certain schools are particularly sought after, such as the Bauman School of Engineering in Moscow or the Moscow Foreign Languages Institute. The average number of applicants per place is five, but for each place at the Moscow Institute of Dramatic Art there were 100 applicants, and at the Leningrad Law Faculty in 1974, there were 40. The number of places available is laid down by the ministry of higher education on the basis of forecasts prepared by Gosplan for 340 different specialities. Admission procedures entail a medical examination and the competition proper, as well as an interview with a jury chaired by the dean or director, where consideration is given to the candidate's 'political maturity'. In addition, instructions are issued setting quotas for each nationality (including discrimination against Jewish students, whose numbers very greatly exceed their numerical importance in the population). Certain newspaper articles have referred to string-pulling on behalf of candidates from influential families.

Between 1928 and 1950, with the exception of the year 1940 when most youths joined the army, 80 per cent of secondary-school graduates were admitted to higher education. Today, full-time students represent no more than 19 per cent of those completing full secondary school (ten years' schooling).

In this scramble for diplomas, there is little equality of opportunity between those in full-time schooling and those who are obliged to combine study with work. While the former can use their free time to broaden their interests, the latter do not enjoy the same advantages and are therefore less well prepared to sit the examinations. Some 74 per cent of students in higher education and specialized technical education receive grants; these vary between 30 and 60 rubles per month (since September 1972), but represent only two-thirds of the cost of a student's upkeep on average, which means that parents have to make up the remainder. Students generally live in hostels and dine in canteens (meals cost 20 rubles a month).

Until 1976, the diploma was initially awarded on a provisional basis, only becoming definitive after an eighteen-month trial period in the student's first posting, which meant that students who refused to accept a posting lost their right to a diploma. This rule was rescinded in September 1976, and the university degree is now awarded by examination.

The teaching profession. The educational system nowadays absorbs approximately 30 per cent of higher-education graduates, which is almost as much as industry (in the broadest sense), i.e. 40 per cent. Women, who now account for 50 per cent of the student population, compared with 28 per cent in 1928–9, make up the bulk of those opting for a career in teaching: they account for 80 per cent of secondary-school teachers (although 70 per cent of these schools have male directors). In the republics with Muslim traditions, the percentage of women teachers is appreciably lower, reflecting the persistence of ancient prejudices regarding the status of women.

The prestige of the teaching profession is still intact. For in the Soviet Union it offers the peasant's son or daughter a means to social advancement, even though the schoolmistress's conditions, obliging her to run two or three primary-school classes single-handed, are not always exactly restful (a rural schoolmistress teaches between 32 and 39 hours per week, not including time taken to prepare classes and correct homework, which brings her effective working week to 60 hours). Furthermore, Soviet schools lay great emphasis on respect for teachers, discipline and a spirit of comradeship. Student participation in the running of courses was very short lived (1918–19). Nowadays, it only survives in the form of student representation on the grant-awarding commission and, for Party members, in meetings of the establishment's primary organization, where teachers and students are represented on an equal footing.

Teachers are assessed on the basis of the number of pupils that pass the examinations leading from one class to the next (rate of transfer, or *uspevaemost'*), which scarcely makes their job any easier, given the diversity of their pupils' backgrounds, and which in addition is liable to depress educational standards. Since 1974, teachers have been periodically assessed by a review panel with powers to decide on promotions and dismissals.

Thus, the Soviet educational system does not escape the dilemma of whether to broaden access to all the different levels and types of education by giving weight to social considerations, or whether to select the brightest on the basis of school results.

Promotion or social selection?

Aspirations and achievements. The universalization of secondary education does not abolish inequality: for there is a selection process at work, between lower- and upper-secondary education, which often determines people's future occupations. Yet, surveys of youth aspirations (regardless of interviewees' social origins) reveal a unanimous desire to pursue studies. However, career intentions differ from one social background to another. A collective-farm worker's son will view even an unskilled job in town as a step up the ladder, whereas one-third of children born to parents belonging to the intelligentsia (scientists, members of the professions) aspire to the same career as their parents.

Regular surveys of the subsequent careers of young people after leaving school seek to analyse the relative prospects for achieving their ambitions of children from different social backgrounds. The situation varies from one province to another, but a certain number of general tendencies do emerge. The least privileged are children born in the countryside: in the province of Novosibirsk, there was no appreciable rise in the percentage of those entering full-time vocational or higher education over an eight-year period. The same survey reveals that 39 per cent of girls continue to work in farming after leaving the rural schools, whereas only 12 per cent of them actually wanted to remain in this sector. Of the 21 per cent of girls wanting to become schoolmistresses or doctors, less than half were actually able to pursue the career of their choice. Among young men in the countryside, 24 per cent had applied for the army or the air force (a much sought-after training course), but only 9 per cent managed to realize their plans; most went into the vocational schools.

Nowadays, rural youth supplies specialized workers and middle-rank supervisory personnel: technicians, construction-plant operators, skilled metal-

TABLE 32   *Career intentions of final-year students and attainment of objectives in the province of Novosibirsk (1963–73) and Leningrad (1964–5) (as percentage of expressed intentions or fulfilment)*

Plans on leaving school	Social origin of pupils' parents								
	Intelligentsia		Industrial workers		Urban clerical workers		Peasants (rural schools)		
	Nov. 1963	Len. 1965	Nov. 1963	Len. 1965	Nov. 1963	Len. 1965	Len. 1965	Nov. 1963	Nov. 1975
Would like to:									
1 Continue studies	93		83		76			76	88
higher									33
vocational									55
2 Reconcile work with study	5		6		15			14	
3 Work	2		11		9			10	12
Occupations envisaged:									
Engineer		40–48		39.9		42.1	36.4		
Researcher, doctor, teacher		35–44		34.9		30.5	26.0		
Specialist	71		60		36				
Worker	25	0.6–2.7	35	8.3	56	3.5	11.7	88	
Farmer	1				4		6.5	12	
Actual status after 1 year:									
1 Continuing studies in the *vuzy* (higher education)	82	73	61	58.3	59		4.4	10	59
Vocational schools)									16
									43
2 Work plus study	3	10.5	3	14.2	3		3.4		3
3 Work	15	16.5	36	27.5	38		55.2	90	38
Average years of schooling of the active population in the USSR	12.2		7.6				7.3		

workers, schoolmistresses, nurses, textile and construction workers. It is still under-represented in the higher schools and universities.

The figures in Table 32 are representative of a major industrial city and a cultural and administrative metropolis, where the intelligentsia is more heavily represented than in the population as a whole. In Moscow, in 1975–6, 49 per cent of students were children of the intelligentsia (compared with 60–70 per cent in 1958 – *Trud*, 10 December 1958), i.e. as many as those from working-class backgrounds, while only 2 per cent were of peasant origin. Another interesting point is that students from secondary schools in Moscow enjoy an advantage in admissions to research institutes (53 per cent of students) and particularly to those run by the Academy of Sciences (69 per cent of students). This is a far cry from the situation in the 1930s, when the

TABLE 33 *Social and educational background of students in Sverdlovsk (6 higher schools) and Leningrad (3 faculties)*

	Sverdlovsk			Moscow	Leningrad	USSR		France
	1963	1969	1982	1976	1967	1970[1]	1979[1]	1973−4[1]
Family background								
Intelligentsia					30.5			5.1
Office workers	44.2	50.2	47.1	54.3	25.1	2.41	1.84	0.6−1.2[2]
Military					13.3			
Blue-collar workers	44.7	47.3	51.9	40.1	25.8	0.65	0.79	0.3
Peasants	8.1	2.5	1.0	5.1	2.2	0.41	0.44	0.6
Sources of recruitment								
Secondary schools	18.9				37.2			
Courses for								
Office worker	40.6				58.7			
Blue-collar worker	40.0							
Peasant	0.5							

Notes: 1 The index of relative opportunity of admission is based on the percentage representation of social groups in the population; this index would be equal to 1 in all cases, if opportunities of admission were equal for all.
2 For France, 0.6 represents the index for office workers, 1.2 that for middle-rank executives.

proletarianization of the universities was at its peak, with working-class students representing 58 per cent and students from non-manual backgrounds 27.8 per cent of the total student population. Looking at the example of Sverdlovsk (Table 33), we find that Khrushchev's reforms have not radically altered the situation (the rise in worker recruitment goes hand in hand with a drop in the proportion of peasants, due to the fact that a great many collective farms have become state farms and that their employees are now classified as 'workers').

Factors of inequality and correctives. Soviet sociologists who have investigated factors capable of accounting for these inequalities have reached the conclusion that the family environment exercises a decisive influence on success in school. The coefficients of correlation between different variables show that school marks obtained correlate most powerfully with the economic situation of the pupil's parents (0.52).

The reason why so few children from peasant and working-class families pursue their studies is presumably their readiness to go out to work at a younger age in order to help their families, and also that, despite recent increases, study grants are inadequate to cover the entire cost of keeping a full-time student. Furthermore, people whose mother tongue is a language other than Russian are handicapped in the competition for places in higher education, where Russian is compulsory. For instance, in the Tatar Republic, 60 per cent of whose population is Tatar and 40 per cent Russian, we find the same distribution of nationalities in the general secondary schools, while in higher education Tatars represent only 37 per cent and Russians 56 per cent; the proportions among doctoral students is 27 per cent and 56 per cent respectively.

A survey of students at the Ufa Aviation Institution, carried out in 1965, showed that parental assistance was given to students by 83 per cent of white-collar families, by 70.1 per cent of blue-collar families and by 31.6 per cent of peasant families. Grants are awarded in the reverse order: to 90.5 per cent of peasants' children, 85.8 per cent of blue-collar workers' and 75 per cent of white-collar workers'. In France, at the same period (1964–5), 19 per cent of students were receiving higher-education grants. It should be borne in mind that many Soviet students spend their summer vacation working in voluntary brigades, where they are paid the going rate for their speciality and sometimes more.

Material conditions are not enough in themselves to account for all the inequalities found in the Soviet Union; for here as elsewhere their roots are primarily cultural in origin. Because residential environment plays a decisive part in determining children's career prospects, it has been necessary to alleviate the handicaps facing rural youth not only by means of special grants (awarded by the collective and state farms in return for a commitment to come back after graduation to work as specialists on these farms), but also by means of special coaching. In August 1969, it was decided to set up an intermediate course of between eight and ten months to provide coaching for the children of peasant and blue-collar workers in preparation for the entrance competitions to higher education, and a 20 per cent quota of places was set aside for them. In 1971, some 50,000 students out of a total of 516,000 full-time students had passed through these special training centres, which suggests that Khrushchev's reforms, most of which were repealed after his departure, did little to threaten the entrenched positions of the intelligentsia.

Soviet opinion is divided as to the appropriate importance to attach to social criteria in the selection of candidates for higher education. Some (such as the sociologist V. Mishin) believe that over-rapid universalization of secondary education, far from improving young people's prospects, actually tends to sharpen their feeling of frustration, because the toughness of the competitions works in favour of the better-prepared pupils, thereby perpetuating the privileges of the intelligentsia. According to him, it would be preferable to introduce quotas of admission based on social criteria. However, M. Rutkevich argues that this practice would be contrary to the principles of equality of all citizens before the law. On the contrary, it is better to select the ablest candidates. These considerations have led to the foundation of special schools for children who are particularly gifted in certain subjects. Inequalities will disappear the day economic development does away with them. In other words, educational policy should be dictated by the medium-term needs of the economy.

The needs of the economy and social demand

It would be mistaken to judge the efficiency of the Soviet educational system in exclusively economic terms. For the final goal of education is not work, but human beings themselves. The moral and intellectual training of the individual is intrinsically valuable, transcending material applications; but this does not abolish the need to adapt to the needs of the community as determined by the planners.

Forecasting job supply and demand. The Soviet constitution, which imposes on everyone the obligation to work, in principle also guarantees everyone the right to work. In actual fact, while adjustment of supply and demand in the Soviet Union is not subject to the vicissitudes of labour-market fluctuations, it nevertheless encounters other difficulties connected with forecasting and labour-recruitment methods.

Right to work and freedom to work are antinomic. The rejects of the school system need not fear unemployment, but they will have to put up with humbler or less gratifying work.

Despite progress in the technique of balanced job projections for each branch of the economy, forecasting specialist-training needs continues to be an awkward business. In some professions, personnel needs can be forecast with a fair degree of precision, as in the teaching or medical professions; but, in technical fields, industrial progress makes it difficult to arrive at reliable estimates. Gosplan bases its calculations on requests for labour sent in by the enterprises. But a factory's field of vision rarely exceeds five years, while it takes a good deal longer than that to train an engineer. An engineer graduating in 1983 will have begun his studies as far back as 1977. But neither the ministry of higher education nor the institutes possess detailed projections of job trends over timespans that long. This explains the difficulties encountered in finding jobs for engineers, and the fact that these graduates often hold down jobs to which they are unsuited by training.

All graduates of the higher schools or *technicums* are ordered to particular jobs by an appointments commission. But this only affects a small percentage of new recruits to the workforce each year.

Until now, most young people have found jobs on the labour market. There is now talk of setting up appointments commissions for secondary-school-leavers, as they compete with other job-seekers. The slack in the labour market represents the equivalent of 223,000 workers annually, or 1.4 million job-seekers experiencing an average of 26 days' unemployment. The privileges enjoyed by workers aged under 18 (shorter working hours, longer annual holidays, facilities for those pursuing their studies) do not make it easier for them to find jobs. In 1957, it proved necessary to establish compulsory quotas in order to induce employers to hire young people (10 per cent of the workforce). Even so, according to Gosplan statistics, 25.2 per cent of young people aged between 16 and 17 and 13.9 per cent of those aged between 18 and 19 were un-employed in medium-sized towns in 1965, compared with 1.7 per cent for other age groups.

The reaction of the government was to set up a state committee for labour reserves, resuscitating the labour commissariat which existed prior to 1931. Since 1969, this has organized a network of labour exchanges in the big cities to centralize offers of employment. Furthermore, the *orgnabor*, which is answerable to this committee, exists to recruit available labour, in town and country alike, to work on two- or three-year contracts on big construction schemes and in the coalmines.

But the adjustment of supply and demand in the labour market is not merely the outcome of the way the market is organized; the ladder of occu-pational prestige leads people to seek careers in occupations that are in scarcest supply: not everyone can become a cosmonaut; conversely, the least sought-after jobs are those that are most necessary. In addition, the vocational schools often offer a limited range of specialities, which means that many students pursue their studies in fields not of their choosing. Here, as elsewhere, we find the classic dilemma between what individuals want as consumers (which deter-mines the structure of production and services, and hence of jobs on offer), and the work that these same individuals are prepared to accept as workers.

It is hoped that better careers guidance will narrow the gap between aspir-ations and the needs of the economy. But, however great the means deployed to revive the status of manual work, and in particular certain occupations such as that of dairymaid, these campaigns are unlikely to alter the scale of prefer-ences. Thus, all that remains to be done is to mechanize manual tasks which, both in the Soviet Union and elsewhere, are the most backbreaking and most shunned. Despite the fact that two generations have now been brought up to respect manual work, everyone yearns, if not for himself then at least for his children, for a career among the intelligentsia.

The content of training and further training. There is controversy among factory managers and economists as to the best way to train the great mass of skilled workers. Until now, most of them were trained in factory-run appren-ticeship schemes, which amounted to a narrow specialized training suited to the needs of the enterprise. The factory school therefore cannot claim to provide the theoretical background essential to the redefinition of jobs under the pressure of technological change. It was for this reason that the vocational schools have been entrusted with this task (doubling their enrolments by 1980).

Factory managers argue that knowledge is less essential than experience gained on the job. Economists reply that apprenticeship in the factory is an expensive solution, when one considers the need for retraining. About 20 million workers attend further-training courses or classes each year; it would be more efficient to allocate the money spent on lifelong training to the schools rather than to the factories. A great deal of attention is currently being focused on educational costs.

Behind this debate, though, there lurks a more fundamental issue, namely should education be proportionate to the present needs of the economy, or should it train personalities capable of adjusting to or even promoting change, without regard to immediate returns? Some people fear that an education in advance of the present state of technological development in industry will merely exacerbate the frustrations of youth and breed social tension, just as educational progress in the republics is sharpening national sentiment (as illustrated by incidents that have occurred at the University of Erivan).

Military service plays an exceedingly important role in the education of youth by relieving these tensions and exalting collective values — in other words engendering and fostering a sense of Soviet patriotism. Since 1938, when the policy of recruiting regiments on a national basis was discarded, the army has become a kind of melting pot and an instrument for Russification, transcending particularism. What is more, the army offers youngsters a second chance to learn a skill where they have not succeeded in doing so before military service. This side of the army's activities has ramifications in civilian life in the form of voluntary associations in support of the army, air force and navy (DOSAAF) which together have close on 80 million members, 20 million of them practising one kind of sport or another. These associations enjoy a virtual monopoly of sport (including shooting), teaching people to drive, running pleasure-boating concessions, etc. The Olympic medals won are a tribute to the efficiency of the organization of military training.

Socialization in the Soviet Union is therefore not restricted to the educational system in the narrow sense of the word; rather, it is an integral part of ideological work, which penetrates, by means of the mass media and social organizations, to every part of society, in a climate of permanent mobilization from which the individual can escape only with difficulty. Education itself is made to serve a political ideology that jealously guards its monopoly, and in Chapter 11, which is devoted to the question of social values, we shall be looking at how this social control is reconciled with the freedom of expression and innovation essential to the formation and fulfilment of the personality.

It now remains to be seen whether the major aspects of the educational system as described above, such as the crucial role of the family, the lengthening of schooling and the specialized schools' monopoly over the transmission of knowledge, are liable to be undermined by technical progress and the transformation of the Soviet family and society.

Certain Soviet educational planners, looking to the future, see the family, which used to constitute a living educational unit in the days when there were several children in the home, as no longer capable of performing this role when reduced to only one or two children living in separate apartments, with little contact with their fellow pupils. It could lose certain of its prerogatives in favour of collective units, which would care for the children all day long or even provide boarding accommodation for them. Thus, the traditional concepts of Marxist educational theory have retained their vitality where education (*vospitanie*) is concerned.

Where the transmission of knowledge is concerned, on the other hand, the single-school system, which was the ideal of earlier generations, is likely to lose its monopoly, for like the family it is no longer able to keep step with the rapid pace of progress in knowledge. The universalization of higher education would mean devoting one-third of one's life to study. Computers are going to make it easier to store knowledge and make it more accessible to all. The training of the future will be not only lifelong but also personalized, in response to the needs and potential of each individual. Diplomas will be awarded by adding up passes in major and minor subjects selected according to taste. This diversification matches that of Soviet society itself.

To conclude, the Soviet educational system is, like those everywhere else, patterned on the overall model of society. As elsewhere, it performs a number of traditional functions, namely:

1 The transmission of knowledge and the generalization of education among broad strata of the population is one of its positive achievements, for this implies a far-reaching transformation of society; a galaxy of artists and eminent scientists, including several Nobel prizewinners, is evidence of the quality and vitality of this education.

2 But, as elsewhere, the educational system also perpetuates the dominant social model: (a) by means of selection tending to ensure the social advancement of children from culturally and economically privileged categories, despite reforms to promote equality; and (b) through respect for authority, work and competition inculcated at a very early age, which serves to reproduce the hierarchical model and the cult of performance, upon which the Soviet model of production is based. Thus, there is no divergence between educational values and those of the factory in the Soviet Union.

NOTES

1 G. Strumilin, *Golos politekhnika*, no. 7, 1912.
2 Mainly, certain military academies and schools in those branches of the economy suffering from labour shortages, to which gold-medal students are admitted without being obliged to sit the competitive examination.

SUGGESTED READING

History

Anweiler, O., *Geschichte der Schule and Pädagogik in Russland vom Ende des Zarenreiches bis zum Beginn der Stalin-Ära*, Berlin, Walter, 1964 (extracts in Katov, G. (ed.), *Russia Enters the Twentieth Century*, London, Methuen, 1973).
Anweiler, O., *Bildungsreformen in Osteuropa*, Stuttgart, Kohlhammer, 1969.

Anweiler, O., *Bildung und Erzichung in Osteuropa im 20 Jahrhundert*, Berlin, 1982.
Bereday, G., *Modernization and Diversity in Soviet Education*, New York, Praeger, 1971.
Berton-Hogge, R., 'L'école d'enseignement général, dix années de réforme', *Problèmes politiques et sociaux*, n. 281, April 1976.
Deyneko, M., *40 let narodnogo obrazovaniya v S.S.S.R.*, Moscow, 1957.
Fitzpatrick, S., *The Commissariat of Enlightenment* (under Lunacharsky), Cambridge University Press, 1970.
Fitzpatrick, S., *Education and Social Mobility in the Soviet Union 1921—1934*, Cambridge University Press, 1979.
Hans, N., *The Russian Tradition in Education*, London, 1963.
De Witt, N., *Educational and Professional Employment in the U.S.S.R.*, National Science Foundation, 1961.

Educational methods

Bronfenbrenner, U., *Two Worlds of Childhood, US and USSR*, Russell Sage Foundation, 1970.
Makarenko, A., *Problèmes de l'éducation scolaire soviétique*, Progrès, Moscow (n.d.).
O'Dell, F. A., *Socialization through Children's Literature: the Soviet Example*, Cambridge University Press, 1978.
Rutkevich, M. N. and Filippov, F. R., *Vysshaya shkola kak faktor izmeneniya sotsial'noy struktury obshchestva*, Moscow, Nauka, 1978.

The sociology of education and social mobility

Avis, G., 'The sociology of Soviet higher education', in *Education and Mass-media in the Soviet Union and Eastern Europe*, New York, Praeger, 1976.
Berton-Hogge, R., 'La promotion sociale et l'école du soir', *Problèmes politiques et sociaux*, no. 157, Dec. 1972.
Lagneau-Markiewicz, J., 'École et changement social: le rôle de l'école secondaire en U.R.S.S.', *Revue française de sociologie*, special number, 1967—8.
Lagneau-Markiewicz, J., *Éducation, égalité et socialisme*, Anthropos, 1969.
Rutkevich, M., *The Career Plans of Youth*, White Plains, New York, IASP, 1969.
Soviet surveys into promotion in education: Aitov, N., *Sotsial'nye issled.*, Vypusk 2, 1965; Shubkin, V., *Voprosy filosofii*, n. 8, 1964; Vodzinskaya, V., *Chelovek i obshchestvo*, Vypusk 2, 1967, Vypusk 6, 1969.

The economics of education and employment

Berton-Hogge, R., 'L'emploi des jeunes', *Problèmes politiques et sociaux*, nos 175—6, May 1973, nos 235—6, July 1974.
Chambre, H., 'Les coûts de l'éducation en U.R.S.S.', *Revue de l'action populaire*, April 1965.
Friedman, G., 'La formation professionnelle en U.R.S.S.', *Arguments*, Nov. 1958.
Komarov, V., 'L'éducation, le développement économique et la formation des spécialistes', in *Textes choisis sur l'économie de l'éducation*, Unesco, 1968.
Revenko, T., *L'enseignement supérieur en Union Soviétique*, OCDE, Paris, 1973.
Voronov, O., 'Le congé éducation payé en U.R.S.S.', *Revue internationale du Travail*, June 1973, pp. 575—85.

Chapter 7

The enterprise

The nature of business enterprises is an essential feature of any society, for we nowadays distinguish the socialist from the free-market capitalist countries on the basis of their respective forms of ownership of the means of production. Marxists hold that the level of technological development, the system of ownership of the means of production, and the social relations that arise in connection with the production process are the prime movers of any social dynamic.

Without necessarily attributing to the enterprise an exclusive or privileged role, we are bound to acknowledge that this basic unit of industrial society conditions to a large extent both family and urban life today. We have already noted, in the foregoing chapters, the intimate links between industrialization and urban growth (it was the factory which gave birth to the town) and the impact of paid work on the resources and pace of family life and leisure and of the requirements of the labour market on the training and education of youth. As we shall see later, social classes and their degree of mobility are very directly dependent on the socio-occupational structure of the population and on economic growth; they spring, in the last analysis, from the different forms of enterprise activity and from the opportunities for promotion created by technical progress, for Soviet enterprises are in a state of constant change.

The enterprise is not an independent variable with a life of its own. Of all the primary structures, it is the one most sensitive to change, and it is this capacity for adjustment which is, in a market economy, the condition for survival. Whereas the family unit is an institution upon which the state is unable to exercise any form of direct action, for the enterprise, on the contrary, state action is of decisive importance, whatever the regime. However, forms and degrees of state control vary according to stages of economic development and the ideologies that shape this development.

THE ENTERPRISE AND HISTORY: TYPES OF INDUSTRIALIZATION AND DEVELOPMENT IDEOLOGY

Whatever the regime, industrialization is first and foremost a process of technological change. We might try to define it as the utilization of energies external to human beings which, when used in conjunction with machines, enable us to intensify our efforts while at the same time binding us (unlike tools) to their demands and their own specific rhythms. This mutation first got under way in the eighteenth century in England and the Netherlands, and subsequently in France, Germany and Russia. But the latter were forced along a different path from the English model, for they lacked the same resources (proximity to iron and coal mines), a colonial empire capable of serving as a market for the products of their industry and that enterprising bourgeoisie which, having grown rich on commerce, launched into colonial or industrial adventures. Russian agriculture was not transformed, as was that of England, by the introduction of clover in animal husbandry, and it proved incapable of supplying the towns with both farm surpluses and an abundant supply of labour, a veritable 'reserve army' of cheap labour resulting from a dispossessed peasantry.

The historical conditions for industrialization in Russia

At the beginning of the nineteenth century, Russia had no colonial empire, and its coal resources in the Ukraine were geographically distant from the iron-working centres of the Urals, which employed wood. It was not until 1871 that the first coke-fired blast furnace was inaugurated, as a result of the opening of a railway linking the Donbas with the Krivoy Rog ores. It took the setbacks of the Crimean war to free Russian farmworkers from their serfdom. The nobles used their income to keep up their lifestyle, not to build an industrial empire. The merchant class, though far from negligible, only rather belatedly managed to organize itself politically. The better off among them were integrated into the privileged classes and never constituted an autonomous force of their own, independent of Tsarist power. This explains why, as in Japan (from the Meiji restoration onwards), the state was the principal driving force behind industrial development.

Russia's first industries were set up under Peter the Great, in the form of government-subsidized manufacturing. He wanted to equip his country with the modern means indispensable to its power: iron and cloth for the army. The desire to equal or even surpass the most developed countries of the west has been a key strain in the industrial policy of all the country's leaders — mercantilist, capitalist or communist — down to the present day. When, in February 1931, Stalin adopted Lenin's slogan 'We must catch up with and overtake the most advanced capitalist countries, or die', and added 'We are lagging 50–100 years behind, we must cover this distance in ten years' (*Questions of Leninism*), he was echoing the Minister of Finance and Economy, Witte, who wrote to the Tsar in February 1900:

> International competition waits on no one: we must take energetic and decisive measures if our industry is to be able to satisfy the needs of Russia in the coming decades . . . the rapidly expanding foreign industries are going to establish themselves on our soil; our economic backwardness could breed political and cultural backwardness. (*Istorik-Marksist*, nos 2–3, 1935, p. 130)

As a latecomer to industrialization, Russia sought to make up for its short-comings by adopting the most up-to-date techniques, which led it from the outset to give pride of place to large enterprises. By 1866, Russia possessed 42 factories employing over 1000 workers in the cotton industry. The spinning mills of the Neva, with 160,000 spindles, were in advance of the largest American firms at that time. In terms of the degree of concentration of factories on the eve of the first world war, Russia, with 44 per cent of the work-force in establishments employing over 1000 workers, ranked ahead of Germany and the United States (15 and 21 per cent respectively).

The economic historian Strumilin[1] has shown that there is a close relation-ship between degree of concentration and proletarian consciousness; that workers' struggles and strikes have always been more frequent in big factories than in smaller workshops. Which is why the Bolshevik Revolution did not suddenly explode in an underdeveloped country, as if by accident, but oc-curred within a specific social context that was already changing under the impact of rapid industrialization. Today, Soviet historians recognize that imperial Russia ranked fifth among the great industrial powers in 1914. It is important to recall the social effects of this development before going on to demonstrate their repercussions on ideology.

The social effects of industrialization

As everywhere, the transition from small-scale manufacturing to large-scale industry gradually eliminated the craftsman and drove sizable numbers of peasants into the towns. Industry and associated activities (transport, build-ing, services) each year attracted to the towns all the surplus labour for which the countryside no longer had any use, initially as seasonal peasant workers, later as permanent urban workers.

The concentration of workers within the confined space of the factory, and the swift elimination of manual techniques, created a separation between place of work and place of residence. Where once there had been interdepen-dence and communication between the different trades in the rural com-munity (not only in the form of exchange of commodities but also in the sense of the perpetuation of a community culture) there now arose a complex system of impersonal, hierarchical relations, in which the individual's personality ceased to be identified with anything but his job and his income. The old solidarity, founded on mutual aid among neighbours and relations of kinship, has given way to a legal system of social security in a society based on competition, efficiency and the conflicts born of a market economy.

But workers instinctively seek if not security at the workplace, at least the old sense of solidarity. This accounts for their ambivalent behaviour and for certain features of the Russian workers' movement, especially the Soviet trade unions. In periods of calm, the young peasant only recently arrived from the village sees the factory as a substitute for the community at home, and the union (legally permitted in 1906), traditionless and organized by the authorities, much more as a mutual assurance society than as a fighting organization. In revolutionary periods, on the other hand, the peasant brings to the city all the anarchic vehemence that slumbers in the peasant world.

The Soviet period did not eliminate the effects of proletarianization in its early decades; rather it accentuated them by speeding up the process of urban development and by abolishing all autonomous economic activity at the end of the NEP. Even today, the population suffers from the notorious inadequacy of 'services' consequent upon the disappearance of the craftsman and the small shopkeeper. Above all, however, the concentration of factories and the proliferation of administration have served to strengthen the bureaucracy — that sickness common in different degrees to all industrial societies, and the chief obstacle to their evolution. Thus, in spite of technical progress, and because of it, there is a widening gulf between those who decide and those who execute.

Reactions and ideologies

As elsewhere, the pressures, excesses and inhumanity of industrialization and bureaucracy gave birth to movements of protest in Russia, from which in turn socialist and reformist ideologies sprang. To begin with, protest was directed against capitalism, held to be the chief cause of the enslavement and violence of industrialization; later, when socialism had established itself firmly, people began instead to question the arbitrariness and inertia of the bureaucracy and to dream of possible improvements to the industrial set-up in order to make it both more efficient and more acceptable to rising generations. A fundamental postulate in both cases is that social progress calls for a thoroughgoing reform of the enterprise.

Russian slavophile and populist circles began criticizing industrialization as early as the middle of the nineteenth century. Both wished to safeguard the Russian people from the evils and upheavals of the western world, as then exemplified in its English version. The more radical among them — the populists — inspired by socialist ideas, thought that it would be possible to build a Russian socialism out of the peasant community tradition and thus to miss out the capitalist phase. Marx himself, when questioned by Vera Zasulich, was hard put to assess the likelihood of a Russian socialism.

In the closing decades of the century, this idealistic intelligentsia was replaced by a more realistic generation, powerfully influenced by Marxist economic thinking. Capitalism, meanwhile, had wasted no time establishing itself, so that the capitalist stage was not only inevitable in the view of the new generation, but necessary even, in order to develop the productive forces before going on to envisage more radical social change. To everyone, except perhaps Lenin, this seemed a very distant prospect.

The confrontation between capital and labour surfaced only rather belatedly, at the end of the nineteenth century, in the form of increasingly violent strikes which culminated in the revolutions of 1905 and 1917. While socialist ideas had taken relatively little root in the Russian proletariat in 1917 — it was fighting more to improve its condition than to transform it — the Bolshevik intellectuals guiding it drew from Marxist ideology the references that were to set industrialization along a new path.

We know that, for Marx, the private appropriation of the means of production was the source of capitalist exploitation, and that it is necessary to substitute for the anarchy of the market economy, which is governed by the law of profit, a 'conscious regulation' of the economy on the basis of the workers' needs. Thus it would be possible to develop the forces of production to the point where, in a classless society, people would no longer be alienated from their work. From this we may deduce the following principal characteristics of a socialist mode of production:

1 Socialization of the means of production, which gives to whomever is in power the means to control production and to distribute its fruits.
2 Planning, to replace the market as the driving force in the economy and set production targets in the light of the needs of the community.
3 Payment based on work done, which implies both the duty to work and also the right to work (full employment is explicitly guaranteed by Art. 40 of the Constitution of the Soviet Union).
4 The development of the forces of production, in order to bring about a radical transformation in the worker's condition.

To sum up, socialism is a theory of social change, founded upon economic development and nationalization of the production system.

It was the putting into practice of these principles which was to inspire the organization of the economy and the policy of industrialization. And many of those who took part in its implementation, working on the big projects around the country, found more than a doctrine in socialism: it had a mystique that fuelled their enthusiasm. It is very likely that this irrational aspect was what enabled ideology to play a key mobilizing role in the realization of the regime's major undertakings.

The stages of Soviet industrial policy

While ideology determines what is desirable, politics defines what is possible in the light of objective conditions. The socialist system has been established by means of a series of phases and experiments in which different solutions have been tried out and those proved incompatible with the goals and priorities laid down by the regime rejected.

1 During the first half of 1918, the Bolshevik government proceeded to nationalize the banks, external trade and large-scale industry (in 1919, the whole of industry passed under direct state control); as early as 27 November 1917, however, workers' control was established in all enterprises employing more than five people. On 15 December 1917, a Supreme Council for the National Economy (VSNKh) was charged with the task (until 1932) of activating and co-ordinating the whole of the economic machine.

With the introduction of war communism, the militarization of the economy entailed the suppression of all workers' self-management experiments. The provisional government had recognized the freedom to organize trade unions and factory committees on 12 April 1917. Consequently, workers' control had been exercised in all enterprises prior to their nationalization. In June 1918, when these nationalizations were completed, industries were combined into unions (cartels), and Lenin initiated a return to order by placing managerial responsibility for the enterprise in the hands of a single manager. Bukharin and Radek, who accused Lenin of establishing 'state capitalism', were rebuked for 'infantile left-wing communism'. In vain, the workers' opposition sought in 1921 and 1922 (at the tenth and eleventh congresses) to give the Russian trade unions a greater measure of responsibility in management. This tendency was condemned for its anarchist leanings, and self-management was thus doomed as definitively incompatible with the Soviet system of central planning. To this day, the enterprise has preserved the unity of command as well as the vocabulary inherited from that heroic age (front, hero of labour, brigade, etc.).

2 The restoration of the market, under the NEP, brought with it a return to monetary accounting (*khozrashchet*) in the factory, which has survived down to the present time. When it became necessary to envisage different approaches to the development of industry in order to restore prewar production levels, a split arose between those who favoured the development of light industry in association with agriculture and those who advocated the development of heavy industry by means of accumulation at the expense of agriculture; Stalin came down on the side of the latter. The first five-year plan (1928–32) was speeded up, producing serious disruption, notably due to the freezing of the markets for farm produce. The introduction of forced requisitioning signalled a fresh confrontation between the regime and the peasantry, ending in the total collectivization of peasant agriculture and the elimination of the kulaks (1929–32). The government deduced from this that the small-scale peasant economy was incapable of satisfying the needs of a fast-expanding socialist sector, which therefore justified the setting up of large collective farms. The

world economic crisis, meanwhile, strengthened the leadership's desire for autarky.

3 The priority given to heavy industry, by means of a series of five-year plans, enabled the country to develop an economic and military potential that was to come through the trials of the second world war victoriously, thanks to the very highly centralized system of control exercised over the factories and the mechanisms for the distribution of products. A high rate of investment has been imposed on the population over several generations in order to achieve the desired levels of development and security. The Soviet Union, having taken the place of Germany in eastern Europe, hoisted itself to the position of a world power and leader of the socialist camp.

4 The explosion of the first Soviet thermonuclear bomb in 1953, and Stalin's death in that year, ushered in a new phase in industrial policy, this time directed towards the search for greater economic efficiency. In place of extensive growth (continuous and massive growth in employment and invest-ment), attention now turned to intensive growth, based on greater labour productivity and more intensive use of plant and equipment (Table 34). This change of direction was due to economic factors: the complexity of industrial relations rendered centralism more costly and wasteful and the depletion of labour resources and a desire to boost consumption, with the phase of basic investment completed and nuclear parity achieved, permitted a diversification of priorities. It also stemmed from the postwar technological revolution: automation and computers were opening up new horizons and giving scientific and technical innovation a preponderant role in growth. For this reason too, the Soviet Union has since the 1960s grown more receptive to trade and exchange with the other industrial countries, and has borrowed their manage-ment methods.

The evolution we have just described is continued in the present-day organ-ization of the enterprise, which is both heir to the past and chief beneficiary of the reforms that make it constantly changing.

THE ENTERPRISE AND ITS ECONOMIC ENVIRONMENT

Before analysing human relations within the factory (microsociology), it is first necessary, in order to understand the climate of these relations, to gain some insight into the macro-economic goals and pressures that govern the organiz-ation of the enterprise. We shall then go on to see how different categories of personnel subjectively experience these goals and pressures.

The purposes and characteristics of the Soviet enterprise

According to the classic model, the enterprise is a place in which various associated activities converge and capital in the form of plant and equipment is concentrated (these are the enterprise's assets) and put into operation by the

TABLE 34 *Characteristics of economic development in the USSR*

	Accelerated industrialization phase		Mature phase	
Industrial output, annual growth rate	16%[1]		7%[2]	
Employment, annual growth rate	9%[1]		2.7%	
Rate of growth of industrial fixed capital	1940 (1929 = 100)	715	1978 (1965 = 100)	285
Output				
producer goods	,,	780	,,	257
consumer goods	,,	360	,,	232
Active population				
in agriculture	1940 in %	54	1978 in %	21
industry	,,	23	,,	39
in services	,,	13	,,	40
National income relative to the USA		31[3]		67
Soviet trade with capitalist countries	1940 (1913 = 100)	21	1978 (1965 = 100)	699[4]

Notes: 1 1928–40.
2 1965–78.
3 Relative to the USA in 1950 = 100.
4 At 1978 prices.

workers, labourers and executives under the control of a manager, who is responsible for guiding the enterprise towards achievement of its goals: namely, to produce and innovate in order to create, at the lowest possible cost, more wealth than it consumes (profit). In a market economy, this profitability is vital, for otherwise the factory cannot survive. Competition forces it to improve productivity or diversify its range of products, which leads it to expand through takeovers and mergers and to innovate, since the test of good management is the ability of the company to adapt to changing circumstances and earn profits – hence the crucial role of investment decisions.

Under Soviet law, an enterprise must have a company *name*, a *Gosbank account* guaranteeing its financial autonomy (*khozrashchet*), that is sufficient receipts to cover its outgoings, and a *manager* responsible to the administration for fulfilment of its *production plan*. It is autonomous in accounting matters, although it does not enjoy full financial autonomy; the goal of the enterprise is not a commercial one, and it may even be run at a loss, with state subsidies. Profit (the difference between costs and revenues) is one management criterion to measure the functioning of the enterprise, but by no means a decision-making criterion. The enterprise is not free to modify its production plan or to invest without permission from the administration.

The administration lays down prices (state committee on prices), wages (state committee on labour and wages), capital expenditures, profits and reserves to be retained in the factory. The state budget creams off a very large proportion of profits in the form of taxes and compulsory levies; as a result, the factory's profit is put to the service of the economy as a whole and not to that of the enterprise. The norms laid down by the administration play the part performed by competition in a market economy. Thus, the Soviet enterprise does not take the risks assumed by a capitalist firm, particularly in respect of investment decisions; its ability to expand therefore depends less on its profits than on credits allocated to it in the budget plan.

Whereas the capitalist enterprise operates within a price system that dictates its constraints through the mechanisms of the market, and is therefore not concerned in the running of other enterprises, its Soviet counterpart is part of an overall plan. Far more than planning, it is this *administrative tutelage* which distinguishes the centrally planned Soviet system from free market economies, in which each company does its own planning. A single decision-making centre, the Gosplan, takes the place of a multitude of arbiters. It is therefore essential to know something about the administrative network exercising tutelage over the enterprise in order to understand how the latter works.

External constraints on the enterprise

Since it is the central authorities which lay down the model of consumption, in other words the things to be produced and distributed, they require a network of channels through which to guide decisions and control production.

Formal channels. 1 *Channels supplying information* on the needs of the population, the capacities of enterprises and likely technical advances. Planners receive information about the population's needs through regular household-budget surveys and market research conducted by certain economic forecasting departments in light industry. In 1965, the budgets of 51,000 households were observed, including 21,000 industrial blue-collar families, 4000 managers' and white-collar workers' families and 26,000 collective-farm workers' families. Despite this large number, which was increased to 62,000 in 1967, the sample is still only imperfectly representative from a social and geographical standpoint as a measure of potential demand, a factor not immediately apparent in analysis of actual budgets. In addition, deputies to the soviets (local, provincial, republic and Union) act as a channel of information by laying problems before the different ad hoc committees. The Party organs play a similar role.

It is the job of the research institutes to lay down scientific norms that will enable planners to determine the amount of goods and services required to satisfy the needs of the population (per capita nutritional norms) as well as the demands of the production system (technical coefficients per unit produced). They are also expected to explore medium- and long-term prospects and to forecast and identify the emergence of new needs, likely technical improvements, etc. The authorities are kept regularly informed of the current situation by the ministries and the Central Statistical Office, which gathers all data concerning enterprise performance and capacity.

Thus in possession of all the information necessary to establish a balance sheet of resources and needs, planners can then draw up a draft plan for submission to the highest political bodies (the Politburo and the Council of Ministers of the USSR).

2 *Channels for issuing directives and adjustments.* In the Soviet Union as elsewhere, it is the government which decides on the main priorities and shape of the plan. The priorities contained in the five-year plan are submitted to the Party congress in the form of directives for approval; annual plans are presented to the Supreme Soviet at the same time as the budget. These key options set growth rates and orders of priority. It is then up to the State Planning Committee (Gosplan) to spell out objectives and ensure their internal coherence by setting overall ratios to be adhered to, in the form of control figures.

Within the limits of these control figures, each technical ministry prepares a detailed breakdown of the plan's objectives for the enterprises under its responsibility. Certain factories making consumer goods are run by urban soviets, while collective or state farms are attached to a 'regional agricultural production unit'. The technical ministries are far more than simple Gosplan transmission belts, for the number of indicators planned by the central organ is tending to decline, so that these administrations are now becoming the true planners, pending the day when, perhaps, this task devolves upon industrial associations through gradual decentralization of the decision-making process.

The enterprises, meanwhile, are invited to submit a counter-draft for discussion with the relevant central office in the ministry (*glavk*). After that, the draft is returned to the Gosplan for preparation of the final version which, after approval by the Supreme Soviet, becomes law. Fulfilment of the plan then becomes a legally binding obligation at all levels.

The nature of the relations that grow up between administration and enterprise during the preparation and execution of the plan determines the very character of the Soviet economic system. Depending upon whether one stresses the bureaucratic and restrictive aspect of these relations, or the procedures of consultation and compromise between the different parties concerned, one will conclude that the Soviet economy is either a 'command economy' or an administrative economy founded on consultation.

3 *Material and financial channels.* In fact, the central administration controls the enterprise less by means of directives and norms than through the centralized system of allocation of industrial products (over 13,000 products,

representing one-third of the total, are allocated; the remaining two-thirds are allocated on a regional basis). In effect, suppliers and clients are not free to choose each other. Enterprises are obliged to submit their requests (*zayavka*) to a state supplies committee (*Gosnab*), which alone has the power to deliver order forms to suppliers and delivery forms to their clients (*naryad*). Because the production plan is tight from the outset, that is, at the upper limit of the enterprises' capacities, resources themselves are stretched, or even in chronically short supply, which thereby strengthens the authority and importance of the allocating authorities. Unlike western enterprises, where manufacturing is generally dependent on the sales departments and smooth relations with the banks, the day-to-day business of a Soviet enterprise is dependent on material supplies, and these are the predominant worry. Obtaining the raw materials and equipment needed to fulfil the plan on time is far more important than loans or profits, for without an allocation voucher money is powerless. Through its financial dealings with the enterprise, the State Bank (the local subsidiary of the Gosbank) is able to exercise control over management: investment allocations or provisions, the wage fund, sales growth, payments to the Treasury out of earned profits, all these movements of funds take the form of written entries in the enterprise's bank account. The bank can extend short-term credit, if necessary, in order to cope with overdrafts or short-term requirements. On the other hand, interest-free long-term investment financing is granted on the basis of programmes stated in the annual or five-year plan.

Industrial investment totalled close on 300 billion rubles in 1970. The enterprises financed two-thirds of this amount (20 billion) internally. But it is important to note that half these funds were used for centralized investments, and so the fact that financing is done out of internally generated funds does not necessarily imply decentralization of decisions.[2]

The primacy of material factors over financial considerations, which by means of physical checks ensures compliance with the priorities laid down by the planners, has its drawbacks too. First of all, administrative procedures become increasingly cumbersome as interindustrial relations grow more complex. Attempts are being made to achieve greater flexibility by allowing enterprises to establish direct links among themselves in the form of long-term delivery contracts which are submitted to the *Gosnab* for approval on a single occasion only. But, with very few exceptions, the Soviets are still far from accepting the idea of a trade in industrial products, which would substitute for the rigidity of the existing vertical channels the flexibility of horizontal relations found in a market economy.

It is possible that at some time in the future contracts between factories will be adopted as a basis for planning in a sort of contractual economy. However, these contracts would have to take into account the limits imposed by the control figures so as not to outrun resources, inventories being permanently monitored by computer. Another solution would be to draw up more realistic plans and less ambitious objectives. The risk of non-fulfilment currently incites factories to guard against this eventuality by building up buffer stocks, or by means of informal procedures verging on the illegal.

Parallel channels. One finds informal relations in all human groups, and these often flow from formal relations: we sort people into friends, acquaintances and enemies. In the Soviet Union, the most important factor in production, and the scarcest, namely labour, is not susceptible to strict administrative planning. Except for managers, who are posted according to the order in which they graduate from the advanced colleges, or promoted at the behest of their superiors, the great majority of workers and specialists are recruited directly by their employers, or, in the big cities, by a central labour exchange. The free play of individual preferences and offers of services thus breeds a labour market.

The freedom of the enterprise to recruit is limited by the wage fund allocated to it, as well as by the pay scales laid down for each occupation by the state committee on wages and labour (the trade unions play a part in setting norms but not wages). Individuals looking for work generally turn by preference to the big employers, which receive more attention from the authorities and therefore offer their personnel greater security and benefits. This accounts for the existence of some measure of competition among enterprises on the labour market, as well as for the sometimes over-rapid labour turnover (*tekuchest'*), with workers moving too frequently from one factory to another since 1956, when the wartime measures mobilizing workers at their place of work were rescinded.

There is a further form of mobility resulting from bureaucratic inertia in the Soviet Union. Each day, thousands of representatives of different enterprises set out for the towns, usually the capital, in order to lobby some government agency or other on behalf of their firms. These public-relations specialists are paid to 'speed up' (hence their name: *tolkach*) the granting of authorizations or the delivery of goods. Unlike our sales representatives, whose job is to sell their wares, the *tolkach* is concerned rather to obtain the materials, credits and plant his or her firm lacks.

One way for a factory manager to secure his or her future is to build up 'reserves' (plant, raw materials, personnel), which merely helps to increase shortages. Another path to the same result is to underestimate one's capacity in order to obtain a less stringent plan, hence one easier to fulfil. Some prefer to guard against the risks inherent in dependence on outside supply circuits by trying to live within a closed circuit, i.e. making their own supplies with whatever comes to hand and bartering with nearby enterprises, or even turning to the black market for the products they still lack. This fosters the development of positively feudal industrial empires, which strengthens the traditional importance of the big enterprise in the Soviet Union. In very many cases, the latter enjoys a monopoly in some product or other. It is this monopoly situation, rather than its size, which determines the true economic importance of an enterprise.

THE INTERNAL ORGANIZATION OF THE ENTERPRISE

The majority of Soviet enterprises are still small or medium in size (with fewer than 200 employees), even though over 60 per cent of output and labour is concentrated in firms employing over 1000 workers. However, under the terms of a decision taken in April 1973, close to half of industrial enterprises will lose their legal status in favour of industrial associations (unions of enterprises), which will result in a considerable reinforcement of industrial concentration in the coming years.

This development is dictated by three preoccupations: (1) to speed up research, development and innovation by concentrating research institutes within the big enterprises; these were until now dependent on the different ministries (which explains why these associations are to be called unions of production and research); (2) to decentralize decisions by conferring upon the union's supervisory board the prerogatives of the former central ministerial divisions (the effect of this will be (a) to transfer the *glavk* personnel to the union, and hence to shift the administrative costs formerly borne by the ministries onto the union, and (b) to reduce administrative staff through the disappearance of small firms absorbed by the union); and (3) to permit the development of computers.

To make these enterprises workable, they are divided, as elsewhere, into a certain number of departments or technical divisions (*tsekh*), namely production, administration and personnel, research and design, planning, and supply and procurement, which are themselves subdivided into units and workshops (*uchastok*). Together, these units are placed under the authority of a general manager, who assumes sole responsibility for the enterprise as regards the administration of the different departments (Art. 4 of the enterprise statutes approved in 1965).

The work of the manager is governed by the obligation to fulfil the enterprise plan (*tekhpromfinplan*), which is itself the synthesis of the different plans for production, finance, supply, innovation, etc., imposed upon the manager by the various bodies to which he or she is answerable. The sheer quantity of these obligations, many of which are incompatible, enables managers to choose from among them and to concentrate on those criteria most likely to show off their management to its best advantage and thus to further their promotion, or else those criteria most profitable to their personnel.

From this point of view, two criteria in particular occupy much of a manager's time: (1) the extent to which the production plan is fulfilled, as measured by value-added and by the smooth performance of delivery contracts; (2) labour productivity, this criterion having replaced that of profitability since 1981 in the allocation of the enterprise's various profit-sharing funds. If the plan is not fulfilled, the enterprise is sanctioned: wages are reduced and bonuses withheld; what is more, profit-based bonuses will be low if profits are insufficient. Consequently, *share of profits*, if not the profit itself, must always be among the factors motivating a Soviet factory manager.

The manager has a duty also to *innovate* in order to improve productivity (trimming production costs improves profitability and hence the amount available for distribution to personnel) and to modernize methods and, less frequently, the product range. But innovation entails certain risks, notably by increasing launching costs, something managers are not always willing to countenance. Thus, the technical ministries are in fact the true promoters of innovation, and it is the senior ministry officials (some of them with vice-ministerial rank) who take the major investment decisions. The counterparts of the western corporation's managing director or chief executive officer are these vice ministers, who are the true chiefs of the enterprises under their juris-dictions. It is they who decide to form new enterprises, appoint the managers and their deputies, draw up the list of personnel required and set prices. It is worth noting that the individual enterprise has no 'import-export' depart-ment, as it has no direct contact with foreigners. It is the technical ministry which deals with foreign suppliers or customers, generally through the relevant departments (central import and export organizations) of the foreign trade ministry of the Soviet Union.

The manager's policies are channelled through deputies and backed by the different committees involved in supervising the running of the enterprise: the Party, the trade union, the permanent production conference, the weekly shop-floor meeting and the people's control committee (see Chapter 10).

Through the intermediary of the organization secretary (*partorg*), the Party constitutes a parallel hierarchy with links to the Party central committee, whose job it is to represent and defend (demands are submitted to the Party and not to the trade union) the higher interests of the regime, but in a much more direct fashion than would the annual general meeting of stockholders in a limited liability company. For the job of the Party is not only to see that directives are executed, but also, more fundamentally, to appoint the key executives of the enterprise, with the exception of the manager and chief engineer, who are appointed by the supervisory ministry (which in turn must obtain the approval of the Party organization at ministerial level). But within the *partkom*, managers are subject to the same discipline as any other Party member. They are thus part of two separate hierarchies: one concerns the sector of industry and is thus the hierarchy of the technical ministry respon-sible for the manager's particular branch of industry; the other is geographi-cal, operating through the Party organization, which makes a manager answerable to the Party committee of the local town or city (and not to the *partkom* of the branch ministry), which gives local Party officials powers to arbitrate such conflicts as may arise between enterprises.

The political function assumed here, not by the trade union but by the Party, reduces the trade union organization to a mainly administrative role.

Since strikes are forbidden, and since wage-bargaining is not in union hands but in those of the state committee for wages and labour, on which the trade unions are represented, the local trade union organization enjoys only limited powers to discuss work norms. The trade union is not an organ for the pressing of claims — the socialist regime has abolished the class struggle in principle — but a mechanism in the service of productivity and the welfare of the workers:

> The principal task of the trade unions is to stimulate the initiative of the masses, to foster involvement, in order to strengthen the economic power, the overfulfilment of plans, the mobilization of the reserves, the raising of the material and cultural level of the workers. (Articles of the rules of the plant trade union committee)

Thus it acts to ensure compliance with labour legislation, standards and rules of hygiene and safety and to arbitrate disputes with management and condemn bureaucratic excesses.

The trade union is also responsible for the running of the social security system; also, eligibility for different benefits and allowances, holiday vouchers for rest homes and holiday camps run by the unions, theatre tickets, etc., are dependent on union membership. This is not compulsory, but no one refuses to contribute 1 per cent of his or her wages per month in order to benefit from the trade union's benefits and advantages. At the Rustavi steel mill, holiday vouchers (12–26 days) are distributed to 1800 people each year, giving the 11,000 employees a holiday at a preferential rate once every 6 years.[3]

The trade union runs the cultural club, with its many amateur activities, workshops and sports facilities. Lastly, it represents the workers in the yearly collective-agreement negotiations, which spell out the employees' production commitments (the trade union plays a leading part in campaigns of socialist emulation) in exchange for social benefits and amenities, which the management agrees to include in its programme. The collective agreement represents as it were the social aspect of the enterprise plan.

Personnel are kept periodically informed as to the degree of fulfilment of the plan, by means of a variety of participatory bodies not unlike those found in German or French law (joint staff-management committees); these can in no way be described as a form of self-management. In 1958, permanent production conferences (PDPS, *postoyanno-destvuyushchie proizvodstvennye soveshchaniya*) were set up in all enterprises employing at least a hundred workers. These conferences, which meet at least every six months, are attended by Party, trade union and Komsomol representatives, as well as delegates of the different categories of personnel. A more direct form of democracy operates on the shop floor, where the brigade meets each week to review events and problems, under the chairmanship of the *master* (foreman). The latter is a key figure in the organization of work, controlling bonus awards, assignments to this or that task, the training of apprentices and shop-floor discipline; indeed, the *master* is largely responsible for the quality of labour relations on the shop floor, as we shall see.

It is not certain that the present form of participation in the enterprise is sufficient to give workers the feeling that their condition has been radically transformed. The state enterprise has not abolished wage labour; wage labourers hire out their labour and, in the capitalist phase of Soviet development, this entails sacrifices.[4] Payment by piece rates, and bonuses for overfulfilment of the plan, are an incitement to hard work, but these are not the only material incentives. One feature particular to the Soviet system is that bonuses depend on group work and make use of non-economic incentives. While profits are distributed on an individual basis, the profit itself is the outcome of a joint effort measured by the efficiency of the enterprise. This is permitted to distribute to personnel out of its own funds ('profit-sharing funds') either bonuses or indirect social benefits ('social and cultural funds'). In this way, workers may share in the profits of the enterprise.

There are two categories of bonus: *legal* bonuses, paid to workers out of the wage fund and the profit-sharing fund, and *exceptional* bonuses to reward outstanding performance, workers at retirement, and so on. Managers with particular responsibility for the satisfactory fulfilment of the plan receive a greater proportion of the annual bonuses, for it is only possible to measure their performance at the end of the year. In 1980, some 59 per cent of the profits earned by industrial enterprises was paid to the state budget, and of the 41 per cent allocated to their reserves, approximately 8 per cent was handed out to workers in the form of bonuses.

Further, appeals are made to the workers' civic sense to encourage them to exceed the plan (socialist emulation), work overtime, forgo one day's holiday (*subotnik*), etc. In certain cases, these campaigns are organized under pressure from the authorities, in conditions that cast doubt on the spontaneous and voluntary nature of people's commitments. On the other hand, there can be no doubt that rewarding the best workers by giving them priority access to rest homes, presenting them with decorations or honorific titles, or publicizing their performances on the front page of the factory newspaper, where one exists, or on the roll of honour is a sign that the moral satisfaction and social prestige felt by the beneficiaries are rooted in a value system that places far greater emphasis on work than is the case elsewhere.

Conversely, 'slackers' or 'parasites' are prosecuted and punished under civil law (by withholding their income in lieu of material damages, although this is restricted to one-third of a person's wages according to Art. 49 of the Labour Code) or under penal law by a scale of punishments ranging from reprimand to withholding earnings, dismissal, demotion or, in extreme cases, dispatch to a disciplinary labour camp. With the end of shortages, emulation and coercion are tending to lessen in importance, while material incentives are becoming increasingly, though by no means overwhelmingly, significant in the psychology of the worker. This emerges from sociological surveys of workers' attitudes to work.

HUMAN RELATIONS AND WORKING CONDITIONS IN THE ENTERPRISE

The impact of enterprise organization on human relations

Certain organizational structures are determined by technological imperatives that are the same regardless of political regime. Thus, the tendency to concentration is universal: in the past 20 years, the optimal size of a steel mill has grown from 1 million to 4 million tons of steel, and will soon have risen to 8 million tons. On the other hand, the quality of human relations in the Soviet enterprise ought to test characterizations of a regime that claims to be socialist and proposes to establish communism. In fact, the belief that a new consciousness ought to replace the development of productive forces led in the beginning to emphasis on economic growth, while the effects on behaviour and social aspects of the quest for economic efficiency were neglected.

An analysis of organization reveals the following factors:

1 The size of an enterprise, its gigantic proportions still further accentuated by recent measures amalgamating existing enterprises, is determined by economic optima and not by considerations of what would be the dimension most favourable to the full development of human relations. 'Concentration entails the subordination of thousands of workers to a single manager',[5] whereas in a medium-sized enterprise, the management is approachable, and daily contact with the rank-and-file workers breeds a friendly atmosphere, giving people the feeling that they all belong to one big family bound by common interests.

2 The size of factories and the centralized nature of the decision-making process demand hierarchical structures and a style of authority that tend to throw up two sorts of barrier, one between the manager and the central officials entitled to interfere in his management, the other between the manager and his or her employees. To be successful, a manager needs a fighting spirit. Even if a manager was inclined to introduce workers' management, he or she would lack the necessary degree of autonomy to do so. Soviet-style centralized planning is incompatible with workers' management. While it is true that the control exercised by Party and trade union do serve to involve workers in the running of the enterprise, the rank and file have no say in objectives or production norms. In a word, the dichotomy between those who decide and those who execute has not been abolished, and attempts to deny this by means of moral exhortation are likely merely to corrupt communication.

3 The criterion by which workers are judged and promoted within the enterprise is that of economic efficiency, as measured by output, and political activism. This tends to encourage competition and to lay stress on **economic**

incentives, at the expense of team spirit and the virtues of co-operation and disinterested work, which are the mainstays of the communist ethic. Here, though in a different form, we encounter the contradiction between the demands of the economy and the goals of society which is common to all industrial societies.

In other words, the factory reforms set in hand by Liberman's proposals in 1962,[6] and implemented in 1965, have mainly been directed at relations between managers and the administration; they have had no effect on the style or climate of industrial relations. Three-quarters of workers asked 'What have you personally gained by the reform?' replied either 'Don't know' or 'Nothing at all', while two-thirds of the engineers interviewed either refused to reply or expressed unfavourable opinions.[7] Judging by reactions and replies to sociologists' investigations, the process of identifying workers with their enterprise and of giving them the feeling of being the masters and not mere employees has hardly commenced, except among an activist minority. This is why each category of personnel experiences the goals of the enterprise and its shortcomings after its own particular fashion.

Stratification inside the enterprise

Sociologically speaking, we may distinguish a certain number of criteria by which to differentiate the workforce of an enterprise.

According to whether a job is skilled or unskilled. Attitudes towards the industrial system differ according to whether the person concerned performs an exacting manual task, entailing a great deal of physical effort (docker, miner, seaman, etc.), or an office job, i.e. a mere executant's job or one entailing responsibilities.

Approximately 12 per cent of industrial workers may currently be reckoned to belong to the supervisory grades (engineers and technicians, foremen) and thus more directly responsible for or associated with decisions; close to 4 per cent are office workers and 84 per cent are blue-collar workers, of which 60 per cent are 'professionals' and 40 per cent unskilled workers.

Engineers are a relatively numerous group in the Soviet Union, with 1 engineer on average to 30 blue-collar workers (compared with 40 in the United States). Between 1928 and 1969, the Soviet Union trained 2.5 times as many engineers as the United States. True, a greater number of Soviet engineers occupy administrative posts. Furthermore, the country has a plethora of managers — 1 engineer on average for 3 technicians — in industry, which sometimes means that engineers starting out on their career are given jobs well below their level of qualification.

What makes for differences between these categories is not only the nature of the work but also attitudes. A person with a scientific background has less difficulty finding a place in an organization, without questioning its rationality, than an untrained worker, seeking simpler explanations suited to the simplified world of his or her immediate experience. Not that the better educated are less critical or frustrated; quite the reverse, for it is among the engineers and young workers graduating from secondary school that we find the most highly developed critical sense.

According to degree of involvement or activism. The role of the Party militants and trade unions is to foster a positive frame of mind and the desire of each individual to become involved in the service of all. This is a difficult art, for activism is not to be confused with the conformism and formalism of a campaign of socialist emulation, nor with the careerism that offers glittering opportunities of promotion to the most zealous, nor with those political or moral harangues that result only in debasing language. Which is why, in the Soviet Union as elsewhere, success is rare; when it does come, it is evidence of that genuine desire to transcend the working man's condition which fires the best and the most disinterested among them.

The activists form the pool from which trade union officials and Party members are recruited. They form a parallel political hierarchy, alongside the professional hierarchy: they are the star workers, innovators, members of an élite, enjoying material advantages, the publicity that surrounds their performance and rapid promotion.

Specialists in the sociology and the psychology of work have paid close attention to factors capable of increasing workers' participation and productivity. For the answer to the problems facing the enterprise does not lie exclusively in more rational decision-making (which could be solved by greater use of computers and programming or simulation techniques, as found in modern management methods), but increasingly in the psychological context which conditions the individual's attitude towards work (degree of job satisfaction, ability to co-operate as part of a team, etc.). As a result, the scope of social action has come to spread well beyond the framework of the enterprise to everything that has some bearing, however immediate or remote, on the behaviour of the worker: family, housing conditions, aspirations and career ambitions.

According to sex and age. Living conditions and aspirations vary according to age and sex. The domestic duties of the working woman (see Chapter 5) restrict the amount of time available to her to improve her professional qualifications or play an active part in the different works committees. This explains why women show a marked preference for jobs liable to make their lives as housewives easier: proximity to the home and flexible working hours. Women are more inclined than men to put up with repetitive work. Men attach greater importance to opportunities of promotion. We find too that women are less involved than men in social activities: only 13 per cent of women attend production council meetings, compared with 35 per cent of men. They would like a shorter working week, not in order to spend more time on their hobbies or increase their earnings by taking a second job, as is the case with men, but in order to spend more time with their children.

Growing numbers of young people in industry (the average age in Leningrad fell from 31 in 1965 to 28 in 1970) attach particular importance to promotion and to 'the harmonious development of the personality', which is a consequence of the raising of the school age. At the Moskvich car factory in Moscow, 66 per cent of workers recruited in 1966 had had between 8 and 10 years' schooling; 10 per cent of unskilled jobs were being performed by high-school graduates. There is a particularly high percentage of young people in the skilled-worker category (8.7 years' schooling), while unskilled workers are generally older (an average age of 46, with 5–6 year's schooling).

For young people who leave secondary school with hopes of going on to higher education, going to work in a factory is a temporary expedient, meant to last only a short while before resitting the examination or finding a job better suited to their qualifications or aspirations. Many continue their studies, despite the difficulty of reconciling factory work with evening classes. Their education also explains why these young people resent more deeply than others the discrepancies between the theory and the reality of the industrial system. They are more demanding than their elders with regard to work organization and hygiene. They believe that their claims are insufficiently represented since there are too few young people on the various committees.

The young are also attracted to pastimes such as sport, films, music, theatre and science. They tend, in the interests of the harmonious development of their personalities, to be somewhat worldly in their attitudes towards work and though they do not go so far as to reject all desire for a career, as occurs in the west, there is a growing preference for unorganized leisure activities, and work has ceased to be the first of their ambitions as was the case with the older generation: their minds are otherwise occupied.

Because young people frequently tend to be nonconformists, it is among them that enthusiasm for socialist emulation is most perfunctory, that indiscipline and even delinquency, absenteeism and instability are most common. Job turnover is twice the national average among the 21–24 age group. Some 65–80 per cent of those who change jobs are young people; but then this is only to be expected at an age when a person is still searching for an aim in life.

Labour mobility: the impact of the social climate

The high job-turnover rate (*tekuchest'*) in the Soviet Union, ever since the repeal in 1956 of the wartime decrees mobilizing workers at their jobs, has driven the authorities to puzzle over the causes of the seasonal upheaval which each year robs the factories of 20 per cent of their workforce on average. One worker in five changes jobs each year. The damage to the economy is considerable, owing to the fact that it takes roughly six months' training for a new recruit to become thoroughly skilled in a new job, besides falling output in the three weeks prior to resignation and the two weeks of unemployment between jobs.

As we have already pointed out, instability is highest among the young, but it is also high among certain seasonal labourers such as construction workers (there is a 32 per cent annual turnover in the building industry). The highest turnover rates are to be found in Siberia and the far north regions, where living conditions are hardly an encouragement to workers to settle down beyond the term of their contract, knowing as they do that under present circumstances they are in no danger of unemployment.

The prime reason for this mobility is the job situation. Each year, the labour market offers considerable scope for changing jobs, because new factories are being built. In this way, a job in the building industry is the rural labourer's first step to obtaining the qualifications necessary for subsequently finding a job in industry. For many people, changing jobs is a means of obtaining promotion (for 5—6 per cent of personnel, on average): often, the only way in which individuals who have improved their qualifications can find a suitable job is by going to work for another factory.

The abundance of jobs on offer has its drawbacks as well as its advantages. Competition between factories to recruit personnel may lead to sizable disparities in pay for a given level of qualification from one enterprise to the next in a single city, which means that everyone will apply for a job in the factory that pays the best wages. This also makes it harder to maintain discipline, as a worker threatened with some form of sanction may ask for dismissal and obtain it within a fortnight. In a country in which the right to strike does not exist, but in which freedom to work is generally respected, the possibility of leaving one's job is often the only means whereby one can express an opinion on living or working conditions. Thus, labour mobility may be seen as a barometer of industrial relations.

Factors of satisfaction and dissatisfaction with work

A great many surveys have tried to elucidate the reasons why workers change jobs and the factors that stimulate them to improve productivity. As well as the motivations of the young, who are concerned to improve their qualifications, for most workers there is the problem of instability, arising from housing conditions (distance between place of residence and place of work, poor provision of transport) and inadequate social amenities (day-care nurseries and kindergartens). Some 30 per cent of workers changing jobs in Leningrad cited reasons of this kind. The percentages are even higher in Siberia, even though wages are 50—200 per cent greater and seniority bonuses may represent 10 per cent of annual pay.

Then come factors specific to the enterprise: poor shift organization (10 per cent of cases), unpleasant or unhealthy work (14 per cent), obstacles to the acquisition of further qualifications or promotion (8 per cent), and too much overtime. The most recent surveys reveal that the style of relations between different echelons of the hierarchy and arbitrary decisions are cited more frequently than poor working conditions, by women especially.

What emerges from these various surveys is that the decisive factor is psychological and may be summed up in the worker's attitude towards work (job satisfaction). Table 35 gives the scale of factors making for positive or negative judgements about work.

TABLE 35   *Order of job-appreciation factors in the USSR*

Soviet workers	*US workers*	*Young Soviet workers (aged 17–25)*		
			Satisfied (%)	*Dissatisfied (%)*
1 Job content	1 Job security	Equipment	29	71
2 Pay	2 Promotion	Hygiene	35	65
3 Promotion	3 Pay	Job content	67	33
4 Organization	4 Job content	Pay	46	54
5 Relations between superiors and subordinates		Promotion	61	39
		Relations with:		
6 Physical toil		workmates	96	4
		management	51	49

As can be seen, the greater or lesser earning power and prestige of different occupations are not overriding motivations. People give priority to job content (the variety and nature of the job) and to working conditions. Such considerations become more important as educational levels improve. Engineers and technicians are the most vigorous critics of organizational shortcomings in industry and attach greatest importance to relations within the hierarchy. This points to the conclusion that wage increases alone would be incapable of solving all the industrial-relations problems within a firm. It is not by improving purchasing power, i.e. their capacity to consume, that workers will be reconciled with their lot as producers, but by improving their working conditions.

Working conditions

In the Soviet Union, as everywhere, working conditions (degree of arduousness, repetitiveness, creative freedom, etc.) are as varied as occupations themselves. However, two features specific to the Soviet enterprise are worth looking at in detail, namely the specific pace of industrial work and the constant accompanying exhortation.

All workers, but especially assembly-line workers, find that the life of the enterprise alternates between moments of intense activity and periods of calm. The work rate is frequently disrupted by shortages of spare parts or absence of stocks due to delayed deliveries of raw materials and plant. The consequent irregularity of factory work, which is reminiscent of the peasant's style of work and is often attributed to the rural background of most of the workers, stems chiefly from the shortcomings of the factory-supply system mentioned above. These difficulties arise not only from shortages of raw materials or spare parts; in certain cases they are attributable to shortages of personnel, as in the Ivanovo textile mill, where it has been necessary on occasion to quadruple overtime work in order to fulfil the plan.

The slackness of the first ten days in the month is made up for by a sudden rush of work in the last ten days (*shturmovchina*), which means overtime, lost weekends and sometimes even additional unpaid holidays when the enterprise overreaches its overtime ceiling (limited by law to 120 hours per worker per year).

Young people continuing their studies deeply resent this alternating pace of life: ten days of overtime can wreak havoc with a study programme, and in certain scientific subjects the result may be irreparable. It is not hard to imagine the discouragement individuals must feel when they have been counting on taking an exam or waiting impatiently for Sunday in order to enjoy a favourite sport. What is more, overtime rates do not always make up for the earnings shortfall resulting from non-fulfilment of the planned volume of production. Lastly, these different factors of stress at work breed morbidity, absenteeism and even alcoholism. Consumers themselves are yet another victim of the *shturmovchina*, as the poor quality of certain goods is a consequence of the relaxation of inspection procedures (OTK) towards the end of the month.

In many factories, the buildings are no longer suited to the machinery being operated in them, and as more and more tools and plant are installed, quarters grow more cramped, noisier, dustier and overheated. However, foreign visitors agree that pilot factories are roomier than in the west.

The Soviets employ a variety of means to improve working conditions, including: (1) ergonomics, which is concerned not to adapt human beings to machine work but to study the organization of production in the light of the worker's own pace (for instance, the assembly line at the Togliatti car factory is slowed down at the start and end of each shift); (2) job enrichment — for example, to break assembly-line monotony, Togliatti workers are free to change places on the line; workers at the Shchekino chemicals plant are encouraged to diversify their qualifications, and savings achieved through cutting down the workforce by amalgamating several jobs in one are credited to the enterprise, an experiment which has been extended to other enterprises; (3) automation or mechanization of the most backbreaking or unpleasant jobs — currently, between 2 and 4 per cent of workers are employed to operate automated production lines.

These different palliatives, which are intended to reconcile economic efficiency with greater job satisfaction, or at least to attenuate its monotony or unpleasantness, are not in themselves capable of breaking down the inevitable barrier between those who execute tasks and those whose greatest reward lies in creative activities of one sort or another.

To complete this picture of working conditions, it is also necessary to form an idea of the special atmosphere of work in the Soviet Union. The Soviet worker is surrounded by a climate of permanent mobilization or politicization. Banners and posters proclaim his solidarity with this or that people in its heroic struggle for independence; slogans urge him to exceed the plan. These campaigns, whose impact on the individual varies considerably judging by repeated criticisms of the 'formal' character of socialist emulation, serve as occasions for ceremonies in which telegrams are sent or read out, resolutions passed, red flags and medals distributed, in order to maintain social pressure and the authority of those whose job it is to distribute rebukes and rewards. As Egnell and Peissik point out, 'the Russian people have gone, practically without transition, from one paternalism to another' (*L'U.R.S.S.*, p. 169).

Hierarchical relations inside the enterprise

As in all groups, these relations are governed by written and unwritten rules, which flow from the nature of the organizations concerned. Starting from the bottom up, the hierarchy is represented by the shop-floor supervisor (*master*), followed by the engineers and executives, up to the manager. Certain enterprises have drawn up a code of conduct for leaders, in the form of recommendations, recalling certain elementary rules of social psychology such as 'rudeness is a sign of weakness, trust your subordinates, do not shrink from punishing, but also learn to compliment with a kind word': an American manager would find nothing wrong in that.

The supervisor. For the great majority of workers, authority is personified in everyday life by the supervisor (*master*) or site foreman. He or she is a key figure in the enterprise for, as in the army, the outcome of the battle, the climate of relations in the team he leads, depends on him. Workers can understand shop-floor problems, and make suggestions on matters affecting their daily life, but they are generally at sea in the welter of general issues affecting the factory as a whole, which are beyond the scope of their experience. Thus, if labour democracy begins on the shop floor, one may easily imagine the heavy responsibility that lies on the *master*'s shoulders in order to make it work.

The qualities demanded of *masters* are awesome: he is expected not only to be a leader, capable of welding his workers into a fraternal, effective group (of some twenty-five people), but also to have the necessary experience to assert his authority. It is his job to distribute the tasks in the workshop, to maintain discipline and to keep everybody working. The weekly meetings, at which the *master* takes the chair, are an occasion to put this direct democracy into practice, with everybody contributing to the decisions and voicing an opinion. To create the necessary climate, he must be able to understand the workers in his team; there is no such thing as a good or a bad worker, as each person contributes to the work of the group in his or her own way: some try to understand what is going on, while others seek to rationalize their efforts. The aesthete and the life and soul of the party are like musicians in an orchestra, who will play well together provided they respect each other and have a sense of equality, comradeship and mutual assistance.

Another of the *master*'s jobs is to train the apprentices under his orders. He is as wary of these beginners, who will take two or three years to meet the production norms, as of the pseudo-'innovators' — who manage to exceed them by means of privileges (such as more sophisticated machinery or priority supplies). This innovator is in fact a troublemaker, for he likes to be treated with special favour and his workmates take a dim view of his over-enthusiastic approach to work which, they know, will end in higher norms all round.

The *master* also acts as middleman between workshop and the other departments. As the person responsible for keeping the team running smoothly, the *master* is constantly busy, always on the look-out for trouble, warning people and foreseeing new problems. His technical skills must at all times be commensurate with the demands of the task in hand, for he has years of experience and practice behind him. There is no real gulf between himself and the engineer, either in material terms (he earns more than a young engineer) or intellectually, for he needs a sound technical background in order to understand plans and blueprints. Indeed, he is often consulted about materials and machinery, with which he may sometimes be more familiar than the engineer himself. The latter in turn is on hand to help workers spell out the details of some suggested technical improvement. This absence of social barriers is very much to the credit of those seeking to build a genuine working community. In order to strengthen the collegial atmosphere still further, it has been proposed to have the brigade-leader or *master* elected by his shift, and some factories have apparently adopted this approach.

The role of the *master* has been upgraded by the gradual spread of autonomous brigades, in the building trade to begin with (the Zlobin method, 1970) and subsequently in industry (in the Kaluga turbine plant, 1978). The autonomous brigade signs a contract with the enterprise, spelling out production objectives, delivery dates and supplies, while leaving the brigade absolutely free to organize its work and recruit and pay its members. This autonomy is conducive to better discipline, since each individual's wages and bonuses depend upon the group result.

Engineers and executives. The engineer's equivalent of the workshop is the design office, institute or research laboratory in which he or she works as part of a team. Human relations are enormously important here, as research workers are heavily dependent on their assistants, as well as on the spirit of co-operation or competition prevailing in the group, on the authorities' receptiveness to innovation and their superiors' opinion of their work. In short, the engineer's career depends upon the degree to which his peers co-operate in helping him to achieve his ambitions and assert himself.

All recruitment to the research institutes is by competition, and contracts are subject to periodic review, which means that no one's job is ever completely secure. Recruitment to factory design offices (KB) is at the manager's discretion, except in the case of the chief engineer, who is appointed by the ministry, which gives him some independence *vis-à-vis* his manager. But while conditions of recruitment to the factory are more flexible, this circumstance may on occasion entail some uncomfortable responsibilities for the engineer. The need to fulfil the plan, overtime and even fines leave him little rest. If he is responsible for a sector of production, much of his time will be taken up in meetings and dealings with officials (in particular to obtain vital supplies), so that less than 50 per cent of his time is spent on his principal function.

Promotion and selection are dependent on the conclusions of a review panel that periodically assesses the performances of executives; in some cases this may result in demotion, so that the executive is constantly under pressure to attend training courses, refresher courses, and so on. It is difficult, in the absence of objective criteria, to assess intellectual work. The questions who ought to be authorized to pass judgement and according to which criteria (number of pages published or productivity gains attributable to innovations) are currently the subject of widespread discussion. Growing attention is being paid to the results of research, given the growing number of engineers and the rising cost of their training. International comparisons in this respect are tricky, as Soviet executives, engineers included, are far more occupied with administrative tasks, and receive far less assistance, than elsewhere. There were 130,000 shorthand typists in the Soviet Union in 1960, compared with 560,000 in the United Kingdom at that time. In France, one-third of engineers work in design offices while two-thirds work in administration, production or sales departments.

Rising up the hierarchy means shouldering greater responsibility, and many people prefer a quiet career in an institute to the hustle and bustle of the enterprise. In any case, as for all officials, the selective promotion of executives tends to favour individual success and personal performance, for it is relative to his or her colleagues that an executive moves up the ladder, and he is little concerned to attach his name to this enterprise or that since his fate is not, as in a western company, bound up with the reputation and prosperity of the firm he works for. On the other hand, the role of the manager in the selective and promotion panel may encourage conformism. Innovators are always a headache to their superiors, for it is always the drawbacks of the proposed change that strike one most forcibly to begin with; they attract hostility for upsetting the factory routine and complicating the job of the manager.

The manager. The manager's personality emerges from what has been said above as a matter of central importance from the standpoints of both economic performance and industrial relations. For he or she is responsible not only for fulfilling the production plan, but also for the housing and welfare of his or her workers. The manager is the boss, the *nach* (short for *nachal'nik*) in workers' slang, setting the tone of the whole enterprise: it is he who bears principal responsibility for the enthusiasm of those under him.

The social background and training of the manager have an undeniable influence on his capabilities and his dealings with people. There are the 'practitioners' (*praktiki*), who have risen to the top without an engineering degree but on the strength of their qualities of leadership and of experience gained in the course of their careers; the 'graduates', on the other hand, attach greater importance to organizational and technical problems. This is the source of the classic confrontation between manager and chief engineer. The latter deputizes for the manager in his absence, and may well take decisions of which the manager would disapprove. The conflict may be one of generations as much as of personality; one may be more of an administrator than an innovator, while the other pays more attention to techniques than to people.

Whatever their background, however, managers have until now been unfamiliar with those skills that in the west go under the name of management sciences or social psychology. This situation is now changing, and a National Institute of Economic Management was founded in February 1970. This top-level academy, which holds further training courses exclusively for senior civil servants in civil government and the managers of big firms, in other words the decision-makers, was modelled on the American business schools. The management sciences have since made further progress in the Soviet Union, and production organization faculties have been opened in certain cities, such as the MIEI (Moskovsky Inzhenerno-ekonomicheskiy Institut), and in 1975 a new degree course was approved leading to a degree in 'management organization' (of enterprises).

It is now planned to recruit managers by competition, which was provided for in a decree signed on 10 June 1918 but was never implemented. But some fear that if selection is confined to certain set channels of training this may restrict opportunities for promotion, and that Soviet managers may end up forming a closed corporation. They point out that managerial talent is something that reveals itself in practice, and that one cannot attribute it to a young graduate until he has shown what he is capable of. There is no substitute for experience. What do workers and executives think of this?

When workers are asked what they think makes a good manager, they cite in the first place (64 per cent) his knowledge of his job; 53 per cent cite his specialist skills while 47 per cent cite his willingness or ability to consult with subordinates before taking a decision. Conversely, they are wary of the manager who has no regard for his subordinates and is intolerant of other people's opinions, who is authoritarian and impatient. The manager must be competent and be a good listener.

Executives take a rather different view. When asked to choose between three types of manager — the liberal type, self-effacing, courteous, attentive, but easily influenced, concerned to avoid problems and therefore liable to put off decisions; the authoritarian type, who, as opposed to the former, is energetic and decisive but not always master of himself; and the democrat, who stands mid-way between the two foregoing, consulting his subordinates but aware of his responsibilities — two-thirds favoured an authoritarian manager.[8]

Doubtless, the manager's job demands a certain strength of character. As the man responsible for the running of all the different departments, he must, like the workshop *master*, be constantly on the lookout to defend the interests of the enterprise in the face of government demands. He must fight to obtain the necessary permits, and to deliver his goods on schedule; and he must be prepared at all times for unforeseen eventualities. This is why Soviet literature tends to depict the manager as a hard man, harsh and irritable, with a fondness for shouting. In his defence, it must be said that much of his behaviour is dictated by the attitude of his superiors towards him. If they take arbitrary decisions, these will inevitably have repercussions lower down. The economic reform has not done away with certain common practices, such as the obligation for the enterprise to prepare its annual plan well before knowing the objectives assigned to it and the resources allocated to it. The frequent and arbitrarily imposed revisions of the plan are an incitement to cheat about reserves. What counts for the manager above all is to keep in with his superiors, hence the obsession with presenting a favourable image come what may: outstanding workers on the front page of *Pravda*, spectacular undertakings or results and optimistic reports.

The manager is a dignitary. In addition to his work at the factory, he is constantly invited to meetings and discussions. He will sit on countless commissions. He will generally be a deputy to the municipal soviet, a member of the trade union presidium, chairman of the board of governors of a children's home, director of a further-training seminar, and so forth; he is a man constantly on the move. This celebrity inevitably encroaches upon his private life, in which public opinion takes an interest. His living standards and privileges — official car, house and personal dacha, travel facilities, and so on — set him apart, like a nobleman under the old regime. His private life must comply with the standards of Soviet morality; otherwise, his subordinates are unlikely to take kindly to his rebukes and verbal exhortations. A chief must practise what he preaches.

Thus, human relations inside the enterprise are heavily influenced by the external social context, including administrative practice and the lifestyle of managers. It appears that the behaviour of the different categories of personnel is to a large extent conditioned by organizational structures, and any speculation on the future of industrial relations in the Soviet enterprise must be based on the likely evolution of these structures.

The future of industrial relations in the enterprise

The Soviets, with their grounding in materialist philosophy, stress that changes in organizations and social relations are primarily dependent on technological change. This, by generating new occupations, will gradually dissolve the barriers between manual and intellectual workers. The narrowing of hierarchical differences will lead to the growth of genuine democracy at work through a less authoritarian style of management. In a word, the Soviets do not conceive of an ethic in isolation from material conditions. Changes in the organization of labour condition human relations.

The industrial system described in this chapter has been organized to achieve rapid results in priority sectors, drawing its inspiration from the rules of wartime economics: unity of command, virtual militarization of labour over a long period, emphasis on administration and logistics, selective promotion of senior personnel and decorations and honorific titles. In order to catch up with and overtake the most advanced industrial countries, the Soviet Union was forced to fight on the terrain chosen by its adversaries, by adopting certain techniques characteristic of the early stages of the industrial revolution – piecework and Taylorism[9] – in order to accustom peasants to factory work by means of simple, repetitive tasks. It also stressed economic efficiency at the expense of far-reaching change in human relations.

Having now achieved a degree of industrialization capable of guaranteeing its security, having rebuilt the country out of the ruins of the second world war and having overtaken the United States in the production of certain key items, the Soviet leadership is now under pressure from international competition to lend greater weight to its own people's aspirations to more comfort. At the same time, dwindling human resources are forcing it constantly to modernize and to devise more qualitative forms of growth demanding greater productivity and inventiveness on the part of the workers. Today, innovation is one of the chief driving forces of economic development.

From this has flowed a whole series of reforms aimed at incorporating computers into the industrial system and improving the co-ordination between research and production. These two imperatives are tending to foster greater industrial concentration (in the form of production and research associations). Great hopes are being placed on computers, which are expected to enable the administration, by means of a network of automated management systems (ASU) to make information-gathering less time-consuming, to cut office staff, improve resource-allocation techniques (linear programming and inter-industrial exchange charts), improve the synchronization of material flows (factory supplies), and also to establish more precise responsibilities in a bureaucracy where everyone blames everyone else for mistakes. Still, computers are not a panacea capable of preserving the existing system merely by improving it. The rationality of a system depends not on techniques but on judicious decision-making. To acknowledge that there is such a thing as management science is to acknowledge that profits and losses do not stem exclusively from the system of ownership of the means of production, but also from good or bad decisions. The change in the ownership system was not enough to change certain behaviour patterns; is the computer likely to have more fortunate effects upon human relations?

Certain Soviet economists and sociologists realize that economic reforms alone are not enough, and that over and beyond the confines of the enterprise everything must be done, however directly or indirectly, to promote greater personal involvement in work. Hence the appearance of additional targets on 'social planning' in the factory's economic plan. This deals with changes to be made in the social structure, qualifications and training of personnel and measures to be taken in order to improve working conditions and safety, housing conditions and social amenities available to workers' families, as well as communist education to develop a sense of involvement.

This social planning does not question the forms of power within the enterprise. Perhaps the associations will give birth to collegial types of management and contractual relations among enterprises, in place of administrative tutelage within the framework of a global plan. But at the same time, the growing professionalism of management tasks is liable to enhance the importance of the specialist, or even to breed a technocracy, should the Party relax its grip. This does not rule out the possibility that within the Party itself, where the administrative and technical strata are heavily represented, power struggles between conservatives and innovators may hold back the pace of reform, since the inertia brought about by habit tends to favour those who fear risk; but time is working against them. However, there seems little likelihood that in a global system, in which initiative may come from below but authority always comes from above (according to the Soviet view, it is through power that the working class exercises its control over the economy), self-management forms of power could arise inside the enterprise. Such forms of management are foredoomed, because of the risk of neo-corporatism they entail. On the other hand, however, it is hard to see how and when it will ever be possible, assuming continuing devotion to the communist ethic of disinterested work, to achieve the passage from today's hierarchic structures to a society without constraint, from democratic centralism to workers' management. The question then arises whether we should reject the anarchist ideals of a socialist society founded upon a federation of workers' associations and communes as utopian visions thrown up by the first industrial revolution, as ideals suited to an age when the relatively undiversified range of industrial techniques may indeed have suggested the possible lowering of barriers between manual and intellectual work and the abolition of hierarchy, as ideals, furthermore, that were born of an age when enterprises were no larger than a community. Or ought we to leave time and education to do their work, knowing that it takes more than one generation to change human behaviour and value systems? Workers' management cannot be instituted by decree: it must be worked for. On this assumption, the existing system of joint supervision is merely a stage in the process. It is designed to teach each and every one the hard lesson of social responsibility, thus helping to select the most active elements in a society which, by virtue of its production system, is still stratified in distinct classes and socio-occupational groups.

NOTES

1 G. Strumilin, *Ocherki ekonomicheskoi istorii Rossii*, Moscow, 1960, p. 539.
2 E. Egnell and M. Peissik, *L'U.R.S.S.: l'enterprise face à l'État*, p. 208.
3 J. Roy, in *Le Monde*, 27 Sept. 1975.
4 'Labour costs in Soviet enterprises are under-valued, which boosts the profits of the enterprise to an unwarranted extent' (sic); *Planovoe Khozyastvo*, no. 3, 1975, p. 49.
5 A. Aganbegian, in *Izvestiya*, 1 April 1975.
6 *Pravda*, 9 Sept. 1962.
7 A. Birman, *Novy Mir*, no. 2, 1968, p. 185; *Izvestiya*, 9 July 1969.
8 21 per cent favoured the democrat and 13.5 per cent the liberal; *Lit. Gaz.*, 25 Aug. 1976.
9 Taylorism is a method of scientific management based on the analysis of the movements of factory workers in order to rationalize them and improve efficiency.

SUGGESTED READING

Economic development

Bergson, A., *Soviet Economic Growth*, Rov Peterson, 1953.
Brinton, L., 'L'autogestion ouvrière en U.R.S.S.', *Autogestion*, special number, 1969.
Carr, E. H. and Davies, R. W., 'The foundation of a planned economy (1926–1929)', in *A History of Russia*, London, Macmillan, 1969–76, 3 vols.
Crisp, O., 'The pattern of Russia's industrialization', in *L'Industrialisation en Europe au XIXe siècle*, C.N.R.S., no. 540, 1974.
Davies, R. W., *The Industrialization of Soviet Russia*, Cambridge, Mass., Harvard University Press, 1979, 2 vols.
Dobb, M., *Soviet Economic Development since 1917*, London, Routledge & Kegan Paul, 1966.
Gerschenkron, A., *Economic Backwardness in Historical Perspective*, Cambridge, Mass., Harvard University Press, 1962.
Lenin, V., *The Development of Capitalism in Russia*, London, Lawrence & Wishart, 1957.

Nove, A., *An Economic History of the U.S.S.R.*, London, Allen Lane, 1969.
Nove, A., *The Soviet Economic System*, London, Allen & Unwin, 1977.
Strumilin, G., *Ocherki ekonomicheskoi istorii Rossii*, Moscow, 1960.
Zaleski, E., *Planning for Economic Growth in the Soviet Union 1918–1932*, Chapel Hill, University of North Carolina Press.
Zaleski, E., *Stalinist Planning for Economic Growth 1933–1952*, Chapel Hill, University of North Carolina Press, 1980.

Economics of the enterprise

Berliner, J., *The Innovation Decision in Soviet Industry*, Cambridge, Mass., MIT Press, 1976.
Chambre, H., 'L'entreprise soviétique (avant la reforme de 1965)', *Économie appliquée*, archives de l'I.S.E.A., vol. 17, nos 2–3, 1964, pp. 369–402.
Chambre, H., 'Le profit en Union soviétique', *Économie appliquée*, vol. 25, no. 4, 1972, pp. 681–747.
Delamotte, J., *Shchekino, entreprise soviétique pilote*, Editions ouvrières, 1973.
Egnell, E. and Peissik, M., *L'U.R.S.S.: l'entreprise face à l'État*, du Seuil, 1974.
Lagasse, C. E., *L'Entreprise soviétique et le marché*, Economica, 1979.
Lavigne, M., *Les Économies socialistes soviétiques et européennes*, Paris, A. Colin, 3rd rev. ed., 1979.
Lowitt, T., 'La rémunération du travail dans l'entreprise soviétique', *Sociologie du travail*, no. 2, 1970.
Meyer, M., *L'Entreprise industrielle en U.R.S.S.*, Cujas, 1966.

Sociology of work

Armstrong, J., 'Administrative behavior: some Soviet and Western European comparisons', *American Political Science Review*, Sept. 1975.
Berliner, J., *Factory and Manager in the U.S.S.R.*, Cambridge, Mass., Harvard University Press, 1957.
Granick, D., *The Red Executive*, New York, Doubleday, 1960.
Granick, D., *Managerial Comparisons of Four Developed Countries: France, Britain, United States and Russia*, Cambridge, Mass., MIT Press, 1972.
Kaidalov, D. and Suimenko, E., *Aktual'nye problemy sotsiologii truda*, Ekonomika, 1974.
Kugel', S. and Nikandrow, O., *Molodye inzhenery*, Mysl', 1971.
Lowitt, T., *Le Syndicalisme de type soviétique*, Paris, A. Colin, 1971.
Ossipov, G., *Industry and Labor in the U.S.S.R.*, London, Tavistock, 1966.
Naville, P., *Le nouveau léviathan: le salaire socialiste*, Paris, Anthropos, 1970, 2 vols.
Sotsial'nye problemy truda i proizvodstva, Moscow and Varsovie, 1969.
Teckenberg, W., 'Labour turnover and job satisfaction', *Soviet Studies*, vol. 30, April 1978.
Zdravomyslov, A. and Rozhin, V., *Man and His Work* (transl. from the Russian), White Plains, New York, IASP, 1972.

Chapter 8

Social classes

Our analysis of primary groups within Soviet society has so far avoided the pitfall of doctrinal prejudice. However, macrosociology necessarily produces a simplified image of this society, and so some reference to ideology is inevitable, whether to conceal certain aspects of social reality (ideology's justificatory function) or, on the contrary, to lay bare the contradictions that the dominant ideology wishes to ignore (ideology's mobilizing function). Our impression so far has been of a highly diverse society composed of many different ethnic groups and cultural spheres, with strong contrasts between town and country, levels of education and styles of family life. Nor is the hierarchic structure of the enterprise sufficient in itself to account for the complexity we observe.

To unravel this tangled skein, we shall begin by examining the Soviets' own doctrinal interpretations of their social structure, since these determine the classifications employed in official statistics, which are themselves the starting point for any form of empirical research.

THE DOCTRINAL APPROACH

Soviet doctrine, in keeping with the teachings of Marx, interprets the Soviet Union's social stratification in terms of the socialist mode of production. Lenin uses the term *class* to denote

> broad groups of individuals which are differentiated one from another by their position, at a given point in history, within the system of social production, by their relationship to the means of production, by their role within the organization of social labour, and, consequently, by the means available to them of acquiring wealth. (*Pol. sobr. sotch.*, vol. 22, 5th ed., p. 388)

The division of society into classes results from the relationship of the different groups to ownership of the means of production. In a socialist state, where ownership of these means is collective, the fundamental antagonisms found in a capitalist society between the owners of the means of production and the exploited proletariat disappear. The only social cleavages that subsist result solely from differences in status or systems of ownership, as between the public enterprises in which the state's blue- and white-collar employees work and the co-operative enterprises which employ collective-farm workers. At its current stage of evolution (the Soviets do not claim to have yet achieved communism and a classless society), Soviet society is made up of two classes, though this differentiation cannot cause opposition between interests because of the nationalization of the means of production.

This abstract bipartite model is scarcely satisfactory.

1 It tends to exaggerate the distinction between systems of ownership, which in fact ignores the similarities in status and lifestyle of collective- and state-farm workers. Though this distinction may have had some meaning in the first decades after the collective farms were formed, it has lost much of that meaning today. It would be more realistic to distinguish differences in the respective lifestyles of city and country workers than seek to contrast two similar categories of agricultural worker.

Is this why the new constitution (Art. 1) states that 'the Soviet Union is a socialist state of the working class, the peasants and the intelligentsia'? This statement does indeed set the peasantry as a whole against the working class. In addition, the intelligentsia is seen as a social category in its own right, whereas it was formerly considered a subgroup within the working class or the collective-farm-worker class.

2 According to classic doctrine, non-manual specialists (the fastest-growing group due to technical progress) were not considered a distinct social class because they stand in the same relation to the means of production as workers or collective-farm workers. However, it is recognized that the intelligentsia, by virtue of its level of income and education, forms a distinct social stratum within the working class because its *function* in the production system and its consumption patterns differ from those of the other strata. In this way functional criteria are introduced into the analysis of social stratification, while the principle of the determinant mode of production is safeguarded, since the latter conditions the nature of work and income. Consumption patterns, to which western sociologists pay great attention, play only a secondary role from this point of view.

3 What is more debatable is the elimination of any reference to political power in social stratification. The division of labour is not confined to the economic sphere alone; power too is stratified and ramified. It is important to know whether all social groups have an equal say in political decisions. However, we shall see in Chapter 10 that the ruling strata are mainly recruited from within the intelligentsia. According to Marx, under a capitalist regime political power flows from the system of ownership (in fact decision-making power

flows not only from capital but also from struggle between groups). Under a socialist regime the reverse relationship is found: power gives control over collective property. Hence, power is no longer a dependent variable but, on the contrary, an essential feature of Soviet society by virtue of the dynamic role assigned to it in the transformation of the social system.

Marxist sociological doctrine cannot be reduced to a determinist theory of the existence of classes. Marx transposes a Hegelian view of the antagonism of opposites and considers that conflict between the two classes is the driving force behind history, seeking to organize it in such a way as to speed up social change.

I cannot take credit [Marx wrote to Weydemeyer in March 1852] for discovering the existence of class, nor for having discovered the struggles between the latter. My originality was to show: 1) that the existence of classes can only be linked to certain specific historical phases; 2) that class struggle leads to the dictatorship of the proletariat; 3) the latter is itself only a transition leading to the abolition of all classes and a classless society. (*Études philosophiques*, Paris, 1947, pp. 125–6)

What distinguishes the history of human beings from that of animals is that society is transformed through the conscious activity of mankind. Success depends on consciousness of the objective conditions of our situation and of the effectiveness of our political organization and equally of our economic situation. Thus, Marxist theory of social change can be summed up in the dialectic of objective conditions and the consciousness, in which the 'line' alternates between, on the one hand, a right-wing opportunist deviation stressing objective conditions and restricting the role of action and, on the other hand, left-wing subjectivism which is voluntarist and heedless of objective conditions.

The subjective factor in history must not be understood as the activity of isolated individuals, but as the collective consciousness which includes the organization necessary for objective conditions to emerge as social change. (G. Gleserman, *Le Développement de la société socialiste, principes scientifiques*, Progress, Moscow, 1970, pp. 32–40)

'The sphere of the subjective factor is greatly enlarged under socialism', states Gleserman (*Le Développement de la société socialiste*, p. 54). It includes the sum of all conscious activity by the masses under the leadership of the directing forces of society: the Party and the socialist government. Henceforward, since society rests upon a common economic basis, namely social ownership, it can act as a single whole. The Party can harmonize the activity and aspirations of the people as a whole around a common purpose. It is clear that transformation of social structures is no longer the result of competition among social partners: it flows from the objective conditions of development and the decisions of the authorities, who lay down common objectives and determine the respective place of each group, its status, rights and obligations, within the common effort. Social structure is here the conscious creation of authority.

The unanimous social consensus which is heralded here would stem from the absence of any antagonism based on objective conditions of the mode of production. However, doctrinal statements cannot eliminate situations of conflict. These are conflicts that result not from subjective relations between people, such as incompatibility of character, lack of modesty, arrogance, delinquency, but from the very nature of social interplay which in any society is, if not always conflictive, at least competitive. When we come to discuss the problem of social control, it will be interesting to see whether conflict is eliminated through the regime's refusal to allow it the opportunity of organizing, or whether it simply assumes different forms from those found in pluralist societies, where recognition of the conflictive nature of social relations is, on the contrary, a fundamental tenet.

To sum up, Soviet doctrine excludes the possibility of opposition of interests between social partners, but does not deny the existence of social groups (social classes or strata). These groups correspond to a specific function in the social ladder, where every individual's place is fixed according to his or her capacity (a meritocracy). Hence the Soviets have taken over the functional justification of social groups for their own use, thus converging towards the integrative view of social reality held by their adversaries. Elimination of barriers between these groups (more precisely between town and country and between manual and intellectual workers) will take time, for it presupposes not only the economic development of the country but also a change in mentality (*peremena soznaniya*). The concept of social structure itself implies duration: thus the formation and transformations of this structure are part of the historical process.

THE HISTORICAL APPROACH

To recognize that the idea of structure implies duration implies admitting — and Soviet authors do not contest this — that the new society which emerged from the 1917 Revolution is heir to its past. This past explains the survival of social groups and mentalities, which can only be modified over time. The new structure is formed by incorporating the original elements and eliminating those considered alien.

Stages in the formation of contemporary Soviet society

If present-day Soviet society is characterized as *industrial* on account of the dominant sector of its economy, *socialist* because of its institutions and *urban* because of its dominant form of civilization, these three fundamental changes occurred at different periods of Soviet history.

Technical aspects of the transition from a rural to an industrial society. The transition began in 1861 with the abolition of serfdom, which released the peasants from bondage to the nobility and freed them for employment in the factories. The movement towards industrialization speeded up in the 1890s and again from 1906 onwards, when the farmworker, freed from his obligations towards the community, was able to choose either to become the owner of his farm or to move permanently to the city. Between 1895 and 1917 the factory labour force trebled, exceeding 3 million in 1917. With the launching of the first five-year plans (over the twelve years 1928–40), the number of workers in industry again trebled, reaching 9 million in 1940. This rapid growth of the industrial labour force before the first world war bore with it the seeds of a second, far-reaching change.

Institutional aspects of the transition from a capitalist to a socialist regime. With this growing industrial concentration and the formation of a stable working class, the workers' demands became organized under the influence of radical ideas and culminated in violent confrontations: that of 1905, when the first general strike occurred and the first soviet was set up, was merely a rehearsal for the Revolutions of February and October 1917. Twenty years were to pass before socialization was brought to its conclusion with nationalization (1918), collectivization (1929–30) and the elimination of social categories hostile (or declared alien) to the new regime: first the nobility, then businessmen and tradesmen, prosperous peasants and certain experts. Then, within the ruling classes, the 1936–8 purges cut broad swathes in the ranks of leading politicians and administrators who were suspect in Stalin's eyes.

It is strangely paradoxical that Stalin's dictatorship should have revealed itself at its harshest just when the advent of socialism was being proclaimed in the 1936 Constitution. During his reign a new hierarchy gradually emerged in the name of economic efficiency. The egalitarianism of the regime's early years was condemned in 1934 in order to encourage the promotion of skilled workers. In 1935, military ranks were re-introduced. In 1940, school fees were re-established in the final years of secondary school and in the universities (between 1935 and 1938 the percentage of students of working-class origin dropped from 45 to 34 per cent, while the percentage of students from the intelligentsia rose from 16 to 22 per cent).[1] In 1939, the Stalin prizes were created to reward distinguished artists, writers and scientists. In 1943 and 1945, the inheritance laws were made more favourable. In short, from out of the ashes of the old regime a new intelligentsia arose, sympathetic to the new regime, conscious of its privileges and of its role in the running of a society that had undergone a profound change in mentality over two generations.

The transition from revolution to bourgeois habits of mind. It was not until 1968 that for the first time the urban population of the Soviet Union outnumbered the rural population. The weakness of the middle classes was one characteristic of the old regime: in 1900 Russia had only 65 towns with more than 20,000 inhabitants, and in 1922 only 16 per cent of the population lived in the towns. The rapid urban growth that accompanied Soviet industrialization brought more than 60 million Soviet citizens into the cities – the equivalent of the country's entire population increase between 1926 and 1960 – thus causing a distinct 'ruralization' of urban life within the space of less than one generation. When the restraints of the Stalin era were lifted following the leader's death, these city dwellers finally gained access to mass-produced consumer goods. Under his successor's government an attempt was made to rectify the most flagrant inequalities (in salaries and housing) and to reinstate socialist legality (amnesty for and rehabilitation of some of those deported), though this in no way undermined the privileges enjoyed by certain categories. The younger generations, who never experienced the hardships of the years of iron, have lost the revolutionary faith of their forefathers. Their ambitions are more immediate and bourgeois. They want to become 'someone', to succeed in the examinations that will open up a career among the intelligentsia.

There was a gap of thirty years between the emancipation of the serfs and the formation of a stable working-class after industrial development had got off the ground. Another generation (1906–56) had to pass before the building of socialism was completed. It took another thirty years to pass from Stalinism to contemporary Soviet society. Few social revolutions provide such a clear example of the truth well known to sociologists: that the unit of measurement in social change is the generation.

The time lag between these three developments provides a classic example of this. As a general rule, technical innovations precede political transformations. The change in attitudes of mind lags still further behind, since it proceeds from gradual adaptation to a new framework of life. In the case of Soviet Russia this rule has been proved over the long term. In the shorter term, on the other hand, we find exceptions that have been decisive for the future.

At the beginning of this century, the institutions of the Tsarist regime had fallen behind the evolution of attitudes. Because of this, numerous historians have imagined a less brutal transition, by means of reforms, towards more liberal institutions. The growing homogeneousness of Russian society, due to the opening up of the civil administration and the army to commoners, progress in education, the beginnings of an independent farming class on the model of the American farmer, very rapid growth in industrial production, the emergence of a business bourgeoisie, all these factors suggest that Russia might have followed a development comparable to that of western democracies had it not been for its fatal ordeal of the war. The thesis of Marxist historians, which is based on the contradictions between economic development (capitalist) and institutions (feudal) and concludes that the old regime was doomed in any event, has at least the advantage of being the theory favoured by the winners.

'Drunk with success', the winners wanted to rush ahead at top speed. Under the new regime, socialist institutions anticipated technological means and the aspirations of much of the population, i.e. the peasants. The bloodiest of the revolutions was not that of October 1917 but the 1929–30 revolution, which, brutally coerced the peasants into the collective farms. Stalin confided to Sir Winston Churchill (as related by the latter in *The Second World War: Hinge of Fate*, London, 1950, p. 498) that collectivization had led to 10 million deaths. To work the collective farms the Soviet Union had only 5000 tractors. Must we conclude that history would have been different had the country started from a different level of development? The historian is not concerned with such questions. Those who would answer this question base their replies on either their faith or their experience, neither of which can be communicated.

Factors in social change

In place of the traditional Marxist interpretation, which accords to the economic factor a decisive or even exclusive role, the present author favours (in order to avoid endless quarelling over which came first, chicken or egg) an analysis in terms of systems, in which the variables only become fully meaningful when mutually interdependent. For the sake of clarity, we shall distinguish the causes, forces and ends that contrive to bring about social change.

The causes. In the history of Russia and the Soviet Union, external factors have always played a decisive role: sometimes military defeat has revealed the regime's weaknesses (e.g. the Crimean war, the Russo-Japanese war, setbacks in the first world war); sometimes the war effort and its attendant ordeals have forced crushing burdens upon the population, curtailing any possibility of development. For 250 years Muscovite Russia had to maintain considerable armed forces on a war footing in order to head off the Mongol powers. When Peter the Great died the Russian Army was three times larger, per head of population, than the armies of any of the western powers.[2] Under the Tsars, the average military budget over the period 1900–13 represented 29 per cent of total expenditure (51 per cent in 1905). Even today, according to western estimates, the proportion of military expenditure represents between 8 and 15 per cent of gross domestic product. And under every regime considerations of defence have been the driving force behind industrialization.

In its turn, industrialization has had the effect of creating an industrial proletariat that did not exist previously and of encouraging the growth of the middle classes. By a familiar cumulative process, urban growth has facilitated educational progress and the birth of the mass media, which propagate new ideas.

Driving forces. The speeding up of material development and the opening up of society to external influences generated change only because certain forces acted as catalysts to shape development in the light of a vision of the future (*ends*). Under the old regime, action by the mass of the people was for a long time hindered by the fact that the peasants were unable to organize themselves politically, and by the numerous legal obstacles to the development of trade unionism (by the law of 1886 strike action was an offence), which was only legally recognized in 1906. However, this state of affairs did not prevent a spectacular increase in the number of strikes in Russia in the final decades before the Revolution. Concentration of enterprises certainly had something to do with the awakening of working-class consciousness. However, the main factor was the influence of the radical intelligentsia, which gave the working-class movement organization, a programme, leaders and ultimately the signal for revolutionary action.

In the non-Russian border areas of the empire, the foreign intelligentsia stimulated the growth of national consciousness, which merged with the demands of the workers and peasants in the Revolution. In most cases, though, the social development of Russia and the Soviet Union was dictated from above, not from the grassroots. Established authority rather than free confrontation between social groups fixed the status of the different classes of the population. In 1722 Peter the Great issued a Table of Ranks. This remained in force until 1917 and established the ladder of civil and military offices. It allowed high officials access to the nobility on a life or hereditary basis and at the same time bestowed on the sovereign and his government control of social promotion. In the same way the status of the different orders within the state (clergy, farmers, merchants) was regulated by the authorities. We shall see in Chapter 9 how the Party has arrogated to itself an equally important role in promotion to posts of responsibility. The Table of Ranks has now been replaced by the *nomenklatura*. As with commoners in the past, this designation by the Party (*vydvizhenie*) provides for the appointment of candidates who need not necessarily possess a diploma, but who have won the Party's confidence. Today, as yesterday, the status of the various sections of society is laid down by the administration: the status of the collective farm (1935, 1969), for example, which lays down the condition of the peasants who work on it. In other words, the rights, obligations and social promotion of the different strata of society are dependent on decisions by the authorities, the sole employers.

Long-term changes in social structure

Any attempt to quantify the changes that have taken place since the beginning of this century runs into numerous methodological difficulties.

The different concepts employed under the old and new regimes. Not only are different concepts used by the new regime but the Soviets often use terms that mean something else in western classifications. For example, the 1897 census is based entirely on the division of society into 'estates or orders': the nobility, the clergy, honorary citizens (those in the professions), merchants and peasants. A residual category of 'petty bourgeois' (*meshchane*) took in city artisans, clerks and workers not included in other estates. Workers who had come from the country continued to be classified as peasants, with the result that under the old regime workers did not form a distinct class. After 1917 the old classification was recast in Marxist terms. The exploiting classes included, in addition to capitalists, prosperous farmers (kulaks). The criterion for classification of a group as exploiter or exploited does not always refer to occupation or to economic criteria, for what defines the relationship of individuals or groups to ownership of the means of production is political action, by which is understood their attitude to the Bolshevik authorities. By this token, any peasant overtly hostile to the regime was classified as a kulak, even if he did not exploit another's labour. The *working-class* (20 million in 1917) must not in Soviet terminology be confused with the *manual workers*. It includes all those who hire out their labour in the widest possible sense, that is producers as a whole, irrespective of type of work or level of qualification.

The term *intelligentsia* was used under the old regime to designate a state of mind rather than a class of society. The intelligentsia was drawn from all levels of society, including the nobility, but mainly from the professional classes, that is the most enlightened strata of the population who were opposed to the regime in force. It reflected a way of life rather than a specific profession. According to the Soviet definition, the intelligentsia is an occupational category characterized by the performance of non-manual work and the possession of corresponding qualifications (higher or technical education). On occasion, the term *highly qualified specialist* is used instead. The Soviets place in this category managerial staff in the production systems, members of the professions (lawyers, doctors, artists, men of letters who belong to a union) and political personnel. The result of this admixture is that the political élite is diluted within a wider social group.

Social stratification and professional classification. Professional classification includes for statistical convenience persons in the same occupation. However, a speciality does not necessarily constitute a stratum of society. For example, accountants include both modest clerks and specialists belonging to the intelligentsia by virtue of their qualifications. Moreover, statistics of population distribution according to class are based on the physical units recorded in censuses, while professional distribution only affects the active population and is derived from conventional units, the annual worker unit already mentioned in Chapter 4 (p. 76). Hence the two series are not homogeneous. Despite this, we have combined them in Table 36 in order to elucidate general trends, which are unlikely to be invalidated by more detailed analysis. From these data we may make the following observations:

1 The disappearance of certain categories, for example the privileged members

TABLE 36   Social class in Russia and the USSR

	Total population (%)				Active population (millions)				Active population in the USA (%)	
	1897	1913	1939	1970	1917	1940	1960	1970	1900	1960
Clergy	0.2									
Hereditary nobility	1.1									
Senior civil servants	0.6									
Merchants	0.3									
Professional classes	0.2									
Total	2.4	4.9								
Peasants:									37.6	6.3
prosperous		11.4								
individual	86	66.7	2.6			8.5	9.9	5.6		
collective-farm workers			47.2	20		29	22.3	17.0		
Artisans					3.5	2.3				
Workers:	11.6	14.7	32.5	55	7.8	19.7	43.5	60.7	35.8	39.6
Industrial					3.6	9.9	18.9	25.6		
Others					4.2	9.8				
Servants and service personnel									5.4	2.8
Office workers		2.3	17.7	25	0	9.5	9.7	12.7	11.1	31.5
Specialists						2.4	8.8	16.8	10.1	19.8
Students						3.1	4.6	11.8		
Total	100	100	100	100					100	100
of which urban population	15	18	33	56					39	69

of the old society and domestic employees. At the end of the NEP the kulaks (prosperous peasants), whose numbers were already greatly reduced in comparison with 1913, disappeared completely. However, individual farming in the form of family farms remained alive. The number of persons of working age employed in the private and domestic sector, in town or country, was almost 10 million in 1960, in other words half the number of industrial workers. In thirty years (1940–70), the family sector had diminished by a third, i.e. appreciably less than the collective-farm labour force. In addition, industrialization has completely absorbed the artisan sector, whose numbers in 1917 were comparable to those of industry in the strict sense. The co-operatives of artisans (1.3 million in 1959) have over the past few years been annexed by the local industrial sector.

Also absent from the official classification are the members of the professions, which in the Soviet Union means members of the various unions (writers, journalists, composers, filmmakers, painters and lawyers) who do not appear on the staff of any public establishment. This group now appears in the statistics under the heading: 'persons with other resources'. In 1970 there were

365,000 such persons, grouped together with domestic staff paid by private individuals (nannies, cleaners).

2 The gradual transfer of the population from agriculture to industry. This development is amplified in the Soviet Union by the fact that the agricultural labour force of state farms is classified as 'workers'. However, if we take into account agricultural workers as a whole (family-, collective- and state-farm workers), 28 million people were employed on the land in 1973 (in conventional units, i.e. more than 30 million in physical units). This is a figure almost equivalent to the industrial labour force. The agricultural labour force has decreased by no more than 16 per cent in 33 years (1940—73). What has changed, however, is the status of the agricultural labour force, which is being transformed increasingly into a worker (state farms) category. While developments in western agriculture have had the effect of strengthening the position of the most skilful and the wealthiest farmers at the expense of the agricultural proletariat (which has left the countryside), in the Soviet Union the reverse may be observed: the elimination of the wealthier farmers from traditional-type agriculture and the departure of young people from the countryside, while one class of agricultural worker has remained on the land, those at the bottom of the ladders of prestige and income. The number of workers in both town and country has increased tenfold, and in 1970 represented 55 per cent of the total population, as against 15 per cent in 1913 and 1928. In this group, the number of metallurgical workers, metalworkers and workers from the mechanical industries increased from 510,000 in 1913 to 14.3 million in 1973, that is 43.5 per cent of the total industrial labour force.

3 Growth of the service sector (office workers and specialists) between 1928 and 1970. This was more rapid than the increase in blue-collar workers, owing to the expanding bureaucracy, the development of services and the formation of an increasingly numerous intelligentsia. It is this last category (of specialists) that has increased, most spectacularly since 1940 (index 700), and the movement gives no sign of slowing down. The number of people of working age continuing their studies has almost quadrupled (index 380), which clearly reveals the desire of society as a whole for culture and social promotion.

4 All these trends are accompanied and reinforced by urban growth, the process being a cumulative one, as already discussed. It remains to be seen whether this urban civilization (which is becoming the common experience of the great majority of the population) serves to level or to diversify the consumption patterns of the main strata of Soviet society.

THE EMPIRICAL APPROACH

To explore beyond these general remarks we shall attempt an empirical approach, based on a number of *objective criteria* that are both quantifiable and identifiable, in order to delimit the frontiers between social groups and to elucidate the factors involved in the stratification of Soviet society. We shall then ask ourselves whether the inequalities observed are experienced as generating class consciousness (*a subjective factor*), capable of breeding conflict, or whether on the contrary, the dynamics of social change, and in particular social mobility, tend to reduce these boundaries.

We shall take as our point of departure the more highly diversified occupational classification used by planners to plan vocational training, employment and consumption, which is good evidence of its operational value.

The nature of work and training: peasants, blue-collar workers, white-collar workers and intellectuals

Four broad divisions may be said to flow from the nature of work.

1 On the basis of the productive or non-productive nature of the work, we may distinguish people occupied in the material transformation of matter in the widest sense, who are considered productive (74.4 per cent of the working population in 1978) and people employed in non-productive activities (in the Marxist sense of the term) which we refer to as services (11.7 per cent of the total in 1940 and 25.6 per cent in 1978). We shall not dwell on this distinction; its effects are purely economic (in particular for the calculation of national income according to the Soviet concept).

2 On the basis of the worker/space relationship, a distinction is made between agricultural workers (on the collective and state farms) and other workers, i.e. blue- and white-collar workers.

3 On the basis of the manual or intellectual nature of work, occupations are classified either as mainly manual (blue-collar workers) or as mainly intellectual (white-collar workers). There is an intermediary range of occupations, for example foremen who are skilled technicians and perform both physical work and supervisory functions of an intellectual nature.

4 Level of qualification serves as a basis for distinguishing work not requiring specialized training from work that does, and finally work requiring advanced studies.

By combining the last three criteria, we obtain a typology that links type of work and training received in four social groups, and within these there are subgroups according to the functions performed in the economy or state administration and based on the scale indicated in Table 37.

Within the main categories of worker, the complex nature of work leads us to distinguish a number of subgroups: unskilled workers, complex-manual workers, skilled machine operators, etc. Similarly, within the 'intelligentsia', we can distinguish, depending on their functions, 'administrators' and supervisory staff, scientific and highly qualified staff and professionals. The dividing line between the 'specialists' (the preferred Soviet term) and the others is a university degree. The diploma of specialized secondary studies usually leads

TABLE 37   *Level of studies as related to nature of work and qualifications*

Level of education among people over 10 in 1973	Active population 1973	Nature of work	Type of occupation	Education received		
				Primary[1]		Higher
	1973	Groups	% in each group	1939	1970	1970
Higher education	6.3	6.5	Intelligentsia, highly qualified specialists	Central admin., civil servants	54	98.7	57.8
				Kolkhoz chairmen	2.3	93.3	29.3
				Factory managers	35.5	96.2	39.3
				Engineers	98.4	99.5	53.0
				Journalists, writers	80.9	99.4	62.8
Complete secondary education	21.3	9.5	Technicians, office workers	Foremen	32.9	92.8	6.8
		10.0		Nurses	63.6	98.1	0.5
Incomplete secondary education (7–8 years)	24.6			Typists	62.4	96.4	0.8
		25.0	Skilled workers	Train drivers	21.1	82.8	0.4
				Lathe and milling-machine operators	32.0	81.8	0.1
				Tractor drivers	2.1	48.6	0.02
Primary education (less than 7 years)	47.8	49.0	Unskilled workers	Arc welders	16.3	69.3	0.1
				Weavers	7.8	72.5	0.1
				Cleaners	0.9	24.8	
				Unskilled kolkhoz workers	1.3	32.8	0.1
	100	100					

Note: 1 Percentage of occupational category concerned having gone beyond primary school.

to employment as a technician (92 per cent of midwives in Table 37), although in 1970 almost half the foremen did not possess this diploma. The majority of white-collar workers have attended secondary school (generally not completed), while in 1970 some 70–80 per cent of workers had gone beyond the primary-school level.

We find that the nature of work demands a particular level of qualification, which leads to the conclusion that training is a fundamental determinant of position in society. There are exceptions to this rule. Thus, among enterprise managers, a university degree is not the general rule and a large number of older people in authority have achieved their position through practical experience (*praktiki*).

In addition, technical progress alters the content of work within a given occupation, making more advanced training necessary. The changes from one generation to another are most apparent in the country areas, where the cultural level lags furthest behind (in 1939 only 2 per cent of collective-farm chairmen had gone beyond the primary-school level). Today almost half the tractor-drivers, and a third of the non-specialist labour force have received (incomplete) secondary training. Some differences seem inevitable, whatever the regime; for example between the doctor who must have advanced training and, at the bottom of the scale, the cleaning woman. But these manual categories are bound to disappear in time.

Pay differentials

Differences in function and qualification within a social group are not necessarily accompanied by differences in income. In a monastic community or a
kibbutz, each person's share in consumption is the same. A similar formula
was applied in the Soviet communes during the period of war communism.
After this shortlived experience, however, the egalitarianism of the early years
was replaced by a policy of income differentiation, based on the idea that in
the socialist stage income should be proportional to each person's contribution
to the collective effort. Socialism should not be confused with egalitarianism,
which would be premature at this stage according to Stalin.

   In the absence of any source of income other than work, it remains to
determine the basis on which pay scales are decided, in the absence of the free
play of labour supply and demand and free contract-bargaining. Economic
considerations, rather than doctrinal preferences for manual labour, proved
decisive: the social utility of the job and the qualifications required. The
disparities in income between the different branches stem from the need to
attract workers to priority sectors or development regions. Hence, the peasants
who form the labour pool have been least favoured, while the miners are the
best-paid industrial workers. (Their salary was 57 per cent above the average
in 1970, as against 20 per cent in France.) For the same reason, blue-collar
workers are better paid than white-collar workers (before 1923 the situation
was more favourable to office workers). Compared with workers in the building trade, salaries of teachers, health workers and 'cultural' workers (mainly
propagandists and librarians − they are at the bottom of the ladder) seem
modest. A decree dated 28 December 1976 was designed to upgrade jobs in the
services sector.

   Within a given branch, pay scales seek to stimulate productivity − hence
the still very large proportion of industrial workers paid on a piecework basis.
References to qualification, which often serve to justify pay differentials, thus
roughly resemble the arguments put forward in capitalist societies, namely the
need to encourage productivity and to reward responsibility.

   Table 38, which gives a range of incomes, shows a narrowing of differentials
since Stalin's death. Low wages have been raised by stages: the minimum was
raised to 40−45 rubles in 1965, 60 rubles in 1968 and 70 rubles in 1975. The
agricultural workers have been the main beneficiaries of this policy. The
collective-farm worker, who in 1960 received only 38 per cent of the annual
wage of a state-farm worker, in 1970 received the equivalent of 74 per cent of
the latter's remuneration. Since 1980, the collective-farm worker has, like
workers in other branches, enjoyed a minimum wage of 70 rubles per month.

   Family considerations seem to have no effect on incomes policy. In the Soviet
Union there is no family allowance, except in the form of an allowance to a
woman remaining at home until her child is one year old, which is envisaged for

TABLE 38 *Soviet pay differentials*

| | Average wage = 100 | | | | | Monthly range (R)[4] |
| | USSR | | | | France | Al'metevsk |
	1932	1940	1960	1978	1970[1]	1967
Managers, senior executives			220	118[2]	251	178.3
Highly skilled specialists	263[2]	214[2]	155	130	137	146.3
Technicians						111.7
White-collar workers	150	111	82	89	87	77.4
trade		76	74	78		
education		98	87	84		
Industrial workers		105	110	110	87	
skilled machine-operators						114.6
skilled manual workers						95.8
unskilled						62.9
Construction		110	116	123		
Agriculture: sovkhoz		63	64	89	60[3]	
kolkhoz		30	50	68		

Notes: 1 After tax (*L'Expansion*, no. 33, Sept. 1970).
2 Average pay for engineers and technicians (ITR) relative to industrial workers' pay (= 100).
3 In the case of France, the figure refers to average earnings of salaried farmworkers.
4 O. Shkaratan, p. 404 (see p. 228).

TABLE 39 *Some examples of pay differentials within a single hierarchy*

	Monthly income (R)	Differentials
Commerce		
Shop manager	200 (1965)	3.3
Warehouseman	60 (1968)	1.0
Agriculture		
Kolkhoz chairman	268 (1974)	3.8
Unskilled kolkhoz worker	70	1.0
Research		
Director of an institute	500–700	4.7–5.6
Researcher at start of career	105–125	1.0
Officials		
Marshal of the USSR	2,000	28.6
Party		
Secretary general	900	12.7
Unskilled worker on minimum wage	70	1.0
Pensioner		
in the town	60	0.64
in the countryside	28[1]	0.40

Note: 1 Not including produce from the family farm.

the tenth five-year plan. Women are encouraged to work, and those who do not are the exception. As a result the difference in per capita family income between managers and workers is widened by the fact that both members of a working couple usually belong to the same social category.

The disparities between categories are not very great in the official figures, which give averages for each group (engineers/technicians, workers, office workers) or branch. If we had accurate information about the highest and the lowest salary instead of the average, we could measure the differences more exactly. Unfortunately the statistics tell us very little that might reveal one group's privileged situation compared to another's: envy is a failing too widely shared in this world, as witnessed by the Frenchman's reluctance to divulge his tax returns. This explains the fragmentary nature of the figures in Tables 38 and 39.

We find that the range of average differentials within a given hierarchy is not appreciably different between the main socio-occupational categories of salaried workers in the Soviet Union and in France. However, the difference between a manager's salary and the wages of lower-level workers, within a single hierarchy, is definitely smaller in the Soviet Union (Table 39) than in France. In France, according to Jacques Meraud, there is a difference of 1 to 25 between a managing director and an unskilled labourer as compared with 1 to 6 in the Soviet Union. A marshal of the USSR earns 28 times as much as the minimum wage-earner. Roy Medvedev, in *Socialist Democracy*, says that in some enterprises pay differentials between senior executives and those of workers may vary from 1 to 10, 1 to 20 in others, sometimes even 1 to 50. 'At national level, the differences may be as high as 1 to 100 if practical advantages, medical care and holidays are taken into account' (*Socialist Democracy*, p. 268). If one considers the situation of retired people — almost 44 million in 1975 — whose average pension is between 50 and 90 per cent of their final salary, differences are still more obvious. This explains why in 1970 some 6 million workers of retirement age supplemented their pension with a salaried job. If we adopt as our criterion of equality the relationship between the highest-paid 10 per cent of the population and the lowest-paid 10 per cent, the difference is, according to our estimates, 1 to 10 in the Soviet Union and, according to Attali, 1 to 8 in the United Kingdom and 1 to 15 in West Germany.

Since the reform of the enterprise in 1965, aimed at placing greater responsibility in the hands of managers and giving them an interest in making profits, bonuses as a proportion of managers' earnings have increased more rapidly than those paid to workers. Among the latter, bonuses rose from 7.2 per cent to 13.4 per cent of their earnings between 1965 and 1971, whereas they represent 20.9 per cent of managers' earnings (as against 10.6 per cent in 1965).

This distribution of profits is statutory. It is not the result of negotiation, still less of confrontation. It stems from profit-sharing schemes in the different categories; in almost half of cases, workers are motivated by means of piece-work or productivity-related wages, while managers are rewarded on end-of-year results (bonuses), in the absence of any other criterion by which to evaluate their work.

In the Soviet Union, income tax plays no redistributive role. Direct tax is levied only on salaries above 70 rubles per month, and the maximum rate is 13 per cent for the highest salaries. In France an annual salary of 5444 francs (70 rubles per month) would also be exempt from income tax, since the ceiling for exemption for an unmarried person was 11,500 francs in 1974. This figure is greater than the average Soviet salary at that time (144 rubles per month, that is 11,170 francs per year). However, indirect taxation does have an equalizing effect in the sense that luxury goods are more heavily taxed (carpets, caviar, spirits and art books) than basic goods and services. Vodka is a prime example of a fiscal product, though this does not seem to deter the impecunious customer.

Transfer payments (grants, scholarships, social security) and other indirect benefits (free schooling and medical care, subsidized rents, reduced fares on public transport) help to increase family incomes to an equal extent for all categories of society, and in no way reduce the inequalities previously observed. In 1974 these social benefits represented 35 per cent of the average salary.

In a regime whose avowed aim is to establish communism, in other words a more egalitarian distribution of goods and advantages, consumption in the form of collective benefits ought in theory to occupy an increasingly large place. The 22nd congress in 1961 envisaged raising this proportion to 50 per cent of income in 1980, in particular with free public transport and housing. It is not easy to maintain a balance between egalitarian measures and the direct stimulants necessary for continued economic growth. This makes Soviet policy appear to fluctuate.

If instead of individual income we consider income per family (1.8 active persons), this is on average 254 rubles of monetary income per month (£213 or $339 at 1982 prices) and 342 rubles including indirect benefits. The minimum needed for a family of four persons to sustain life is considered to be between 300 and 400 rubles per month,[3] and so a great many families, particularly in the countryside, are below this minimum level and must supplement their resources by means of produce from their family farm or by a second job. Almost all families have two income earners, but as working-class families usually have more dependent children than the intelligentsia, the discrepancy in per capita income is increased.

In situations of scarcity, income differentials are less important than access to goods. It matters little how high or low rents are if one does not have an apartment of one's own. In other words, the decisive element in behaviour depends upon income, and this is why consumption patterns, however difficult to measure, are the best guide to the strata of Soviet, or any other, society.

Lifestyles

Type of work and income condition *quantifiable* living standards, though these are not necessarily class characteristics. Hence, to be complete, our analysis requires *qualitative* criteria, which concern the education and cultural habits of the different groups and reflect their lifestyles.

These signs – language, dress, rules of polite behaviour, the snobbery and non-conformism of one or another sphere of society – are subtler and depend on *subjective* appreciation. Concepts such as 'bourgeois', 'worker' or 'intellectual' do not correspond to precise sociological definitions. This difficulty is no excuse for confining ourselves to *objective* criteria only for stratification (system of ownership, type of education, qualification and income), as this is presented in Soviet analyses. These imponderables nevertheless remain significant.

Under the old regime the westernized bourgeoisie was recognizable by its dress. Today this distinctive sign lives on among the various categories obliged by regulation to wear uniforms: school-children, soldiers, post workers, railway workers, sea and river shipping company staff, airline staff, miners. As everywhere else, styles of dress set the provinces apart from the capital, where smart young people try to ape western fashions. Here, blue jeans are evidence neither of progressive views, a reaction against the bourgeoisie, nor of a counter-culture. On the contrary, they reveal that the wearer belongs to the *jeunesse dorée*, in short they are a sign of status. However, at the doors of certain restaurants patronized by foreigners, commissionaires in gold-braided uniform refuse admission to unsuitably dressed people. The older generation has had trouble coming to terms with women in trousers. The bureaucrat is recognizable by his raincoat, felt hat and leather briefcase. A cap, pea jacket and open-necked shirt is the distinctive dress of the blue-collar worker. The peasant woman wears leather boots in summer, felt boots in winter, and a scarf knotted about her head in all seasons. However, there are many other more subtle characteristics, such as hairstyle, shape of tie or the colour of an umbrella, symbolizing membership of different artistic or privileged circles, who come into contact with foreigners.

Among the different elements of Soviet lifestyle, income counts less than access to goods. Not all groups can in fact procure what they need with equal facility, because there are many different distribution circuits for goods, some of which are better stocked than others. Country dwellers are less well provided for than city dwellers. Muscovites are privileged in comparison with the provinces. In addition, various shops and dressmakers in the capital are reserved for a few privileged customers: foreigners, members of the intelligentsia, senior officials. Differences in living standards between the capital and the average-sized provincial town are more bitterly felt than differences between the various strata of population within the same town. These observations

lead us to identify a number of cultural disparities between different nationalities, between town and country, between the intelligentsia and the working
classes.

Cultural differences between nationalities. In the Soviet Union, these do not
generate class differences because, as a general rule, nationals within the
autonomous republics are organized according to the same socio-occupational
hierarchies. The situation would be quite different if recruitment to specific
occupations were reserved to a dominant (or a dominated) nationality. There
do indeed exist different aptitudes at national level, with the result that on any
given worksite, for example, one may find a high proportion of Ukrainians or
Tatars in a particular occupation. The Caucasian peoples are highly prized
building-workers, since for generations they have been skilled masons. But there
is nothing to indicate that these specialities cause conflicts in terms of national
feeling. A recent inquiry among the Tatars revealed that more than two-thirds
of them were indifferent to the nationality of their superior. However, the
predominance of Russians in the central apparatus of the Party and in the
federal government poses a more general problem that is not only social but political. This will be examined when we come to discuss nationalism (Chapter 11).

Opposition between urban and rural ways of life. At the present time this is the
most obvious gulf within Soviet society. Today, as yesterday, despite considerable progress, dress, language and behaviour identify peasants who have
not yet adapted to city life. Even the country intellectual is influenced by
country habits. This is the result of the inadequate supply facilities in the rural
areas, but also of the specific rhythm of life, of village relationships and of the
importance of gardens and family farms in supplementing income. A. Sakharov
says that this sideline income gives country dwellers an advantage over office
workers and the broad strata of the city intelligentsia, who have only their low
salaries to live on.[4]

All of these differences define a rural style of consumption. There is a
greater tendency to save than in the town. However, the cultural level remains
lower, despite the creation of clubs to replace the old *izba* libraries. Industrial
workers spend three times more than collective-farm workers on leisure and
culture. The situation varies from one region to another and according to
qualification (thus in the province of Moscow 85 per cent of managers own a
television set, as against 25 per cent of unskilled collective-farm workers).

The contrasts observed between one group and another depend also on
habitat. Specialists generally live in the regional centres, where the administration has its offices and where amenities are better than in the smaller towns,
where 78 per cent of unskilled personnel live. Behind the goods symbolizing
urban civilization, one senses a change in mentality: the washing machine is
evidence of a desire to lighten the woman's workload, the television set a desire
to break out of isolation and establish a permanent link with the town.

The gulf between the upper strata (intelligentsia) and the mass of workers.
Estimates of the number of people belonging to the top category vary from one
author to another. Thus, Mervyn Matthews reckons that this category contains
227,000 elite personnel (i.e. 750,000 people including their families), while
Janina Markiewicz-Lagneau puts the figure at 8–12 million. We shall adopt
an unquantifiable criterion, distinguishing between those who in their professional life are called by their patronymic (Ivan Ivanovich), which shows that
the bearer belongs to the upper station, and those called by their family name
(Ivanov).

We have already noted the family lifestyles characteristic of the various
urban strata, as determined by education and income. We have amalgamated
them in Table 40 on the basis of a socio-occupational stratification designed to
bring out the scale of inequalities in housing, heritage and cultural habits.

TABLE 40   *Range of living conditions (housing, property, leisure) 1967–70*

	Accommo- dation $m^2 \times capita$ in Kazan	Property		Leisure (as % of free time) in Byelorussia		
		Necessities[1] Kazan (%)	Library[2] (% of households)	TV	Cinema	Theatre
Managers, top officials (*rukovoditeli*)	7.8 (= 135)	37.3	90			
Highly skilled specialists	7.0 (= 127)	35.9	90	19.4	10.5	5.5
Technicians		38.2	80	20.9	13	4.7
White-collar workers	6.0 (= 107)	43.8	38	25.5	14.8	
Skilled workers	6.6 (= 117)	41.7		24.8	11	
Unskilled workers	5.6 (= 100)	44.2	25	25.5	5.8	

Notes: 1 This percentage reflects the value of a sample of basic necessities (table, wardrobe, bed and bicycle) as a
proportion of total family property.
2 The Soviets define a library as consisting of 100 books at least.

Possession of an official car identifies the beneficiary's ranking within the
civil-service hierarchy according to make of car. (Distribution of private cars
according to social category is not made public. It is known that in 1965 in
Pskov only 2 per cent of households owned a car and 16 per cent a motorcycle,
as against 66 per cent and 27 per cent respectively for French households at
that time). Dignitaries have their own chauffeur, and even domestic staff. To
the list of privileges must be added official living accommodation, whose size
and comfort depend on rank; priority tickets (*postoyannaya propiska*) for
entertainment and travel; special waiting-rooms in stations; limited editions;
special showings of films to which the public is not admitted; dining-rooms
reserved for notables in restaurants in provincial hotels; the *obkom*'s procurement office for direct deliveries to the home; and a pass (*bronya*) to jump
queues.

Home decoration is a fair indication of the difference between members of the intelligentsia and those with 'petty-bourgeois' tastes. The intelligentsia (particularly the young) frequently adopt a starkly functional style. Entry to the bourgeoisie on the other hand finds expression (especially among recent arrivals from the countryside) in a proliferation, space permitting, of objects, plants and photographs, in keeping with the previous generation's tastes.

Certain members of the intelligentsia view their surroundings merely as a means to distinguish themselves from officials in the political apparatus and from run-of-the-mill specialists. Official statistics record the latter as part of the intelligentsia; the others, however, look upon them as merely 'intelligent', that is people who are educated, but who lack the open-mindedness and moral rectitude that were the attributes of the intelligentsia in the limited sense of the term before the Revolution. They profess to scorn the unscrupulous ambition and aggressiveness of those who sacrifice family to career. But, like them, they rely upon a network of social relationships to enable them to fulfil their ambitions whether to get their children into a specific school or to obtain a seat for a concert. They pride themselves on their knowledge of art and philosophy, collect old icons, and some can even afford a servant.[5]

However, these privileged categories do not form a 'club' of well-off families like the old aristocracy. They have taken from the latter various traditions, such as heavy meals, a taste for entertainment, use of a dacha and the habit of taking a detached view of official stereotypes. But they come from professional circles that are too different in their interests (scientific, literary and artistic) to constitute a social class. They share an openmindedness that finds discreet expression in the debates in the columns of the literary reviews. The only exceptions are a few committed rebels in the tradition of the old regime. In comparison with their elders, they appear much more conservative, more concerned to take a few quiet hours off for themselves, far from the worries of factory or office. What distinguishes this intellectual élite from the newly rich is its absence of ostentation and acquisitiveness. The latter have always been considered the distinguishing marks of a petty-bourgeois mentality.

Dialogue between the intelligentsia and working class is not easy, however informal their social relationships, to judge from the difficulty experienced by contemporary Soviet writers in producing works in which the working class can recognize itself (as it once did in Gorky's novels). A diploma does seem to create a barrier, just as rank (*chin*) did in the past. To get beyond this hurdle is to become 'someone'.

The prestige ladder

Before analysing subjective evaluations of social prestige as revealed in the job preferences of young Soviets, we might try to note some objective signs of the hierarchy of prestige. In any society, a parade or procession reflects an order of precedence. National ceremonies to mark 1 May, the order in which the different groups march past, the people who watch from the platform, all reveal a society's image of itself: the importance of the army, the pre-eminent role played by members of the Politburo and the Party apparatus, the popularity of gymnasts, the desire to honour those who have distinguished themselves in socialist work and competition, and also the fact that the whole population participates in the procession, quarter by quarter. In the same way the rules governing the wearing of decorations (which number around forty) avoid establishing an order of precedence between civil orders which are worn on the left side of the chest, and military medals which are worn on the right. In Soviet railway carriages there are five different classes: these arise more from the practical requirements of long-distance travel and degrees of comfort rather than from social differentiation. Fares do, however, range from the basic fare to three times that amount for a journey of 500 kilometres, which inevitably implies a degree of selection.

The official scale of prestige does not always coincide with young people's spontaneous choices of profession and career aspirations. To belong to the Party apparatus counts less than a job that makes one a member of the intelligentsia. Manual work, which is extolled in the mass media, comes bottom of the Soviets' scale of preferences. These largely confirm data obtained from similar surveys in western countries.

Soviet surveys carried out among students in the final years of secondary education show that the scientific professions remain the most prestigious, though the humanistic careers (doctor, teacher) are tending to improve their ratings. Indeed, there are similarities between Soviet replies in the 1950s and similar surveys carried out in West Germany and the United States. Surveys in the rural areas (in the province of Tambov) indicate that girls would prefer to become teachers and doctors, while boys want to become drivers, pilots, soldiers, engineers, mechanics or sailors. These replies should be compared with those given by peasant children in the 1920s when their career ambitions aimed no higher than to become a tailor or joiner.

The most highly valued professions are those requiring advanced education and a maximum of creative ability (Table 41). The scale of prestige does not coincide with the commonest occupations (lathe-operator ranks only 55th out of 80), or with power (the technical intelligentsia has more prestige than the administrative intelligentsia), or with the manual trades extolled by propaganda: miner, tractor-operator, dairy maid. The jobs of miner or tractor-driver are passed over in favour of that of chauffeur. The cobbler precedes the printing-worker. A military career is more prized than that of university professor, illustrating the prestige of the officer corps within the nation. Children's nannies, on the other hand, are impossible to find: domestic work is looked down upon in the Soviet Union, as elsewhere.

TABLE 41   *Scale of occupational prestige*

	USSR			USA	West Germany
	Novosibirsk	Leningrad	Displaced persons		
	1970	1965	1950	1950	1950
Research worker (research)	1[1]	1[1]	73[2]	89[2]	1[1]
Aviator	2				
Engineer (radio-technician)	3	2	73	84	10
Geologist	7	4			
Doctor (medicine)	8	11	75	93	2
Factory manager			65	82	5
Career officer			58	80	8
Teacher	12		55	78	11
Accountant			62	81	
Shop assistant	70	75			
Office worker	74	76			
Kolkhoz chairman (farmer)			38	76	11
Farmworker		78	18	50	38
Printing worker		79			
Unskilled worker			48	60	26
Local-council worker	73	80			

Notes: 1 In order of preference (Leningrad, from 1 to 80; Novosibirsk 1 to 74; West Germany 1 to 38).
2 Number of points (maximum USSR DP 75; USA 93; minimum USSR 18, USA 33).

Social relations

Do differences in material situation, culture, occupation and prestige affect relationships between groups? The reply is negative according to official ideology, which seeks to foster an ideal of social harmony, banishing all antagonisms. It is not denied that conflicts can arise, but they are held to result from individual factors and not from group confrontations or the workings of institutions.

Reality is more complex. Surveys of interpersonal relationships confirm that there are no impenetrable barriers between groups, but that friends and spouses tend to be chosen from within the same group. People often choose friends out of a need for advice or support, and this would explain the tendency to confide in an older or better-educated person than oneself.

Forms of sociability vary from one social group to another. At Akademgorodok, high-level scientific staff devote 61.8 per cent of their contacts to conversations revolving around cultural affinities, 16.9 per cent to visits to relatives and only 6.4 per cent to neighbourhood contacts. On the other hand, service personnel in this same town prefer contacts with neighbours and relatives (64.8 per cent of relations). The frequency of neighbourhood relations in this category can be explained by the frequence of mutual practical help in the least-skilled categories, where salaries are lowest: people rely more on their family and neighbours to look after the children and to borrow money or objects.

'The big problem in the Soviet Union is learning to trust one's neighbour.'[6] The Soviets look for sincerity, honesty and simplicity, in short authentic personal contact, in friendship. They do not confuse friendship with sociability: the latter may be gay and familiar, but it is merely superficial.

When Soviet authors write about working life, they tend to present problems in psychological terms, as the result of conflicts of individual temperament at the factory, building site or laboratory, in particular between conservatives and innovators. However, there are also objective causes of tension between groups, namely unequal access to resources such as food supplies, housing and higher education. This scarcity inevitably exposes certain occupations to temptation. Shop and service employees would not readily change their jobs, even though they stand at the bottom of the ladder of social prestige: no other occupation could offer them so many tangible opportunities. A few are led astray into unlawful trading. No occupation is immune to corruption and speculation, although these are severely punished when discovered.

Disputes at work are in theory arbitrated by the trade unions, which act as factory inspectors. Strikes are illegal, but according to foreign observers in the Soviet Union they do break out sporadically when production norms are raised (for workers on piece rates) or when difficulties arise in procuring food. The Soviet press hints at the need to reinforce discipline and to improve industrial relations whenever new measures are announced or in statements made on the occasion of Party or union congresses. However, shortcomings are attributed usually to individual failures, to a lack of integration or a weakening of social control, but not to class conflicts.

This denial of any manifestation of conflict — in a society that is diversified in terms both of occupation and of cultural and national traditions — lends exceptional importance to the functions of control and social integration performed by the state apparatus. Do those who perform this function constitute a separate class? Later on we shall devote a whole chapter (10) to the question of whether the distinction between leaders and led creates a gulf in society or whether — as the official thesis maintains — the political élite is recruited from all social groups.

Conclusions

After this analysis of social stratification we may hazard a few general remarks.
1 Reality appears to be more diverse than any simple official division of society into two groups, workers and peasants, would suggest. Neither of these two classes is homogeneous. Economic growth and technical progress are altering job content and workers' qualifications, likewise the numbers of people employed in administration and services.

2 If by classes we mean groups that appropriate for themselves the labour of others, or who pass on their privileges to their descendants through the accumulation of capital, this type of domination does not occur in the Soviet Union.

3 However, this does not exclude appreciable disparities between socio-occupational groups (see Table 42). Moreover, these inequalities accumulate: inequalities in living standards (housing and income) seem less far reaching than differences in education, types of leisure activity and heritage, which reveal themselves in lifestyles.

TABLE 42   *Range of inequalities, 1967 (unskilled workers = 100)*

	Education[1]	Income		Housing Kazan	Property		Party membership
		Kazan	Leningrad		Car/ piano	library	
Highly skilled specialists	340	207	152	139	295	360	535
Technicians	300	146	131	125	247	320	529
White-collar workers	260	97	116	107	95	152	210
Skilled workers	200	130	136	117	121		383
Unskilled workers	100	100	100	100	100	100	100

Note: 1 Educational inequality is calculated on the basis of the average number of years' schooling in each group.

4 Although these differences are smaller than in western societies, given consumer conditions and the minimal opportunities for diversified use of income in the Soviet Union, the privileges of the higher category stand out against a background that is frugal in comparison with what we are accustomed to.

5 The egalitarian aims of the regime's early years have been replaced by a functional justification of the social hierarchy. This is generally felt to reward merit to the extent that social mobility offers equal opportunities for all. But, on the other hand, because of the role played by the administration in social promotion, any restrictions on social mobility could well breed a classic dichotomy between 'us' (the governed) and 'them' (those who govern). This is amplified by a conflict between generations when management posts are occupied by older people on the verge of old age.

6 The most strongly resented barrier is that of the university degree. Like the Table of Ranks in the past, the degree is associated with prestige and sometimes with income. It is associated with a lifestyle that tends to be transmitted from one generation to another through culture. We may see in this the beginnings of a process of social reproduction, evidence of which we examined in Chapter 6 on the educational system (which favours the children of the intelligentsia) and in Chapter 5 on the family (endogamy is more frequent than exogamy). Some sections of the intelligentsia go so far as to justify their privileged positions on the grounds of an ideology that vaunts the moral mission of this particular class and its dynamic function in social development.[7]

7 In a society where property is in theory collective, the security of the group and the individual is no longer founded upon ownership. As in feudal society (when the land was the property of the sovereign) it grows out of a network of relationships. The inevitable bureaucratization that centralism and large-scale organizations entail does not preclude personal links. A successful career and a comfortable material situation depend not only on qualifications but also on an individual's skill as a navigator and on the favourable or adverse winds that symbolize a person's dealing with the authorities. No one's position is ever definitive, and this gives Soviet society its great mobility.

NOTES

1 Barrington Moore, Jr, *Soviet Politics: The Dilemma of Power*, New York, Harper & Row, 1965, p. 238.
2 R. Pipes, *Russia under the Old Regime*, London, 1974, pp. 115 and 120. The author states that in the eighteenth century two-thirds of the Russian population was occupied in feeding the military.
3 R. Medvedev, *On Socialist Democracy*, London, 1975, p. 268.
4 *My Country and the World*, p. 19.
5 Y. Trifonov, *Bilan préalable*, Paris, Gallimard, 1975, pp. 20, 38, 57, 61, 66.
6 V. Bukovsky, *Le Monde*, 8 Feb. 1977.
7 G. Pomerants, cited by R. Tokes, *Dissent in the USSR*, Johns Hopkins University Press, 1975, pp. 181−6.

SUGGESTED READING

Social structure

Connor, W., *Socialism, Politics and Equality: Hierarchy and Change in Eastern Europe and the USSR*, New York, Columbia University Press, 1979.
Hegedus, A., *The Structure of Socialist Society*, London, Constable, 1977.
Klassy sotsial'nye sloi i gruppy v S.S.S.R., Moscow, Nauka, 1968.
Problemy izmenenya sotsial'noy struktury rabochego klassa S.S.S.R., Moscow, Nauka, 1968.
Senyavsky, S., *Problemy sotsial'noy struktury sovetskogo obshchestva, 1938−1970*, Moscow, Mysl', 1973.
Shkaratan, O., *Problemy sotsial'noy struktury rabochego klassa S.S.S.R.*, Moscow, Mysl', 1970.
Strimska, Z., 'Projet socialiste et rapports sociaux en U.R.S.S. et dans les pays socialistes', *Revue des études comparatives Est−Ouest*, vol. VII, 1976, no. 3, pp. 107−235.
Yanowitch, M., *Social and Economic Inequality in the Soviet Union*, White Plains, New York, Sharpe, 1977.

Workers and intellectuals

Churchward, L. G., *The Soviet Intelligentsia*, London, Routledge & Kegan Paul, 1973.
Kahan, A. and Ruble, B., *Industrial Labor in the USSR*, Pergamon, 1979.

Lane, D. and O'Dell, F., *The Soviet Industrial Worker*, Oxford, Martin Robertson, 1978.

Lewin, M., 'L'État et les classes sociales en U.R.S.S. (1929–1933)', *Actes de la recherche en sciences sociales*, no. 1, Feb. 1976.

Markiewicz-Lagneau, J., 'La fin de l'intelligentsia? Formation et transformation de l'intelligentsia soviétique', *Revue des études comparatives Est–Ouest*, vol. VII, 1976, no. 4, pp. 7–71.

Matthews, M., *Privilege in the Soviet Union: A Study of Elite Styles under Communism*, London, Allen & Unwin, 1978.

Promyshlennye rabochie Komi A.S.S.R. 1918–1970, Moscow, Nauka, 1974.

Rabochiy klass i industrial'noe razvitie S.S.S.R., Moscow, Nauka.

Sovetskaya intelligentsiya (istoriya formirovaniya i rosta 1917–1965), Moscow, Mysl', 1968.

Teckenberg, W., *Die soziale Struktur der Sowjetischen Arbeiter Klasse im internationalen Vergleich*, Munich, Oldenburg, 1977.

Voslensky, M., *La Nomenklatura*, Paris, Belfond, 1980.

Chapter 9

Social mobility

The analyses in the preceding chapters reveal a dual trend: first, the hierarchical diversification of Soviet society with regard to income, education and lifestyle, which works to the advantage of the intelligentsia; secondly, a certain fluidity in personal relationships which lessens the social distances between groups. We might conclude from this that the existence of a hierarchy is accepted as a functional necessity and is not perceived as class differentiation, since mobility gives everyone the feeling that they occupy the place due to them, and that through their merits and labour they can hope to rise to the greatest heights. The terms for social *change (peremeshcheniya)*, which the Soviets use to refer to social mobility, implies that what is involved is a simple transition from one type of occupation to another, not promotion which would presuppose the existence of a social ladder. Soviet behaviour — in particular the appreciation of the place of different occupations in the scale of prestige — does not bear this statement out. Social mobility does however exist alongside occupational mobility; in a large number of cases the two types are combined.

DIFFERENT TYPES OF MOBILITY

Job mobility is first and foremost an economic necessity. Had it not been for the large-scale transfer of peasants to industry and internal migration, the development and opening up of the country would have been out of the question. Technical progress, moreover, spawns new professions, while old occupations disappear. Some of these swings are planned and controlled (recruitment of workers, admission to various schools, selection by the Party of personnel for *nomenklatura* posts). Others are spontaneous and not much controlled (rural depopulation, redundancy and firing of workers, choice of workplace and residence). However, job mobility cannot be bought, as happens in France, for example, when a journeyman buys the business of his former artisan boss, thereby himself becoming a boss.

Social mobility is what improves or reduces an individual's or a group's position on the scale of status. It takes the form of promotion when, for example, a foreman becomes an engineer. However, occupation is not the only channel of social mobility; marriage to someone from another stratum can produce the same result. Political advancement of an ethnic minority, or conversely the disgrace attached to certain origins (such as having a kulak or nepman – a private dealer during the NEP – for a father) or the fact of being related to a convict, may lead to downward social mobility. Antisemitism is an unacknowledged form of discrimination in the normal workings of social mobility. We shall refer to upwards social mobility as *vertical mobility*.

Horizontal, or geographical, *mobility* is often a prerequisite of professional mobility. Movement from one region to another will not necessarily alter a person's status; in certain cases, however, this spatial mobility also involves social promotion, in particular where the rural exodus brings peasants into urban occupations.

GEOGRAPHICAL MOBILITY

Some 10 million inhabitants of the suburbs commute daily to the cities (see Chapter 3). Seasonal migrations affect activities like fishing, forestry, the building industry and, most of all, agriculture. At harvest time around 900,000 city dwellers, in addition to between 400,000 and 600,000 students, flock to the countryside. The number of seasonal workers is estimated at between 1.5 and 2.8 million.

A further 12 million people on average change their residence every year, that is 5 per cent of the total population: 6 million city dwellers move to another town, 1.5 million rural inhabitants change their villages, 1.5 million leave the town for the country and 3 million leave the land and move to the town. This results in an annual net loss from the countryside of 1.5 million per year over the long term (1926–70). During the past few years rural depopulation has tended to speed up (1.9 million in 1970), though without reaching the record levels of the 1930s (2.6 million in 1930; 4.1 million in 1931; and 2.7 million in 1932).

On the occasion of the 1970 census a survey of geographical mobility revealed that 28 million Soviet citizens had changed their homes over the previous two years. Among these the Russians were the most mobile (8.7 million, that is 6.7 per cent of the Russian population), while only 1.4 per cent of the formerly nomadic Turkmen and Uzbeks had moved. The rate of population renewal is particularly high in eastern Siberia and the far east (9 per cent of the total during the 1960s). Compared with the Americans, however, the Soviets are much more stable: according to Vance Packard, 40 million Americans (23 per cent of the population) change their address at least once a year (*A Nation of Strangers*, McKay, 1972).

Fluidity among the industrial labour force also produces migration. This reached its height in 1956, when a decree of 26 June 1940 mobilizing personnel at their place of work was rescinded. Average annual labour turnover in industry is currently running at 20 per cent. This percentage is much higher in the eastern regions, which creates particular problems. Not only is the population of Siberia and the far east not increasing at the desired rate, but it does not settle down easily. Too many workers leave their jobs and return to more hospitable parts, to be replaced by new arrivals. The far eastern towns alone record almost half a million arrivals per year, and almost as many departures. The net result of these migratory movements during the 1960s was unfavourable to the settlement of Siberia. However, thanks to measures taken to improve living conditions in these regions, the outflow has dwindled in western Siberia and the situation is tending to stabilize in eastern Siberia. Among those coming to settle in Siberia and the far east between 1951 and 1970, there were 213,800 peasant families, maintaining the tradition of agricultural colonization.

In order to control these spontaneous migrations more effectively, sociologists have enquired into the motivations of emigrants and immigrants. The results obtained vary, depending on whether the region is recently developed (like that of the Tyumen oilfields in western Siberia, where because of the housing shortage only a fifth of personnel recruited between 1960 and 1970 settled permanently), or a rural area like Novgorod, where the rural exodus is motivated by a desire for social promotion and occupational training.

Because the chief contributing factor to the rural exodus is the desire for social promotion (to acquire a trade and to study) the categories most concerned are the younger generations and the better trained. Thus the sample studied by Staroverov (*Sotsial'no-demograficheskie problemy derevni*, p. 101) reveals that young people aged between 16 and 29 (who represent only 10.6 per cent of the resident active population) accounted for 69.4 per cent of those leaving the villages. Similarly, those with more than seven years' schooling (23.2 per cent of the resident population) represent 64.4 per cent of emigrants.

The Zaslavskaya survey (*Migratsiya sel'skogo naseleniya*, p. 160) of Siberian rural society partly confirms Staroverov's data. However, inadequate working conditions rate more mention (24 per cent of replies) than the desire to continue one's studies (16.7 per cent). It is estimated that for the country as a whole 68 per cent of children who leave the country schools do not return to their villages, and 90 per cent of those who complete advanced school do not return to the land.

The fact that geographical mobility is greater early in a career is not specific to the rural exodus. Everywhere, youth is a period of learning, and young people go through a series of experiences before settling down to a job to their taste. In western Siberia (Tyumen) the average age of immigrants posted there at the end of school or called up by the Komsomol is 23; the average age of those who migrate of their own free will is 30–32.

Rural depopulation is beneficial to the extent that it reduces overpopulation in some areas and supplies the labour necessary for mass employers like the building industry and coalmining. In most cases, although housing conditions are often less satisfactory in the towns than in the countryside, emigrants obtain higher salaries and – most important – enjoy better vocational training. This is why the youngster who wants to 'go places' must go via the town.

Movement away from the country has also negative effects: nowhere is such movement in proportion to the needs of agriculture, since it is determined by the supply of non-agricultural jobs. This is felt particularly in the industrialized areas (central and northwestern Russia, western Siberia), where development of agricultural production is currently held back by labour shortages. Between one census and the next the Ukraine, the RSFSR and Byelorussia have lost at least half their rural youth. Since it is young people who are leaving, the population remaining on the land shows a heavy bias towards the old, for many people return to the country on retirement. In the sample studied by Staroverov, the female population aged 50 and over represents 36 per cent of the rural population (as against 25 per cent in the population of the Soviet Union as a whole in 1970). Between the ages of 40 and 49, women form 61.4 per cent of the village labour force, while below the age of 18 men outnumber women. The ageing process is also depressing birthrates. In the provinces of Novgorod, Kalinin and Pskov, deaths outnumber births.

The rural exodus also deprives agriculture of its specialists, as mobility is greater among this category than among others; this concerns tractor and lorry drivers especially, as they can easily find work on building sites. The farms lost 3.6 million drivers in the space of 5 years.[1] Artisan carpenters and electricians are also in very short supply in the countryside. Some villages are deserted, and many peasant families have dwindled to a single member living on his or her own (in the province of Kalinin, 25 per cent of the heads of the family farm were women living alone).

Administrative controls were introduced to regulate the rural exodus, by making the issue of passports to country dwellers dependent on the employer's authorization. The effects of this measure (which dated from December 1932) were unfortunate, tending to hasten the departure of the under-16s, who require no passport in order to move to the towns. This discriminatory measure restricting the mobility of the rural population was highly unpopular, without proving a real obstacle to migration. Young conscripts avoided returning to their villages after demobilization, so as not to lose their freedom of movement. The regulation was abolished on 1 January 1976, since when all rural inhabitants not previously in possession of a passport have been issued with one.

The authorities can also influence the rural exodus by indirect means. The rise in farm wages is an inducement to remain on the land only for those workers with little prospect of improving their lot in the towns. But it cannot retain those with qualifications, who leave for the towns in the hopes of making a career there. Investment in the form of creating jobs in rural industries or to improve living conditions may, on the other hand, provide an incentive to stay on the land for young people yearning for standards of comfort and leisure comparable to those in the towns. Interestingly, the exodus has slowed down considerably in rural areas close to the regional centres and major trunk routes, while it is more intense in isolated villages.

VERTICAL MOBILITY

Vertical mobility may be defined in two ways: in the sense of *intergenerational mobility*, when a person moves out of his or her parents' social group onto a higher rung of the social ladder; and *individual mobility*, when a person changes his or her social status in the course of a career by means of qualification and function.

Intergenerational mobility

Available data concerning the social origins of the various socio-occupational categories in the Soviet Union reveal that, out of every 100 skilled workers more than half (55.6 per cent) are of working-class origin, while the greater proportion of unskilled workers came from the peasantry. Some 54 per cent of qualified managers have a white-collar background, while most white-collar workers (57.9 per cent) come from blue-collar families. In other words the mobility drift is from country to town, channelling the children of peasants towards unskilled jobs. From this category they move on to become skilled workers. In the second generation, the latter are to be found as middle-rank supervisory staff (technicians).

From mobility rates, we may state precisely what percentage of children from a given social group (total = 100) have remained in their group of origin, and how many have moved into an upper or lower stratum (Table 43). The availability of data for calculating these rates in terms comparable with figures for mobility in France is rather limited (comprising figures for the province of Kazan, 1967). However, the fact that these same data have been used by a Soviet sociologist in a general study are an indication of their representativeness.

In order to analyse the mobility rates given in Table 43, we must start from the respective percentage of each group in the population as a whole. This means that, if social mobility were ideal, the sons of people in Group I (higher managerial) remaining within their group of origin should not exceed, respectively, 3.2 per cent in the Soviet Union and 8.5 per cent in France and should

TABLE 43 *Comparative mobility rates, USSR and France, 1960s*

Social status of sons		I	II	III	IV	V	Total
Social status of father							
Gr. I skilled senior executives and managers (professions, factory managers and owners, big-shop keepers)	USSR	16.7	55.7	4.4	21.2	2.0	100
	France	44.5	32.0	11.0	6.9	4.8	100
Gr. II middle-rank executives (*master*), technicians, artisans	USSR	7.6	42	12.2	30.9	7.3	100
	France	12.9	40.2	10.0	21.5	15.3	100
Gr. III White-collar workers	USSR	7.2	34.9	12.7	39.8	5.3	100
	France	9.5	31.4	16.3	29.5	13.3	100
Gr. IV Skilled workers	USSR	2.4	10.7	15.1	58.9	12.9	100
	France	3.1	20.6	9.2	41.8	25.1	100
Gr. V Unskilled workers	USSR	1.4	14.5	11.4	59.8	12.9	100
	France	1.6	13.8	8.5	31.6	44.4	100
Farmers: sovkhoz workers	USSR	0.8	8.5	8.5	64.4	17.8	100
agricultural labourers	France	1.2	12.3	6.5	21.5	58.5	100
kolkhoz workers	USSR	0.9	6.5	10.5	59.2	22.4	100
farmers	France	3.7	19.8	12.1	19.1	45.3	100
Total	USSR	3.2	17.0	11.2	51.6	13.2	100
	France	8.5	25	10.2	26.7	29.6	100

be distributed within the other groups in proportion to the overall percentage. In reality we find that 16.7 per cent in the Soviet Union and 44.5 per cent in France remain within their group of origin. Thus, in comparison with the ideal rate, the children of senior managers are 5.2 times more likely *in both the Soviet Union and France* to preserve their original status. Workers are the most stable (64.8 per cent of total personnel in the Soviet Union) since 72 per cent of the workers remain within the same group in the second generation. Only 2.4 per cent of the sons of skilled workers and 1.4 per cent of those of unskilled workers were able to rise to a higher group. We also find broad similarities between France and the Soviet Union with regard to mobility in the middle strata (middle-rank supervisory grades and white-collar workers) and agricultural workers.

Social mobility in the Soviet Union does not appear to be fundamentally different from that of the main industrial countries, judging by the rates in Table 44.

A Soviet worker of rural origin who does not wish to remain in the country will, 82 per cent of the time, find a manual occupation, while in France 50 per cent will find non-manual jobs. Middle-rank managers and supervisors are three times more likely to become senior managers in the United States than in the Soviet Union, while the chances of a worker of working-class origin gaining such promotion are five times greater in the United States than in the Soviet Union.

In the absence of data on the movement of city dwellers towards the country,

TABLE 44   *Comparative interoccupational mobility rates*

	USSR 1967	France 1964	USA 1967	Japan 1956
From agriculture to manual occupations	81.7[1]	48.3[1]		
		36.5[2]	55.2[2]	22[2]
From manual to non-manual occupations	27.7	27.8	36.9	33
From non-manual to manual occupations	36.8	32.7	27.6	21.0
From working class to higher groups	1.9	2.2	10.0	6.9
From middle-class to higher groups	7.5	11.8	20.9	15.1

Notes: 1 Not including agriculture.
2 Including agriculture.

we shall indicate the pattern of this mobility only within the rural world; the figures in Table 45 are based on surveys carried out by the Soviet sociologist J. Arutjunjan.

The rate of mobility of groups from 'tractor drivers' upwards is greater than the theoretical average; on the other hand, unskilled manual workers are very stable, since 79 per cent of their children who remain in the country do not alter their status on starting their working life. In addition we find that in Kalinin province almost half the managerial grades (middle and higher) are from non-peasant strata. Hence the towns tend to supply the managers and white-collar workers in the services sector in the countryside, which indicates inadequate training of élites of rural origin.

Individual mobility

Individual mobility − which measures a worker's promotion in the course of his or her career − varies with degree of qualification and type of activity.

In the collective farms, a man's chances of promotion are greater than those of a woman, judging by the results of a survey carried out by J. Arutjunjan on a

TABLE 45   *Rural social mobility*

	Father's status	% from rural background		Children's status (first job)					
		Kolkhoz	Sovkhoz	I	II	III	IV	V	VI
Gr. I	Managers and senior executives	50	47.1	22.8	17.5	5.3	8.8	1.8	42.1
Gr. II	Middle-rank executives	60	63.6	17.9	16.7	11.5	11.5	7.7	34.6
Gr. III	White-collar workers	90.8	47.1	16.8	7.4	18.8	7.4	4.2	45.4
Gr. IV	Skilled workers, tractor drivers	88.6	54.9	8.0	5.3	13.3	25.3	9.4	38.7
Gr. V	Manual labourers	85.5	79.3	6.2	4.5	10.0	10.7	10.7	58.0
Gr., VI	Unskilled workers	89.5	86.1	4.5	4.2	3.9	6.0	2.4	74.0
Total		87	78	7.1	5.6	6.1	7.8	3.7	69.7

pilot farm in the Ukraine in 1964.[1] This study shows that, for 100 men beginning their careers as managers (Group I), 60 still retained this position at the end of their careers, 20 had become skilled workers (tractor-drivers, etc.) and 20 ended their careers as unspecialized collective-farm workers. Some 46 per cent of the men who had started out in unskilled posts rose to a higher group (32 per cent became tractor-drivers, mechanics or lorry-drivers), while 95 per cent of women starting out in the same conditions had failed to improve their situation by the end of their careers. Mobility rates tend to diminish with age. They are highest around the age of 27. From 50 onwards mobility ceases (retirement age is in theory 55 for women and 60 for men, but in rural areas these norms are not strictly observed due to labour shortages and relatively meagre retirement pensions.

We must also bear in mind that transformation of a collective farm into a state farm can represent promotion for some categories of worker, though their qualifications may not alter: state-farm personnel carry a passport, for example, which means they enjoy greater facilities for travel than the collective-farm workers.

In the factory, similar studies have shown that a worker's promotion is bound up with his initial level of education. Thus, in a mechanical engineering factory, milling-machine operators with ten years' schooling rose to a higher level within a year, while those with only seven years' schooling took on average three years to make the same progress. We also find that women are promoted more slowly than men. According to Soviet sociologists, this is because women put family considerations before their careers.

In the office, promotion of managers poses a number of specific problems resulting from: (1) the structure of the hierarchy, which is based on age and is pyramidal, with a handful of incumbents, usually over fifty, at the top; (2) research staff are not particularly eager to take on posts of responsibility within the administration, as higher salaries and other advantages are not sufficient compensation for the longer working days and the many worries involved in carrying out the plan; and (3) the difficulty of choosing objective criteria for evaluating candidates' work and capabilities.

Responsibility for selection is left with the manager, assisted by Party and union representatives. This is likely to produce a mandarinate, lead to favouritism or result in the thwarting of an innovator's or potential rival's career. To remedy these problems, which are inherent in any public or private administration, there are a certain number of procedural checks designed to correct abuses and inequalities in the promotion of individuals.

The regulation of career mobility

We have already indicated that admission to higher education — the means to promotion — is by competitive examination. This system also governs access to employment in scientific research. The selection committee is presided over by the head of the establishment, but the scientific staff must ratify his choices by a vote.

Every three years, scientific staff have to be re-examined (*attestatsya*) before a committee which reviews each individual's record (*otzyv*) and subsequently decides on promotion, maintenance or downgrading, sometimes even dismissal (decree of the State Committee on Science and Technology, GKNT, 5 May 1969). This committee's decisions are subject to appeal before the supervisory administration, which has to give its verdict within five days. It has been proposed to extend this periodic review to all industrial managers. To encourage greater mobility of personnel, there is talk of downgrading 10 per cent of officials each year, and of promoting an equivalent percentage, thus avoiding long waits for vacant posts. An experiment carried out in an industrial combine in Lvov has confirmed the value of this procedure. However, the difficulties too are stressed, in particular the working out of objective criteria for awarding marks to staff according to such factors as professional conscientiousness and innovative capacity.

Appointment to certain posts such as shopfloor supervisor or foreman by means of election is also being studied. In a Riga factory the entire staff votes for a list of candidates drawn up by the personnel department, i.e. under Party and union supervision.

All appointments to posts of responsibility are vetted (*vydvizhenie*) by the Party apparatus and the union. Originally, this system made it possible to promote trusted people without reference to their level of education — their career records and loyalty being considered a better guarantee. In fact, we have here a system of *co-option*, which is still in force for all management posts contained on the list known as the *nomenklatura*, which reserves the choosing of a candidate to the central or regional authorities of the Party, according to the level of the post in the administrative hierarchy. In the case of a city like Leningrad, the *nomenklatura* contains 3000 posts, which are filled by the regional committee of the Party. This rule probably only concerns a limited percentage, approximately 2 per cent, of higher officials and specialists. We might recall here that in France the prefects, university vice chancellors, ambassadors and heads of the larger nationalized industries are all appointed by the Council of Ministers. In Spain the Opus Dei, and elsewhere freemasonry or 'the old school tie', have played a covert role in selection; similarly in private business 'introductions' play a considerable part.

Is Party membership essential for certain jobs? According to published data on the composition of the staff of the Party apparatus of the Leningrad region executive committee (1962–6), we can reckon that almost two-thirds were neither Party members nor candidate members. On the other hand, the chairman, his deputy and the secretary to the executive committee all have to be Party members, likewise 95 per cent of departmental heads; among *ispolkom* specialists (inspectors, experts, etc.) the percentage of members and candidate members falls to 28 per cent, and to 9 per cent among office staff of the total Soviet working population. (Party membership represented 12.4 per cent of the total Soviet working population in 1971.) In the case of 'reserved' jobs (*nomenklatura*), we find that more than half the appointed holders are members of the Party or the Komsomol.

We may conclude from this that, though it is not compulsory to have a degree and be a Party member in order to qualify for a *nomenklatura* job, the great majority of senior officials today are experts with an advanced training. Some 90.8 per cent of Party, state and union leaders, 85 per cent of factory and company managers and 99 per cent of heads of cultural and scientific establishments hold higher-education degrees or are graduates of specialist secondary establishments. Thus, Party regulation of social mobility does not appreciably alter the trends identified in the previous chapter.

NOTES

1 V. Boldyrev, *Itogi pezepisi naseleniya SSSR*, Moscow, 1974, p. 70.
2 'Essai de sociologie du village', *Archives internationales de sociologie de la coopération*, no. 32, July–Dec. 1972, pp. 120–74.

SUGGESTED READING

Social mobility

Lebin, B. and Perfilev, M., *Kadry apparata upravleniya v S.S.S.R.*, Leningrad, 1970.
Markiewicz-Lagneau, J., 'Les problèmes de la mobilité sociale en U.R.S.S.', *Cahiers du monde russe et soviétique*, vol. VII, no. 2, 1966.
Rutkevik, M. N.and Filippov, F. R., *Sotsial'nye peremeshcheniya*, Mysl', Moscow, 1970.
Yanowitch, M. and Dodge, N., 'The social evaluation of occupation in the Soviet Union', *Slavic Review*, Dec., 1969.
Yanowitch, M. and Fisher, W. (eds), *Social Stratification and Mobility in the U.S.S.R.*, White Plains, New York, 1973.

Rural exodus

Berton-Hogge, R., 'L'Exode rurale en U.R.S.S.', *Problèmes politiques et sociaux*, no. 385, March 1980.
Gol'tsov, A., 'Regional'nye problemy sovremenoy migratsii sel'skogo naselenya', *Voprosy Ekonomiki*, no. 10, 1969, pp. 64–74.
Perevedentsev, V., *Metody izucheniya migratsii naseleniya*, Moscow, Nauka, 1975.
Staroverov, V., *Sotsial'no-demograficheskie problemy derevni*, Moscow, Nauka, 1975.
Wadekin, K. E., 'Internal migration and the flight from land in the U.S.S.R. (1939–1959)', *Soviet Studies*, Oct. 1966, p. 131.
Zaslavskaya, T. I., *Migratsiya sel'skogo naseleniya*, Moscow, Mysl', 1970.

Chapter 10

Social integration: the political system

The word *politics* is commonly associated with certain facts, such as elections, speeches, and so on. We could even say that any social fact is political, because society is, by its very nature, conflictive. According to Marxist doctrine, the state is born of the need for some form of authority, purportedly above society, to resolve these irreducible conflicts (Engels, *The Origins of the Family, Private Property and the State*). Looked at in this light, politics grows out of the impossibility of achieving social integration by means other than coercion; hence, on the contrary in a classless society conflicts disappear and the state itself will wither away.

Here, we shall be using the term *politics* in its narrow sense, namely its *integrating function* in the social system. Government imposes this cohesion upon the different groups composing society by means of a variety of norms (laws) and by coercion (police, judiciary, army) — the attributes of power — which regulate behaviour (the *normative function*), as well as by means of a variety of objectives that translate social demands into political measures (the *political function*). It is aided, in this twofold function, by a set of shared values. The more widely held and internalized these values are, the less need is there for external coercion. In this way the value system complements the political system, and they work together to perform this same function of social integration. Political power and ideological action take on increasing importance in proportion to the extent of the changes one wishes to make to traditional values (cultural revolution).

The excessive role played by the state has been pointed out in earlier chapters, namely in its economic role as sole employer, in its monopoly of education and in its role as the arbiter of social selection. Any attempt to broaden the discussion beyond mere description of political institutions runs into three major difficulties: (1) the legalist approach, attempting to get to grips with real life through a study of constitutional or administrative law, will prove illusory, since the Supreme Soviet, which is the highest organ of power according to Article 136 of the 1977 Constitution, is merely a façade behind which the Party's Politburo wields the real power; (2) the systemic approach, favoured by western political sociology, generates models that are ill suited to the reality of communist regimes; and (3) the way things really work in the Soviet Union, decision-making procedures especially, is surrounded by even greater secrecy than other spheres.

To avoid prejudicing the outcome of our analysis, we shall begin by looking at the history of the Soviet political system, which, like any other political system, was not built in a day; no one planned it or created it; rather it was born of circumstances. It did not spring up on virgin soil but is heir to a secular tradition. The functions that it has assumed have been dictated by the country's level of development and its external environment, in consequence of which emphasis has been placed on the economy and the demands of national defence. Nevertheless, history cannot account for everything: the ideology or political culture that underpin state action, and the functions it performs, also dictate the forms in which power is organized and their relations with society.

POWER AND HISTORY: THE FORMATION OF THE POLITICAL SYSTEM

The problem of origins is never a simple one, for history is merely a sequence of causes and effects. Some historians delve far into the past, back to Muscovy; others point to the conditions of underdevelopment and to those that gave birth to the new regime. None of these factors is sufficient to account for *all* the features of the Soviet system.

Russian national tradition

According to Tibor Szamuely (*The Russian Tradition*, London, Secker & Warburg, 1974, pp. 11–22), this national tradition grew up under Ivan the Terrible, who achieved a synthesis of the Muscovite landlord system, Mongol despotism and Byzantine Caesaro-Papism in the form of Russian autocracy. Even the Tsar, who himself seems to foreshadow Stalin, appears to have been a mixture of farsightedness and crazed paranoia. Even in this patrimonial state, the land belonged to the sovereign, who wielded absolute control over his subjects through a corps of privileged and devoted officials (*oprichnina*).

This narrow-minded, servile, venal bureaucracy, still relatively small and inefficient, was never subjected to any separation of powers (into executive, judiciary and legislature). In the Oriental tradition, the power of justice was in the hands of the sovereign, and his subjects were obliged to assist him in this task by reporting any deed that was detrimental to the interests of the state. Pre-publication censorship, introduced in 1826, in fact dated back to the monopoly over all printed matter in the empire held by the monarch until 1783. He alone decided what was fit for his subjects to read. Control over public morality was in the hands of the Church and the political police, which was placed under the authority of the imperial chancery (third section) in 1826. This police was responsible for authorizing all workers' or students' associations; it had the power to judge without other form or process, and to deport, whoever was suspect in its eyes. The 1845 criminal code provided for the conviction of an individual on grounds of his or her presumed intentions. These measures still figure in the penal code (Art. 70 of the RSFSR code, 1960). Thus, the present-day regime inherited its autocratic administration and the instruments of a police state from the old regime.

Leninism is also heir to the Russian revolutionary tradition. Bolshevism arose as a counter-culture, as a reaction against police intolerance and repression, before growing, from 1917 onwards, into a counter-society. For these extremists, formal liberties do not exist. Their claim to act in the name of the people means that 'the minority, because of its moral and intellectual development, always prevails over the majority. Consequently revolutionaries, as members of a minority, ought, inasmuch as they remain revolutionaries, to retain their hold on power' (Tkachev in Szamuely, *op. cit.*, p. 301). Tkachev was much more the forerunner of Bolshevism than was Marx. His revolutionary catechism served Lenin as an inspiration in the organization and role of the Party, which were in turn to be Lenin's personal stamp on the Soviet system, namely democratic centralism and the leading role that the Party exercises in the name of the proletariat.

In the teeth of fierce opposition from his opponents, Lenin imposed an élitist, centralized conception of Party organization in the debates on the Party constitution held in 1903–5. He argued that this form of organization was demanded by the illegal activities and secrecy required to protect the Party against infiltration by police informers and provocateurs. In any case, Lenin had nothing but mistrust for the spontaneity of the masses: 'The proletariat, if left to itself, is only capable of a trade-unionist consciousness' (*What is to be done?*); in other words, reformism. An organization in which the base rules the top leads to anarchy; revolutionary centralism, as opposed to democratism, flows from the top downwards. Only an intellectual élite is capable of rising above immediate economic demands. It is this élite which embodies the class consciousness of the proletariat (Lenin, *Oeuvres complètes*, vol. V, p. 484–90). The Party was to be the conscious vanguard of the proletariat, fit to guide society by its ability to stand outside and above it. The Party was to be unique because, as a class, the proletariat could only be represented by a single party. Since the twenty-first Party congress in 1959, the concept of the dictatorship of the proletariat has been supplanted by the doctrine of the *state of all the people*, with the Party continuing to occupy the leading role. These principles are expressed in Articles 1 and 6 of the new constitution adopted in 1977.

These two currents, autocratic and revolutionary, merged in 1917 to produce a totalitarian system. For Marxism-Leninism supplied the bureaucracy with an ideological monopoly such as it had never enjoyed under the old regime.

The absence of a democratic tradition is also cited; perhaps it would be better to speak of a liberal tradition, for there existed a centuries-old direct democracy at village level in the form of the *obshchina* or *mir*, but this peasant organization was incapable of extending beyond the village boundaries; and peasant movements were for centuries anarchist in inspiration. The first soviet was a spontaneous creation of the 1905 revolution. Liberals and democrats who tried to establish a constitutional regime in the country encountered, on the other hand, only failure. The experiment in parliamentary government which followed the 1905 revolution did not outlast the first and second Dumas (10 May 1906–3 June 1907). The pseudo-constitutional monarchy fell victim to its own purblindness and carried the entire burden of responsibility for the war. The provisional government set up by the liberals and democrats after the February (15 March by the Gregorian calendar) revolution was itself swept aside on 25–26 October (7–8 November) by the tiny minority of the military revolutionary committee, a product of the Petrograd soviet, which led the popular insurrection.

Political and economic conditions at the birth of the regime
The success of the October *coup d'état* cannot be ascribed solely to the weakness of its opponents. It enjoyed the backing of the crowd, disappointed by the long wait for promised reforms whose implementation had been postponed pending the calling of the constituent assembly, and increasingly won over by the Bolsheviks' calls for peace on any terms and land distribution. The first acts of the Bolshevik government, led by Lenin, were to declare peace and to decree the right of the peoples to self-determination (25 October) and the nationalization of the land (26 October).

The signing of the Treaty of Brest–Litovsk (March 1918) served as a pretext for foreign intervention, which fanned the flames of the civil war that had broken out in November 1917, especially in the south and in Siberia. These circumstances left a deep mark on the new regime, triggering the militarization of the economy and the strengthening of the executive and coercive machinery in order to stem the tide of anarchy that had followed the collapse of the traditional structures of government. A decree signed on 20 December 1917 set up the Vcheka, the extraordinary commission to combat the counter-revolution, sabotage and speculation; this was attached to the NKVD in 1918 and soon spread as its network ramified, throughout the country. The Vcheka has changed its name several times: to OGPU in 1924, and to KGB (committee for state security) in 1954, as which it now controls the 'organs' of security. The NKVD became the MVD in 1946, but in 1953 it lost responsibility for the labour camps – GULAG in official terminology – which were placed under the control of the ministry of justice. These camps, set up by decree on 15 April 1919, had by the outbreak of the second world war come to hold at least 3.5 million inmates – counting only people employed in economic activities (estimates based on official data used in the 1941 economic plan).[1]

Thus, relations between the Bolshevik party and the masses underwent a change in the aftermath of the seizure of power. The days of 1917 had taught it that political action could not be dissociated from permanent mobilization of the masses. It was essential to keep their attention riveted on precise objectives and to brighten the prospect of the future with glorious visions. But militarization of the economy turned out to be incompatible with workers' control (not to be confused with self-management); it entailed bringing the unions under state control and the condemnation of the theses of the workers' opposition (Shlyapnikov and Kollontai) at the tenth congress (1921). This faction — the same congress banned organized tendencies inside the Party — proposed to grant to the unions broad management powers in the workplace and to have all officials elected, rather than appointed by the Party. In 1921, the central committee delegated its powers as executive organ to the seven-member politburo.

The determination to hold on to power bred from the earliest days of the revolution a solidarity of interest among the members of the central machinery and the Party activists. Even so, the instinct for self-preservation or the urge to power do not explain everything: the economic functions which the ruling group had assumed, the need to forge a powerful state and build a nation on the ruins of the empire were to prolong mobilization well beyond the civil war.

The revolutionary effort sought not merely to modernize society but to transform it radically, substituting for traditional beliefs a new ideology with scientific claims. In the name of science, it was impossible for Marxism–Leninism to tolerate the expression of beliefs that it held to be outdated. By enshrining a state ideology, the Soviet regime laid claim to a monopoly formerly enjoyed by the Church, namely the power to define culture, to define good and evil, to reward and to punish. This ideology, which is really a secular religion, with its devoted, disciplined militants, has replaced the old state religion while preserving certain of its myths, such as infallibility (of the Party) and the omniscience of its leaders: a dogmatic and totalitarian form of socialism.

Stalinism

In a country that has never known any constitutional limitation on power, the concentration of the ideological, political and economic functions into the hands of a single group produced the excesses of the Stalinist period, when the Party became identified with its leader.

Terror: its role and its causes. Terror has become a means of social change permitting the elimination of opponents, generating a climate of insecurity that undermines all the values by which people might cling to their habits or certainties. It reached its zenith at the time of collectivization when, confronted with the mounting problems of the NEP, the Party decided to do away with peasant property, in other words the very foundations of Russian society. The reservations which many people in the country, and in the Party, had over these 'administrative methods' are not unconnected with the purges of 1934–9, when 4 or 5 million Party members and officials were arrested on political grounds, 400,000 or 500,000 of them being executed without trial. When the eighteenth Party congress opened in April 1939, a mere 37 survivors of the 1827 delegates to the seventeenth congress of 1934 were present.

Commentators have also looked to psychopathology for an explanation of Stalin's cruelty. The dictator's paranoia does not explain how the 'little father of the peoples' came to be the focus of a cult. As with many peoples with no experience of universal suffrage, the legitimacy of power, to the Russians, stems from the virtues ascribed to a charismatic leader; the little father (*batyushka*) was the affectionate term by which the good people had formerly referred to the Tsar. So the 'personality cult' seems to have been the result, rather than the cause, of society's underdevelopment. The concentration of roles and the 'overdevelopment' of power may be viewed as a technique employed by Stalinism to wrest the country from its underdevelopment.

The Party becomes an omnipotent bureaucracy. It is still an open question whether Lenin, in condemning war communism, intended through the NEP to introduce an original stage in socialism, founded on a resumption of dialogue with the masses ('the alliance of the proletariat and the peasants'), and on co-operative forms of economic organization and a long-term cultural revolution,[2] or whether he intended the NEP to be as it turned out, namely a temporary retreat. Unquestionably, the abandonment of the NEP involved the state in direct managerial responsibility for the economy, for which it was unprepared.

The launching of the first five-year plan in 1928 merely increased the need for managers. The ranks of specialists of the old regime, decimated by emigration and purges, were no longer adequate to the task. It became necessary to recruit from among the skilled workers graduating from the *rabfaki*[3] and the non-commissioned officers of the Red Army, who owed their social promotion to the Party and were thus all the more devoted to it. In other words, from having been in its early days an élite, the Party was turning into a vast administrative machine. The swelling of Party ranks following Lenin's death is a reflection of its twofold transformation, functional and sociological. 'The new state system is undoubtedly the most important result of the [first] five-year plan.'[4]

Lenin's death was followed by massive recruitment (the 'Lenin levy'), which gave increasing influence in the Party to Stalin's nominees who, like him, brought with them only a modicum of theoretical background. The Party's

TABLE 46　*Evolution of Party membership (excluding candidate members)*

Under Lenin		Under Stalin	
Jan. 1917	23,600[1]	Jan. 1928	914,307
Jan. 1918	115,000[1]	Jan. 1932	1,769,773
Jan. 1919	251,000	Jan. 1941	2,490,479
Jan. 1924	350,000	Jan. 1952	5,853,200

old guard were socially more homogeneous, with their noble or bourgeois origins, their rigid ethic and their contempt for the petty-bourgeois mentality, and had a generally sound Marxist culture and experience of the rigours of clandestine activity or exile. The new wave of Party members was not averse to material advantages such as a car or special rations (fairly rare at that time), which accompanied their jobs; these people needed precise directives, and identified more easily with Stalin's simplistic logic than with the sophisticated dialectic of a Bukharin. With these people there grew up a rough-and-ready style of command which amounted to 'leaning' on one's subordinates in order to obtain results, regardless of cost.

As the economy grew, so the bureaucracy spread. Once in existence, it was governed by its own internal logic, which required that it strive to perpetuate itself even after the conditions that had brought it into being had ceased to obtain. This is why this feature has persisted down to the present day – an ailment common to all modern societies – despite the many reforms enacted since Stalin's death to restore socialist legality and enhance the efficiency of the administration.

The return to socialist legality

Nikita Khrushchev's speech to the twentieth Party congress (February 1956). Khrushchev reviewed in his speech the history of the Party over the previous decades and revealed that, in order to secure his power, Stalin had not hesitated to frame and liquidate anyone he suspected of opposing him. This confession, which proved hard to keep secret, was a token of the new leader's determination to abjure terror. The *Osoboe soveshchanie* (*Osso*), the special NKVD commission set up in 1934 to pass sentence without trial, was abolished. Huge numbers of prisoners were amnestied. But the system of repression itself, with its assortment of labour camps (harsh, reinforced, general), remained in being. Some 10,000 political and religious prisoners are still held captive (Amnesty International, *Prisoners of Conscience in the USSR*, 1975), working in conditions that make a nonsense of the official claims to re-educate prisoners. At the same time, other, more subtle, methods such as internment in psychiatric hospitals have drawn the attention of world opinion to the misuses of psychiatry, as repression ceases to be on a mass scale and becomes more selective and individual. Even so, Soviets go less in fear of arbitrary arrest than in the past.

Although certain political trials are still held in secret, the machinery of justice is becoming more settled, thanks to the work of Soviet jurists.

Restoring legality inside the Party. Since 1956, this has found expression in the regular holding of congresses and central committee plenums, by more diversified social recruitment and by a return to the sources of Leninism. The centenary of Lenin's birth was an occasion for celebrations bordering on worship. Special deference is also paid to the general secretary of the Party, although this can no longer be attributed to the mysticism of the masses. The personalization of power in the Soviet Union, as in all countries that possess nuclear weapons, is dictated by the rules of the strategy of deterrence, which calls for an immediate riposte in case of major conflict. However, the functions of general secretary of the central committee and chairman of the council of ministers have been separated, so that a single man no longer, as in Stalin's time, controls both Party and administration. On the other hand, the new constitution adopted in 1977, which gives legal expression to these reforms, does allow the head of the executive to be head of state as well, i.e. to be chairman of the presidium of the Supreme Soviet.

Attempts to deconcentrate the administrative machine have been either shortlived or limited in their effects. In 1957, a large number of technical ministries were replaced by a hundred or so regional economic councils with competence in general matters (*sovnarkhoz*), co-ordinated by a state economic commission. After Khrushchev was ousted, it proved necessary to re-establish the ministries, but a similar attempt is currently in progress, with the formation of regional unions of enterprises.

The return to legality also facilitated a 'thaw' (the term is taken from the title of Ilya Ehrenburg's novel, published in 1954) in the intellectual sphere, and in particular the publication in 1962, with Khrushchev's permission, of Alexander Solzhenitsyn's novel *A Day in the Life of Ivan Denisovich* in the magazine *Novy Mir*, whose editor at the time was A. Tvardovsky. The speech delivered by L. I'ichev, the ideological chief, to intellectuals on 17 December 1962 marked the end of this spring. The trial of the writers Daniel and Sinyavsky in 1965 ushered in a period of repression of intellectuals and opponents. Even so, the mere fact that these dissidents dared to come out into the open, and that their trials were held in regular courts, illustrates the extent of the change that had occurred.

As we shall see, in the analysis that follows, the political system still retains, despite all these adjustments, two fundamental characteristics: democratic centralism (the subordination of the Party and the administration to the central organs) and the rejection of the separation of powers. Are we to conclude from this that underdevelopment alone is not enough to account for the permanence of this state of affairs, and that what really makes this a totalitarian political system is its ideological monopoly, which is a fully fledged religion of the state?

THE ORGANIZATION AND FUNCTIONS OF POWER

Soviet doctrine distinguishes two types of power: *social power* (*obshchestven-naya vlast'*), which is supposed to be the political expression of the masses, as manifested in all kinds of relations between state and society; and *political power* (*vlast'*), or the *machine* (*apparat*), which translates this popular will by means of a body of institutions which together form the state.

The organization of the state is dictated by its functions: (1) to convert social demands into political action, through the intermediary of the Party, which is the nerve system of society as a whole; (2) to arbitrate between and integrate these demands in the form of objectives (this being the function of the political decision-making organs); (3) to implement these through the agency of the central and local organs of the administration; (4) to supervise the execution of policy by means of a series of specialist control organs (financial, judicial, police); and (5) to organize ideological work by explaining the Party line and policies in order to obtain public support with the aid of the mass media and the various mass movements.

These mass movements are run by Party members (*aktiv*) and act as a relay for its policies. Together, the Party and its auxiliaries form what are referred to as the *social organizations*. They participate in the mechanisms of the political system by selecting the information to be transmitted further up the hierarchy, recruiting cadres and exhorting the populace, transmitting the directives that emanate from the central authorities and ensuring their implementation.

The Party

Although the 1977 version of the Soviet constitution, like its predecessor in 1936, places full power in the hands of the Supreme Soviet (Art. 136), it is the Communist Party which is the 'leading and guiding force in Soviet society; it is the central element in its political system and in all social and state organizations' (Art. 6). Thus, the Party occupies a central position in the political system, both as the political decision-making organ and as an instrument of control and influence; other institutions are mere auxiliaries, whose role is to serve the objectives of the Party and to bring about far-reaching changes in society. The Party is the arbiter of the people's aspirations.

Party membership. When the twenty-sixth congress met in February–March 1981, the Party had 17,480,000 members, which means that an average of 360,000 people had joined each year since the previous congress in 1976 (compared with an annual average of 762,000 between 1962 and 1965, against approximately 255,000 deaths or non-renewals of Party cards and with 300,000 expulsions in five years).

A third of the membership has been recruited since 1965, while only 17.8 per cent of the members had joined prior to 1946. The 26–40 age group is in a minority (38.4 per cent compared with the over-40s, who represent 56 per cent, of whom the over-60s represent 10.6 per cent). The proportion of women has increased from 19 per cent in 1952 to 23 per cent in 1973.

The social composition of the Party is changing too (Table 47), and the concern to attract people with the requisite skills accounts for the high percentage of specialists and the relatively higher percentage of people with either a full secondary education or a higher-education degree (60 per cent of Party members, compared with 32 per cent of the population as a whole).

The Communist Party of the Soviet Union is made up of fourteen parties of the socialist republics (the exception is that of the RSFSR, whose organization is amalgamated with that of the Union). Nationalities are not altogether equally represented in the Party and the population, however, for there is a higher proportion of Russians, Jews and Tatars in the Party than in the population as a whole (61.2 per cent of the Party membership is Russian, while Russians only account for 52 per cent of the total population; 13 per cent of all Jews are Party members, which is twice as many as for the population as a whole).

TABLE 47 *Social composition and educational level of Party membership*

Social group	Party members (%)				Popu-lation 1979	Educational level	CP members		Popu-lation 1970
	1924	1930	1957	1981			1956	1973	
Peasants (kolkhoz)	28.2	20.2	17.3	12.8	14.9	Less than 7 years	42.6	17.1	43.0
Blue-collar workers	44.1	65.5	32	} 43.4	60.0	7–8 years' study	24.6	23.0	25.1
White-collar workers	27.7	14.3	50.7		} 14.6	10 years	23.3	36.1	24.9
of which specialists			26.4	43.8	} 10.5	Higher education	9.5	23.8	7.0

The functions of Party members. Three categories of Party member can be distinguished:

1 Rank-and-file militants, full or probationary members. Probationary members are trainees who have belonged to the Party for at least one year, are at least 18 years old and are recommended by three members; in addition, their candidature must be approved by a majority of at least two-thirds of the primary organization, and this vote needs to be ratified by the higher echelon. Joining the Party carries with it the obligation to educate oneself by assimilating Marxist-Leninist theory, by playing an active part in building communism and combating bourgeois ideology.

2 The *aktiv* category consists of Party members exercising managerial responsibilities inside the Party machine or in enterprises or institutions and occupying positions reserved for the *nomenklatura* in mass organizations (Komsomol, the unions and the soviets), to which they have been elected on the Party's nomination; they represent between 20 and 50 per cent of the total Party membership.

3 Members of the apparatus (*apparatchiki*) are full-time salaried employees working at different levels in the Party, accounting for 3.2 per cent of total membership.

Consequently, 96.8 per cent of the Party membership operates in the workplace, for it is in the enterprises that the primary Party cell is organized — eighty-one members on average in an industrial enterprise, half as many in a collective farm. The percentage of Party members varies according to function or occupation: 94 per cent of collective-farm chairmen, 75 per cent of deputies to the Supreme Soviet, 60 per cent of lawyers, 33 per cent of engineers, 25 per cent of teachers and 20 per cent of doctors.[5]

Only a small group of between 200,000 and 250,000 members whose names are included in the special *nomenklatura* (*nomenklatura partiinykh organov*) have specifically political functions, which involve in particular the selection of cadres for all reserved jobs in the administration, enterprises and social organizations. At the higher echelon, this élite guides the political work of the central organs of the Party, the politburo and the secretariat of the central committee.

The decision-making organs: the politburo and the secretariat of the central committee

According to its statutes (revised on the occasion of the twenty-third congress), the Party holds its congress every five years. At the twenty-sixth congress, in 1981, 4994 delegates elected the central committee. Originally, this committee was composed of 22 members (in 1917) and was the Party's executive. Today, it has 470 members, 319 full members and 151 candidate members; the plenum, a vast political forum rather than a decision-making gathering, meets twice yearly.

Since the civil war, the function of the executive has been performed by the political bureau (known as the presidium of the central committee from 1956 to 1966). It is currently made up of fourteen full members and eight candidate members, including the principal Party leaders (the general secretary of the Party, four members of the secretariat and the first secretaries of the most important republics or cities), representatives of the administration (the chairman of the council of ministers, a vice chairman and a few ministers) and representatives of the state (members of the presidium of the Supreme Soviet). This is almost a government in its own right, and meets weekly; the secretariat is responsible for the day-to-day running of the Party machine.

The secretariat consists of ten members (of whom five are members of the politburo) and prepares briefs for discussion by the politburo, with the aid of its different specialist sections, which together form a rather large unit of roughly 1000 people, working under the general secretary.

The general secretary of the Party is officially appointed in the same way as the political bureau and the secretariat, i.e. by the 5000 or so delegates to the Party congress; the top leadership is elected by a show of hands, the central committee members generally confining themselves to ratifying the list submitted to them by the outgoing leadership. In practice, the decision is thus made by co-option among the full members of the political bureau (fourteen in 1981), probably with the six candidate members taking part along with those of the secretaries who are not members of the former organ (five). These twenty-five people include the leaders of all the major state and Party organs, the Party leaders from the principal republics, the head of government and his chief assistants and, since 1973, the army and police chiefs. Despite the soundness of the supreme leader's position, the general secretary's personal authority is a good deal less than that of a president of France or the United States. True, he is not answerable for his deeds before a genuine parliament, but he cannot alter the composition of the politburo at will, nor can he make it adopt major political changes against its wishes.[6] It is worth remembering that in June 1957 Khrushchev relied on the central committee to overturn a majority decision of the political bureau against him; on that occasion, the central committee was called upon to arbitrate a political crisis. But in 1964, Khrushchev was forced to yield in the face of his colleagues' opposition, which runs counter to the notion that the general secretary wields apparently absolute authority.

We have little information concerning actual decision-making procedures, and what we do have is open to all possible interpretations. Some see the leadership turning to ideology as a system of reference, while others believe that the policies of the Soviet Union are dictated by objective conditions, entailing one adjustment after another. The pragmatism that inevitably accompanies action does not rule out the pursuit of long-term objectives. A driver is forced to follow the bends in a winding road, but that does not affect his chosen destination.

The secretariat of the central committee is assisted in its day-to-day business in each republic by the central organs of the fourteen parties, which are organized along the same lines as the Union Party. Responsibility for the running of public affairs lies with the council of ministers of the Soviet Union and the different state committees and ministries that it comprises.

The central administration of public affairs: the council of ministers of the Soviet Union

The administration is responsible for giving practical shape to the directives and decisions of the Party. Because its competence covers practically every area of life, the Soviet government is unprecedentedly large. The council of ministers contains about 100 members: the chairman of the council, 1 first vice chairman, 10 vice chairmen, the 15 chairmen of the councils of ministers of the Union republics, 15 presidents of the state committees and 61 ministers. In each republic, the administration is organized along similar lines, except that there are only half as many ministerial portfolios, as thirty Union ministries (including railways, foreign trade, merchant marine, aviation and arms industries) have no counterpart in the republics. As in any modern state, the list of ministries and state committees is frequently modified.

To streamline the running of this council, the new constitution (Art. 131) provides for the creation of an inner cabinet, taking the name of the presidium of the council of ministers and comprising, in addition to the chairman of the council of ministers, the first vice chairmen of the council and the vice chairmen, making a total of a dozen people, instead of thirty-odd.

The present trend is to an increase in the number of state committees, because these tend generally to perform an intersectorial role, serving to co-ordinate the work of government, as opposed to the more specific sectorial competence of the ministries. We have already mentioned the importance of some of these, such as the Gosplan, the Gosnab, the Gostroy and the state committee for science and technology, when discussing the workings of the enterprise. The role of the committee for state security is notable for the fact that its chairman belongs to the political bureau of the central committee.

The state bank — Gosbank — with its network of 4000 branches in the provinces is directly responsible to the central management in Moscow; in other words, the Union government exercises absolute financial control over every enterprise and institution in the country. As envisaged by Lenin, this single, tentacular, state bank was supposed to be the paramount instrument of economic control (Lenin, *Can the Bolsheviks Retain Power?*, 1 October 1917). Along with the central telegraph office, the state bank was one of the first strategic centres occupied by the Red Guards in Petrograd during the October days. The nationalization of all the banks in Russia, which merged with the state bank (December 1917), predated that of transport (January 1918) and of all industry (June 1918).

The government works mainly through ordinances (*postanovlenie*), for in principle legislative power resides in the Supreme Soviet, which votes on general legislation; the business of government mainly involves the responsibility for all enterprise and institutional managers, who are answerable to specialized administrations in the ministries (*glavki*). The separation between the political decision-making organs (politburo) and administration means that the highest Party organs are not responsible for the execution of policy. But in fact the two hierarchical networks, those of the Party and the administration, live in symbiosis at the central level, since the chairman of the council and several ministers are also members of the political bureau. Similarly, in the regions, each enterprise is simultaneously answerable to a central government agency responsible for a specific sector and, at the territorial level, to the Party organization in the city in which it is located. These two streams ensure the *centralization* of power.

Furthermore, local, regional and Union administration is subject to control by deputies, who are elected to the soviets by all Soviet citizens, which is a means of justifying the adjective *democratic* affixed by the Soviets to this centralism.

Local, regional and republican authorities, and the first secretary

Local power emanates from the executive committees (*ispolkom*), which are elected for two and a half years by the village soviet deputies (*sel'sovet*) or the city soviet (*gorodskoy sovet*), whose powers are akin to those of the French town hall or departmental assembly (or the British county or district council). The executive committee is assisted in its work by a certain number of specialist commissions which supervise local administration. Like administrative employees, the elected members of the executive committee are paid on a full-time basis, but most of the people sitting on commissions are unpaid. Each administration (*otdel*) (e.g. the hygiene department) of the soviet is, by virtue of a dual mechanism of hierarchic subordination, answerable both to the *ispolkom* and to a central government agency (for instance, the republic's health ministry). The militia is controlled by the soviet and the ministry of the interior; the courts, on the other hand, are the sole responsibility of the public prosecutor. These local administrative departments run the schools, the hospitals, places of amusement, shops and markets, buildings and land, and sometimes even municipal industries. Consequently, each higher administrative echelon has a right to intervene in local affairs and can overrule a decision taken by the soviet.

In fact, the person with the widest powers in the region is the first secretary of the *obkom* (of the *raikom* in the countryside). His is the awesome responsibility for simultaneously supervising activities pertaining to the *ispolkom* and those of all the industrial enterprises, which are also subject to the authority of distinct central-government agencies. The bureau or committee of the *obkom* (comprising around ten members) consists of: the *obkom* Party secretaries, the first secretary of the main city, the chairman of the *ispolkom* and the first secretary; the chief of police, the military commandant of the region and the chief editor of the local newspaper.

By virtue of these responsibilities, the first secretary acts as co-ordinator and arbiter at the regional level, helping to solve the profusion of day-to-day problems that arise in the region's enterprises. For this reason, the first secretary often has a technical training bearing some relation to the principal sector of industry in the region. It is his or her job to lobby the central organs in support of requests for credit or allocations of resources necessary to the smooth running of the enterprises in his area; it is he, in the final analysis, who will be held responsible for the results obtained in his region. This makes his situation at once powerful and precarious: powerful, because he is the representative of the political authorities and answerable to them only; precarious, because he is personally committed to the eminently political job of integrating often incompatible social pressures into the realities of everyday life. More than sixty RSFSR *obkom* first secretaries are full or candidate members of the central committee of the Party.

Figure 7   The fifteen Union republics of the USSR

Notes: 1 Republic capital.
2 National capital.

National and Union representative bodies: the Supreme Soviet

Every five years, all Soviet citizens aged eighteen and over, are called upon to elect by direct, single-member, majority secret ballot, the deputies to the soviet in their own republic (Union or autonomous) as well as the deputies to the Supreme Soviet (voting takes place twice in one day). The Union parliament consists of two chambers, each with the same number of deputies (750): the *Soviet of the Union* and the *Soviet of Nationalities*. In the latter assembly, 480 deputies represent the Union republics, 220 deputies are elected by the autonomous republics and 50 come from the national districts, thus slightly curtailing the weight of the RSFSR, which has only 243 seats in this body compared with 424 in the Soviet of the Union.

The practice in elections is to present a single candidate in each constituency. The Party takes care to ensure that candidates are representative, in terms of social origins, and to safeguard a satisfactory balance between continuity and the necessary renewal of deputies. To be a candidate, one has to be aged eighteen or over, and be nominated by a general assembly of workers in the enterprises and public bodies, after a debate which serves as a kind of substitute primary election. Sometimes this takes place in a somewhat artificial climate of excitement and even frenzy, lasting throughout the campaign up to polling day. The voter is handed a ballot slip without an envelope, and he can, if he so wishes, go into the polling booth and cross out the name of the candidate proposed. Once elected, the deputy continues to exercise his usual occupation; all he receives is an allowance for official expenses and free transport on the Soviet Union's air, rail and river networks.

The Supreme Soviet appoints the members of the government (council of ministers), the prosecutor general, the general arbitrator[7] and the Supreme Court of the Soviet Union. It ratifies constitutional texts and federal laws (*zakony*), which often take the form of general laws, to be supplemented by specific codes laid down by each republic; it ratifies decrees and approves the annual budget and plan. As it only meets in ordinary session twice a year, for a few days at a time, the Supreme Soviet delegates the work of legislation to fourteen specialist commissions. Parliamentary sessions bear no resemblance to debates in western-type parliaments. The deputies take it in turns to mount the rostrum, according to a strict timetable, reading carefully prepared, often identical reports, and there is no genuine debate. Voting is by show of hands, in an atmosphere of perfect unanimity. For the provincial dignitary, this excuse for a trip to the capital is well worth the boredom of a few parliamentary sessions.

The Supreme Soviet elects a 37-member presidium for the duration of the legislature and to represent it when the assembly is in recess. Consequently, the presidium can exercise legislative powers by means of decree (*ukazy*), declare war, ratify treaties and receive foreign ambassadors, and reprieve criminals. In other words, it is invested with the function of national representation of a head of state, in the person of the chairman of the presidium. This is more than an honorific post, since it was from this that L. Brezhnev, chairman of the presidium from 1960 to 1964, acceded to the top leadership position of general secretary of the Party which from 1977 until his death in 1982 he combined with that of chairman of the presidium.

To relieve the chairman of the presidium of the Supreme Soviet of some of his countless duties, the new constitution has provided for the appointment of a vice chairman of the presidium; it is the latter who receives certain foreign visitors, welcomes ambassadors, presents decorations and in general assumes all minor official obligations.

Specialist supervisory organs

The general task of supervising the administration, which is performed by the Party organization and the soviets at their respective levels, does not altogether do away with the need for more specific supervisory bodies.

Financial supervision, which is carried out by the Gosbank inspectors, is facilitated by the fact that all enterprise accounts are kept by the Gosbank, which appoints the chief accountant in each enterprise; thus the manager of the enterprise does not control its accountant.

Supervision of the administration is in the hands of a people's state control committee, which is responsible for eliminating all shortcomings and mal-practices in the administration and enterprises. For this purpose, it runs an extensive network of 7 million people's inspectors, publicly elected for two years and supervised by the local people's control committees. These are em-powered to upbraid and rebuke officials and, where necessary, place matters in the hands of the prosecutor's office to initiate appropriate legal proceed-ings. In addition, the new constitution has also set up a state arbitration court, responsible for arbitrating economic disputes arising between organizations, enterprises and the administration; the general arbitrator of the Soviet Union is, like the general prosecutor, elected for five years by the Supreme Soviet. He is assisted by a staff of regional arbitrators.

Supervision of the judiciary is exercised by the state prosecutor's office and the courts, which are independent of the local soviets but still subject to the authority of the central organs. The general prosecutor is appointed by the Supreme Soviet for a period of five years and reports on his work to the pres-idium of the Soviet. His functions are twofold: (1) he supervises (*obshchiy nadzor*) all the country's courts through the prosecutors (whom he appoints) in each of the republics and the circuit and city prosecutors (who are appointed by the republic prosecutors), as well as the entire administration and all social organizations; he also presides at appeals against certain illegal de-cisions, which he is empowered to overrule; and (2) he acts as state prosecutor and initiates criminal, administrative or disciplinary proceedings against offenders.

The courts are presided over by judges elected for five years and assessors recruited from among the population and elected for two years. The latter do not necessarily possess a legal training, whereas the judges are professional jurists, although the fact that they are appointed by popular vote means that they can be removed. Once again, elections are based on the single-candidate principle; the Supreme Soviet appoints the Supreme Court judges (the *Verkhovniy Sud*), while people's court judges in the cities are elected by the same voters as elect the city soviet. There is also a network of people's juris-dictions in the enterprises (*tovarishcheskiy sud*) to sanction petty offences against opinion rather than against the judicial codes.

The police are divided into two streams: the military (identified by the 'red piping' on their uniform), which are controlled by the ministry of the interior, and the 'organs' of the KGB (state security committee), responsible for terri-torial surveillance, recognizable when in uniform by their 'blue piping'. They are concerned with 'marked' people and are assisted by informers (*stukachi*). But the vast majority of Soviet citizens escape this surveillance, though know-ing full well it could be applied to them. However, the sense of personal insecurity engendered by these untrammelled powers does entail a far more fundamental difference from western bureaucracies than the contrast result-ing from lower living standards. Even so, however excessive these police methods and certain judicial investigative procedures may appear, it would be just as dishonest to avoid all reference to them as it would be to imagine a society governed by force alone.

Access to the mass media is a state monopoly which is exercised by specialist enterprises (press, publishers, film studios, etc.), administered by ad hoc state committees (radio and television, publishing, cinema) and the ministry of culture. All these media, which are available for information and propaganda campaigns, are supervised by the department of agitation and propaganda (*agitprop*) of the secretariat of the Party central committee. This is the main driving force behind all ideological activity, and more especially behind the press.

The sheer size of the information industry is undeniably impressive. The television network operates 132 broadcasting centres and 6 channels, broadcasting to two-thirds of the national territory by means of 1600 relay stations; and *Pravda*, with its circulation of 10 million, is the biggest-selling newspaper in the world.

The chief editors of the leading newspapers and magazines meet weekly in Moscow to announce general instructions for the whole of the Union's press. News items are handled by the news agency Tass, which issues a number of special bulletins for certain privileged clients. Foreign publications are screened by the customs and the censor's office. Unauthorized works are stored in a special division of the central libraries (*spetskhran*), to which access is restricted.

Before publication, Soviet periodicals and books must obtain the censor's certificate of approval (*glavlit*) which is printed in small print in each book, together with the authorized number of copies. It is the publisher who deals with censorship. After reading the manuscript, the censor will invite the publisher, if necessary, to come and discuss 'doubtful or delicate points'. He will suggest corrections, which the publisher then proposes to the author, who never comes into direct contact with the censor.

Does this mean the public has no influence on decisions taken by the political system and that the latter operates without any feedback? The Party's preeminent role in breathing life into every organization, enterprise and public administration imposes upon it a twofold duty of communication: first, it must explain the Party line to the general public, but secondly it must convey grassroots reactions to the top leadership. In the absence of a separation of powers, the sole guarantee that information will reach the leadership relatively undistorted and in good time, before real life begins to diverge from the authorities' image of it, is the existence of a profusion of parallel channels, including the soviets, the mass organizations and the supervisory organs. The growth of opinion polls since the 1960s suggests that these traditional channels have proved inadequate as a means of keeping the leadership fully informed as to the state of the country.

This political system is perfectly organized to mobilize resources and men for the achievement of objectives laid down in the Party programme, but three major shortcomings may be noted.

1 The absence of any constitutional mechanism to ensure regular renewal of the top leadership. Candidates are not chosen by universal suffrage but by a system of co-option, which gives rise to both a gerontocracy and the elimination of members by humiliation (e.g. Malenkov, the 'anti-Party group', Khrushchev) or, in the past, even by means of criminal procedures (Beria's execution was the last in a long series of political murders).

2 The absence of legal redress against unconstitutional administrative measures, as in cases of violations of public freedoms guaranteed under the Constitution; the Supreme Court is not a constitutional court, but an appeals court to which only the state prosecutor and presidents of the supreme courts of Union republics are entitled to refer cases.

3 The absence of a separation of powers between the political, economic and cultural spheres means that none of the functional groups – administration, enterprises, educational institutions, press, etc. – is able to act autonomously; whatever is administrative, economic or cultural is also political, which is why any reform that might be envisaged in any one of these spheres directly affects the Party itself. Thus, the ability of the system to adapt itself depends, in the final analysis, upon the wisdom of the men who carry the heavy responsibility of leading the Party.

POWER AND SOCIETY

Needless to say, official doctrine denies this totalitarian model. According to this doctrine, the democratic character of the system – the state of all the people – is evidenced in (1) the fact that the population participates extensively in political life through the mass organizations; and (2) the fact that the political élite is recruited from among all social groups. What finally determines the nature of institutions and the political system is the existence, or otherwise, of a dialogue between rulers and society.

Participation in political life

Forms of participation. 1 *Membership of mass organizations or associations.* More than any other revolution, the Bolshevik programme has sought to modify relations between rulers and society, drawing them closer by permanent mass mobilization. The Party is assisted in this task by a series of auxiliary organizations which perform ideological tasks by addressing more homogeneous publics.

The trade unions, which are organized into 25 occupational branches, had 113 million members in March 1977. Practically every worker belongs to a union in order to enjoy full social-security rights. It is difficult to say precisely how many union members are activists, but half are reported to participate in campaigns of socialist emulation designed to stimulate a 'communist attitude to work'. The formal character of this type of involvement is attested by generally poor levels of productivity.

The Komsomol, the communist youth organization for those aged between 14 and 28, has a membership of around 35 million, or roughly one-third of this age group. Like the union activists, the Komsomol activists form a nursery for future Party members.

Some of the professions, for example, journalism, writing, architecture, painting, singing and filmmaking, are organized into unions. The Writers' Union, for instance, has a membership of over 7200, but one does not have to be a member of this union in order to be published or receive fees. These unions have their own property — rest homes, clubs, blocks of flats — which supply members with a certain number of services in exchange for the obligations they shoulder. For example, the college of lawyers charges clients a fixed scale of fees and withholds roughly 30 per cent in order to pay court-appointed lawyers.

It is an open question whether the fact of belonging to a union, which though not compulsory nevertheless comprises virtually all workers or members of a profession, ought to be regarded as a form of political participation. When a Frenchman or an Englishman pays his social-security contributions, he does not feel that he is performing a political act, even though the national insurance boards in France, for instance, enjoy a broad measure of independence under state supervision and are generally jointly administered by workers' and employers' representatives.

2 *Voting in elections to the soviets.* Voting by the entire electorate is far more frequent in the Soviet Union than under parliamentary governments since the local soviets are elected every two and a half years.

Whereas the Party and the unions are active at the place of work, the election campaign is held in places of residence: neighbourhoods and villages. The 'agitators' give free rein to their activism in the housing estates (*agitpunkt*) and public gardens (*agit-ploshchadki*), which are transformed into so many election headquarters. The election-day turnout is an impressive 99.98 per cent of registered voters (1974), and results are no less remarkable, with candidates regularly polling 99.97 per cent of the votes. One would quite likely meet with disapproval were one to abstain from an operation designed less to discover the voters' wishes (since the list contains only one candidate) than to demonstrate how unanimous society is. Which is why election day looks more like a popular holiday than, for example, a dreary French Sunday poll.[8]

In the Soviet Union, the participation of the population has the same significance as a believer's membership of some religious body and his involvement in its ceremonies; it illustrates the perfect communication that exists between all who share in the same faith and the same ideal. But it should not be seen as a western-style election in which voters are asked to choose between different political programmes, implying a choice between different models of society, which is precisely the justification for having more than one candidate in democratic regimes.

3 *Criticism and self-criticism.* While individuals have no opportunity of expressing disagreement with the major political options and candidates proposed to them through electoral channels, they are nevertheless free to express their views on the vast subject of everyday life and work, by drawing attention to abuses or by suggesting improvements.

The pre-election meetings to select candidates are an occasion for those taking part to present their grievances (*nakazy*). At the same time, complaints (*zhaloby*) and suggestions (*predlozheniya*) may be formulated and submitted to the administration, which is obliged to examine them. In the event of illegal actions, the citizen is entitled to lodge a complaint with the prosecutor or the courts.

Soviet people are also in the habit of writing to their newspapers. Some of these letters get published, but only after selection by the editor, so that they can scarcely be regarded as a true reflection of public opinion. In certain cases, a journalist will be dispatched to conduct his own inquiries. Government agencies criticized are entitled to reply.

Article 58 of the new constitution permits individuals to claim damages for injury suffered as a result of illegal administrative action, and Article 49 protects them against prosecution for exercising their right to criticize.

Meetings held at a place of work also offer those taking part an opportunity of expressing criticisms and making proposals (*kriticheskie zamechaniya i predlozheniya*), which may produce a response on the part of the people thus assailed (self-criticism). Furthermore, deputies to the soviets are expected to report back periodically to their voters, thereby maintaining contacts with the rank and file. Mass participation, therefore, is not merely a display of self-satisfaction and stirring speeches; it can also serve as a useful corrective for certain mistakes in points of detail or engender initiatives that can be subjected to experiment and perhaps even generalized.

Thus it would be wrong to say that the Soviet political system has no place for debate, even political debate. One finds traces of it in the specialist publications, which often publish opposing points of view on theoretical and practical issues. But debate on the major political questions is never held in public.

The degree of participation. The degree to which citizens take part in public life can be measured not only in terms of election turnouts but also by the place occupied by social and political activities in the lives of different strata of the population.

Surveys of the way people use their free time carried out between 1965 and 1968 in certain cities showed that, among both men and women, political activities come last on the list, regardless of educational level. This does not necessarily mean that they are disinterested in the affairs of the country, for men spend a good deal of their free time reading the papers. However, foreign observers have noted that Soviet men tend to begin their newspapers at the back, with the sporting news and practical guides.

Television clearly wins out over the newspapers, especially among women. Programme preferences and the number of hours spent viewing vary according to age, profession and education. Most people buy a television set in order to relax, which is why games, sports broadcasts, films, variety shows and drama are more popular than the news, discussion programmes and programmes about work and the economy.[9] On public holidays, television devotes its entire programme to the celebrations. The freedom of choice available to the viewer necessarily entails a profound change in methods of ideological action. Gone are the days when the best way of swaying the relatively uneducated masses was to hold meetings designed to create the necessary climate. The printed media breed a sense of detachment and distance between the reader and the world outside. Television, on the other hand, is capable of engaging the viewer in a more immediate experience. It is no longer possible to count on the contagion that is capable of gripping an audience; it has now become necessary to employ some kind of rational argument to keep the viewer glued to his set. As a result, mass media techniques are changing both the habits of the general public and propaganda methods.

The degree to which one takes part in public life depends on whether or not one is a Party member. A survey conducted at Saratov showed that 92.5 per cent of the Party membership were 'active', compared with 14.5 per cent of the population as a whole.[10] It is worth pointing out that family income also exercises some influence, as the amount of time spent on public activities rises from 35 minutes per week for the head of a family with a monthly per capita income of less than 50 rubles, to 1 hour 5 minutes in families whose per capita income exceeds 75 rubles. Does this mean that one's sense of involvement in public affairs is a function of one's social position, and that here, as elsewhere, public life is the preserve of a political élite?

The political élite

Description and membership. In a hierarchic system, where bureaucratic circuits proliferate, it is not easy to identify the dividing line between governors and governed. We may all regard ourselves as superior to someone and inferior to someone else. Where, therefore, does the political élite begin?

Official statistics supply part of the answer to this question. At the 1970 census, 405,784 people, i.e. 0.35 per cent of the working population, were classified as belonging to the 'leadership' group (*rukovoditeli*), including leaders of primary Party organizations and chairmen and secretaries of rural soviets. If we confine ourselves exclusively to the personnel of the Party machine and the regional, urban and central-government agencies, this total drops to 220,000. Furthermore, the Labour Yearbook (*Trud V SSR*, 1968, pp. 28–29) gave the figure of 1,640,000 employees in central and regional government, including 68,000 in the judiciary, representing 2 per cent of the working population. But the political élite is not confined to these categories. It would be unreasonable to extend the definition to cover all supervisory personnel (*nachal'stvo*) in the country's enterprises and institutions (over 1,500,000 people), for not all collective chairmen and shop managers can seriously claim to belong to the establishment. Which is why certain analysts suggest that the criterion defining the ruling group, or political élite, should be all those individuals occupying a post deemed sufficiently important to be included on the official list of posts drawn up by the Party central committee, i.e. some 30,000–40,000 people. This list includes not only high-ranking Party apparatus and administrative personnel but also army officers and leading members of scientific and cultural organizations. Alec Nove remarks that if, under certain other regimes, ownership of property is a means to acquiring power, in Soviet society the élites are recruited by co-option, which tends to make the *nomenklatura* the instrument of the leadership.[11]

While the political élite is being recruited increasingly from among the intelligentsia, the two are not conterminous. The intelligentsia forms a far more stable stratum, and certain sections of it actually prefer to keep out of politics. Furthermore, the position of a leading official may prove only temporary, and it can never be transmitted to his or her children. True, the children of high officials do find it easier to acquire a comfortable position in the intelligentsia or administration, as witnessed by certain well-known examples. Although not dependent on political opinion or the electorate, an official is never assured of a political future. This insecurity distinguishes the *apparatchik* from a member of the intelligentsia who has no public function. On the other hand, the *apparatchiki* enjoy a certain number of privileges attaching to their function, less in the form of higher pay, which is scarcely better than that of a manager in industry, than in the form of comfortable homes, cars and services. They also enjoy opportunities of travel abroad, and have priority access to rest homes. Above all, they enjoy the rare privilege in the Soviet Union of being informed and listened to.

However, a person does not attain a position of authority without personal sacrifice. While political personnel may hope for rapid promotion, this is the reward of total devotion to the Party line. This means they must give all their time to the task, as well as not being afraid to reveal themselves, including their family life. A public figure may at any moment be called upon to account for his or her conduct. Each must be an example, the archetype of the positive hero found in Soviet literature.

These leaders are generally recruited among industrial managers, for the fact of having run a major enterprise or construction site is the best apprenticeship in leadership. Others get an early start on the Party ladder after graduating from the advanced Party schools (22 regional schools and the central committee advanced Party school between them train an average of 5000 *apparatchiki* annually).

Social composition. The Party central committee may be regarded as the body most representative of the political élite, according to the narrowest definition of this term, since its membership is restricted to fewer than 500 people. Table 48 gives the composition of the central committee. The higher organs of the Party account for over one-third of the membership, including the entire politburo and secretariat, which belong to this committee as of right. Roughly 30 per cent of the posts are assigned *ex officio*, as, for example, those of chairmen of the councils of ministers of the Soviet Union and of all the republics, those of almost all ministers and state committee chairmen, and that of state prosecutor. On the other hand, social organizations and economic and cultural activities are insufficiently represented, and in most cases by candidate members. This serves to underline the fact that the political élite is not to be confused with the intelligentsia (managers and representatives of the professions and intellectuals).

The changes that occur in the composition of the central committee from one congress to another give a measure of the rate of renewal of the political élite. The quickest turnover occurred between 1956 and 1961, during Nikita Khrushchev's government, when half the central committee was replaced between these two dates. The rate of renewal dropped to 39 per cent between 1961 and 1966, to 24 per cent between 1966 and 1971 and 26 per cent between 1971 and 1976. Between 1918 and 1930, the rate of renewal never exceeded 17 per cent, while the record was 77 per cent, between 1936 and 1939, in the

TABLE 48   *Composition of the central committee of the Communist Party of the USSR, 1971–81*

	Full members		Increase or decline (%)
	1971	1981	
Party: central apparatus	18	43	+ 139
republics and regions	72	99	+ 38
Central and republic administrations	76	83	+ 9
Soviets	14	12	− 15
Military	18	27	+ 50
Soviet ambassadors	15	12	− 20
Social organizations: trade unions	2	5	+ 150
Komsomol	1	1	nil
Intelligentsia: unions and associations	9	17	+ 89
Factories: directors and executives	7	3	− 57
workers and kolkhoz workers	9	15	+ 67

wake of the 'purges'. In 1981, only 17 per cent of the full members elected were new to the position.

John Miller has analysed the nationality of 259 people occupying the post of first or second secretary in the Union or autonomous republics between March 1954 and March 1976. The majority were non-Russians (134, compared with 125 Russians). In the Ukraine, Byelorussia, Armenia and Estonia, these posts are always occupied by nationals of these republics. In central Asia, the post of first secretary is traditionally given to a non-native, who is assisted by a Russian as second secretary. In certain cases (Kazakhstan, Moldavia), we find the reverse pairing. Lithuania, Latvia, Georgia and Azerbaijan, all of which had nationals as first and second secretaries in the period following Stalin's death, have all recently seen the latter post go to Russians. We cannot put this duality down exclusively to considerations of political control, for we find that the non-Russians generally come from occupations connected with ideology or culture and are therefore suited to 'communication'; while the Russians, who generally have a technical background, tend rather to concentrate in economic responsibilities.

Interest groups. One needs to tread carefully when transposing western patterns, founded on the notion of pressure groups, to Soviet political life. There are several reasons for this: (1) it is often misleading to present certain individuals involved in political debate as necessarily being the spokesmen for latent groups; (2) unlike what happens in pluralistic regimes, where pressure groups operate outside the power system, by seeking to exert either covert influence (lobbies) or public influence (trade unions) on decisions, the workings of the political system are here confined to the Party; in other words the process is almost entirely secret, barring a few generally rather small groups, such as the Jews or Germans wanting to emigrate, Crimean Tatars, etc., who draw attention to their situation by means of public demonstrations; (3) the fact of acting inside the Party means that the different groups recruited by co-option and who form the political élite have not only common interests but also a common political culture.

Even so, it is reasonable to suppose that differences of temperament, age and political experience must inevitably arise inside the Party machine; some elements are presumably more conservative, others more liberal. The commonest debate revolves around the allocation of resources and apportionment of credits. One merely has to read the minutes of meetings of the Supreme Soviet or Party plenums to observe the frequency of discussions arising out of requests for credits. Regional first secretaries generally act as spokesmen for factory managers and local councils in dealings with central government. Party representatives and managers, so far from being at loggerheads, actually tend to work in unison, because they are both equally concerned with the economic success of their region. There is no reason, therefore, to regard the Party apparatus and 'technocrats' as being mutually antagonistic.

The position of career soldiers is particularly respected under the Soviet regime, even though they held only 33 central committee seats in 1981 (i.e. 8 per cent of the seats, compared with 10.7 per cent in 1952). The officer corps is the only social group to have maintained a certain élitist tradition, because practically every member of it has passed through the military academies. The abolition of political commissars has not diminished the Party's supremacy over the army. In practical terms, the Party organization inside each barracks is answerable solely to the central committee. And the army has always co-operated loyally with the Party, asserting itself only in periods of crisis (to restore the balance of power in Khrushchev's favour in 1955) or when cuts in personnel or military spending were felt to be contrary to the national interest. It will be recalled that in 1955, General Zhukov, who was then immediately promoted to the rank of Marshal by Khrushchev, intervened in his favour against the chairman of the Council of Ministers, Malenkov. He was appointed minister of defence, while Marshal Bulganin became chairman of the council of ministers. Eleven generals were then promoted to the rank of marshal. But Zhukov's rise was shortlived; accused of 'Bonapartism' at the October 1957 plenum, while on a visit to Yugoslavia, he was dismissed from his post.

One might think that, by tradition, career soldiers would tend to be conservative in outlook and hostile to over-rapid reform; but on the other hand, new weapons technology means that, like industrialists and scientists, their concern is for efficiency and that military experts carry the greater weight in decisions in any way connected with the defence of the nation. One should be wary of underestimating the patriotic feeling which the army both schools and incarnates; possibly even more so than the Party, it is the firmest cement of Soviet society.

Future prospects

Having come to the end of this analysis, it is tempting to examine from a few general observations how the Soviet system is likely to evolve. Such prognoses as we are able to make flow from the nature of that system. For those who are inclined chiefly to define the regime in terms of its centralism and its totalitarian ideology, change can come only from above. They focus on changes in the top leadership and on real or imagined conflicts within it. The stability of the regime can only be shaken in the awesome event of a major international crisis. For while on the one hand the bureaucracy (which is the result of the statist organization of the economy), with its considerable inertia, rules out any kind of far-reaching evolution; on the other, the absence of any alternative allowing the citizen to express himself gives to the term *democracy* a rather special meaning, referring to participation rather than to political choice. As a result, the system entails a permanent politicization of every aspect of social life, without any group having yet managed to win autonomy for itself, as any kind of fractionalism is regarded as incompatible with the spirit of unity.

For those who are more attentive to relations between government and society and to the contingent nature of the political system, the emergence of a diversified and educated industrial society inevitably breeds factors of change, which are already perceptible in youth behaviour patterns and the renewal of the political élites. The generation of revolutionaries has been replaced by a body of men and women of whom most belong to the new technical intelligentsia or to the bureaucracy.[12] Can we expect to see a secularization of official ideology, which has been elevated into a state religion, under pressure of rationalist demands for the introduction of greater efficiency into the old structures? The political line seems increasingly to be the outcome of compromise, for, as in all developed societies, economic decisions involve choosing between alternative resource allocations and all social life is competitive, even conflictive, by nature, appearances to the contrary notwithstanding: this makes the future unpredictable.

These two visions are not mutually exclusive, for real life is a mixture of dogmatism and pragmatism; but these are insufficient to serve as a basis for diagnosis. The future is determined not only by economic structures or social processes, it is also the product of man's will, that is, of the values that guide everyday behaviour and conspire to unite or divide a society. The Soviet political system is designed to bring about rapid change in the structures of society and, from this standpoint, it has proved itself effective. Has it been equally successful in achieving that supremely delicate mutation, namely a change in people's mentalities?

NOTES

1 N. Jasny, 'Labour and output in Soviet concentration camps', *Journal of Political Economy*, Chicago, Oct. 1951.

2 'On Cooperation', an article by Lenin, dated 26 Jan. 1923, in *Pol. soch.*, vol. 33, 5th ed., p. 427.

3 Workers' faculty, i.e. preparatory classes devised as a means of bringing worker students up to the normal standard of university entrance.

4 M. Lewin, 'L'État et les classes sociales un U.R.S.S. 1929–1933', *Actes de la recherche en sciences sociales*, no. 1, February 1976, pp. 2–31.

5 M. Matthews, *Class and Society in Soviet Russia*, 1972, p. 220.

6 M. Tatu, in *Le Monde*, 15 Jan. 1975.

7 Arbitration tribunals are involved in contract disputes arising, for example, when goods are supplied late or are of bad quality.

8 French elections are held on Sundays, and no political campaigning is permitted on that day (Transl.).

9 V. Sappak, *Televidenie glazami sotsiologa*, Moscow, 1970.

10 Matthews, op. cit., p. 243.

11 A. Nove, 'Y a-t-il une classe dirigeante en U.R.S.S.?', *Revue des études comparatives Est-Ouest*, vol. 6, no. 4, 1975, pp. 5–44.

12 The high percentage of Party members belonging to the intelligentsia is indicative of a trend in which positions of responsibility are being reserved increasingly for graduates of higher education. At the present time, 90 per cent of regional first secretaries and cadres aged under 50 have completed university education. However, this 'young generation' accounts for only 6.3 per cent of the total membership of the new central committee (1981), compared with 57 per cent in 1956.

SUGGESTED READING

Evolution and growth of the political system

Auty, R. and Obolensky, D., *An Introduction to Russian History*, Cambridge University Press, 1976.

Bettelheim, C., *La Lutte des classes en U.R.S.S. (1917–1941)*, Maspero-Seuil, 1974, 1977, 1982, 3 vols.

Carrère d'Encausse, H., *Lenin: Revolution and Power* (vol. I), *Stalin: Order through Terror* (vol. II), London, Longman, 1981.

Elleinstein, J., *Histoire de l'U.R.S.S.*, Éditions sociales, 1972–5, 4 vols.

Elleinstein, J., *Histoire du phénomène stalinien*, Grasset, 1975.

Fainsod, M., *Smolensk under Soviet Rule*, Harvard University Press, 1958.

Ferro, M., *La Révolution de 1917*, Aubier, 1967, 1976, 2 vols.

Ferro, M., 'En U.R.S.S.: la naissance d'un système bureaucratique', *Annales*, March–April 1975, pp. 243–7.

Heller, M. and Nekrich, A., *L'Utopie au pouvoir*, Paris, Calmann-Levy, 1982.

Medvedev, R., *Let History Judge: The Origins and Consequences of Stalinism*, London, 1971.

Pethybridge, R., *The Social Prelude to Stalinism*, London, Macmillan, 1974.

Seton-Watson, H., *The Russian Empire 1807–1917*, Oxford University Press, 1967.

Solzhenitsyn, A., *The Gulag Archipelago*, London, Fontana, 1974.

Sorènson, J., *The Life and Death of Soviet Trade Unionism*, 1969.

Organization of the state

Brown, A., 'Policy making in the Soviet Union', *Soviet Studies*, no. 1, July 1971, pp. 120–49.

Gelard, P., *Les Systèmes politiques des états socialistes*, vol. 1: *Le Modèle soviétique*, Cujas, 1975.

Gelard, P., *L'Administration locale en U.R.S.S.*, P.U.F., 1972.

Hough, J. and Fainsod, M., *How the Soviet Union Is Governed*, Harvard University Press, 1979.

Kulikova, G., 'Povyshenie roli mestnykh sovetov', *Istoriya S.S.S.R.*, no. 5, 1976.

Lesage, M., *Les Régimes politiques de l'U.R.S.S. et de l'Europe de l'Est*, P.U.F., 1971.

Sharlet, R., *The New Soviet Constitution of 1977*, Brunswick, Ohio, 1978.

Nature of the political system

Brown, A. H., *Soviet Politics and Political Science*, London, 1974.

Brus, W., *Socialist Ownership and Political Systems*, London, Routledge & Kegan Paul, 1975.

Brzezinski, Z., 'The nature of the Soviet system', *Slavic Review*, vol. 20, no. 3, 1961 (see remarks by Alfred Mayer and Robert Tucker in the same issue).

Carrère d'Encausse, H., *Le Pouvoir confisqué: gouvernants et gouvernés*, Flammarion, 1980.

Fischer, G., *The Soviet System and Modern Society*, New York, Atheron Press, 1968.

Lane, D., *Politics and Society in the U.S.S.R.*, London, Weidenfeld & Nicolson, 1972.

Meyer, A., 'Qui gouverne l'U.R.S.S.?', *Revue française de science politique*, no. 6, 1967, pp. 1062–79.

Rigby, T. M., Brown, A. and Reddaway, P. (eds), *Authority, Power and Policy in the USSR*, London, Macmillan, 1981.

Political élites

Alleluyeva, S., *En une seule année*, Laffont, 1970.

Frank, P., 'The C.P.S.U. *obkom* first secretary, a profile', *British Journal of Political Science*, vol. I, 1972, pp. 173–90.

Hough, J., *The Soviet Prefects: The Local Party Organs in Industrial Decision Making*, Cambridge, Mass., Harvard University Press, 1969.

'L'élite du Parti entre l'idéologie et la spécialisation', *Problèmes politiques et sociaux*, nos 142–3, 1972, pp. 5–34.

Levin, V. and Perfilev, M., *Kadry apparata upravleniya v S.S.S.R.*, Leningrad, 1970.

McAuley, M., 'The hunting of the hierarchy: R.S.F.S.R. *obkom* first secretaries and the central committee', *Soviet Studies*, vol. 25, no. 4, Oct. 1974, pp. 478–501.

Morozow, M., *L'Establishment soviétique*, Fayard, 1972.

Nove, A., 'Y a-t-il une classe dirigeante en U.R.S.S.?', *Revue des études comparatives Est-Ouest*, vol. 6, no. 4, 1975, pp. 5–44 (commentary by Maria Hirszowicz, *Soviet Studies*, no. 2, 1976, pp. 262–73).

Rigby, T., *Communist Party Membership in the U.S.S.R. 1917–1967*, Princeton University Press, 1968.

Schapiro, L., *The Communist Party of the Soviet Union*, 2nd edn, London, Methuen, 1970.

Souvarine, B., *Stalin: A Critical Survey of Bolshevism*, London, 1939.

Tatu, M., *Power in the Kremlin, from Krushchev's decline to collective leadership*, London, Collins, 1968.

Citizens and interest groups

Friedgut, T., *Political Participation in the USSR*, Princeton University Press, 1979.

Hill, R., *Soviet Political Elites*, Oxford, Martin Robertson, 1977.

Hough, J., 'Political participation in the Soviet Union', *Soviet Studies*, vol. 28, no. 1, Jan. 1976, p. 320 (commentary by F. Rigby, *Soviet Studies*, April 1976).

Kolkowicz, R., *The Soviet Military and the Communist Party*, Princeton University Press, 1967.

Langsam, D. and Paul D., 'Soviet politics and the group approach', *Slavic Review*, March 1972, pp. 136–41.

Miller, J., 'Cadres policy in nationality areas', *Soviet Studies*, Jan. 1977, pp. 3–36.

Mink, G., 'L'opinion publique en U.R.S.S. et dans les démocraties populaires', *Problèmes politiques et sociaux*, no. 260, June 1975.

Skilling, G. and Griffiths, F., *Interest Groups in Soviet Politics*, Princeton University Press, 1971.

Sokoloff, G., *L'Économie obéissante, décisions politiques et vie économique en U.R.S.S.*, Calmann-Levy, 1976.

Unger, A., 'Soviet mass political work in residential areas', *Soviet Studies*, no. 4, 1971, pp. 556–61.

Unger, A., 'Political Participation in the USSR: YCL and CPSU', *Soviet Studies*, vol. 33, Jan. 1981.

White, S. *Political Culture and Soviet Politics*, London, Macmillan, 1979.

Chapter 11

National cultures and social values

The number of institutions involved in the control and mobilization of society underlines the importance that the leadership attaches to social integration. The Bolsheviks won power because they were able to channel the aspirations of the people. Economic growth and the raising of living standards featured neither in the April Theses nor in the grievances of the masses; their common denominator was the hope of a society freed from exploitation. Doubtless this undertaking did imply structural reform, but above all it demanded a transformation of collective mentalities: a long-term task, for it takes more than a single generation to change the way people think.

Socialization begins very early on in life and continues throughout adulthood by means of intensive propaganda, exhorting everyone to work better and harder for the triumph of communism. The purpose of this political work is to internalize social values so as to develop a consensus. In the absence of this legitimacy, the government would be faced with a cool, passive population, whereas faith, as they say, can move mountains.

Although Marxism–Leninism is the only philosophy that can be expressed freely in the Soviet Union, it does not follow that social values coincide with official doctrine. We must therefore try to define the relations that have grown up between national culture and the dominant ideology and the way in which these values are incorporated into the behaviour of Soviet citizens; lastly, we must try to identify certain signs of insufficient integration or social anomie.

NATIONAL TRADITIONS AND MARXIST–LENINIST IDEOLOGY

It is impossible to explain contemporary Soviet society if we begin with Marxist ideology. If, on the other hand, we begin with the history of Russia, we may gain insight into why the Bolsheviks adopted Marxist philosophy. It will be necessary here to review briefly the principal strains in the Russian national tradition, not only because the dominant social values are heirs to this tradition, but also because this tradition has left its stamp on the Soviet interpretation of Marxism.

Sources of national character

For all peoples, history is the source of the collective consciousness. Therefore the peoples making up the Soviet Union share no common tradition. The stamp of Islam and Iranian culture on the peoples of central Asia, the originality of Georgian and Armenian culture, based as they are on independent churches and an enlightened intelligentsia, and the regular contacts between certain borderlands and Europe, are referred to here only for the record. For we shall confine ourselves to Russian culture, not in the hopes of encapsulating a particularly fertile intellectual history in a few lines, but in order to detect what, in the present-day accumulation of social values, has its roots in tradition, or traditions rather — for two must be distinguished.

1 *Folk culture*, which is essentially parochial, offers the individual a *religious* explanation of the world at the same time as a set of moral principles. From this stem those habits of submission to the natural order that foster fatalism, as well as the feelings of compassion and fraternity which are still alive to this day, even if the underpinning morality is no longer explicitly drawn from the New Testament. This traditional culture is also a *community* culture: it teaches the superiority of the group over the individual, the individual learns that he or she is nothing without the community, whose decisions are sovereign. Religious rites, festivals, folk art (songs, dances) are all community events.

2 *Urban culture*, under the influence of, or in reaction against, ideas imported from western Europe, seeks to found a nation by trying to discover Russia's specific mission (Slavophiles, pan-Slavism). This imported culture is a rationalist one. It marks the beginnings of the movement towards the secularization of the collective consciousness, which in western Europe first emerged towards the end of the middle ages. Here, dialectics replaced scholastics. Not that this change met with no resistance. Certain prophets, among them Dostoevsky (in *The Idiot* or *The Devils*), tried to withstand the rationalist tide and western corruption, which they believed conducive to decadence. The intelligentsia was aware of the gulf that stood between it and popular culture, and it sought to build a bridge between itself and the people. The slogan 'go to the people' meant for some the return to the wisdom of the evangelists (Tolstoy), while for others it signalled the awakening of class consciousness (populism, Marxism); certain reformed Marxists were to seek a way out in Christian humanism, associating the demands of the individual with his community-oriented vocation (Berdyaev). These different attempts were not only political in nature; they gave rise to literary and artistic currents, some of which, such as the School of Itinerant Painters, paved the way for socialist realism.

Marxism–Leninism

Marxism is far more than an attempt to bridge two currents; it seeks to bring about a radical transformation in mentalities. From Herzen, the first socialist, the Russian Marxists borrowed the idea that Russia had a mission to open up the road to socialism for the whole world. The term Leninism only came into currency under Stalin, when Marxism became dogma and began to incorporate into its doctine all the different measures taken to build 'socialism in one country'. It was then that Leninism came to be identified with Soviet policy. Once promoted to the position of the dominant ideology, Marxism–Leninism was bound to come up with three responses: to redefine history, to found a new morality, and to develop a style appropriate to its ambitions.

Marxism–Leninism and history. The role of a culture is to enable the individual to take his bearings, in order to gain a fuller understanding and control over the world around him. Which is why all ideologies, religious or secular, are interpretations of history and a reflection on the meaning of history.

Soviet Marxism does not claim to make a clean sweep of the past. Lenin said that Marx's doctrine was the legitimate continuation of the best outpourings of the human spirit in the nineteenth century: German philosophy, English political economy and French socialism. No mention of Russian thought appears in this reference. It subsequently became necessary to admit into the pantheon the entire Russian democratic and revolutionary tradition (Herzen, Belinsky, Chernishevsky, Dobrolyubov) along with the great classic writers: Pushkin, Tolstoy, Chekhov, Shota Rustaveli (a twelfth-century Georgian writer), Alisher Novoi (a fifteenth-century Uzbek), etc. However, debate continues as to the permissible scope of this reassessment of the past.

There is a whole current of thought which may, with caution, be described as neo-Slavophile or populist, which holds that the sources of a national tradition worth preserving are first of all moral and spiritual. Russian patriotism, which had come to the fore at the height of the people's struggle against serfdom and subsequently against capitalism, has its roots in childhood memories, love of nature and the land.[1] Critics of this current, however, fear that too broad a perspective would qualify some of the great figures of Russia's spiritual tradition for admission to the pantheon, saints such as Serafim Sarov, John of Kronstadt or the icon painter Rublev.[2] Yet others fear a revival of nationalism and its attendant ills: antisemitism, xenophobia and intolerance.

For official doctrine, the nation's past, whether history or literature, must be interpreted in the light of the class struggle, for it is this which gives meaning to history and distinguishes what is 'progressive' from what is reactionary.[3] Because Soviet patriotism was forged in struggle, it would be regrettable if the exaltation of tradition or popular wisdom found in certain contemporary novels were to stimulate a withdrawal into the past, which might even turn against Marxism itself and present it as an imported doctrine, foreign to national tradition (as Solzhenitsyn suggests in *Lenin in Zurich*).

There can be no ideology without a vision of the future. Like religion, it is duty-bound to supply answers to the problem of the meaning of life and death. The disarray of traditional institutions (the family, churches) in the face of over-rapid change may account for the appeal of a doctrine that claims to know the secret fate of history. What drew people to Bolshevism in the early hours of the revolution was not the reassurance supplied by ideology; far more important was the humanist element in the Bolshevik programme, i.e. that aspect of Marxism which more nearly resembles an eschatological, hence idealist, vision than its materialism.

Two generations later, 'Marxism must be created afresh each day' (Suslov), and the goal recedes just as one imagines one is attaining it. Khrushchev announced the transition to communism for 1980, but the eleventh five-year plan (1981–5) makes no mention of the transition to the promised land. Vision, then, or mirage: Marxism–Leninism has evolved into a secular religion. Unanimity around the Party (*splochennost'*) has taken the place of communion in the Church (*sobornost'*); the vision of a regenerated humanity on earth, as the outcome of a collective effort to transform the world, has taken the place of the promise of individual immortality. It is the individual's work which perpetuates the memory of the deceased, while those who have not contributed to the cause are never mentioned, their names disappear from the history books and encyclopedias; if need be, photographs are retouched to banish all trace of undesirable witnesses. Outside the Church there is no salvation: the founder alone has earned the right to an immortality contrived for the benefit of the masses who shuffle endlessly through the mausoleum in which he rests.

As in all great religions, the message is universal in its claims. Like them, it aims at reconciling men of all races, not through compassion but through the common struggle against exploitation and ignorance. Like the Church, it believes in the infallibility of its mission, which confers upon it awesome power to define good and bad.

Marxist morality and law. Marxist morality rejects the notion of a universal truth or immutable morality incumbent upon all men at all times; all that exists is relative moralities. Marxist axiology derives from social ends, and is therefore contingent. Morality is social because its standards vary from one age to another, as does society itself. This is not a condemnation of morality, quite the contrary, for the new man or woman is the supreme embodiment of the virtues that are required of each in the building of communist society. Compared with traditional conceptions, the two salient features of this morality are:

1 The fact that it is a morality of action as opposed to idealism, which believes

that a problem has been resolved once it has been analysed and worked through in thought. It is not the ideal which influences reality; in order to do so, it must flow from reality as it is observed. Unlike the utopian approach, which starts out from an ideal model, Marxist morality claims to transcend reality through achieving consciousness of it. In other words, the aim is not to anaesthetize reality by means of external moral action, but to embody the dialectics of necessity: to become the spokesman of the world's suffering.

2 The fact that it marks a total break with bourgeois society. An act is no longer judged by its intention or by reference to a higher norm, but by reference to history. In the final analysis, it is the end which passes judgement over the means and which, unfortunately, also justifies them, so that morality is ultimately tied to political doctrines. Is an assassination in a good cause any less a murder? To ask this question is to raise the problem of sanctions.

Moral values are merely justifications of the sanctions provided for in law; but law itself is no more absolute, and public liberties can only be guaranteed if the activities of individuals do not obstruct the ends of society. Freedom is only permissible if it tends in the direction of allegiance to and participation in the common enterprise; outside the community, it has no existence.

This particular conception of law and freedom may account for the disagreement between East and West on the subject of individual freedom. To be sure, the Soviet Constitution (Art. 50) recognizes freedom of speech, freedom of the press, freedom to hold meetings, freedom of association and even the freedom to demonstrate; but the exercise of these freedoms is only guaranteed by law on condition that they 'conform to the interests of the worker and contribute to the consolidation of the socialist system'. In Marxist eyes, the freedom, equality and fraternity called for in the Declaration of the Rights of Man are merely abstract rights, for they assume a split personality in human beings: as citizens they enjoy political rights, but as workers they are alienated from economic power. The proletarian state abolishes the duality of social and political life and considers work to be the sole criterion of value, and hence of rights. There are no rights independent of society, and to call for individual freedom is practically tantamount to making demands prejudicial to society. One can imagine, therefore, the ambiguous situation in which lawyers find themselves and their limited freedom for manoeuvre in the Soviet judicial system: in principle, they are expected to defend their clients, but they may not do so in a manner liable to damage the interests of the state.

We need not conclude from this that the rules of morality and public law deliberately turn their backs on traditional morality. For while the foundations of morality and law are different, moral desiderata remain the same: honesty, hard work, discipline, achievement. Newspapers, films, indeed everything that conveys some symbolic content, exalts virtue. There are no advertisements encouraging people to consume; there is no exploitation of sex for commercial purposes; no beauty contests or cosmetics adverts.

The symbolic expression of values: socialist realism and rites. Morality is simply one form of consciousness as expressed in thought or through the aesthetic imagination. The creative artist, whether engaged in some form of literature or the visual arts, is expected to contribute to the process of ideological change and to represent reality in a true and historically concrete manner, in other words in a revolutionary perspective. What distinguishes this realism from that of the nineteenth-century realist authors is its 'socialist' inspiration.

> When confronted with socialism, the western individualist or the sceptical Russian intellectual find themselves in more or less the same situation as intelligent, cultivated Roman patricians in the face of all-conquering Christianity. They view this new faith in a crucified God as barbaric and naive . . . what liberty can a religious man demand of his God? (Abram Tertz [A. Sinyavsky], 'Le Réalisme socialiste', *Esprit*, Feb. 1959, pp. 338–43)

Works of art may vary in manner and subject, but they all share certain features: first, the happy end, because even if the end may be unhappy for the hero, the goal that transcends the individual is always assured of final victory; and second, the didactic intention, whether to exalt work or to struggle against remnants of the old man in the individual consciousness.

Socialist realism acts as a kind of system of reference by which to subordinate art and letters to the political objectives of the Party. Still, the function of the work of art goes beyond mere propaganda. Because it penetrates into private life, it is the writer's duty to create stereotypes of good and evil and to idealize reality by presenting it, not as it is, but as it will be, as it should be: a simplified, optimistic vision of reality, shot through with the conflict between positive and negative.

The positive hero is the central figure who illuminates the stage. He is the incarnation of unconditional loyalty to the Party, self-abnegation in the service of the community, patriotism, vigilance in unmasking the enemy, love of work, discipline, modesty, optimism, moral steadfastness, and the capacity for self-criticism and self-education in the light of the teachings of the great masters of Marxism–Leninism. The character who personifies evil must be presented as a focus for the reader's hostility. Frequently, the repulsion that his political attitudes are supposed to inspire is projected in the form of repellent physical or moral features, so that he can in no way be idealized: he is always presented as a man of the past, selfish, hypocritical and corrupt. 'Everything about the kulaks is repugnant, their person to begin with, then the fact that they have no soul, the fact that they stink, and are enemies of the people. . . . No pity for them, they are not men' (Vassily Grossman, *Zhizn' i sud'ba*, 1970).

A number of writers supply archetypes for the collective consciousness through the school curriculum, including M. Gorky, A. Tolstoy, N. Ostrovsky, M. Sholokhov, A. Fadeyev, V. Mayakovsky, D. Bedny, Isakovsky, C. Simonov and N. Tikhonov. Gorky and Mayakovsky occupy close to half the curriculum between them, the former, because he pioneered the Manichean vision that has served as the inspiration for all socialist realism: on the one hand, the hypocritical 'petty bourgeois' (*Meshchane*, 1901) and, on the other, the 'outcasts' — thieves, bandits, redeemed by their generosity, their rejection of security, and transfigured by their hope of a glorious future. Mayakovsky was the great poet who joined the Party, rejecting the aesthetic effects of bourgeois culture, and set out in search of new means of expression attuned to the sensibilities of the masses. Chapaev, the Civil War hero (in Furmanov's novel, 1923), Oleg Koshevy in *The Young Guards* by Fadeyev 1946–51) and Nikolai Ostrovsky, the author of the autobiographical novel *How Steel Was Tempered* (1932–4), are all classics, and have been joined in more recent years by A. Blok, Yesenin, Tvardovsky (*Za dal'yu dal'*, 1960) and Leonid Leonov (*Russky les*, 1955). Not that this list necessarily coincides with that of the most popular authors in the Soviet Union.

Theatre and cinema, which combine the ability to express movement, action and the atmosphere of a public meeting, are the revolutionary art forms *par excellence*. In the field of theatre production, the formal experiments of Meyerhold, the art of Stanislavsky, of Eisenstein and Vakhtanov, and the iconoclasm of Mayakovsky's and Bulgakov's plays introduced a breath of fresh air in the first decade of the cultural revolution. These were popular spectacles, whereas futurism in literature, cubism and abstraction in painting (Kandinsky and Malevich) or constructivism in architecture met with incomprehension on the part of the general public. Individual experiment and art for art's sake were obliged to step aside in favour of realism as tailored to mass taste.

All revolutions are also festivals. The revolutionary 'days' were moments of high drama, as vast mass rallies or demonstrations symbolize the union of the people behind its leaders. But demonstrations lose their spontaneity with the passing of time; they are meticulously organized, even rehearsed. The festival then turns into a lifeless official ritual, except when some unexpected event occurs and sweeps habit aside, such as the homecoming of the cosmonauts, Stalin's funeral or the visit of General de Gaulle, providing an occasion for the expression of popular feeling. Today, the great public holidays are, like the liturgical holidays of the past, based on the agricultural calendar: the new year, the first of May, the anniversary of the Revolution; in the countryside, the harvest festival marking the end of work in the fields. However, these official feasts have not altogether supplanted the traditional religious feasts (Easter, the Feast of St John at midsummer, Pentecost (*Troitsa*) and Christmas for the Christians; Rosh Hoshana, Yom Kippur and Pesach for the Jews, etc.), or the family ceremonies occasioned by the big events in life: birth of a child, marriage, death. Attempts are made to devise new rituals, such as on the occasion of a young man's call-up to the army or on taking up one's first job, or to replace the traditional marriage rites by a lay ceremony. Nowadays, it is considered good form for young married couples to lay a wreath at the war memorial, as an act of fidelity recreating a new symbolism on the remains of the old symbols.

Relations between ideology and society are not only one-way. The regime's aesthetic has been shaped by the aspirations of the new middle classes, whose sole model of reference was the grandiloquent style of the new rich under the old regime and the classicism of the homes of the nobility. Throughout the length and breadth of the Soviet Union, Stalinist architecture reproduced the heavy columns of the Bolshoi and the Admiralty spire.

More fundamental has been the alliance that has grown up in the collective consciousness between Marxism–Leninism and patriotism. The transition from one to the other became manifest in the second world war (commonly referred to in the Soviet Union as the 'patriotic war') and signalled the awakening of the fatherland in danger. M. Sholokhov's *And Quiet Flows the Don*, which won the Stalin Prize in 1941, symbolizes this reconciliation, for it is set in the Cossack community, which had split at the time of the civil war. Eisenstein's films, *Alexander Nevsky* (1938) and *Ivan the Terrible* (1944–6), and Alexis Tolstoy's historical novel, *Peter the Great* (1945), all form part of the same process. The restoration of the Patriarchate of the Russian Orthodox Church in 1943 marked the normalization of relations between the religious hierarchy and the state.

This assimilation is facilitated by the fact that Marxism and patriotism employ similar mechanisms of social integration: the dramatization of situations in order to stimulate popular acquiescence and mobilize hostility towards the enemy (the parasite, the traitor, the foreigner); a Manichean vision of society and history (he who is not with us is against us); the cult of heroes of the past (revolutionaries and the great men of the national pantheon).

Does this mean that the communist message of universalism has failed, and that ideology has only managed to penetrate the masses by picking up the cast-offs of nationalism and chauvinism? To answer this question we must examine the way Soviet people actually react to the ideals offered to them. For, while an ideology may be totalitarian, a society can never mirror that ideology.

SOCIAL BEHAVIOUR

The only reason why the sociologist is interested in ideology and individual motivations is for the influence that these are capable of exercising on collective attitudes and images. This is the most delicate subject of all to investigate owing to the extreme diversity of behaviour patterns: those observed in Moscow cannot be transposed to the provinces, while traits that are characteristic of people of a certain age or nationality are not applicable to others. Even so, some sociologists have sought to explain Soviet society in terms of national temperament.

National temperament as an explanatory factor

This approach, based on some supposed psychology of peoples, is the oldest of all approaches. Montesquieu tried to attribute 'the first of all empires' to climatic factors in order to determine laws and customs. There has been an unbroken tradition of associating institutions with the character of a country's population going all the way back to Helvetius. The Marquis de Custine was a talented exemplar of this line of investigation, and Jules Legras later attempted to describe the 'Russian soul'. Hedrick Smith concludes his latest best-seller, *The Russians*, with this observation: 'Times have changed, not men.'

American sociologists have conducted systematic surveys of displaced Soviet citizens after the second world war and endeavoured, on that basis, to construct a typical or modal personality capable of accounting for the connivance that takes place between individuals and their institutions, as well as the difficulties encountered in integration.

Some of the answers reflect the ambivalence of modern man, with his simultaneous desire for economic security and progress, equality of opportunity for all and freedom for each person to assert his or her personality. For instance, these émigrés claim to want a more liberal regime, in the spirit of the NEP, but are not hostile to a strong government capable of setting noble aims for the nation. They appreciate job security and the guarantee of education for all, the collective ownership of the means of production and, consequently, state control of the economy (agriculture aside); in a word, they are proud of the social conquests and results achieved by their country, Germany's conqueror. Moreover, this attitude, expressed in this case by political refugees, illustrates the difficulty of dissociating, in the Soviet mind, attachment to the regime from love of the fatherland. Far more recent surveys of Soviet Jews who have emigrated to Israel confirm these attitudes: most of the population acknowledges the material progress achieved and believes that the leadership does have the interests of the people at heart.[4]

Analysis of answers to questions about the family, social relations and authority provides some pointers to the model Russian personality: (1) the effective need for personal contact with others, the need of a sense of belonging, which makes people both more dependent and vulnerable, but also more expressive and warmer-hearted; (2) the desire for involvement in a communal undertaking, giving people an opportunity of identification with the community and accounting for their acceptance of an authority that satisfies their moral demands; (3) a lower degree of self-control, a kind of impulsiveness in which depression and exaltation alternate, coupled with greater indulgence of other people's weaknesses. This presumably accounts both for submission to authority and the individual's sense of affective frustration under the present regime. The ancient village community has been replaced by an impersonal, suspicious bureaucracy, obsessed with controls. Nothing can be more trying for someone who is ready to give of his person than reservations and doubt — which are a positive virus in interpersonal relations — *vis-à-vis* anyone outside the narrow circle of friends and relatives.

Now, if these explanations were based on some assumption of psychological determinism, they could not explain why society changes; they are ill-adapted to a sociological approach, in which it is the group which determines the character of the individual, and not the reverse. The 'modal' character is itself the outcome of a social environment.

Traditional society as an explanatory factor

Under cover of the supposed national temperament, what in fact emerges are the features common to all traditional societies. What facilitates submission of the individual to authority is the fact that human rights have never succeeded in asserting themselves under a patriarchal, and subsequently paternalist, regime. The climate inside the Soviet enterprise reflects the paternalism found in all infant industries, where managerial consciousness precedes the birth of workers' consciousness. The loyalty and devotion that the Party exacts from its members resembles the family ethic, in which self-criticism and keeping disputes inside the family are the rule ('one does not air one's quarrels outside the Izba' [*sor iz izby nel'zya vynosit'*]). Another leftover from peasant tradition is the personalization of power and the quasi-religious cult of Lenin, as formerly of the Tsar. It might be added that the very idea of an economy based on needs, on a national scale, as opposed to a profit-centred economy is perfectly compatible with the peasant family economy, which is also based essentially on needs.

According to Geoffrey Gorer, the environment fashions certain features of the modal temperament in the very first weeks of a child's existence. Ambivalence, in the form of oscillation between apathetic submission and violent revolt, between abstinence and indulgence of the senses, are here seen as the expression of a diffuse anxiety, of a persecution complex even, whose roots go back to the way Russian babies are swaddled. Because it is held tightly bound for most of the day, the infant only recovers freedom of movement when being changed; this, alternation between long periods of privation and complete freedom leaves its stamp on him throughout his life.[5]

Leaving such simplifications aside, it is undeniable that education marks the personality and that changes in educational models from one generation to another do as a result influence behaviour. In this respect, the present ideal, as personified by the positive hero, bears no kinship whatever to the traditional type as incarnated in the liberal intelligentsia. Although we find in Chernishevsky's hero, Rakhmetov (in *What Is To Be Done?*), an asceticism in the service of a cause that is very reminiscent of the great figures of Russian spirituality, zeal here has replaced charity. He is the forerunner of yesterday's 'Bolshevik' and the communist of today: unyielding, determined, even aggressive. These models are the antithesis of Goncharov's 'one man too many', as personified in *Oblomov*, unsure of himself, passive, phlegmatic, wanting a quiet life; good yet ineffectual. Could it be that warmth, simple-hearted relations or love of nature are mere remnants of pre-industrial society?

Obviously, the discipline that has been imposed on the Russians to stop them reverting to their natural tendencies has not been altogether successful in dissipating a certain measure of nonchalance and lack of enthusiasm at work, except when they are motivated by powerful emotions. No regime can hope to reshape the collective consciousness overnight. This accounts for the variety of behaviour patterns observed from one generation and one social milieu to the next.

How do traditional values and habits coexist with the new ways of thinking? How does a secular and 'scientific' conception of existence cohabit with a dogmatic interpretation of Marxism, and what is the place, if any, of irrational values? How do love of work and devotion to the community combine with self-interest and the requisite degree of competitive spirit? How does the creative impulse find expression within the limits laid down by the official canons? All this now needs to be investigated.

The search for a world view: science and religion

In the Soviet Union, as elsewhere, scientific progress has deeply influenced our mental universe. People take pride in their technological achievements, and this has reinforced their belief in the power of science to overcome all obstacles. But this evolution contains within itself the seeds of a threat to official orthodoxy.

For either ideology ossifies into a set of formulae which, by dint of being hammered into people's heads in compulsory classes on Marxism—Leninism, become nothing but clichés, supplying their own corpus of quotations alongside those of the authors of the programme themselves; or, alternatively, the ideology displays its vitality through its capacity to adapt. Just as Christianity successively incorporated Caesarism, Aristotelianism, liberalism and perhaps, tomorrow, socialism, so the Soviets are now having to cope with new areas of investigation that did not even exist in Marx's time: the psychology of the unconscious, demography, genetics, cybernetics. In a world of rapidly expanding knowledge, dogmatism exacts a heavy toll, as witnessed by the sorry episode of Lysenko's dictatorship over the biological sciences in the Soviet Union.

In certain subjects, such as the economic or legal sciences, there have been signs in the past two decades of a rationalism seeking to break through the shell of dogmatism. Similar movement is detectable in thinking on fundamental problems affecting individual action and duty. The moral conscience is no longer defined as being bound up with a social ideal or with concrete programmes of social transformation, but as the capacity to express an 'ideal' order, or things as they ought to be.[6] Freedom is conceived of as the capacity for self-detachment, as a universal and objective tendency of being. Human creativity is thought to be the most powerful of human aspirations. To be sure, the individual will is conditioned by the character of the social system in which he or she lives, but, conversely, the social system is shaped by the character of those who make it up. In other words, humanity transcends the social system, and its destiny (*prizvanie*) is to be free.[7] Doubtless we should distinguish here between ideology, which is a fighting science, and philosophical thought, which culminates in the logic of absolute ideas: still, these new departures do appear to be significant and hold out the promise of fruitful investigations for the future.

The transition from these public debates and published writings to the content and climate of Soviet people's mental world is not an easy one to make, for it is within the hidden depths of each individual's intellectual and moral exigencies that a new world-conception (*mirovozrenie*) is evolving. In spite of this, certain works of contemporary Soviet literature do reveal spiritual yearnings; materialism and rationalism do not provide a sufficient definition of the collective consciousness. Writers such as Alexander Blok, Sergei Yesenin, Boris Pasternak, Anna Akhmatova or Marina Tsvetaeva are popular surely because poetry gives us a glimpse of the irrational which, for some people, substitutes for the religious dimension. Others have turned to the great works of pre-revolutionary world and Russian literature for a response to, or merely an echo of, their own questionings, notably through the mouths of Alyosha and Mitya Karamazov or in the writings of Berdyaev.

Churches are not allowed to minister to their congregations outside their places of worship, which are state property. The state has the power to authorize associations (*dvadtsatka*, which take their name from the *twenty* adult members required by law), which apply to the local authorities to perform acts of worship. The administration of the sacraments at home (such as Baptism) is forbidden. The liturgy is thus the sole form of religious activity permitted in the 7500–8000 churches (compared with 39,000 in 1925), 5400 Protestant communities, 1200 mosques and 60 synagogues (compared with 3000 in 1917) open to the public.

While both the Constitution of the Soviet Union and the state claim to respect individual freedom of conscience, neither the Party nor the school, on the other hand, are 'neutral' in their attitude towards belief, which they consider contrary to a scientific conception of the world. In the name of science, atheist propaganda is carried on by means of numerous lectures and publications, including *Nauka i religiya* (Science and Religion), with a circulation of 200,000, compared with the 25,000 copies circulated by the *Bulletin* of the Patriarchate of the Orthodox Church, the only periodical that this Church is allowed to publish. The actual effectiveness of anti-religious propaganda is not very obvious, judging from the fact that teachers are the only more or less regular readers of this kind of literature (13 per cent of them, according to one survey).[8]

It is chiefly among the older age groups of the population that religious beliefs are professed (70 per cent of all 'faithful', according to Ilichev when he was editor of *Agitprop*); but this is not borne out by a survey of the rural communities in the province of Moscow, judging by the uniformity of percentages in the 31–50 age group (see Table 49). Given the possible consequences of 'belief' for one's career, it is possible that retired people are less secretive about this sort of thing. Nor is it certain that religious belief is merely a hangover from the past, given the high percentage of working-class children (47 per cent) brought for Baptism in Moscow and Leningrad, and the fair proportion of men and young people aged between 20 and 40, recognizable by their dress as belonging to the intelligentsia, present on religious feast days. According to estimates made by the Director of the Moscow Institute of Scientific Atheism, 15 per cent of the urban population and 30 per cent of the rural population practise some kind of religion, making a total of some 40 million Orthodox and 600,000 Protestant believers: which comes as something of a surprise in a country that has proclaimed its atheism for two generations now.

TABLE 49   *Soviet attitudes towards religious belief*
(as % of total replies)

	Believers	Uncertain or indifferent	Atheists
Province of Voronezh, 1964–66			
Town	7.9	32.7	59.4
Countryside	15.6	44.8	39.6
Engineers and technicians	0.6	11.0	88.4
Workers	22.2	57.4	20.4
Kolkhoz workers	14.7	55.9	29.4
Province of Moscow, 1970			
Men	16		
Women	45		
Women aged under 31	16		
31–35	47		
36–40	40		
41–50	45		
51–60	65		

This situation has led the officials in charge of ideological work to examine the reasons for the 'survival' of religion. The closure of the churches has failed to solve the problem, since 'one still finds a large number of believers in regions where there are neither churches nor priests'.[9] If, despite the destruction of the 'social bases' of belief, this still persists, then one is forced to acknowledge that it cannot merely be the result of family influences. Often, it results from the discovery of the moral conscience in the face of the trials and injustices of existence. No theory of society is capable of withstanding the test of life itself. Svetlana Alleluyeva and Andrei Sinyavsky were both baptized at the age of forty. Many of the works of Soviet literature that have been banned in the Soviet Union in recent years reveal the vitality of a religious tradition thought to be extinct, notably in the spiritual experiences of writers such as Pasternak, Solzhenitsyn, Nadezhda Mandelshtam and V. Maximov, the religious poetry of Tsvetaeva, the testimonies of Krasnov-Levitin, and others.

Does this mean that the Soviet Union 'is the greatest volcano of Christianity', as Monsignor Etchegaray[10] has described it? Clearly, a church in which the writings of evangelists are copied out by hand is not about to give up the ghost. But to form a clear idea of the real scope of religion in Soviet society, one must beware of underestimating the persistent influence of the school, in which religion is depicted as a form of obscurantism. For a great many Soviet citizens, the world of religion is akin to mythology; they view it as a collection of poetic symbols, stripped of their meaning in the works of art expressing them. How many of today's enthusiasts for the preservation of the national heritage and for the restoration of churches and monasteries, or who share today's fashionable taste for icons, are genuinely concerned with something deeper than mere aestheticism? Perhaps the great explorations of the heartland of Russia also express a periodic need to live a more authentic kind of life, in closer contact with nature, that other gateway to, or mirror of, the mysteries of life.

The moral quest: being and having, the self and others

Even more so than in the past, private life has become a sanctuary for the Soviet citizen. As in all industrial societies, the individual generally looks to his family for the effective gratification that is as vital to him as bread. In the company of his friends and relatives, the Soviet citizen can shake off his everyday conformism. Now, the question is: does this natural way of behaving lead to the same excesses? — excessive concern with material things and self-centred concentration on one's personal interests. In other words, has the moral climate of communism, which places the highest value on work and devotion to the community, managed to steer industrialization clear of the pitfalls of the consumer society and individualism?

Acquisitiveness. This undoubtedly takes up more of the Soviet citizen's time than in our own society owing to the inadequate system of distribution and to chronic shortages. Queues in front of or inside shops are part of the daily scene, especially in the provinces. But this does not mean to say that the Soviet people attach any symbolic value to objects, or that their acquisition is becoming a primary motivation. Quite the contrary — the intelligentsia has traditionally despised the passion for accumulation which, in its eyes, is the sign of the petty-bourgeois mentality (*meshchanskaya kul'tura*).

If by consumer society one means a regime in which the dominant class manipulates the symbols of community life, with the intention of encouraging the population to consume or to amuse itself, then we may, without fear of contradiction, say that Soviet society is not of this order. The regime gives priority to work, not to consumption, in its scale of social values. There is no brash commercial advertising, and no snobbishness or conformism, no 'keeping up with the Joneses'. Indeed housing conditions represent a major obstacle to any such ambitions.

Even so, the fact that the theme of 'petty-bourgeois' habits and 'fashion', and the general attitude of Soviet people to material things, attracts the attention of the press and literature is revealing in what it tells us about changing living standards, and about housing conditions in particular. Consumers are becoming more demanding because they are better informed, and because they now have some choice before them.

When choosing, Soviet people do not allow themselves to be swayed by some false notion of status. They buy the inevitable consumer durables that are part and parcel of our technical civilization, for example television sets, refrigerators and tape recorders; but, where other articles are concerned, they shun standardization in favour of the item of clothing that matches their personality, or some symbol that conjures up their favourite atmosphere. The taste for antiques, icons, furniture, lamps or rugs flows less from any desire to imitate their forebears than from a need for a sense of permanence and authenticity, as a reaction against mass-produced goods; perhaps, too, they yearn for the quieter times of another age, in an attempt to flee the present. What for some is a sign of originality is gradually becoming a fashion.

Fashion changes rather more slowly in the Soviet Union, but it still retains its symbolic value as a means of social identification: a country girl will put on a satin dress for an evening out, while her cousin in the city will prefer a more 'outdoor girl' style; artists do not dress like physicists. Films are not without influence on the formation of these stereotypes.

In response to those who express distaste at the invasion of petty-bourgeois values, one also finds people ready to advocate enrichment through honest work, in terms reminiscent of the Protestant ethic of early capitalism:

> In the old days, my uncle used to be called a kulak because he owned a cow and two horses; today, where is there a home without a television . . .? What is the harm in people saving to buy a car or carpets, since they have

earned their money by honest labour? Show me a rich man today? Let him serve as an example! (B. Kachenovsky, 'Ode to a businessman', *Lit. Gaz.*, 10 April 1976)

This apology for enrichment is fairly new, for wealth has always been associated with dishonesty in the popular imagery. The first owners of private cars in the Soviet Union were not always particularly well thought of.

Certain writers turn their backs on the moral issues, preferring to examine the question in sociological terms. They do not deny the influence of western consumption patterns; however, they do observe that it is primarily among those sections of the population whose work is least gratifying that material objects play a compensating role. The case of a couple that dreamed of getting their two daughters into higher education is cited; the daughters failed to gain admission and, for want of the right connections, they did not marry into the intelligentsia. Thus, lacking the necessary abilities to qualify for a prestigious job in the intellectual sphere, the petty bourgeois seeks consolation in material things. Acquisitiveness is not necessarily the property of a single class; it can take more subtle forms among the intelligentsia, and the collector and bibliophile are as common in the Soviet Union as elsewhere.

The moral and social consequences of the spread of the private car have also attracted the attention of economists and sociologists. While, for the great majority of Soviet people, car ownership is beyond their means, others will scrimp and save to buy one. For the car is more than a mere object of utility, it is also a prestigious symbol. It strengthens people's sense of property and gives rise to disputes: that parking space in front of my house belongs to me!

There is little likelihood that the individual sense of what is his or hers and what is not is about to disappear from the collective consciousness; after all, for thousands of years, the most representative type of human being has been the one with an acute sense of property. As a result, people can be extremely casual in their attitudes towards public property, especially in the countryside or on building sites. Alienation, when associated with acquisitiveness, can lead to desocialization. Having may compensate for some lack of being. Now being manifests itself in relations with one's fellow men, and that is the test of morality.

Soviet behaviour in personal relations. These are no exception to the rules observable in any society. In previous chapters, we have reviewed the whole range of attitudes, from rejection of others in an effort to preserve one's personal and family life to distrust and manipulation of others in order to benefit from their knowledge and domination of others by people whose chief concern is to assert themselves at all costs. Our problem is to find out to what extent social conditions are responsible for these different types of egoism.

The models and habits of the past have an undeniable influence on the style of command of those officials (*rukovoditeli*) who have copied the harshness of the old dignitaries (*barskoe otnoshenie, zhestkoe rukovodstvo*) in their dealings with subordinates. The latters' obsequiousness, and peasant distrust of outsiders, also bear the signs of centuries of serfdom. Foreign observers are struck, however, by the generally very free tone of social relations. In restaurants, in places of amusement or in the train, Soviet people have no hesitation in striking up a conversation with their neighbours, whatever their origins. The taxi-driver will invite his fare to sit beside him, not on the rear seat, because they are equals.

Sporting activities develop an ability to externalize, and a sense of team spirit. Also, relations between the sexes are far less complex-ridden, even though an appearance of prudishness is maintained. In this connection, the press is far more respectful of people's private life than in other countries. Compared with the raucous eroticism of western advertising, Soviet illustrated magazines and films are positively Victorian in their restraint.

The ethos of socialist emulation sometimes finds individual expression in ways incompatible with team spirit. The winner of this kind of campaign will receive a certificate 'for his success', but workers tend to take a dim view of words like *success* or *career*, with their go-getting overtones. Efficiency, a spirit of enterprise and a sense of initiative may be eminently necessary qualities, but they are not always encouraged because, in the popular view, they are associated with the material advantages that reward the most enterprising. Many people are incapable of acknowledging that the value of an individual may be measured solely by his contribution to the common task. In other words, the Soviet citizen is not immune to the competitive nature and alienating temptations of modern society; like any individual in any society, the Soviet individual is forced to choose between being, appearance and having, between self-assertion and acceptance of others.

The search for an authentic style: communication and creativity

An article published by V. Pomerantsev, 'On Sincerity',[11] marked the beginnings of the literary and artistic thaw. The title itself underlines the problem facing the Soviet man of letters or artist: how to create within the canons of socialist realism. How can one be true to oneself, while keeping within the social bounds tolerated by censorship? We do not intend here to explore the vast field of contemporary Soviet literature and art, but rather to try to show how people arrive at a compromise between personal expression and the social code.

The first rule for anyone wishing to be published in the Soviet Union, and elsewhere, is self-censorship. Failing that, one's manuscript is liable to moulder in some desk drawer or to be passed around in typewritten form (*samizdat*, meaning 'published by oneself'). But there are various ways of circumventing the prohibitions.

1 Indirect speech: sometimes an author will place his true point of view in the

mouth of a negative character, a stranger or a drunkard, and convey messages that the informed reader will have little trouble detecting, in an otherwise conventional setting.[12]

2 Utopian or fantastic writing, i.e. transposing situations into an imaginary world, apparently unrelated to reality, enabling the writer to give free rein to his fancy.[13]

3 The use of poetry to express powerful feelings in full, which makes this one of the most popular genres.

4 The production of plays with a message and satires, often by foreign authors, by avant-garde theatres.[14]

5 Children's books are another window onto the world of the imagination.

Some themes touch on sensitive points, where the writer comes into conflict with received ideas in connection with the Soviet conception of the world and morality.

The inevitable hiatus between personal experience and the ideal poses a serious problem to many people who have doubts about the way the last world war was conducted. Many works treat both the heroism and the shortcomings of their fellow citizens with bold realism.[15] The theme of the labour camps and the purges also haunt those who experienced these tragedies, either directly or indirectly, and who wish to produce their own testimony in an effort to re-establish socialist legality.[16] Among the humiliated and downtrodden of Soviet society, the peasants, and particularly the fate of the peasant women, have attracted a great deal of attention: the theme of country life has been, and still is, a very popular one in the Soviet literature of the thaw period (see the list of suggested reading at the end of Chapter 4). It strikes a national chord by its exaltation of rural Russia, with its rustic charms and ancient joys; but it also manifests its attachment to certain moral values which have their roots in the wisdom and the self-denial of country people.

The emergence of personal concerns in literature, dealing with conjugal and family life, not merely with social themes in the news, is evidence of the efforts of certain authors to broaden the range of creative writing in the past two or three decades.[17] Not all their attempts have been crowned with success, and Pasternak's *Doctor Zhivago* (1955) is still banned in the Soviet Union.

By no means everyone accepts official aesthetic canons. 'Art is not the same thing as ideology, it has a content of its own'.[18] Painters are far more dependent on official constraints than writers are, for if they reject them they have no hope of having their works shown. Well-known painters keep the works they create for themselves at home, with no intention of submitting them for exhibition. Compared with their western colleagues, they are plainly better trained in the techniques of execution, thanks to the tough school of Russian academicism (Repine), and less concerned with money worries. Exhibitions provide an opportunity of exchanging views with the public, through the visitors' book and public discussions. Those that do not enjoy these advantages are confined to the narrow circle of their friends. They are not alone in this. The most original, albeit the least visible, feature of Soviet intellectual life is the evenings of prose and poetry readings, reminiscent of nineteenth-century circles.

The dividing line between permissible personal expression and protest is not always easy to draw, as policy towards arts and letters is itself fluctuating. One principle stands, however, namely that one may criticize reality as long as one places it in a historical perspective that points to the radiant future of communism; criticism must therefore be optimistic and constructive.

SUBCULTURE, ANOMIE AND DISSIDENCE

In any society, the intelligentsia and youth will, to different degrees, tend to be critical of the habits and values handed down from generations past. What gives to society its continuity and its vitality is the compromise that people arrive at between tradition and the renewal of social norms. Not everyone manages to strike a happy medium between their personal demands and the social code. Failures of social integration result in various forms of social anomie, or even delinquency. In a regime as closely controlled as this in all its aspects, manifestations of opposition to established values are, if not rare, at least very difficult for an outside observer to detect. We shall confine ourselves merely to listing the more visible aspects.

The generation gap: fathers and sons

It is hardly surprising that, in a country that has evolved so swiftly in the century that has elapsed since the abolition of serfdom, cultural gaps should ever widen from one generation to the next. Turgenyev was the first to introduce the theme of 'fathers and sons' into Russian literature, in 1861 when he published his novel with that title. It re-emerged in acute form at the time of the civil war, and has since continued to be a topical one. Today, in addition to the customary conflict between the retrograde past and the new values, the younger generations have taken since the twentieth congress to asking questions about the origins and experience of Stalinism, rejecting the hypocrisy and ready-made slogans of their elders. In the film *Zastava Il'icha* (1963), Khutsiev makes it clear that fathers are no longer in a position to advise their sons.

'How should I live?' the son questions the spirit of his father, killed in the war.

'How old are you?' replies the father. 'Since the fathers are guilty, they are in no position to give lessons to the young' (*Izvestiya*, 24 March 1963).

To which the older generations reply with the familiar lamentations over the selfishness of the young: 'These children are too spoiled, they have no notion of the values of things, and they are too impatient'.[19] They are criticized for their thirst for life, their disorderliness, their nihilism, their presumptuousness, their quest for an easy way of growing prosperous at the expense of their parents or society. But there is worse yet, as an official report points out:

> Over the last fifteen or twenty years, the inner world of the individual has suffered even more from voluntarism and subjectivism than from the economy. For it is an open secret that there has occurred among the young a certain reappraisal of our convictions and our values; the soul and the consciousness of our youth have been seriously undermined. (E. A. Shevarnadze, first secretary of the central committee of Georgia, *Zarya Vostoka*, 23 Jan. 1976)

Once we go beyond facile generalizations, we are forced to observe that Soviet youth, like youth everywhere, is anything but a homogeneous social group with its own counter-culture. The press, literature and foreign observers with first-hand experience of life among Soviet students have identified a wide variety of types. The most classic is depicted by F. Abramov in his two short stories 'Alka' (the city girl) and 'Pelageya' (her mother, a peasantwoman), for the contrasts between the two generations are more evident in the countryside: the dwindling respect for work among a certain section of Soviet youth, the freer relations between boys and girls, the declining attachment to the family heritage, scant regard for what others think, greater importance attached to appearances and fashion. As everywhere, Soviet youth is divided into those who are concerned solely with their own little world, at the risk of becoming bourgeois, and the cynics, the go-getters — the conformists and those who set out to explore new avenues. It is from among this last category that the literary and artistic avant-garde is recruited.

Nevertheless, whichever category it belongs to, Soviet youth shares a certain number of common features that distinguish it from its parents. It is generally better educated and better informed; technology is part of its world, although not necessarily the be-all or end-all of life; hence its taste for science fiction and for a certain form of poetry inherited from futurism. Young people dislike speeches and go to meetings less frequently; their loyalty to the regime rests upon formulae learned by rote. But because dogmas are unquestioned truths, they seek their answers in every direction.

> All progress is reactionary if man falls.
> They shall not buy us like a lifeless toy,
> like a clockwork nightingale.
> What counts in life is the human being. . . .
> Techniques and power are mortal
> that take precedence over us.
> A lasting thing upon earth,
> as the glimmer of a vanished star,

a steady radiation.
We called it soul.
(Poem 'Oza', by A. Voznessensky, *Projet*, March 1969, p. 349–52)

The influence of western models is external. The clothing, the gadgets, the crime stories, the jazz and rock music, gangs of friends and relaxed gatherings in cafés are all part of a universal subculture, stretching from San Francisco to Novosibirsk, although in the Soviet Union its extent is circumscribed by the general standards of Soviet society. Soviet youngsters are unlikely to wake up tomorrow morning to find that pop culture and posters have dethroned the official faces in the popular imagination or imagery. It is worth noting, nevertheless, that a survey of young people's plans for the future showed that the desire to travel abroad ranked third, after the desire to find interesting work and to obtain a higher-education degree, but ahead of the need to meet the man or woman of their lives or to own a car.[20]

Sociologists have begun to take an interest in youth less because of the emergence of this subculture, which is highly unlikely to degenerate into a counter-culture, than because of the different ways in which failures of social integration manifest themselves among young people (absenteeism, alcoholism, delinquency).

Social norms and the individual

Alcoholism. Soviet citizens are not alone in their fondness for alcoholic beverages, nor is the taste a recent one. In the Caucasus, the habit of drinking wine or cognac at mealtimes is reminiscent of the French; alcohol is an integral part of family life and does not produce the same social consequences as it does among the Russians. For the *muzhik*, on the other hand, alcohol represents a kind of white magic, bringing gaiety into his life.

> The Russian does not like to drink in silence, sitting in a corner, or in small amounts at fixed times of the day: you can leave that to the American and French alcoholics, who drink in order to get drunk and befuddle the brain. They gorge themselves like pigs and then fall asleep. We drink to warm our souls, and it is only then that we come alive. After drinking, our souls rise above lifeless matter, but this we have to do in the street — a tortuous provincial street whose winding curves lead straight into the blue skies. . . . What's the use of freedom if the Russian man cannot let himself go as he pleases? (Abram Tertz [Sinyavsky], *Lyubimov*)

One sign that times are changing is that the consumption of alcohol has grown to disturbing proportions. Per capita consumption of alcohol is now three times higher than it was under the Tsars, while sales quadrupled between 1940 and 1973. According to official statistics, present consumption represents four litres of pure alcohol per head of population, but this is probably a gross underestimate, ignoring the contribution of clandestine moonshine stills.

The social consequences of this are well known: alcoholism is blamed for delinquency (56—80 per cent of thefts and robberies, 90 per cent of murders), a good third of all road accidents and two-thirds of accidents at work, and it is the reason given for half of divorces. In spite of everything, when asked to investigate the causes of alcoholism, Soviet sociologists do not regard neuroses as the commonest cause of the problem. Drunkenness is not, as in the west, a sign of individual maladjustment, or a means of escape from personal problems, but essentially a social habit, a form of sociability, part of the art of living. People like to drink with friends before leaving to do their military service, on completion of their studies, on payday (*den' poluchki*), and they will invite their foreman to join them in a drink to celebrate their first pay. This is the way they celebrate every event in life, sad or gay; if someone does you a good turn, you offer him a drink; the bottle has become a form of currency in black-market transactions.

One consequence of the laws regulating the sale of alcohol in restaurants, cafés and shops (between 11 am and 7 pm) and the prohibition of alcohol in works canteens and in the vicinity of places of work has been to lend greater importance to the street. Not everyone can afford to buy a bottle of vodka in a shop, so people club together to buy one and empty the bottle in a public garden or in the shelter of some doorway before going home. Does this mean, as some people argue, that all that is needed is to open more drinking places and organize people's leisure time better in order to channel their sociability into less degrading forms? Meanwhile, hardened drinkers are picked up by the police in their vehicles and treated to a course of bicarbonate of soda in a 'drying-out cell'. The deterrent effect of this method is rather limited. Despite all the campaigns against drink, the habit is too well rooted in custom and is viewed with a great deal of indulgence, both by the general public and the administration itself. In the 1970s, the indirect tax on sales of alcohol provided the state with revenues of between 21 and 23 billion rubles, representing approximately 7.3 per cent of national income.[21] What this does not tell us is whether or not this habit conceals a deeper ill encountered everywhere in modern civilization, namely boredom.

Delinquency. Forms of delinquency vary from one society to another: opportunity makes the thief. In the Soviet Union, the commonest form of delinquency is damage to or theft of property, probably because the sense of property is associated with the private sphere, and to a much smaller degree with the public sphere: 'Stealing from the state isn't stealing!' While in the west certain frustrations and the resulting crimes may be put down to the temptations of a consumer society, in the Soviet Union it is the shortage of goods, rather, which lies at the root of delinquency. Another significant difference lies in the fact that in our own societies, it is the idleness of young people, brought about by unemployment, which may lead to delinquency; in Soviet society, this idleness would be thought utterly abnormal, for someone who does not work is a parasite and may even be prosecuted as such.

Comparison of crime and delinquency rates in France and the Soviet Union (Table 50) reveals certain forms of offence that do not exist in the Soviet Union (bounced cheques, for example) or exist to a considerably lesser degree (traffic offences). Crimes against property, on the other hand, are more frequent, while those against people figure less frequently in Soviet statistics than in our own. The sale of arms is presumably more strictly regulated than, for instance, in France. Admittedly, the rather vague heading *hooliganism* may conceal all sorts of violence or misdemeanour.

TABLE 50 *Patterns of offences and crimes in the USSR and France*

	% of offences		Age of delinquents in the USSR (%)	
	USSR 1967	France 1968		
Offences against property	33	25.5	under 18	7
Assault	17	24.3	18–25	31
Offences against the state	9.5	9.0	26–30	20.6
Economic offences	5	9.0	31–40	30
Traffic violations	5	24.0	41–50	7
Hooliganism, offences against morals	24	2.5	51–60	2.6
Miscellaneous	6.5	5.6	over 60	1.8
	100	100		100

Juvenile delinquency was particularly widespread in the early years following the Revolution (*bezprizornye*), but now seems to be declining; it is frequently committed by gangs of youths. There are also networks of fences and black-marketeers to dispose of either illegally produced or stolen goods. Underworld slang is evidence of the existence of organized crime.[22] There does not seem to be much drug addiction or prostitution, while sexual procurement is unknown.

Another distinguishing feature of each society is the attitude of its mass media and judicial system towards delinquency. Violence is not exploited for commercial purposes in the Soviet Union, and the press only reports a crime when the guilty person has been caught and punished. As for the penal system, this has moved from an optimistic and relatively indulgent attitude towards the culprit in the direction of greater severity, i.e. in the opposite direction from western penal practice. Previously, the only crimes regarded as incorrigible were those committed against the regime, and other offences were thought to require environmental therapy. Great hopes were placed on transforming the social factors that breed crime. Deprivation of liberty was supposed to be carried out in conditions enabling the individual to achieve rehabilitation through work, one notable means being the communes for the re-education of juvenile delinquents, pioneered by A. Makarenko.

The death penalty was abolished in May 1947, presumably as a reaction against the blood-letting of the last war. Little by little, however, capital punishment was reinstated, in 1950 to punish traitors and spies, in 1954 for murderers and in 1961 for economic crimes. Hooliganism, which in 1922 carried a one-year prison sentence, brought a two-year sentence in 1926 and, since 1965, three to five years imprisonment. The courts do take mitigating circumstances, and social background in particular, into account, but the delinquents, not society, are regarded as largely responsible for their actions.

The lack of general criminal statistics for the Soviet Union makes it impossible to say whether the crime rate is higher, equal to or lower than that of other countries. Also, definitions of crime differ from one type of society to another, as does the degree of non-conformity tolerated. To what point is an individual entitled to be different from others? The hippy counter-culture, which in the west is often nothing but a lucrative marginal fringe show, would be regarded as the very essence of parasitism in the Soviet Union.

Standards of tolerance differ particularly sharply when it comes to demands which would be regarded as political rights in other countries but which are not viewed as such in the Soviet Union. Where, in our society, we define freedom as the right to non-interference in private life, in the Soviet Union it is accepted in its positive sense only: it is the duty of the individual to do right, i.e. to conform to social standards. In the same way as a person has no right to be stupid or to believe what is held to be wrong, the deviant is, in the last resort, regarded as an abnormality.

Dissidence

While delinquency concerns *behavioural* disorders, *dissidence* is the term used to refer to people whose *opinions* place them in political opposition to the established regime. Their reasons are varied. Some would like to see reforms carried out and demand respect for individual or national rights within the framework of existing institutions; others reject the established system as a matter of principle. These different forms of opposition did not originate in the 1960s; what is new is that they are now coming out into the open.

Religious dissidence. From the outset, the Patriarch Tikhon declared the Orthodox Church's opposition to the Bolsheviks when he uttered his anathema against 'the declared or secret enemies of Christ's truth', thereby provoking a schism with those who favoured a 'renovated' Church. When he joined the Soviet cause in 1923, he was not followed by the various 'integrate' factions represented in the 'true Orthodox Church' (*istino pravoslavnaya cerkov*). With its clergy deported, the Church found itself, like some of the sects, a religion without priests. The sects, on the other hand, with their isolated communities, were more successful in preserving their traditions, at least until the period of collectivization. During the 1920s, the authorities played the sects off against the established Orthodox Church (in a policy of divide and rule); but once the latter had fallen beneath the sway of the authorities they changed tactics and began to back the hierarchy against the schismatics. Thus, for example, in 1946 the Ukrainian Uniates (Catholics) were forcibly absorbed into the Orthodox Church.

The council for religious affairs, which is attached to the council of ministers of the Soviet Union, acts as intermediary between the Church hierarchy and the state. According to certain reports, it intervenes discreetly in the appointment of Church dignitaries, for the churches are the only institutions not subject to the Party *nomenklatura*. At a local level, it supervises the associations of worship (*dvadtsatka*). The Protestant communities, with their traditionally more democratic ecclesiastical structures, took longer to be brought under control. A council of Evangelical and Baptist Christians, embracing all the Protestant communities (Lutherans, Baptists, the Pentecostal assemblies and Mennonites) was formed in 1961, but this organization is not recognized by the Baptist activists (*initsiativniki*), dissidents who refuse to accept the limitations imposed by Soviet legislation on the religious instruction of children, freedom of assembly and preaching. The principal leaders of this movement either have been or are in prison.

The other Christian communities are equally divided between allegiance to the established regime and their personal convictions. The Catholic clergy of Lithuania have protested against infringements of religious freedom. A petition addressed to Brezhnev and to the secretariat of the United Nations was signed by 17,000 Catholics. The clergy are now half as numerous as in 1940, and the Kaunas seminary is only entitled to receive 30 seminarists, representing a maximum of 5 or 6 ordinations per year.

State intervention in the affairs of the Orthodox Church at parish level has also provoked reactions. The most spectacular protests have been the 'Open letter to the Patriarch' in 1965, the statement made by eight prelates, among them Archbishop Yermogen of Kaluga, in the same year and Solzhenitsyn's 'Open letter to the Patriarch Pimen' on 22 March 1972. The latter is an indication that laymen such as Solzhenitsyn and Anatoly Krasnov are following a by no means negligible tradition in asserting the demands of the religious conscience. Others, in less spectacular manner, bear witness to their faith by preaching in defiance of intimidation and harassment.

Yet, the Party directives of 11 November 1954 on freedom of conscience stated that a believer could be a good citizen. This tolerance was shortlived. Religious repression was particularly severe in the period 1959–64, when the official in charge of ideological work at the time, Leonid Il'ichev, expressing concern at the 'extent of the persistence of religious belief', declared: 'We have no right to wait for it to disappear of its own accord'.[23] However, in regions where religious tradition is part of a national culture, as among the Georgians and the Armenians (which both have their own venerated independent churches) or among the Muslims of central Asia, the authorities display greater flexibility, taking care to avoid the kind of repression likely to trigger a popular nationalist movement. In Georgia, 70 per cent of collective-farm workers interviewed, 50 per cent of workers and 20 per cent of members of the intelligentsia declared their attachment to the traditional marriage rites, compared with only 1 per cent among the Russian working class in Nizhniy-Taguil.

Nationalist feeling. The revival of Russian patriotism could hardly fail to awaken national feeling among all the peoples of the Union who, at some moment or other in their history, had experienced independence.

Sometimes, nationalism spills over into chauvinism. Always the first victims are the Jews. Antisemitism is a throwback to traditional Russian society. Today, as in the past, the Jews are the scapegoats for all the ills afflicting the country. While pogroms have disappeared, synagogue burnings, defamatory publications (e.g. T. Kichko's *Judaizm bez prikras*) and certain forms of discrimination have not been eliminated. For instance, a nationalities quota restricts access to certain institutes of higher education and certain professions for Jews.

Since the foundation of the state of Israel, which received the blessing of the Soviet Union at the time, antisemitism has found an ally in the Soviet government's anti-Zionist policy. Although Jewish communities have lived in Russia for more than a thousand years, and despite their vital contribution to Russian culture, the Jews are regarded as a distinct nationality, even though they have no territory, no language, often no religion even, of their own. Hebrew-language culture is forbidden, and the only language permitted to be taught in Jewish schools is Yiddish. Some idea of the extent of the decline of Yiddish is given by the fact that in 1974 only 5 books (7000 copies in all) were published in the language in the Soviet Union. Nevertheless, thanks to the support of world opinion, the Jews have managed to obtain the right to emigrate. Since 1969, approximately 250,000 Jews have left the Soviet Union – though not without difficulty for those engaged in certain scientific activities.

In the non-Russian republics, Party plenums and government or Party-machine reshuffles are a frequent occasion for references to 'bourgeois nationalism' and warnings against 'idealizing the past' or 'local particularism'. It is not always easy to detect whether these criticisms are aimed at a desire for greater economic and cultural autonomy, or at fully fledged nationalist demands. The highest proportion of abstentions and adverse votes in elections is found in the Baltic republics, even though these states have the highest living standards in the Soviet Union. But it is precisely this economic and cultural difference which is felt to be burdensome. What the Russians see as a short-coming in their system is interpreted by the nationalists as a failure attribu-table to the Russians. Through the opening up and industrialization of these countries, Russian immigration has led to the growth of large, pervasive Russian communities. The non-Russian authorities claim the right to appoint nationals to *nomenklatura* jobs, and it is precisely this that is opposed by all those who fear that choosing officials on the basis of nationality would tend to strengthen nationalism.

But it is in the cultural sphere that susceptibilities are keenest. The local intelligentsia view with misgivings the imposition of Russian as the compulsory language (in place of Finnish in Karelia) or as a second language. Restrictions placed on national traditions, such as the celebration of certain anniversaries (22 March, the date of birth of Shevchenko for Ukrainian patriots), cannot but breed resentment and protest: 'one cannot graft onto a national tradition what is contrary to the ideals rooted in history, which are the aesthetic expression of a people's achievements' (*Novy Mir*, no. 2, 1971, p. 242). But those who actively protest against Russification, such as V. Morozov, Chornovil in the Ukraine, Parinor Airityan in Armenia, are prosecuted.

In central Asia, the ties that bound the peoples to Turkish or Iranian culture have been cut by the Soviets. The Muslim people's national epics and certain of their folk legends were eliminated from the corpus of authorized works in the 1950s, albeit not without resistance. And in some recent novels local writers have tried to recall their brilliant past.[24] National feeling seems to be less powerfully developed among the Tatars of Kazan, bilingualism and emi-gration having scattered them throughout the territory of the RSFSR, prevent-ing them from withdrawing into themselves. National consciousness remains very strong, on the other hand, among the Crimean Tatars who were deported to central Asia in May 1944 and who are still refused the right to return to the Crimea, even though they have been cleared of allegations of treason. The trial of their leader, Mustafa Djemiliev, marked the beginning of a campaign for the defence of national rights in the Soviet Union, in the course of which General Grigorenko was also arrested.

The defence of human rights. While nationalist and religious currents have their roots in tradition, the human-rights movement is more recent in origin. The twentieth congress awakened hopes of greater tolerance, and liberal youth gathered in Moscow's Mayakovsky Square to listen to its favourite poets trans-formed it into a kind of forum. The path from literature to politics is a familiar one to the Russian and Soviet writer. Rejected for official publication, the flowering of writings born of this period found its way into 'self-published' editions (*samizdat*), i.e. typewritten or photocopied publications. Some of these were published in anthology or review form, such as *Phoenix* (Yuri Galanskov), *Sintaksis* (poetry by Joseph Brodsky) and *Tetrad* (A. Krasnov). The best of this very heterogeneous collection of works, which also included older forbidden writings, found its way abroad for publication. A good proportion of these writings are not literature at all but take the form of requests addressed to the authorities, manifestoes or accounts of events (*Chronicle of Current Events*), for example trials, activities which the authorities regard as criminal.

The trial of the writers Sinyavsky and Daniel in February 1966 signalled the beginning of a period of repression that was to give birth to the intellectual dissident movement, rather in the manner of the Dreyfus affair in France. It was expected that the two writers, who had pleaded innocent, would be amnestied; instead, they were sentenced to heavy terms of imprisonment, under Article 70 of the RSFSR penal code, for having published abroad works held to be defamatory to the regime. (Article 70 condemns 'agitation and propaganda conducted with the aim of undermining or weakening Soviet power or of committing particularly dangerous offences against the State, the dissemination for the same purposes of calumnies denigrating the political and social regime of the USSR as well as the dissemination, preparation or keeping for the same purposes of such literature'.) The sentence aroused a storm of protest, which revived debate over the writer's condition in Soviet society; in particular, Solzhenitsyn wrote an open letter to the fourth congress of the writers' union demanding the abolition of censorship and protesting the banning of *The First Circle* and *Cancer Ward*.

Censorship has led to the increasingly frequent publication abroad of Soviet works (*tamizdat*) and the proliferation inside the Soviet Union itself of *samizdat* publications. The *samizdat* almanac *Metropole* (1979) was seen as a truly literary manifesto, owing to the calibre of its signatories.

The intervention of the Warsaw Pact troops in Czechoslovakia, in 1968, was the occasion of a further manifesto by the dissident intelligentsia, which pleaded not only for creative freedom but also for the whole gamut of individual and collective rights: the right to emigrate, as well as rights of self-determination. The trial of A. Ginzburg and Y. Galanskov, two opponents of the intervention in Czechoslovakia, triggered a fresh wave of petitions, followed by the trial of Larissa Daniel and Pavel Litvinov.

It was in 1968 also that Andrei Sakharov, of the Russian academy of sciences, published in the United States his *Reflections on Progress, Peaceful Coexistence and Individual Freedom*, which revealed that a portion of the scientific intelligentsia desired reforms that would introduce the economic efficiency and political freedoms necessary to enable the regime to maintain its position in the world. His thinking was spelled out more clearly in the manifesto which he signed in March 1970 with Roy Medvedev and Valentin Turshin: this was nothing short of a 15-point political programme addressed to the secretary general of the Party and the president of the presidium of the Supreme Soviet. These intellectuals do not regard themselves as opponents of the socialist regime, but on the contrary as citizens concerned to contribute to its image through a democratization of its institutions. Sakharov wrote further letters to the highest authorities on 3 March and 7 October 1971. Gradually, Sakharov, who was to become the leading spokesman of the Committee for the Defence of Human Rights (founded in November 1970) after Solzhenitsyn's expulsion, tended to draw away from the regime and to turn increasingly for support to public opinion and the international organizations.

Inevitably, the repression of dissidents and their sympathizers lead to a radicalization of the movement. What had begun with Roy Medvedev as a critical reflection on the workings of Soviet institutions, gradually became a search for alternatives to the regime (as exemplified in particular by the authors of *From under the Rubble*, 1975). But these pathetic efforts are a far cry from a fully fledged opposition. For the battle being waged by the dissidents is not a political one: in essence, it is a moral resistance based on a reaction to the gulf between real life and the high-flown words of officialdom. Dissident groups and individuals are neither uniform nor organized. They have no leader, they have no political programme, and the authorities can throttle outbursts of dissidence fairly rapidly, by expelling the leading personalities and denouncing them to the population as traitors to their country or as foreign agents.

Dissidence does not appear to be a movement with roots in the masses. It is more a way of thinking, a moral attitude, than an organized resistance. What unites the dissidents is the harassment and imprisonment to which they are subject. Their strength lies in the depth of their conviction and the relations of trust that bind them in their activities, which of necessity demand great secrecy. It is by no means certain that the working people, with their anti-intellectual traditions, sympathize with the demands of this handful of intellectuals, whom they regard as privileged individuals, or even as traitors.

However, recent strikes, although isolated until now, suggest that the working class is not immune to this upsurge of demands. A spontaneous trade-union movement has grown up out of protests against infringements of the labour laws; these have met with instant and violent repression, the leaders being imprisoned or expelled. The movement has been obliged to modify its methods accordingly. The situation is not comparable to that in Poland owing to the dispersal of Soviet industrial centres over a vast expanse of territory, and to the wide diversity of nationalities, which hamper the emergence of a unified movement. Nor is there as yet any evidence of an alliance between the dissidence of intellectuals and workers' demands. In any case, the dissidents never address the people, turning always to the authorities or to world opinion. Their protests would reach a far vaster audience were they to link up with more sensitive and more popular themes, for instance by appealing to national feeling. It took more than a generation, in the last century, for the demands of the radical intelligentsia of the 1860s to find expression in organized movements. We are free to believe that history repeats itself, that it is pre-ordained and written on a parchment whose secret is guarded by the keepers of the temple, or, on the contrary, that its workings are unpredictable.

NOTES

1 V. Chalmaev, 'Velikie iskaniya', *Molodaya Gvardiya*, nos. 6—7, 1970.
2 A. Dement'ev, *Novy Mir*, no. 4, 1969, p. 219.
3 A. Yakovlyev, 'Protiv Antiistoritsizma', *Lit. Gaz.*, no. 15, Nov. 1972.
4 D. Lane, *The Socialist Industrial State*, p. 86.
5 G. Gorer and J. Rickman, *The People of Great Russia*, London, 1949.
6 E. Huber, 'La philosophie en URSS', *Projet*, no. 113, March 1977, pp. 35—55.
7 Z. Kakabadzhe, *Chelovek kak filosovskaya problema*, Tbilissi, 1970, p. 136.
8 A. Klibanov (ed.), *Komkretnye issledovanie sovremennykh religiozhykh verovanya*, Moscow, 1967, p. 93.
9 N. Kelt, *Komsomol'skaya Pravda*, 15 Aug. 1965.
10 Archbishop of Marseille and former secretary of the French Episcopal Conference (Transl.).
11 *Novy Mir*, no. 12, 1953.
12 A. Belov, *Affaire d'habitude*, Paris, Julliard, 1970.
13 M. Bulgakov, *The Master and Marguerite*.
14 Mayakovsky, *The Bug*; Y. Shvartz, *The Naked King*; etc.
15 V. Nekrassov, *The Trenches of Stalingrad*; C. Simonov, *The Living and the Dead*, *One Is Not Born a Soldier*; V. Bykov, *Dead Men Suffer*; Y. Bondarev, *The Silence*; A. Nekrich, *22 June 1941*.
16 A. Solzhenitsyn, *A Day in the Life of Ivan Denisovich*; L. Chukovskaya, *The Empty House*.
17 V. Nekrassov, *Kira Georgievna*; I. Vinogradov, 'Pod odnoi vechnoi temy', *Novy Mir*, no. 8, 1962, p. 238.
18 *Novy Mir*, no. 2, 1971, pp. 242—4.
19 Iossif Gummer, *Izvestiya*, 27 Sept. 1975.
20 *Chelovek i obshchestvo* (Leningrad), no. 3, 1968, p. 200.
21 V. Treml, 'Alcohol in the USSR: a fiscal dilemma', *Soviet Studies*, April 1975.
22 M. Diomine, *Le Blatnoy*, R. Laffont, 1975.
23 L. Il'ichev, 'On the development of a scientific conception of the world and atheist education', *Kommunist*, no. 1, 1964, pp. 23—45.
24 D. Matuszewski, 'The Turkey Part in the Soviet Future', *Problems of Communism*, vol. 31, no. 4, 1982, pp. 76—82.

SUGGESTED READING

History of ideas

Berdyaev, N., *The Russian Idea*, London, 1947; Boston, 1962.
Besançon, A., 'Dissidence de la peinture russe, 1860—1922', *Annales*, March—April 1962, pp. 259—65.

300   *National cultures and social values*

Besançon, A., *Le Tsarevitch immolé: La symbolique de la loi dans la culture russe*, Plon, 1967.

Besançon, A., *Éducation et société en Russie dans le second tiers du XIXe siècle*, Mouton, 1974.

Billington, J., *The Icon and the Axe: An Interpretive History of Russian Culture*, London, Weidenfeld & Nicolson, 1966.

Chambre, H., *Le Marxisme en Union soviétique*, du Seuil, 1955.

Chambre, H., *L'Évolution du marxisme soviétique*, du Seuil, 1974.

Grier, P., *Marxist Ethical Theory in the Soviet Union*, Reidel Dordrecht, 1978.

Jeu, B., *La Philosophie soviétique et l'Occident*, Paris, Mercure de France, 1969.

Laloy, J., *Le Socialisme de Lénine*, Paris, Desclee de Brouwer, 1967.

Marcuse, H., *Soviet Marxism*, London, Routledge & Kegan Paul, 1969.

Pascal, P., *Les Grands Courants de la pensée russe moderne*, Lausanne, L'Age d'Homme, 1971.

Scherrer, J., 'Les sociétés philosophico-religieuses et la quête de l'intelligentsia russe avant 1917', *Cahiers du monde russe et soviétique*, nos 3–4, 1974.

Scherrer, J., 'Intelligentsia, religion et révolution: premières manifestations d'un socialisme chrétien en Russie, 1905–1907', *Cahiers du monde russe et soviétique*, no. 1, 1977.

Simmons, E., *Continuity and Change in Russian and Soviet Thought*, Cambridge, Mass., Harvard University Press, 1955.

Venturi, F., *Roots of Revolution: A History of the Populist and Socialist Movements in Nineteenth-Century Russia*, New York, Knopf, 1960.

Currents in literature

Aucouturier, M., 'Le léninisme dans la critique littéraire soviétique', *Cahiers du monde russe et soviétique*, no. 4, 1976.

Dunham, V., *In Stalin's Time: Middle Class Values in Soviet Fiction*, Cambridge University Press, 1976.

Frioux, C., 'Le progressisme dans la littérature soviétique', *Politique d'aujourd'hui*, no. 2, Feb. 1969, pp. 112–17.

Heller, L., *De la science fiction soviétique*, Lausanne, L'Age d'Homme, 1979.

Heller, M., *Le Monde concentrationnaire et la littérature soviétique*, Lausanne, L'Age d'Homme, 1974.

Hingley, R., *Russian Writers and Soviet Society 1917–1978*, London, Weidenfeld & Nicolson, 1979.

Hollander, P., 'Models of behavior in Stalinist literature', *American Sociological Review*, vol. 31, no. 3, June 1966, pp. 352–64.

Peter, H., *Anthology of Soviet Satire*, London, Collet's, 1972–4, 2 vols.

Ross, N., 'Utopie et anti-utopie dans la littérature soviétique fantastique', *Annuaire de l'U.R.S.S., 1970*, C.N.R.S., 1971, p. 599.

Schneidman, N. N., *Soviet Literature in the 1970s*, University of Toronto Press, 1979.

Zamoyska, H., 'Problèmes et affrontements de la littérature soviétique non conformiste', *Revue de la Défense nationale*, Aug.–Sept. 1972, pp. 1279–98.

Religions and cultures

Bennigsen, A. and Lemercier-Quelquejay, C., *L'Islam en Union soviétique*, Payot, 1968.

Biddulph, H., 'Religious participation of youth in the USSR', *Soviet Studies*, vol. 31, July 1979.

Chafarevitch, J., *La Législation sur la religion en U.R.S.S.*, du Seuil, 1973.

Dunn, D., *Religion and Modernization in the Soviet Union*, Boulder, Colorado, Westview Press, 1977.

Hayward, M. and Fletcher, W. (eds), *Religion and the Soviet State*, Pall Mall, 1969.

Klibanov, A., *Istoriya religioznogo sektanstva v Rossii*, Moscow, 1965.

Klibanov, A., *Religioznoe sektanstvo i sovremennost'*, Moscow, Nauka, 1969.

Kochan, L. (ed.), *Jews in Soviet Russia Since 1917*, Oxford University Press, 1970.

Lane, C., *Christian Religion in the Soviet Union: A Sociological Study*, London, Allen & Unwin, 1978.

Marchadier, B., 'Opposition et dissidence traditionnaliste dans l'Église orthodoxe en U.R.S.S.', *Cahiers du monde russe et soviétique*, nos 3–4, 1975, pp. 365–82.

Marshall, R. (ed.), *Aspects of Religion in the Soviet Union, 1917–1967*, Chicago, 1971.

Martin, A., *Les Croyants en U.R.S.S.*, Fayard, 1970.

Pascal, P., *La Religion du peuple russe*, Lausanne, L'Age d'Homme, 1973.

Struve, N. A., *Christians in Contemporary Russia*, New York, 1967.

Vardys, S., *The Catholic Church: Dissent and Nationality in Soviet Lithuania*, Columbia University Press, 1979.

Yodfat, A., 'Le statut légal de la religion en Union soviétique et son incidence sur la religion juive', *Istina*, no. 1, 1972, pp. 57–76.

Deviance and delinquency

Bellon, J., 'L'enfance délinquante en U.R.S.S.', *Cahiers du monde russe et soviétique*, vol. no. 1, 1959.

Connor, W., 'Alcohol in Soviet Society', *Slavic Review*, Sept. 1971, pp. 570–88.

Connor, W., *Deviance in Soviet Society*, New York, Columbia University Press, 1972.

Diomine, M., *Le Blatnoy*, R. Laffont, 1975.

Feifer, G., *Justice in Moscow*, New York, Schuster, 1964 (the author, as a research student in Moscow, was able to attend fifty trials).

Mead, M., *Soviet Attitudes towards Authority*, McGraw Hill, 1951.

Youth

Berton-Hogge, R., 'La jeunesse soviétique', *Problèmes politiques et sociaux*, nos 269, 274, 1975.

Ikonnikova, S., *Molodezh, sotsiologicheskii i socialnyi analiz*, Leningrad, 1974.

Kerblay, B., 'Les problèmes de la socialisation en milieu rural soviétique', *Cahiers du monde russe et soviétique*, vol. 21, nos 3–4, 1980.

'Sotsial'nye problemy molodezhi', *Chelovek i obshchestvo*, Leningrad, Vypusk VI, 1969.

Dissidence

Agourski, B., Barabanov, Borissov, Chafarevitch, Korsakov and Solzhenitsyn, *From under the Rubble*, Boston, Little, Brown, 1975.

L'Affaire Guinzbourg-Galanskov, du Seuil, 1969.

Amalrik, A., *Will the Soviet Union Survive until 1984?*, London, Penguin, New York, Harper & Row, 1970.

Amalrik, A., *Voyage involontaire en Sibérie*, Paris, Gallimard, 1970.

Boukovsky, V., *Une Nouvelle Maladie mentale en U.R.S.S.: l'opposition*, du Seuil, 1971.

Bukovsky, V. and Gluzman, S., *Manual of Psychiatry for Dissidents*.

Etkind, E., *Dissident malgrè lui*, Paris, Albin Michel, 1977.

Kouznetsov, E., *Journal d'un condamné à mort*, Gallimard, 1974.

Medvedev, Z. and Roy, *A Question of Madness*, London, Macmillan, 1971.

Meerson Aksenov, M. and Shragin, B. (eds), *The Political, Social and Religious Thought of Russian Samizdat*, Belmont, Mass., Nordland, 1978.

Un Observateur à Moscou, du Seuil, 1970.

Plyashch, L., *History's Carnival: A Dissident's Autobiography*, London, Collins and Harvill, 1979.

Sakharov, A., *Progress, Coexistence and Intellectual Freedom*, London, 1968.

Sakharov, A., *Sakharov Speaks*, London, Collins, 1974.

Sakharov, A., *My Country and My World*, London, Harvill, 1975.

Solzhenitsyn, *Letter to Soviet Leaders*, London, Collins, 1974.

Solzhenitsyn, A., *The Oak and the Calf: Sketches of Literary Life in the Soviet Union*, London, Collins, 1980.

Solzhenitsyn, A., Cahier de *L'Herne*, edited by G. Nivat and M. Aucouturier, 1971.

Syndicalisme et libertés en Union Soviétique (an anthology ed. by O. Semyonova and V. Haynes), Maspero, 1979.

Tokes, R. (ed.), *Dissent in the U.S.S.R.*, Johns Hopkins University Press, 1975.

Zinoviev, A., *The Radiant Future*, London, Bodley Head, New York, Random House, 1981.

Zinoviev, A., *Nous et l'occident*, Lausanne, L'Age d'Homme, 1981.

Conclusion

Past and future

Throughout this exploration of Soviet society, we have constantly encountered two major themes, namely the modernization of traditional society and its revolutionary transformation, aimed at raising up from the ashes of the old regime a society different from the western model. These two evolutionary processes work at different paces. The changes brought about by modernization (industrialization, urban growth, the spread of education) first began to take place in the nineteenth century. From the beginning of the twentieth century, the revolutionary movements that emerged from this slow, peaceful transformation were to alter its course and give fresh impetus to the historical process. In the aftermath of the NEP, the political system (which, as an instrument for mobilizing resources and directing the activity of the nation, was remarkably effective) took precedence over the construction of the economic base. Today's predominantly urban, educated, industrial society, achieving standards of comfort commensurate with its level of technical development, emerged only after Stalin's death. But here, as elsewhere, people's mentalities have lagged far behind these transformations, the collective consciousness has been only partially remodelled by official ideology. It is still deeply marked by the trials of history and by ingrained habits. Soviet culture has not broken with the past: it has re-interpreted it, still drawing from it that love of the fatherland which, more than Marxism–Leninism, is the true cement of national unity.

Students of Soviet society have tended to stress one or another of these three faces: that of modernization, many of whose characteristics it shares with all industrial societies; that of national culture, which spotlights the factors of continuity and stability; or that of the revolutionary regime, which, on the contrary, underscores the differences between the present-day Soviet Union and the past, or between the Soviet Union and 'liberal' societies. These three views serve as the basis for a typology of interpretations of Soviet society.

Those who focus chiefly on certain inevitable resemblances between Soviet society and our own, whether because of the techniques they use or because of similarities in aspiration, may be tempted to stress this *convergence*, each system borrowing certain features from the other, where these may help to bring about improvements without altering its nature. Those who, while not denying these similarities, are conscious above all of the differences in tradition and culture, will be inclined to emphasize factors of permanence and continuity. Political scientists, lastly, believe that it is in interpreting ideology and, above all, in the renewal of the political élites that pointers to any possible evolution in the regime are most likely to emerge; although, given the efficiency of the system of internal control and social integration, the chances of change, even in the medium term, appear slender to say the least. All these analyses generally agree on one point — that the interdependence of the different variables in the social system is such that attempts to foretell the future are extremely uncertain.

To this should be added the fact that Soviet ideology, economy and politics have not developed in isolation, but in constant confrontation with opposing ideologies, and in tenacious competition with the capitalist societies, and that, like it or not, Soviet society is not immune from outside influences or reactions. The relative isolation in which Soviet citizens live used to be a factor of stability: it is hard to imagine freedoms one has never known. Slowly rising living standards, which the population is able to measure for itself, bring with them the hope of further progress, while the world outside is painted in its darkest colours. Is this to say that economic, political and military competition between the Soviet Union and the capitalist world, which constantly forces the country to perfect its technology and thus to open the door to trade and co-operation with the outside world, simultaneously entails the introduction of corrupting influences into the Soviet Union? Some diplomats have opted for precisely this gamble: incapable of halting the expansion of Soviet power, they hope at least to be able to guide it into channels that will lock it into the world economy.

Like all scenarios that predict hoped-for changes, this one is based on patterns borrowed from western societies. It has yet to be demonstrated that such patterns are equally applicable to the 'socialist' societies: the German Democratic Republic, which is technologically the most advanced of the socialist countries and, by virtue of its interzone trade, the most permeable to western influences, is not the most liberal country in the eastern bloc. But while the regime does appear to be assured of a high degree of stability, Soviet society, on the other hand, is changing: it is becoming more diversified, more complex, better educated and hence less docile, less coherent, less determined, less predictable.

Upon this imposing, well-ordered façade, time continues in its work, for nothing can resist it. The foundations guaranteeing the stability of the edifice look unshakable: on the one hand, there is an ubiquitous, all-powerful Party that will brook no formation or association outside its control; on the other, there is a population whose essential needs (security, education, health, leisure) appear to be satisfied and which in any case has no opportunity of choosing an alternative. The intelligentsia, which elsewhere stands for contention, is here integrated into the system; far from being alienated, it is on the whole closely associated with the regime.

Yet each of these strengths contains within it the seeds of weakness. Bureaucratic centralism breeds inefficiency, wastage and unofficial dealing. Ideological totalitarianism leads to double thinking and double standards of behaviour. Job security, for those who accept the established order, discourages effort and breeds apathy. The spread of education breeds a tendency to criticism − of the privileges enjoyed by the élite, in particular − and new aspirations among the young. In the peripheral republics, these aspirations could take on a nationalist colouring. For patriotism, to which the authorities constantly appeal, is a two-edged sword, one which can prove extremely difficult to wield. The problem of the nationalities, which has until now been brushed aside or channelled by excitement over the economic development of the republics, is liable to produce a backlash as a result of population pressures, unless the local élites obtain a satisfactory measure of autonomy. The dominant position of the Soviet Union in eastern Europe offers it a reassuring measure of protection, while its political and ideological influence over certain Third World governments allows it to continue to play its messianic role. But this dominant position carries with it dangers of its own, for, unlike ancient Rome, Soviet power is not embodied in a superior civilization acceptable to the culturally more sophisticated peoples of Europe; yet, at the same time, it is likely to lull Soviet leaders into overestimating their strength.

In conclusion, our attempt at appraising the different factors of stability and change suggests that while the evolution of Soviet society is undoubtedly conditional upon objective factors, such as steady economic growth and expansion of its military might, the transformation of production and organizational techniques and the demographic dynamics of its different populations, it is still more powerfully shaped by *subjective* assessments of this evolution made by individuals and groups. Which is why the future of Soviet society, like that of any other society, is surely not dependent solely on economic determinism or ineluctable social processes (to which some people are convinced they possess the key). Like the history of the past, that of tomorrow depends upon the choices people make: up till now, these choices have been confined within strictly limited bounds, but we do not have to look far into the past to see that no regime in history has ever managed to limit the human brain to a single track. Today, as in the past, in the Soviet Union, as elsewhere, a tiny minority of people refuses to allow the human spirit to be walled up in a single moment of history, or to identify culture with the narrow world of ready-made ideas. Nor has humanity ever been able to resist looking beyond rational explanations for a meaning to existence, for science is incapable of producing a model, ideal human being. It is in this struggle of the intelligence, between ideology and utopia, in this unceasing quest of the will between the real world and the ideal, that the fate of a society lies.

General bibliography

INTRODUCTION TO THE STUDY OF SOCIAL SYSTEMS

Aron, R., *Le Développement de la société industrielle et la stratification sociale*, Paris, C.D.U., 1956–7, 2 vols.

Bottomore, T. B., *Sociology: A Guide to Problems and Literature*, London, Allen & Unwin, 1971.

Duverger, M., *Sociologie de la politique*, Paris, P.U.F., 1973.

Grosser, A., *L'Explication politique: une introduction à L'analyse comparative*, Paris, A. Colin, 1972.

Janne, H., *Le Système social: essai de théorie générale*, l'Université libre de Bruxelles, 1967.

Mendras, H., *Éléments de sociologie*, Paris, A. Colin, 1967.

Shchepansky, J., *Elementarnye ponyatiya sotsiologii*, Moscow, 1967.

GENERAL STUDIES OF SOVIET SOCIETY

Bell, D., 'Ten theories in search of reality', in *The End of Ideology*, London, Macmillan, 1960, pp. 315–54.

Black, C. (ed.), *The Transformation of Russian Society*, Cambridge, Mass., Harvard University Press, 1960.

Black, C. (ed.), *The Modernization of Japan and Russia*, The Free Press, Macmillan, 1975.

Breslauer, G., *Five Images of the Soviet Future*, Berkeley, University of California Press, 1978.

Brown, A., Fennel, J., Kaser, M. and Willets, H. T. (eds), *The Cambridge Encyclopaedia on Russia and the Soviet Union*, Cambridge University Press, 1982.

Cohen, F., *Les Soviétiques: classes et société en U.R.S.S.*, Paris, Éd. sociales, 1974.

Davies, R. W., *The Soviet Union*, London, Allen & Unwin, 1978.

Gleserman, G., *Le Développement de la société socialiste, principes scientifiques*, Progress, Moscow, 1970.

Hollander, P., *Soviet and American Society: A comparison*, Oxford University Press, 1973.

Inkeles, A., *Social Change in Soviet Russia*, Cambridge, Mass., Harvard University Press, 1968.

Kassof, A. (ed.), *Prospects for Soviet Society*, New York, Praeger, 1969.

Lane, D., *Politics and Society in the U.S.S.R.*, London, Weidenfeld & Nicolson, 1972.

Lane, D., *The Socialist Industrial State*, London, Allen & Unwin, 1976.

Leltchouk, V. and Poliakov, Y., under the direction of Protopopov, A., *Histoire de la société soviétique*, Éd. du Progrès, Moscow, 1972.

Matthews, M., *Class and Society in Soviet Russia*, London, Allen Lane, Penguin Press, 1972.

Meissner, B. (ed.), *Social Change in the Soviet Union*, Indiana, University of Notre Dame Press, 1972.

Nogee, J. (ed.), *Man, State and Society in the Soviet Union*, London, Pall Mall, 1972.

Pankhurst, J. and Sacks, P. (eds), *Contemporary Soviet Society: Sociological Perspectives*, New York, Praeger, 1980.

Sorlin, P., *The Soviet People and their Society, from 1917 to the Present*, London, Pall Mall, 1969.

SOCIOLOGY IN THE SOVIET UNION

Chagin, V. A., *Ocherk istorii sotsiologicheskoy mysli v S.S.R.* (Essay on the History of Sociological Thought in the USSR) *1917–1969*, Leningrad, 1971.

Dunn, S. P., *Sociology in the U.S.S.R.: A Collection of Readings from Soviet Journals*, White Plains, New York, IASP, 1966.

Simirenko, A., *Soviet Sociology: Historical Antecedents and Current Appraisals*, London, Routledge & Kegan Paul, 1967.

La Sociologie en U.R.S.S., members' reports from the Soviet delegation to the 6th International Sociology Congress, Progress, Moscow, 1966.

'La Sociologie en U.R.S.S.', report from the mission of French sociologists, 16–26 November 1971, *Revue française de sociologie*, Paris, C.N.R.S., vol. XIV, no.3, Sept. 1973, pp. 396–409.

Sotsiologiya v S.S.S.R. (Sociology in the USSR), under the direction of Ossipov, Moscow, 1965, 2 vols.

Weinberg, E., *The Development of Sociology in the Soviet Union*, London, Routledge & Kegan Paul, 1974.

REVIEWS AND PERIODICALS DEALING WITH SOVIET SOCIETY

French language

l'Aternative, Maspero.

Annuaire de l'U.R.S.S. (Centre for the study of the USSR and Western countries at the University of Strasbourg, since 1962).

Cahiers du monde russe et soviétique, Mouton, E.H.E.S.S.

Économies et sociétés, Cahiers de l'I.S.E.A., Droz, Geneva.

Le Courrier des pays de l'Est, Documentation française.

Notes et Études documentaires, Documentation française.

Problèmes économiques, Documentation française.

Problèmes politiques et sociaux, Documentation française.
Revue des études comparatives Est-Ouest, C.N.R.S.

English language

Problems of Communism, Washington D.C., US Information Agency.
Slavic Review (published from 1948 to 1961 as *American Slavic and East European Review*), Colombus, Ohio.
Soviet Sociology, White Plains, New York, IASP, since 1962.
Soviet Studies (University of Glasgow); the tables contained in the 25 vols to 1974 have been published in ABSEES, University of Glasgow, Jan. 1974.
Survey, London, since 1956.

German language

Osteuropa, Stuttgart, since 1951.

Italian language

L'Est, CESES, Milan.

Russian language

Chelovek i obshchestvo (Individual and Society), review published irregularly by the University of Leningrad; about 10 issues published to 1982.
Problemy nauchnogo kommunizma (Problems of Scientific Communism), anthology of the work of the Academy of Social Sciences of C.K.K.P.S.S.
Sotsial'nye issledovaniya, review published irregularly by the Institute of Philosophy of the Academy of Sciences of the USSR and the Soviet Sociological Association; continued since 1974 by *Sotsiologicheskie issledovaniya* (quarterly).
Sovetskaya Etnografiya (Soviet Ethnography) (quarterly).
Voprosy filosofii (Questions of Philosophy), quarterly review with a regular section on sociology.

Mention must also be made of the leading general periodicals, namely *Kommunist* (the Communist Party's theoretical review); *Partiinaya zhizn'*, *Sovetskaya yustitsiya*, *Sovetskoe gosudarstvo*, and in particular the literary reviews *Novy mir*, *Nash Sovremennik*, *Oktyabr*, *Yunost'*, *Znamya*, not forgetting the weekly *Literaturnaya Gazeta*, whose articles and essays (*Ocherki*) make a lively contribution to our knowledge of contemporary Soviet society.

Readers not familiar with Russian may nevertheless keep abreast of much of this output with the aid of the *Current Digest of the Soviet Press*, New York, Joint Committee on Slavic Studies, since 1950.

BIBLIOGRAPHIES AND LIBRARIES SPECIALIZING IN THE SOVIET UNION

French-language books and periodicals dealing with the Soviet Union

de Bonnières, L., *Le Guide de l'étudiant en russe*, Paris, Institut national d'études slaves, 1977.

European Bibliography of Soviet, East European and Slavonic Studies, Paris, Institut national d'études slaves, annual since 1975.

L'URSS dans les publications de la Documentation française, bibliography 1945–65, Paris, Documentation française, 1967.

Le Guide du slaviste, Paris, Institut d'études slaves, 1969, contains a list of dissertations on Russia and the Soviet Union presented in France since 1824.

English-language publications on the Soviet Union

The American Bibliography of Slavic and East European Studies, published by the University of Indiana from 1961 to 1969, and subsequently by Ohio State University, Columbus.

Simmons, J. S. G., *Russian Bibliography, Libraries and Archives*, Oxford University Press, 1973.

Specialist centres in France with either a reading room or a library

Association France-U.R.S.S., 61 rue Boissière, Paris 16ᵉ.

Bibliothèque de documentation internationale contemporaine, Centre Universitaire, 2, rue de Rouen, 92 Nanterre.

Centre de documentation sur l'U.R.S.S. et les pays slaves, E.H.E.S.S. Maison des Sciences de l'Homme, 54 bd Raspail, Paris 6ᵉ.

Centre d'étude des pays de l'Est, Université libre de Bruxelles, Institut de sociologie, Solvay, 49, rue du Châtelain, Bruxelles (publishes a *Bulletin* three times a year).

Centre d'étude des relations internationales, section U.R.S.S. et Europe de l'Est, Fondation Nationale des Sciences politiques, 27 rue St Guillaume, Paris 7ᵉ.

Centre d'étude sur l'U.R.S.S., la Chine et l'Europe orientale, Documentation française, 31, quai Voltaire, Paris 7ᵉ, primarily covering the period after 1955.

Centre de recherches sur l'U.R.S.S. et les pays de l'Est, Université de Strasbourg, place d'Athènes, Esplanade, 67 Strasbourg.

Service de Recherches juridiques comparatives du C.N.R.S., 25, rue Paul-Bert, 94 Ivry-sur-Seine.

Specialist centres and libraries in the United Kingdom

Birmingham University Library, P.O. Box 363, Birmingham.

Bodleian Library, Oxford.

British Library of Political and Economic Science, London School of Economics, 10 Portugal St, London WC2.

British Library Reference Division, Great Russell St, London WC1.

Cambridge University Library, West Road, Cambridge.

Centre for Russian and East European Studies, Alexander Baykov Library, University of Birmingham, P.O. Box 363, Birmingham.

Great Britain–USSR Association, 14 Grosvenor Place, London SW1.

Institute of Soviet and East European Studies, University of Glasgow, 9 Southpark Terrace, Glasgow.

Keston College, Heathfield Rd, Keston, Kent (extensive collection of *samizdat* material).

Marx Memorial Library, 37a Clerkenwell Green, London EC1.

National Library of Scotland, George IV Bridge, Edinburgh.

School of Slavonic and East European Studies, University of London, Senate House, Malet St, London WC1.

Society for Cultural Relations with the USSR, 320 Brixton Rd, London SW9.

Taylor Institution, St Giles, Oxford (university's main collection in modern and mediaeval European languages and literature).

Index

Entries in italics refer to figures and tables.